Sacred Gifts,
Profane
Pleasures

❖

MARCY NORTON

Sacred Gifts,

A HISTORY OF

Profane

TOBACCO AND CHOCOLATE

Pleasures

IN THE ATLANTIC WORLD

Cornell University Press

Ithaca and London

PUBLICATION OF THIS BOOK WAS MADE POSSIBLE, IN PART, BY A
GRANT FROM THE PROGRAM FOR CULTURAL COOPERATION BETWEEN
SPAIN'S MINISTRY OF CULTURE AND UNITED STATES UNIVERSITIES.

Copyright © 2008 by Cornell University

First published 2008 by Cornell University Press
First printing, Cornell Paperbacks, 2010

Printed in the United States of America

Library of Congress Cataloging-in-Publication Data

Norton, Marcy.
  Sacred gifts, profane pleasures : a history of tobacco and chocolate in the Atlantic world /
Marcy Norton.
     p. cm.
  Includes bibliographical references and index.
  ISBN 978-0-8014-4493-7 (cloth : alk. paper)
  ISBN 978-0-8014-7632-7 (pbk. : alk. paper)
    1. Tobacco use—Latin America—History.   2. Tobacco use—Europe—
History.   3. Tobacco industry—Latin America—History.   4. Tobacco industry—Europe—
History.   5. Chocolate—Latin America—History.   6. Chocolate—Europe—
History.   7. Chocolate industry—Latin America—History.   8. Chocolate
industry—Europe—History.   9. Europe—Civilization—Latin American influences.
  10. Latin America—Civilization—European influences.   I. Title.
HV5770.L29N67 2008
394.1'4—dc22   2008012196

Cornell University Press strives to use environmentally responsible
suppliers and materials to the fullest extent possible in the publishing
of its books. Such materials include vegetable-based, low-VOC inks
and acid-free papers that are recycled, totally chlorine-free, or partly
composed of nonwood fibers. For further information, visit our
website at www.cornellpress.cornell.edu.

Cloth printing   10   9   8   7   6   5   4   3   2   1

Paperback printing   10   9   8   7   6   5   4   3   2   1

For my parents

Contents

❖ ❖

Maps, Tables, and Illustrations

Maps, Tables, and Illustrations

Acknowledgments

❖ ❖

This book has been twelve years in the making. My debts of gratitude to erudite scholars, magnanimous institutions, wise teachers, generous colleagues and editors, and loving friends and family are enormous. In addition to the names listed below, I give my thanks to the help, generosity, and kindness offered to me by so many others.

Research for this book was made possible by fellowships and awards from the University of California, Berkeley; the Fulbright Program; the Mabelle McLeod Lewis Memorial Fund; the Huntington Library; the John Carter Brown Library, and the George Washington University. I was given the precious gift of uninterrupted time for writing by fellowships from the Shelby Cullom Davis Center for Historical Study, and the John W. Kluge Center at the Library of Congress. My fellow fellows at these institutions, my classmates at Berkeley, and my colleagues at GW have been vital sources of intellectual stimulation and moral support. This project also matured with the help of participants and audiences at various conferences and seminars, in particular those at two sessions of the International Seminar on the History of that Atlantic World at Harvard University. I am extremely appreciative of the exceptional research assistance provided by Vikram Tamboli (Kluge Center) and Natalie Deibel (GW). I also must single out the assistance offered by Michael Weeks, who runs the GW History Department with miraculous efficiency.

The staff at libraries and archives in Spain, the United States, and England were crucially helpful. In particular, I want to thank the Bancroft Library (Susan Snyder), the John Carter Brown Library (Norman Fiering and Susan Danforth), and the Huntington Library (Roy Ritchie).

Acknowledgments

As this project has seen me pass through several stages of the academic life cycle, I have depended on generous mentors. Peter Sahlins was a smart and supportive advisor. James Amelang—whose name is ubiquitous in the acknowledgement pages of books on early modern Spanish history for very good reasons—is, quite simply, an amazing mentor whose erudition is perhaps only surpassed by his generosity. Many endnotes in this book have their origins in his e-mails. I am also grateful for the learning and encouragement offered by Jordan Goodman, Anthony Grafton, Richard Kagan, Ken Mills.

This book very much was born in Berkeley. It carries other geographic traces, too: Madrid, Seville, Santa Fé, NM, and the District of Columbia. In all of these places, I found new and old friends who shared with me ideas, food, and love, for which I can only begin to express my gratitude. Like the rest of the book, this list proceeds in roughly geographic and chronological order (and omits far too many): Sarah Moseley, Vinnie D'Angelo, Elizabeth Gessel, Jeffrey Becker, Jennifer Kagiwada, Alison Barth, Wayne Wu, Diana Selig, Ethan Pollock, Katharine Norris, Pablo Urrutia Jordana, Guillermina Achleitner Dichino, Laura Cunniff, Gay White, Susan Seastone, Marcela Estevez, Jovita Baber, Daviken Studnicki-Gizbert, Adam Rothman, Antonio Barrera-Osorio, Paula de Vos, Alison Games, Johanna Bockman, Andrew Zimmerman, Stephanie Smallwood, Liz Langston and Amy Searight.

The esteemed colleagues and dear friends and family who read this book in its many phases of development are heroes to me: various anonymous reviewers, Tyler Anbinder, Gillian Weiss, Carol Benedict, Kathy Camp, James Amelang, Alison Kalett (editor extraordinaire), Rita Norton, David Carl Andrew Keitt, K. K. Roeder, Kent Norton, and Claudia Verhoeven. I want to acknowledge Katy Meigs for her copy-editing and all of the terrific people at Cornell University Press, particularly Michael J. McGandy and Ange Romeo-Hall, who have shown such patience and commitment to this project.

The generosity of the George Washington University History Department and donor Benjamin Klubes helped make possible the reproduction of the images.

I am very lucky to have such a loving and generous family. There is no way to adequately express my thanks to Virginia, Louisa, Daniel, Sharon, Julia, Kent, and Rita.

Abbreviations:
Archives, Libraries,
Collections

Seville

ADS	Archivo de la Diputación, Sevilla
AFTS	Archivo de la Fábrica de Tabacos, Sevilla
AGI	Archivo General de Indias
AGI Consul.	Consulados
AGI Contrat.	Contratación
AGI Contad.	Contaduría
AGI Indif.	Indiferente
AGI Mex.	Audiencia de México
AGI SDom.	Audiencia de Santo Domingo
BCol.	Biblioteca Colombina

Simancas

AGS	Archivo General de Simancas
AGS DGT	Dirección General de Tesorero
AGS CJH	Consejo y Junta de Hacienda
AGS Rentas Cont. Gen.	Rentas, Contaduría General

Madrid

AHN	Archivo Histórico Nacional, Madrid
AHN Cons.	Consejos
AHN Est.	Estado
AHN Inq.	Inquisición
AHN Rent.	Rentas
AHPM	Archivo Histórico de Protocolos de Madrid
AVM	Archivo de la Villa de Madrid
AVM Sec.	Secretaría
BN	Biblioteca Nacional

BN VE	Varios Especiales
PRB	Palacio Real, Biblioteca
RAH	Real Academia de la Historia

London

BL	British Library
BL Add. Mss.	Additional Manuscripts
BL Eg. Mss.	Egerton Manuscripts

Mexico

AGN	Archivo General de la Nación, Mexico City
AGN Inq.	Inquisición

United States

Banc.	Bancroft Library, University of California, Berkeley
HSA	Hispanic Society of America Library, New York City
Hunt.	Huntington Library, San Marino, California
JCB	John Carter Brown Library, Brown University, Providence, Rhode Island
NYPL Arents	New York Public Library, Arents Tobacco Collection

Other Abbreviations

FC	*Florentine Codex*
est.	estampa
exp.	expediente (file)
inv.	inventario (inventory)
leg.	legajo (bundle)
lib.	libro (book)
no.	numero (number)
r.	ramo (folder)
sig.	signatura (shelf mark)

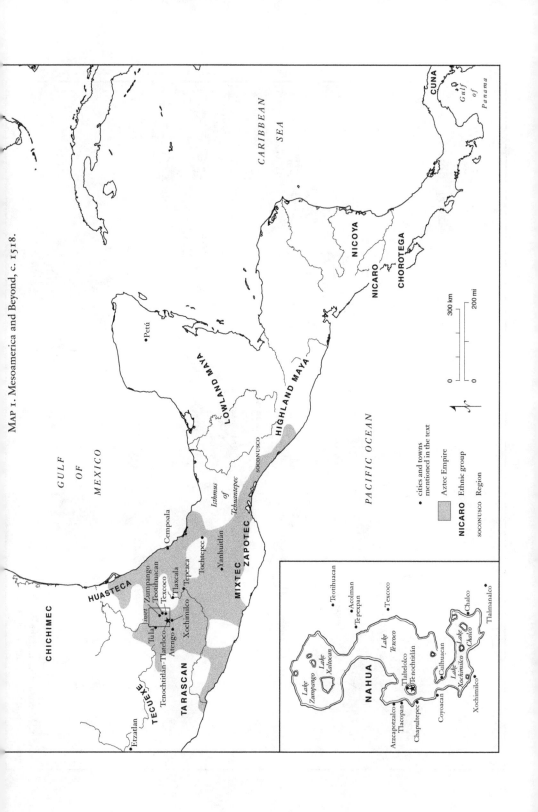

MAP 1. Mesoamerica and Beyond, c. 1518.

CHICHIMEC

TECUEX

Etzatlan

TARASCAN

HUASTECA

GULF
OF
MEXICO

Tula
Tenochtitlán—Tlatelolco
Atengo
Xochimilco
Metztitlán
Zumpango
Teotihuacan
Texcoco
Tlaxcala
Tepeaca

Cempoala

Tochtepec

Yanhuitlán

MIXTEC

ZAPOTEC

Isthmus
of
Tehuantepec

SOCONUSCO

PACIFIC OCEAN

Petú

LOWLAND MAYA

HIGHLAND MAYA

CARIBBEAN
SEA

NICOYA

NICARO

CHOROTEGA

CUNA

Gulf
of
Panama

• cities and towns
  mentioned in the text

▨ Aztec Empire

NICARO Ethnic group

SOCONUSCO Region

300 km

200 mi

0

0

Lake
Zumpango

Lake
Xaltocan

Teotihuacan

Acolman

Tepexpan

Texcoco

Lake
Texcoco

Atzcapotzalco
Tlacopan
Chapultepec

Tlatelolco
Tenochtitlán

Coyoacan

Culhuacan

Xochimilco

Lake
Xochimilco

Chalco

Lake
Chalco

Tlalmanalco

NAHUA

Xochimilco

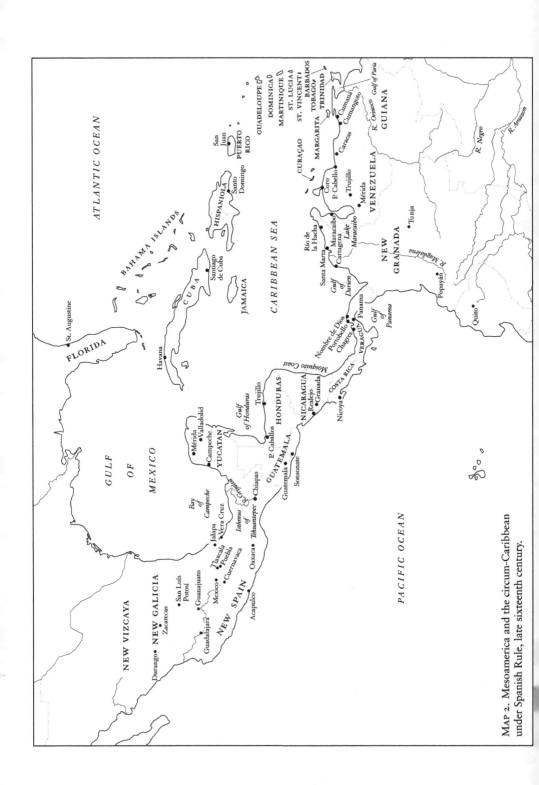

MAP 2. Mesoamerica and the circum-Caribbean under Spanish Rule, late sixteenth century.

Sacred Gifts, Profane Pleasures

❖

Introduction

If, in 1491, you had crossed the Americas north to south, visiting the far-flung communities between the sub-Arctic tundra and the southern shores of South America, one thing you would have noticed was the ubiquity of tobacco.[1] In some places, you would have seen people sucking on dried leaves mixed with crushed seashells, while elsewhere you would have passed others inhaling snuff or puffing on corn-husk cigarettes, long-stemmed pipes, or cigars. In many places, people applied tobacco topically to treat wounds and infections or ingested tobacco concoctions to fight parasites.[2] Despite Amerindians' diverse uses for tobacco and its wide geographical distribution, I suspect you would have noticed a common element: Across the western hemisphere, people saw it as essential to their physical, social, and spiritual well-being.

During your travels southward, at some point before you arrived in the Aztec Empire in central Mexico, you would have begun encountering chocolate consumers.[3] In this chocolate zone, which stretched at least as far south as present-day Nicaragua and Costa Rica,[4] people, at least the powerful ones, consumed a beverage made from the dried fermented seeds of the fruit of the *Theobrama cacao* tree. The fact that the cacao seeds ("beans") functioned as currency throughout the region would have tipped you off to its value. You might also have noticed that in this region people saw chocolate as similar in nature to blood—both of them were liquids coursing with life-giving force. Chocolate, reddened with the spice achiote, was prescribed for hemorrhages, shared during marriage ceremonies, and offered in sacrifice to thirsty, sensuous deities. Tobacco, not infrequently, accompanied the consumption of chocolate.

Figure 0.1. Drinking vessel (detail). Maya, Late Classic period, 600–750 CE. This image reflects the longstanding Mesoamerican tradition linking smoking tobacco and drinking chocolate. Monkeys were vital to cacao ecology since they spread the seeds; they were also associated with creativity in traditional Mesoamerica beliefs. Guatemala, central Petén lowlands. Earthenware: red, black, and brown on orange slip paint. 20.8×11.8 cm. Private Collection. Photograph © 2008, Museum of Fine Arts, Boston.

If, in the same year, you had visited Europe, you would not have encountered these two quintessential American goods, for neither existed outside of the western hemisphere. Their spread eastward was one of the consequences of the chain of events sparked by Christopher Columbus's accidental discoveries. For some, the infiltration of tobacco and chocolate by the early seventeenth century into Madrid, the seat of the Spanish Empire, defined a new epoch. In 1627, the courtier Francisco de Quevedo, a biting satirist and devotee of both goods, made an ugly joke of it. "The devil of tobacco and the devil of chocolate," he wrote, "told me that they had avenged the Indies against Spain," wreaking more harm with snuff, smoke, and chocolate drinks than the conquistadores "Columbus and Cortés and Almagro and Pizarro" had wrought across the Atlantic. He observed how these goods had transformed his compatriots' bodies: tobacco habitués afflicted by "snuffling and sneezing" and chocolate-indulgers with gas and dizziness. Quevedo believed these physical symptoms marked an even more disturbing metamorphosis. European tobacco and chocolate aficionados had become idolaters. In emulating the inhabitants of the New World, they had transferred their faith in Christ to these "entrancing," diabolical substances (which chocoholics "venerated" while smokers were "apprenticed for hell").[5]

Though when Quevedo wrote this passage tobacco and chocolate were only at the beginning stages of their Old World conquests, he was prescient about their path toward global dominance. A recent study found that caffeine and nicotine are, respectively, the first and third most widely consumed psychoactive substances in the world.[6] Nicotine's ranking is due, of course, to the spread of tobacco. Chocolate is not, strictly speaking, a caffeinated substance since it contains only trace amounts of caffeine, but it is rich in caffeine's molecular relative, theobromine. Moreover, one cannot understand the triumph of coffee and tea without chocolate, for the latter was the first stimulant beverage used in Europe, and Europeans' initial experiences with chocolate informed, perhaps even precipitated, their subsequent adoption of these other beverages.

Quevedo's obscene joke introduces the question that drives this book. What, exactly, did it mean for Europeans—bound as they were to an ideology that insisted on their religious and cultural supremacy—to become consumers of goods that they knew were so enmeshed in the religious practices of the pagan "savages" whom they had conquered? In asking this question, I am reframing the history of the Atlantic world.

1492 RECONSIDERED

The year 1492 marks a dramatic rupture in the history of the world. The millennial isolation of the globe's two hemispheres came to a sudden end.

The new era in world history is most often told as a story of European conquests, which, of course, it was: Old World pathogens killed native American peoples; colonial regimes displaced native societies; settlers and merchants exploited New World resources; scientific experts inventoried flora and fauna.[7] Across the genres of history—environmental, economic, political, and cultural—the Americas figure as a land of objects to be possessed, subdued, converted, exploited, and catalogued. However, there are counterstories that make clear that native Americans (and enslaved Africans), though they suffered greatly as a consequence of European conquests and colonial systems, were not passive victims. Colonized subjects actively participated in the making of the American societies that emerged in the aftermath of European invasions. In this book, I argue that the history of tobacco and chocolate reveals that this was a phenomenon with repercussions for the other side of the Atlantic ocean. Like its American counterparts, European society was profoundly affected by the new era inaugurated in 1492.

Given the importance of tobacco and chocolate to both pre-Columbian Amerindian societies and "post-Columbian" European societies, it is somewhat surprising that they have not occupied more prominent positions in general histories of the Atlantic world. Part of the reason, I suspect, is the tendency, one initiated in the sixteenth century, as will be seen, to view both goods as neutral resources, products of the natural world, devoid of cultural content.[8] Yet they are no less *cultural* artifacts than, say, guns or writing. Tobacco and chocolate—as they are used today and as they were used when Europeans arrived in the fifteenth and sixteenth centuries— would not exist without knowledge and techniques developed over millennia in the western hemisphere. Some speculate that when the inhabitants of tropical northern South America invented agriculture with slash-and-burn techniques perhaps eight thousand years ago, tobacco, on a par with maize and cotton, was one of their earliest crops. The earliest archaeological evidence for the human use of tobacco are seeds from Peru that date from 2500 to 1800 BCE, and, more indirectly, tubular stone pipes from eastern North America that date as early as 2000 BCE.[9] Neither of the two most prevalent species of tobacco at the time of the European invasions, *Nicotiana rustica* and *Nicotiana tabacum*, existed in the wild, so it seems likely that humans in the distant past hybridized them from naturally occurring species.[10] "Tobacco," however, was much more than a plant; it was manufactured using technologies of cultivation, curing, and processing. Smoking, which was a favored Amerindian method of ingesting tobacco, was also a technology, and one that many believe did not exist in Europe prior to 1492.

Figure 0.2. Vase (detail). Maya, Late Classic period. This detail from a Mayan court scene shows two palace attendants smoking together. 24×18 cm. Rollout Photograph K8469 © Justin Kerr.

Figure 0.3. Ceramic vessel (detail). Maya, Late Classic period. By pouring from a height, this woman was probably making foamy chocolate. She is in the Maya underworld presided over by God L (not pictured here). Guatemala, northern Petén. 21.5 × 16.6 cm. Princeton University Art Museum. Rollout Photograph K511 © Justin Kerr.

"Chocolate" is the consequence of countless breakthroughs in plant domestication, experimental hybridization, cultivation techniques, and fermentation and curing technologies, not to mention a complex set of social
rituals surrounding its manufacture, distribution, display, service, and
consumption.[11] Cacao derives from the *Theobrama cacao* tree, a
distinctive-looking arboreal specimen with a multistemmed dark trunk
from which small flowers emerge directly and become largish, oblong, stri-
ated pods of a reddish color.[12] Then, as today, "chocolate" is many steps of
intervention away from raw cacao. First, one must remove the dark seeds
from the pulpy fibrous interior of the cacao pod for drying and fermentation and then grind and heat the "nibs" or "beans." Of course, chocolate is
more than processed cacao. For both the Europeans and the pre-Columbian
Indians featured in this book, chocolate was almost exclusively a beverage,
one that mixed cacao, water, and a panoply of other ingredients, such as
maize, achiote, and vanilla.

The origins of the human use of cacao are mysterious and contested. It is
not clear whether cacao was first cultivated in South America, Mesoamerica, or independently in both.[13] The oldest known vessels that yield chemical traces of chocolate preparation (discovered in the Ulua River Valley of
Honduras) date to about 1100 BCE,[14] though linguistic evidence suggests
that its invention was much earlier. Inhabitants of the Gulf Coast (Olmec
or their descendants) provided the loan word *kakawa* that appeared in
Mayan languages as *kakaw*, Nahuatl as *kakaw-atl* (or *cacautl*), as well as
similar variants in most other Mesoamerican languages.[15] Whether they
inherited chocolate from Gulf communities or predecessors in Honduras,
the Mayans of the Classic period (250–900 CE) have left behind abundant
physical and symbolic traces of cacao and chocolate, such as the vessels
with identifiable residue of theobromine, or those inscribed with glyphs
proclaiming *kakaw*, or those decorated with gods awaiting foamy chocolate or chocolate gods who themselves sprout cacao.[16]

BEYOND BIOLOGICAL DETERMINISM
OR CULTURAL CONSTRUCTIVISM

In this book, I offer a revisionist account of how Europeans assimilated
tobacco and chocolate.[17] The prevailing explanations for why and how
these things made their transoceanic, transcultural migration fall into two
categories: biological determinism and cultural constructivism. In the
former tradition, the addictiveness of these two substances is what explains
their eventual global success. Tobacco is primarily understood as a vessel
for nicotine and cacao as one for theobromine, or because scientists are not
sure that theobromine constitutes an addictive substance, they defer to

chocolate's "innate" sensory appeal.[18] In this tradition, tobacco's addictiveness or chocolate's intrinsic hedonic qualities explain the alleged ease with which they attract new devotees, leading one historian to refer to their role in history as the "Big Fix."[19]

The most compelling rebuttal to the theory that Europeans instantly recognized the aesthetic and psychoactive attractions of tobacco and chocolate is that empirically they did not. Those Europeans who had only scant exposure to the chocolate drink found it, by and large, disgusting, as indicated by the experience of a Milanese adventurer, Girolamo Benzoni. Encountering chocolate in Nicaragua in the middle of the sixteenth century, Benzoni wrote that it

> seemed more a drink for pigs, than a drink for humanity. I was in this country for more than year, and never wanted to taste it, and whenever I passed a settlement, some Indian would offer me a drink of it, and would be amazed when I would not accept, going away laughing.[20]

He found tobacco even more repugnant: "I cannot imagine that the Devil could vomit something more pestilent. . . . Going through the provinces of Guatemala and Nicaragua, I have entered the house of an Indian who had taken this herb . . . and immediately perceiving the sharp fetid smell of this truly diabolical and stinking smoke, I was obliged to go away in haste, and seek some other place."[21] The initial revulsion that so often characterized European first encounters with tobacco and chocolate is part of the reason Europeans did not use these goods on a wide scale until the seventeenth century. While the powerful chemical compounds may contribute to their enduring attraction, they clearly cannot account for why people begin to consume tobacco and chocolate or for the particular manners in which they use them.[22]

Rightly suspicious of explanations that hinge on biological destiny, other scholars have emphasized the role of culture to explain the introduction of these goods into the Old World. Accordingly, they argue that tobacco and chocolate were "Europeanized" materially and symbolically. From this tradition comes the oft-repeated (and incorrect) contention that Europeans transformed chocolate to suit their palates by sweetening it with sugar, exiling maize, and replacing American spices with those from the Old World. In the case of tobacco, many claim that it was granted a passport to Europe only because it was perceived as a medicine and because Amerindian symbolic investments were repudiated. It is often said that tobacco and chocolate were first accepted in Europe as medicinal goods and only later did European consumers discover their social and recreational attractions.[23]

In contrast, I argue that the European (and African and mestizo and Creole) embrace of tobacco and chocolate was not the consequence of addictive properties or purposeful efforts to make them fit aesthetic or ideological norms. Rather, the material forms of tobacco and chocolate first consumed by Europeans closely resembled Indian concoctions. Likewise, Europeans did not welcome tobacco and chocolate in spite of the meanings that Indians attributed to them, but often *because* of them. New tastes emerged out of the social matrix created of Atlantic Empires.

As this book will illustrate, a taste for tobacco or chocolate, before 1492 and afterwards, entailed more than a dependence on the effects of nicotine or other psychotropic substances. A taste for chocolate meant a desire to drink a red, frothy, flower-fragranced liquid, to feel the smooth surface of a lacquered gourd or porcelain cup against your lips, made warm by its heated contents. To taste tobacco was to smell the mingled odors of pungent tobacco and botanical extracts and to feel nasal passages pricked sharply or bronchial passageways brushed by smoke. Taste encompassed the sense that a certain time of day or a particular situation (gathering of friends, a formal feast, a respite from labor, beginning of a trek, solitary meditation) required the presence of one good or the other. The human mind associates sensory experiences with memories; better yet, "taste and smell alone . . . bear unflinchingly, in the tiny and almost impalpable drop of their essence, the vast structure of recollection."[24] Nor are these "recollections" solely personal and idiosyncratic but they are also collective; they include a culture's convictions about the natural order of things.

In pre-Columbian America, the sensory experiences induced by tobacco and chocolate concretized notions about relationships between humans and between humans and the spirit world. When Europeans and others came into contact with these goods, they learned not only about what tobacco and chocolate should taste like, smell like, look like, and where and when they should be consumed, but also about these more abstract associations. As a result, a history of these goods is a bridge between material and symbolic levels of experience.

MESTISAJE AND MODERNITY

The social milieu of the Americas and Europe's Atlantic hubs created an environment where people became unintentionally habituated to tobacco and chocolate. A central theme in this account is that of syncretism, a term most often applied to colonial societies where the cultures of the conquerors and conquered mingle.[25] However, syncretism, meaning an amalgamation of beliefs and practices emerging from different cultural traditions, defined why and how tobacco and chocolate arrived in Europe, as well as how and why they endured in America. European uses of the goods had their origins in native American technologies, material forms, therapeutic knowledge, and symbolic investments. Equally important in understanding the European assimilation of tobacco and chocolate was the fact that colonial and Christian discourses discouraged and denied the desirability of emulation of "idolaters" and "savages." In other words, conquistadores, scientists, and theologians formally repudiated the syncretism that underlay the reception of the American goods. Understanding this dynamic of syncretism and its disavowal can help us understand not only tobacco and chocolate but also the broader phenomena in which they were enmeshed: conquest ideologies, religious practices, colonial identities, scientific research, trading networks, state building, secular rituals, and discourses of the supernatural.

The story begins in the lands of Aztec, Mayan, and other Mesoamerican groups at the beginning of the sixteenth century in the years before the Spanish conquests. Though often divided politically and linguistically, these people were bound together in their common usage of tobacco and chocolate. Appreciated for their powerful sensory, mood-altering, and medicinal effects, these goods anchored rituals of religious and social significance as well as those of quotidian efficacy. Then, Spanish conquest, epidemic disease, and the imposition of a colonial regime transformed the Americas.

Chapters 2, 3, and 4 illuminate a central paradox of early colonial society in Spanish America. On the one hand, the ideology legitimating Spanish conquest depended on an absolute distinction between European and Indian identities. In published chronicles and histories, tobacco and chocolate became symbols of Indian otherness, the former epitomizing diabolically inspired paganism and the latter evoking an idealized lost epoch of "noble savagery." And for the first generation of Indians, tobacco and chocolate featured powerfully in resistance efforts; they anchored pre-colonial rituals and stories threatened with extinction. On the other hand, the reality of colonial experience led to an increasingly pervasive blurring of bloodlines and cultural traditions.

For colonists and Indians alike, tobacco and chocolate also exemplified the process of syncretism that was going on everywhere. For native Americans, as well as increasing numbers of free and enslaved Africans and those of mixed ethnicity, both goods provided a means to adapt Christianity to traditional beliefs and practices and offered a material bridge between old and new religious and cosmological traditions. Likewise, social relations in American settings made colonists susceptible to native influence. European soldiers relied on Indian allies, colonists on concubines and domestic servants, and missionaries on their converts to minister to their bodily needs.

Through these encounters, Europeans learned to hold a pipe, dip snuff, and scoop the foam off of chocolate. They also learned when, why, and what one should think when using the novel substances: they discovered that tobacco and chocolate shared among strangers symbolized friendship, that tobacco had healing properties, and that chocolate brought honor or assisted the pursuit of love. Colonists become adept students of Indian culture without even knowing it.

Chapters 5, 6, and 7 investigate the systematic entrance of tobacco and chocolate into European discourses and markets. Initially, sixteenth-century academic medicine offered stiff resistance to American goods, particularly those that had obvious social and sacramental, as well as medicinal, uses. It was a turning point, then, when in 1571 the Sevillan physician Nicolás Monardes published a book celebrating New World materia medica that praised tobacco above all. The reaction of physicians such as Monardes to tobacco and chocolate reveals, I argue, that colonial science was defined by, on the one hand, its practitioners' fascination with and dependence on native American knowledge and, on the other, the discourse of European supremacy.

Tobacco and chocolate did not enter European markets in significant quantities until the 1590s. Their transformation into European commodities is sometimes explained as a consequence of their "medicalization." Quite to the contrary, their arrival into European society was predicated on their social character; demand for the goods flowed from the emergence of trans-Atlantic communities of habituated consumers encompassing elite networks of colonial officials, well-traveled missionaries, and merchants, and plebian networks of mariners. On the supply side, the commodification of tobacco and cacao took opposite routes. With official encouragement, colonists in New Spain and Guatemala modeled their organization of cacao production on pre-conquest systems in the domains formerly controlled by Aztec and Maya elites. Tobacco, in contrast, was commodified in spite of rather than because of the policies of the Spanish Crown. The organization of tobacco production for Atlantic trade occurred initially in the eastern Caribbean, a colonial backwater by the late sixteenth century, a place where unlikely alliances formed between autonomous native American communities, English and Dutch privateers, Portuguese merchants, and desperate Spanish settlers.

In Chapters 8, 9, and 10, I examine the period from the 1630s through the eighteenth century, when the use of tobacco and chocolate was thoroughly entrenched in Iberian society. Reversing its initial apathetic or even antagonistic stance toward these goods, the Hapsburg state in the 1630s made them the basis for lucrative "vice" and "luxury" taxes designed to remedy its chronic fiscal woes. The implementation in 1636 of a royal tobacco monopoly allowed the state unprecedented reach into civil society. The seventeenth-century state grew as the result of actions by interest groups—particularly a group of merchants-cum-state financiers—as much as it did as the result of royal bureaucracy. An examination of the state through the lens of tobacco also becomes an investigation of Portuguese New Christians, many of them "crypto-Jews," who administered the monopoly and whose own syncretic religious prerogatives dictated in significant ways the organization of the state institution.

By the early seventeenth century, the consumption of tobacco and chocolate permeated Spanish society in both the New and Old Worlds. Along with material practices heavily indebted to native American and Creole antecedents, Spaniards absorbed ritual practices and symbolic connotations connected to pre-Columbian tobacco and chocolate, crediting them as agents that could cure physical maladies, assuage emotional discomfort, bind people with social ties, proclaim honor, or allow catharsis. In pre-Columbian America, tobacco and chocolate linked humans to divine forces and their uses reinforced foundational cosmological beliefs. In post-Columbian Europe, they undermined institutional Christianity. Yet, they also brought an enchanted animism to the secular realm. They were, in fact, among the first commodity fetishes of the modern world.

Despite the predilections of some—modern observers as well as Quevedo—to see the lethal legacy of tobacco as "Moctezuma's revenge," my objective is not to settle scores. Rather, it is to see what happens if one tells the history of empire in reverse of conventional narratives, from the periphery to the center. Recreating the trajectories of tobacco and chocolate over the course of two centuries leads to many corners of the early modern Atlantic world, places where one finds determined and frightened soldiers, zealous missionaries, resourceful plantation slaves, defiant Mesoamerican nobles, adaptive Indian commoners, mestiza love sorceresses, unsubjugated Carib Indians, cosmopolitan European humanists, crypto-Jewish Portuguese traders, lofty Sevillan merchants, worldly clergyman, scrappy sailors, reforming financial ministers, the patrons of smoky taverns, and the guests of well-appointed noble mansions. Taking tobacco and chocolate as our guides, these individuals' struggles and stories become not isolated anecdotes but nodes of an expanding social web created by the accidents of empire.

1

Experiencing the Sacred
and the Social

❖ ❖

There was much that dazzled Bernal Díaz del Castillo (1492–1580?), a soldier who accompanied Hernán Cortés in his military campaigns in central
Mexico, about Tenochtitlan and the neighboring cities: "These great towns
and temples and buildings rising from the water, all made of stone, seemed
like an enchanted vision." There were the "palaces in which they lodged
us . . . spacious and well-built," whose exteriors gleamed with fresh coats
of lime and displayed stone friezes and bright paintings of great artistry,
and whose interiors were paneled with fragrant wood and draped with
woven cotton textiles. There was the great marketplace of Tlateloco, which
"astounded with the great number of people and the quantities of merchandise and the orderliness and good arrangements that prevailed . . .
every kind of merchandise was kept separate and its fixed place marked for
it," the variety ranging from human chattel to precious stones and tropical
feathers to hides of jaguars and other fearsome cats to foodstuffs (meat,
fowl, vegetables, legumes, honey, salt) to "pottery of all kinds, from big
water-jars to little jugs." There was the ceremonial precinct ("bigger I think
than the Plaza at Salamanca"), "surrounded by a double masonry wall and
paved, like the whole place, with very large smooth white flagstones." At
its center, surrounded by smaller shrines and clean-swept courts, loomed a
"great temple" where Aztecs worshipped "their war god," sculpted out of
precious stones, who was "very tall and very fat" with "terrible eyes," "gir-
dled with huge snakes," and another "half man and half lizard . . . the god
of seedtime and harvest." In these shrines he reported seeing incense braziers "in which they were burning the hearts of three Indians whom they
had sacrificed that day" and "walls so caked in blood and the floor so

bathed in it that the stench was worse than that of any slaughter-house in Spain." Yet from the temple top he also admired the feats of civil engineering ("the bridges that were constructed at intervals on the causeways"), the evidence of prosperity in the busy canoe traffic, and aerial views of the temples and shrines in neighboring cities "that looked like gleaming white towers and castles: a marvelous sight."[1]

Even these riches and the sophistication of the marketplace, this beauty of the construction and landscaping, these achievements of civil engineering, and the horrors of human sacrifice that captured Díaz's imagination and inspired his reminiscences did not keep him from lavishing the most attention on the splendors of the court of Moctezuma, the ruler of the Aztecs. He began with his litter, "a marvelous sight" that included a "canopy of green feathers, decorated with gold work, silver, pearls, and jade." Moctezuma was "magnificently clad in their fashion," wrote Díaz, describing the sandals (a privilege restricted to nobility) and his fine cloak. Attending the ruler "were four great caciques who carried the canopy above their heads, and many more lords who walked before the great Moctezuma, sweeping the ground on which he was to tread, and laying down cloaks so that his feet should not touch the earth. Not one of these chieftains dared to look him in the face." Díaz detailed his armories, aviaries ("I cannot possibly enumerate every kind of bird that was in it or describe its characteristics"—though he mentioned the green-plumed quetzals and "beautifully marked ducks"), and gardens with flowers, "sweet-scented trees planted in their order," and medicinal and useful herbs ("a wonderful sight"). He discussed the skilled craftsmen Moctezuma employed, the stonecutters, masons, carpenters, jewelers, feather workers (members of the latter two "counted in the same rank" as Michelangelo), and "the great number of performers whom Montezuma kept to entertain him" ("dancers and stilt-walkers and some who seemed to fly as they leapt through the air"). Still, Díaz lingered particularly on "the way his meals were served" to illustrate the sumptuous grandeur of Moctezuma's court. Díaz described the beauty of the dining implements—the carved stool on which the ruler sat, the red-and-black painted pottery in which his food was served, the wooden screen worked with gold that protected his privacy as he ate—and the quantity and variety of the dishes ("more than thirty prepared in their native style"). He also mentioned the "great chieftains" who attended him, old men who stood respectfully while he ate, "four very clean and beautiful girls" who brought him water to clean his hands, and the jesters and acrobats who amused him.

Yet tobacco and chocolate surpassed all of these instances that showcased the Aztec ruler's ability to marshal resources and deference from his subjects. To exemplify the sumptuous grandeur of the royal court,

Díaz wrote how the beautiful, freshly bathed serving girls brought Mocte-zuma

> a certain beverage made of cacao in cups in the manner of fine gold; they said that it was to have success with women but then we could not look into that. But what I did see was that he was brought about fifty big containers filled with cacao and its foam, and the women served him with great respect.

He added that

> as soon as the great Montezuma had dined, all the guards and many more of his household servants ate in their turn. I think more than a thousand plates of food must have been brought in for them, and more than two thousand containers of chocolate frothed up in the Mexican style, and the infinite quantities of fruit, so that with his women and serving-maids and bread-makers and chocolate-makers his expenses must have been considerable.

Díaz was almost finished here with his account of Moctezuma's victuals and entertainments, when he added a few more critical elements he had almost "forgotten." The last one was that "two more very handsome women" placed "on his table three tubes—well painted and gilded—filled with liquidambar and tobacco, and when he finished eating, after they had danced, sang, and removed the table, he took small amounts of smoke of one of the tubes, and with these he became sleepy."[2] In the conspicuous denouement of a lengthy and elaborately choreographed feast, Moctezuma "ennobled"—to use the anthropologist Victor Turner's term—tobacco and chocolate with the stature of his office and the sumptuous formality of the setting, while the experience induced by their consumption grounded and concretized the notion of rank and caste stratification.[3] That well-crafted tobacco pipes and rich chocolate foaming in fine vessels expressed, even conferred, exalted status was grasped very quickly by the conquering Span-iards, themselves products of an intensely stratified and status-conscious culture. Even in his bawdy and half-joking aside about chocolate's aphrodi-siacal qualities, Díaz conveyed the Mesoamerican association of chocolate with sexually charged vitality. He captured Mesoamericans' understand-ing of tobacco pipes as vessels of olfactory and kinesthetic pleasure and languid contentment.

Like memories, strongly held beliefs become anchored in the body through their enmeshment with somatic sensations. Every time a Meso-american saw a tobacco gourd affixed to a rendering of a deity, or on a priest, or on a midwife, he or she had the divinity made concrete rather than abstract, grounded in the amazing powers of the healing, numbing, pain-relieving plant. The sweet pungent smell of pipes and cigars gave the divine a location in the olfactory organ. The intense, complex flavors of chocolate, combining bitter, musky, floral, and sweet notes, gave the celestial realm a flavor. An abstract understanding of the universe became real and precise through the sensory experiences of ritual and everyday practice. The effects went both ways. The imputation of social and sacred qualities to tobacco and chocolate (ennoblement) was a consequence of their appearance and reappearance in rites that expressed beliefs about the world.

CULTURAL UNITY IN MESOAMERICA

At the time of the Spanish invasions, the Mexica (as the Aztecs are properly known) controlled an expanding empire. Originating as one among many Nahuatl-speaking tribes that migrated south to the high-altitude plateaus of central Mexico, by the early fourteenth century they had founded Tenochtitlan, exiling or mingling with the residents of a preexisting community. By 1470 the Mexica and the city-states Texcoco and Tlacopan, in a partnership known as the Triple Alliance, succeeded in subordinating most neighboring communities in central Mexico, as well as parts of the Gulf Coast, much of Oaxaca, and Soconusco, a prime cacao-producing region along the Pacific seaboard of the modern state of Chiapas stretching to Guatemala. In 1473 the Mexica annexed an adjacent island-lake city, Tlateloco, making it another ward of Tenochtitlan, albeit a resentful one.[4] It is telling about regional integration as well as Mesoamerican notions of empire that among the tribute levied by Mexica from conquered groups were cacao, chocolate-drinking vessels, and tobacco pipes (figure 1.1).[5]

Despite their political and military supremacy, the Mexica, whose culture was a by-product of successive rounds of migration and acculturation, were recent arrivistes in Mesoamerica. Sustained contact over thousands of years in Mesoamerica resulted in a common set of practices and beliefs centered around tobacco and chocolate. That cacao beans functioned as currency throughout this entire region underscores the common and high esteem in which chocolate was held by peoples otherwise separated by language, geography, and warfare.[6] An indication of Mesoamerican cultural homogeneity where chocolate was concerned was the fact that an enslaved woman brought to the Mexica capital might be spared a fate as a sacrifice victim and instead be chosen as a wife if she was an adept chocolate maker (and chocolate making was exclusively women's work). As a former subject of the Aztec Empire explained, "If a woman [slave] could embroider, or if she prepared food well, or made good cacao—from her hand good food, good drink came—[or if she were] a clear speaker, she also was set aside. The nobles took [women like her] as wives."[7] The dominant cacao concoction

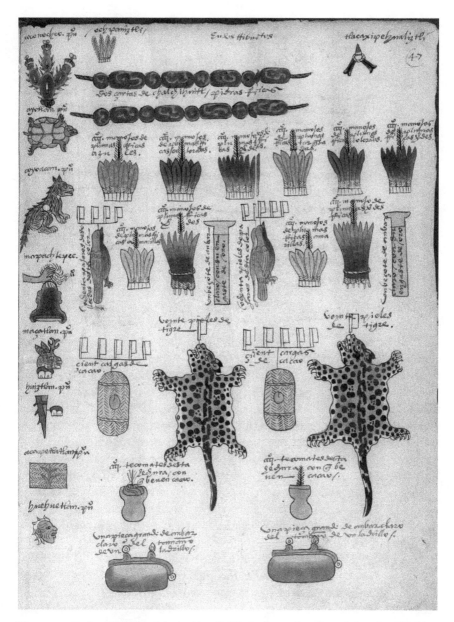

Figure 1.1. *Codex Mendoza*, fol. 47r (detail). The baskets of cacao and chocolate-drinking vessels were among the goods Mexica rulers levied from their tributaries. Shelfmark: MS. Arch. Selden A 1. Hand-painted manuscript. Reproduced by permission of the Bodleian Library, University of Oxford.

was a beverage, or rather, several kinds of beverages, some hot and cold, some mixed with maize and some without, and some spiced with chili peppers and fragrant flowers. Though there are allusions to innumerable variety in Mesoamerican chocolate drinks, colonial dictionaries suggest standardization in classes of cacao beverages.[8] Zapotec (one of the Oaxacan languages), Nahuatl, and Maya speakers attached different names to common compositions, such as "the beverage of cacao with maize," "the beverage of cacao with chili peppers," "the beverage of cacao alone," and the "beverage of cacao with dried and ground flowers."[9] The most luxurious chocolate was described as "finely ground, soft, foamy, reddish bitter." This concoction included a beloved aromatic triumvirate of tropical flowers: vanilla (*tlilxochitl*); a spice the Nahuas called "flowery ear," "divine ear," or "great ear" (*xochinacaztli, teonacaztli,* or *hueinacaztli*); and *mecaxóchitl*, which gave the drink resinous, spicy, flowery notes, collectively reminiscent to early modern Europeans of allspice, nutmeg, ambergris, cinnamon, rose, and anise.[10] The presence of chili warmed the throat (not unlike the heat offered by a swig of whisky); achiote (annatto) tinged the drink red and imparted a slightly musky flavor (sometimes compared to paprika and saffron); and wild bee honey sweetened it. A foamy head—which could be scooped with a turtle-shell stirring spoon—capped the beverage (figures 0.3 and 1.2).[11] The visual pleasures of chocolate extended to the paraphernalia used for its consumption, such as the special vessels exclusively used for chocolate drinking that Moctezuma levied as tribute (figure 1.1).[12] Appreciation of psychotropic effects of chocolate were articulated in a Mexica proverb that declared chocolate "gladdens one, refreshes one, consoles one, invigorates one. Thus it is said: 'I take cacao. I wet my lips. I refresh myself.'"[13] Since the cacao tree has a restricted growing range, many pre-Columbian consumers only procured its fruit or seeds through long-distance trade or tribute. Cacao was extensively cultivated in Veracruz, Tabasco, and in the Pacific coastal zone stretching from Mexico to El Salvador, though smaller orchards were also tended in the Yucatán Peninsula and Oaxaca.[14]

Mesoamericans also shared common ground in their use of tobacco, distinguishing it into two broad categories: the "smoking tubes"—as the Spanish literally translated the Nahuatl term—that were often enjoyed in proximity to chocolate drinks, and the pulverized tobacco often enhanced with powdered lime (an alkaloid substance often obtained from seashells or ashes), which was ingested internally or applied topically. (For smoking tubes see figures 0.1, 0.2, 1.3, 1.8; for pulverized tobacco, figures 1.11, 1.12, 1.13.) The specialization of craftsmen underscores the distinction made between these two categories of tobacco products. The huge market in Tlatelolco had an area designated for "those who sell smoking tubes"

ynċia mexicana

Figure 1.2. *Codex Tudela*, fol. 3r. A page from a manuscript created c. 1553 that depicts a woman making chocolate. Like the woman in a Late Classic Mayan vase (Figure 0.3), she produces the coveted foam by pouring from a height. Hand-painted manuscript. Reproduced by permission of the Museo de América, Madrid.

and another for "those who sell *picietl*," referring to the pulverized form of tobacco.[15] The smoking devices engaged all of the senses. Pipes fashioned out of reeds ("long, of an arm's span") were painted and gilded and then covered with charcoal and clay dust, which dispersed when lit to reveal fanciful designs—maybe a flower, fish, or eagle.[16] The olfactory pleasure derived from pungent tobacco was heightened with the addition of aromatic essences such as liquidambar, pine resin, bitumen from the sea, and flower extracts.[17] "Destined for fondling in the hand," the smoking devices offered tactile enjoyment.[18] Beyond these satisfactions Mesoamericans recognized the pipes' mood-altering properties, such as when one commended the "fragrance of flowers and [tobacco] smoke" as a singular source of "contentment and happiness" in the world.[19]

The seller of ground *picietl* took dried tobacco leaves, crushed them with a stone, mixed in lime (ten parts tobacco to one part lime), and rubbed them with his hands.[20] The lime—an alkali substance, like the ashes and pulverized seashells used elsewhere in the Americas—heightened the tobacco potency, increasing the effect of nicotine.[21] This form of tobacco, too, had its required paraphernalia, the tobacco gourds (*yetecomatl*) that appeared ubiquitously in depictions of divine entities, priests, and penitents, and, among the Maya, special ceramic flasks.[22] This tobacco was valued for its entrancing, stimulating, and pain-mitigating effect. Mexica medical experts explained that "it makes one drunk, it aids one's digestion, it dispels one's fatigue," or, alternately, "it intoxicates one, makes one dizzy, possesses one, and destroys hunger and a desire to eat."[23] *Picietl* also denoted the fresh green leaves used to treat wounds, headaches, and insect infestations. Tobacco for the most part was grown locally, but certain varieties seemed to be specially prized, such as that from Xochimilco, and the crafted pipes that Moctezuma levied as tribute.[24]

AN EXEMPLARY FEAST

The reconstruction of a Mexica merchant's celebration illustrates with splendid precision the way that formalized rites imputed social and sacred qualities to tobacco and chocolate, and the way, reciprocally, the sensory experience created by tobacco and chocolate contributed to the concretization of an abstract understanding of the universe, as it did to a social ethos that emphasized caste stratification, kin solidarity, and gender differentiation. The ethnographic project overseen by Franciscan friar Bernardino de Sahagún (1499–1590) is the source of the reminiscences on which this reconstruction is based. Sahagún served as a missionary in New Spain from 1529 to 1590, and though sometimes termed "the father of modern ethnography," his own purpose was to compile information that would be "useful for the indoctrination, the propagation and perpetuation of the Christiani-zation of these natives of this New Spain."[25] Sahagún secured the assist-ance of native informants, beginning with ten cultured elders and four young men, fluent in both Nahuatl and Spanish and so culturally hybrid. The informants themselves relied on pictorial screen-fold books that had survived Spanish book burnings: "All things we discussed they have shown to me by means of paintings, for that was the writing they had used, the grammarians saying them in their language and writing the statement be-neath the paintings. . . . Most of these books and writings were burned at the time of the destruction of the other idolatries, but many hidden ones which we have not seen did survive and are still kept."[26] The results of the third round of research and investigation are known as the *Florentine Co-dex*, and its book 9 is devoted to the activities of the long-distance mer-chants, the *pochteca* of Tenochtitlan and Tlatelolco. The seeming clarity of the recollections, including many partial and complete formal speeches, may be explained by the fact that merchants appear to have survived the conquest better than did other elite Mexica.[27]

It was customary for a merchant to throw an extravagant multiday cele-bration when he became sufficiently prosperous.[28] In fact, according to the reminiscences of those interviewed by the curious friar, a merchant was compelled to become the host of sumptuous feasting and entertainments "when his possessions, his goods, were already many" as a way to honor the divine forces who "hath shown me mercy [with] his property, his pos-sessions, his goods." The *pochteca* were a distinctive and fairly closed group in their broader communities, with their own guild, neighborhood, and endogamous marriage practices. They were also a cosmopolitan bunch, with contacts and experiences throughout Mesoamerica. They provisioned the Mexica with the most desirable commodities, "green stones, emerald-green jade, fine turquoise, amber, gold; and all manner of feathers . . . the skins of fierce animals, rugs of ocelot skins, and gourd bowls, incense bowls, tortoise-shell cups, spoons for stirring cacao." To procure these and other precious objects (such as ingredients for chocolate), the merchants journeyed hundreds of miles, as far as the "coast lands" of the Gulf or to Mayan areas such as the Isthmus of Tehuantepec or Soconusco on the Pa-cific Coast (where some of the most prized cacao was cultivated).[29]

After the decision was made to sponsor festivities, the merchant began to think about chocolate and tobacco: "First he set down for this purpose the cacao beans, the "divine ear" spice, the tubes of tobacco, the turkeys, the sauce dishes, the carrying baskets, the earthen cups."[30] That the ingre-dients to make chocolate (the cacao beans and "divine ear" spice) and "tubes of tobacco" appear first on the list signaled their ceremonial cen-trality. Smoking and chocolate drinking recur throughout the festivities, like an insistent repeating pattern in fabric or a subtle but pervasive riff in a song.

The staging of the activities took place mostly in and around the merchant's home. The walkways were swept and festooned with flower garlands, and the guests began to arrive. The guest list included the leading merchants who had trained the host and his parents who had nurtured him and those dependents who were less fortunate ("one or two poor, destitute, who are my kinsmen") and accomplished singers whose voices would add luster to the music. The host also made sure to invite his social superiors—members of the aristocracy whose noble blood put them above the merchants and warrior heroes who had distinguished themselves in battle.[31] Merchants, as wealthy commoners, and the nobles and warriors, existed in uneasy interdependence. The merchants' wealth and their highly valued trading contributions to Mexica society made them a powerful group of commoners. However, warriors and nobles resented the power merchants could exert because of their control of essential resources: there were still bitter memories from the famine year of 1454 when even nobles were forced to sell their children into slavery, bought by merchants who still had "plenty, who prospered; the greedy, the well-fed man."[32] And warriors scorned the source of the merchant wealth—trade—rather than battlefield virtuosity.

The warriors articulated these status distinctions with their dress, showing off exclusive finery forbidden to commoners—the smooth cotton cloaks elaborately embroidered, lip plugs and earrings of turquoise and gold, and brilliant glossy feathers. It was the reward of warriors to smoke sweet-smelling pipes and sip rich chocolate, as well as to carry fragrant flowers, wear cotton cloaks, and adorn themselves with precious stones and feathers.[33] They also symbolically usurped the merchant's prerogative of playing host, the generous dispenser of largesse. The warriors performed as "welcomers, attendants, receptionists, ushers" and served first those of highest ranks, "the commanding general . . . all the lords, eagle warrior guides, or the noblemen." As they distributed first the elegant pipes according to a choreographed protocol ("they took the pipe in right hand, on the part covered with carbon, and in the left hand carried the plate used to rest the pipe") they handled the offerings as their armaments, so that the pipes stood in for their spears, the pipes' resting trays, their shields. They paid homage with words as well as gestures (" 'My beloved noble, here is thy cane of tobacco.' ") (See figure 1.3.) And the honored recipient put the pipe between his fingers and began to inhale deeply. After the pipes, the warrior-welcomers distributed flower bouquets, tamales, and other victuals. The first banquet of the festivities ended with chocolate, served with equally exacting protocol tied to nuances of status and worthy of precise

Figure 1.3. *Florentine Codex*, Laur. Med. Palat. 219, c.336r (detail). This artist combines European and Mesoamerican stylistic elements to portray the serving of tobacco pipes at the beginning of the merchants' feast. Hand-painted manuscript. Biblioteca Medicea Laurenziana, Florence. By permission of the Italian Ministry of Cultural Heritage and Activities. No further reproduction is permitted.

recollection: the cup of chocolate simulated the sword, and the accompanying "stirring stick and gourd rest" represented the warriors' shields. At the feast, the noblemen drank from exquisite green-lacquered gourd vessels, while the rest of the guests made do with "only earthen cups."[34]

If, in the first phase of the celebrations, tobacco and chocolate were woven into rites that articulated social differentiation based on bloodlines and battlefield virtuosity, in the next phases they expressed the ties binding humans to the divine. During an interlude between feasting, some of the celebrants proceeded to the ceremonial precinct, where the supernatural forces responsible for Mexica triumph and imperial wealth were worshipped.

Situated inside its walls, rising from a large expanse covered in meticulously swept white flagstones, was a stepped pyramid, mirroring the mountains beyond. The devotees ascended the pyramid of Huitzilopochtli, whose domain was war, death, and, so, Mexica triumph and made offerings of flowers and "tubes of tobacco," and then they left similar offerings at other shrines.[35]

As night fell, the sounding of shell trumpets signaled the beginning of a nocturnal bacchanalia. Now only the men gathered in the courtyard patio for singing and dancing (figures 1.4, 1.5, 1.6).[36] They consumed only chocolate and hallucinogenic mushrooms sweetened with honey ("And once again chocolate was drunk"). Those experiencing the mushroom-induced hallucinations "danced, then they wept." Their visions foretold the future, not only their own but also "what would befall those who had eaten no mushrooms." They discovered how they would die, to what sins they would succumb, to what glories they would experience:

> One saw in vision that he would die in battle; one saw in vision that he would be eaten by wild beasts; one saw in vision that he would be rich, wealthy; one saw in vision that he would buy slaves—he would be a slave owner; one saw in vision that he would commit adultery—he would be struck by stones . . . one saw in vision that he would live in peace, in tranquility, until he died.

When the hallucinations wore off, the men shared their new-found knowledge about their own and others' destinies.[37]

When "the division of the night arrived, when it was exactly midnight," gods were again propitiated; this time paper effigies spattered with sacred rubber represented deities, and they were sacrificed, burned. And "once again chocolate was drunk; two or three times during the night chocolate was served. And so they danced all night; indeed they sang until the dawn broke."[38] Through their moving, singing, and imbibing, the revelers entered a sacred space. They experienced union with divine forces, as the mushroom-induced hallucinations extended their consciousness to allow foreknowledge of the future and the chocolate induced a mood of stimulating pleasure that was thought to match the kind of consciousness enjoyed by joyful gods. Songs expressed the sacred connection of the chocolate, evoking the blooming cacao tree in the realm of the gods. In song the gods spoke through the celebrants: "My song is woven with red and fragrant flowers / where the tree sprouts there is the dance with the narcotic cacao / dancing beside the drum, diffusing fragrance, parceled out."[39] Through other lyrics, the gods commanded: "Suck the honey of our flowers / garland

Figure 1.4. Diego Valadés, *Rhetorica christiana* (Perugia, 1579) (detail). Valadés, probably the son of a Nahua noblewoman, did the engravings himself in his guide to evangelizing the Indians of central Mexico. In this scene he portrays many elements of pre-Hispanic ritual, including a warrior's dance that included chocolate. Shelfmark: BV4209.V34.R5 1579. Reproduced courtesy of the Bancroft Library, University of California, Berkeley.

Figure 1.5. Diego Valadés, *Rhetorica christiana* (detail). A close-up view of the chocolate making, suggestive of the *Florentine Codex*'s insistence that chocolate drinking fueled the nocturnal revelry.

CACAO

Figure 1.6. Diego Valadés, *Rhetorica christiana* (detail). The chocolate theme reappears; here is depicted the cacao and its "mother" tree, thought to provide shade for the delicate cacao trees, and the cacao drying and fermenting in the background.

yourselves with our bouquets / our fans and our tobacco pipes / and live, delighting in our drums / enjoy, enjoy."[40]

The break of dawn signaled an end to this cathartic bacchanal. Before it came, however, it was important that the celebrants "quickly–swiftly" bury the "gifts which have been mentioned"—the flowers, tubes of tobacco, and incense ashes—in the middle of the courtyard, accompanied by singing and drumming.[41] It was feared that if they were not honorably disposed of in a timely fashion, they could be contaminated by someone of "vicious life" (adulterers, thieves, gamblers, drunkards).

More festivities ensued the following day, with rounds of pipe smoking and eating. Yet chocolate—and dancing—was conspicuously absent on day two. Sahagún's informants were explicit about this: "They served them no chocolate, but only *atole* with *chia* [a staple cereal]. . . . Now there was no more dancing." The symbolic logic that precluded chocolate related to the gendering of chocolate and maize when juxtaposed to each other. In contrast to the all-night dancing marathon fueled by copious amounts of chocolate of the first night, on the second day it was women who presided over the rituals: at the midday banquet they processed through the courtyard bearing baskets on their shoulders filled with dried maize grains, and later they stood ceremoniously "in places by the door, holding the grains of maize in the folds of their skirts."[42] The symbolically laden pairing of cacao and maize had deep roots in Mesoamerica, existing at least since the Classic Maya period.[43] In this instance, the juxtaposition suggests a relationship of essential reproductive forces—maize and woman providing the bulky flesh of life, and chocolate and man fertilizing it with the vital essence. Chocolate, however, reappeared at the conclusion of the festivities. For it was expected that the successful host would ensure the "distribution of leftovers," for "nothing more would be to his merit; nothing more would be his reward." Only by giving away chocolate and pipes, as well as other banquet foods and serving ware, potlatch-style, did the host ensure that future banquets would be held.[44]

SOCIAL COMMUNION AND DISTINCTION

It is likely that many elements of this celebration characterized festivities that took place throughout Mesoamerica.[45] In particular, the roles performed by tobacco and chocolate resonated with associations widespread within Mexica—and Mesoamerican—society. Iconography and inscriptions on surviving pottery from the Classic Maya period similarly depict tobacco and chocolate as essential accoutrements to court society, indicating that the correspondence between power, chocolate, and tobacco pipes was of ancient origin and widespread (figures 0.1, 0.2, 0.3).[46] Diego Durán, a missionary ethnographer, went so far as to claim that in Mexica society chocolate was the exclusive privilege of the nobility, accomplished warriors, and wealthy merchants: "Thus the common man was rewarded to distinguish him from the noble . . . even less he could drink chocolate (which is a native drink) unless he was a lord or chieftain."[47]

However, various sources make it clear that on special occasions, humble men and women also had opportunity to enjoy the goods, albeit less frequently and with items of lesser quality. In descriptions of baptismal feasts celebrated by nobles or merchants, Sahagún noted that the chocolate servers not only offered the luxurious beverage to the high-ranking guests but also "put aside chocolate for their servants."[48] His haughty, apparently high-born informants also reported that those with lesser means hosted feasts similar to their own, but qualified that the provisions were of inferior quality, using "only old, withered flowers" and "leftover, bitter sauces." They bought cheap market pipes that "flake off; they crumble" or stretched their resources by reusing tobacco pipes meant for only one use (at least in the eyes of the privileged).[49] Or they scrimped when making chocolate by pouring in more water, which, according to the condescending wealthy, compromised the quality of the foam ("the bubbles burst") and made the resulting beverage only fit for "water flies."[50]

Though the merchant's feast offers a prime example of how tobacco and chocolate worked in rites that marked distinction, it also demonstrates how their service created or affirmed interpersonal bonds. When elite merchants dined and danced with members of the hereditary aristocracy and accomplished warriors—social groups with whom they had long-standing conflicts—they used tobacco and chocolate to override difference and ignore long-standing enmities, however temporarily. This usefulness of tobacco and chocolate to elide social distance is also reflected in their ubiquity in the formalities surrounding diplomatic meetings, such as those between Mexica representatives and envoys from enemy or subject city-states. It was protocol in Mexica courts to welcome foreign dignitaries and emissaries with tobacco and chocolate; when a Mexica ruler, Ahuizotl, received a neighboring lord and tributary "they brought [the ruler of Texcoco] water for his hands; it was a celebrated custom among them to bring water for guests and travelers. And after washing their hands, they gave him the usual royal fare, with the accustomed drink of cacao, and flowers and smoking tubes, not only to him, but to all of the great lords and personages, who were lodging [in the palace] according to their rank."[51] When the elite long-distance merchants from twelve different cities at Tochtepec (Veracruz) assembled to decide on important matters (such as when to hold a sacrificial feast for Huitzilopochtli), they concluded their meal with ritual consumption of tobacco and chocolate.

But the best glimpse of how tobacco and chocolate served to create and symbolize bonds when most needed comes from the aged merchants' reminiscences of the elaborate farewell and homecoming ceremonies they staged before and after members of their group set off on their travels to foreign lands that would keep them away from home for weeks or months at a time. The long trips brought many afflictions: "They traveled exhausted by the heat and the winds; they traveled exhausted; they went exhausted; they went sighing, walking wearily, in great affliction. Their foreheads burned; the sun's heat held them; they went exposed to its rays. They went encountering the deserts; they climbed up and down the gorges, the mountains." They risked "ambush" by foes in foreign lands, to be slain and "served up with chili sauce." Sometimes they were "enclosed in enemy lands" and had to lose their identities to escape detection; it was yet another hardship to dissimulate, going native "in their array, their hairdress, their speech."[52]

Under these conditions of physical stress, mortal danger, and psychological suspension, leave-taking and returning were straining, anxious affairs. The merchants and their kin found assistance in ritualized ceremonies of departure and return. Chocolate and tobacco played a vital role in mending affective ties loosened by time spent apart and diminishing the alienation induced by the immersion in foreign lands. Tobacco and chocolate were served during this farewell banquet:

> And when they had come together, thereupon their hands [and] mouths were washed. When hands had been washed, thereupon food was served. When food had been eaten then once again were hands [and] mouths washed; thereupon chocolate was served [and] drunk. The tubes of tobacco were offered them. And when this was done, then [the host] sat before them: he besought them; he said to them: "Ye have sent yourselves; ye have suffered fatigue. . . . I beseech your revered motherliness [and] fatherliness. For yet, with this, I abandon your beloved water flowers, your beloved neighborhood, your beloved city."[53]

Precisely, drinking chocolate and smoking tobacco marked an intermission after the meal—distinctly separate from the meal, since it followed the hand washing that marked the boundaries of eating—and before the formal, ritualized speech making. (This ordering of rites also marked the court ceremonies described by Durán.) The theme of these speeches was the sadness the merchant would experience while away from his familiar milieu and the risks he would face while on his travels. The elder dutifully reminded the outbound merchant that he might "perish in the midst of the forest [or] the crags . . . thy poor bones scattered in various places" or, if he was lucky, only endure bad travel fare—"the unseasoned, the saltless, the briny [food] . . . the wretched, soggy maize." He cautioned the traveler to behave honestly and respectfully while way and, if he should return intact and with riches, to not succumb to pride. He advised him how to behave among strangers (to not slander) and survive in the wilderness.[54] In the farewell ceremony tobacco and chocolate played a crucial role. In consuming them collectively, the merchant and his people enacted the communal bond just as that bond was going to be temporarily severed. The merchants' leave-taking and return ceremonies were representative of broader Mesoamerican customs.[55]

Chocolate also had a pronounced role in social consecrations of a particular type—those binding men and women in betrothal, marriage, and sexuality. Díaz, of course, famously titillated his readers with the description of Moctezuma heightening his sexual prowess with chocolate. It is hard to trust this salacious aside, but other evidence corroborates the fact that chocolate was used in ritual contexts associated with sexuality and domestic unions, such as the pointed equation made between men and chocolate and women and maize at the merchant's feast. Chocolate also conjoined men and women uniting in matrimony, symbolizing the exchange of "blood flowing between intermarried families."[56] When they wanted to represent marriage in painted genealogies, Mixtec (Oaxaca) artists depicted vessels overflowing with foaming chocolate, reflecting the Mixtec idiom for royal marriage, in which "a royal vessel was placed before the nobleman" (figure 1.7).[57] Scholar Eric Thompson wrote that "the expression *tac haa*, is roughly translatable as 'to serve chocolate,' which the Motul [Maya] dictionary translates as 'to invite the father of a girl whom one's son wants to marry to discuss the marriage and serve him drink.' "[58]

SACRED FORCES

Just as tobacco and chocolate worked in the service of defining and articulating social relationships, so they connected, mediated, and explicated the relationship between humanity and divinity. As in so many societies, Mesoamerican ones simultaneously held different—though not necessarily contradictory—understandings of the workings of the cosmos.[59] The most immediately accessible view is of a cosmic system in which a community of deities—imagined as monstrous human-animal hybrid forms—created and sustained the earth. Collectively, they were responsible for the flow of water and light, sun, oceans, mountains, vegetation, creatures, the inventions of useful tools, and the success of particular groups and individuals. Tlaloc, for instance, associated with agriculture and fertility, ensured (or not) that rain fell to nourish tender maize stocks. Behind the great burning orb of the sun and also the smaller, still vital, domestic hearth fires was Xiuhtecutli. The Mexica credited Huitzilopochtli with showing their wandering forebears where to found their city.

Figure 1.7. *Codex Vindobonensis Mexicanus I*, fol. 35 obverse (detail). A page from one of the surviving pre-Columbian Mixtec books that illustrated cosmology and genealogy. The vessel with a foamy beverage likely represented a serving of chocolate, and its sharing by the royal couple signified their marriage. Hand-painted manuscript, 26.5×22cm. Reproduced with permission of Österreichische Nationalbibliothek, Vienna.

If people were to survive, to flourish—to get sufficient rains, to succeed in hunting and fishing expeditions, to have mother and child survive labor, to take captives in war and escape captivity themselves, to prosper through trade or craft—it was required that they properly venerate and propitiate these and other fearsome, demanding gods. Tobacco and chocolate, then, functioned as tribute—neither the most nor the least important among many gifts expected by and hankered after by hungry, thirsty, sensual gods. As mortal subjects expressed their subservience and ensured the quality of life to their mortal lords, so people were tributaries to their gods. This is perhaps the most straightforward way to understand the smoking pipes delivered to Huitzilopochtli during the merchants' celebrations and the ubiquity of tobacco and chocolate as offerings throughout the calendar of feasts and other ritual propitiations.[60]

Tobacco and chocolate were also mediums that connected people to divinity because, in consuming the substances, humans attained corporeal states that approximated those experienced by gods. Mesoamerican gods inhabited celestial planes that floated above earth (the universe was envisioned as series of suspended, layered disks; see figure 3.1), except those who lived on the planes below, such as Mictlan, where a god of death supervised the deceased. They donned distinct garb. And they, like reveling humans, passed time smelling flowers, sipping chocolate, caressing pipes, and inhaling smoke.[61] Such a characterization survives in the recollections about the rites for venerating Tezcatlipoca, one of the most omnipotent deities.[62] For the annual celebration held in his honor, the priests selected a slave to impersonate the god. The unlucky honoree (for he would be sacrificed) had to meet exacting criteria; he had to be one who had "no [bodily] defects, who had no blemish, who had no mark, who had on him no wart [no such] small tumor." His aesthetic perfection also needed to be manifest in his courtly refinement; as Sahagún's informants recalled, "there was taken the greatest care that he be taught to blow the flute, that he be able to play his whistle; and that at the same time he hold all his flowers and his smoking tube." Before this ritual sacrifice, Tezcaltipoca's human impersonator was forced to circulate through the streets of Tenochtitlan, where "he would go playing the flute, he would go sucking [the smoking tube], he would go smelling [the flowers]."

Songs that survived the conquest as oral tradition, later recorded as Nahuatl texts, corroborate this vision of gods as pleasure loving.[63] These allow a deeper understanding of the place of music, dance, chocolate, and tobacco at the merchant's feast:

> I sing
> To Him, who is my God
> In our place where the lords command
> The flowering chocolate drink is foaming
> The one which intoxicates men with its flowers
> . . .
> The flowering chocolate drink is foaming,
> The flower of tobacco is passed around,
> If my heart would taste them
> My life would become inebriated
> But here on
> The earth
> You, O lords, O princes, if my heart would taste them
> My life would become inebriated.[64]

These verses identify the "place where the lords command" as one characterized by the synesthetic abundance, where one sensory delight—song,

Figure 1.8. *Florentine Codex* (Laur. Med. Palat. 218, c.84v) (detail). For the feast celebrating Tezcaltipoca, a slave was selected for his physical beauty. He was taught to behave with the utmost courtliness (knowing how to play the flute, smoke a pipe, and smell flowers in a refined manner), and he was honored as Tezcaltipoca. The celebration culminated in his sacrifce. Hand-painted manuscript. Biblioteca Medicea Laurenziana, Florence. By permission of the Italian Ministry of Cultural Heritage and Activities. No further reproduction is permitted.

smell, taste, drunkenness—melds into the next.[65] And if, as the accounts of the merchant's feast and other preconquest sources suggest, these songs were accompanied by draughts of chocolate and bouquets of tropical flowers held aloft, the lyrics described a synesthesia being experienced by those vocalizing the lyrics. The sensory delights—epitomized by chocolate—bind the gods and earthlings. In experiencing the hedonistic pleasures of the gods, the inebriation of the senses, the celebrants experience divinity.

There is at least one more way that tobacco and chocolate worked in the Mesoamerican religious system: sacred, life-giving force also resided in the substances themselves. This explains why during the merchant's feast the revelers were careful to bury the smoking tobacco pipes, in order to keep them free of contamination with blasphemous forces.

The idea that sacred energy—*teotl*—inhered in cacao and chocolate is manifest in their associations with the heart and blood.[66] And so to understand the place of offerings of chocolate requires a brief examination of the role of blood sacrifice in Mesoamerican cultures. Gods received blood by different means. Self-mutilating priests drew their own blood, piercing earlobes, legs, and genitals. There were frequent sacrifices of quail—decapitated. Mesoamericans also practiced human sacrifice, but its prominence and frequency was not constant across time and place. Accompanying, maybe assisting, the Mexica's rise to regional dominance,

Figure 1.9. *Codex Fejérváry-Mayer,* p. 1. This is the first page of a pre-Columbian sacred book from the Mixtec-Puebla region. It depicts the four world directions, with each division presided over by a pair of gods, sacred trees, and birds. Cacao—facing toward right side—is the sacred tree of the south. Hand-painted manuscript, 17.5 × 17.5 cm. © National Museums Liverpool, World Museum.

was human sacrifice. Many of the celebrations culminated with the ritual killing, sometimes resulting in thousands dead at a single event. Captive warriors and enslaved children requisitioned from tributaries featured prominently in the ranks of the victims. Atop temple shrines, priests plunged obsidian blades into prone victims and held aloft still-beating hearts; they slit throats of children above coursing streams. So, in order to ensure that the earth would continue to provide harvests, Mexica and other Mesoamericans replenished the thirsty earth with blood offerings.[67]

Chocolate enters this belief system as a metaphor, surrogate, and exchange item for blood. Chocolate's material form did not exist independently of its symbolic associations. The Spanish conquistador and chronicler Gonzalo Fernández de Oviedo y Valdés (1478–1557) explained that the Nicoya (Costa Rica) reddened chocolate with achiote so it would resemble blood. Parsing Nahua proverbs, Sahagún explained that "heart, blood was said of cacao, because it was precious."[68] The connection helps account for why Nahua health experts prescribed chocolate for those who lost blood, whether through hemorrhage, cough, or urine. These associations had an ancient and widespread lineage. In Mayan iconography, cacao beans are visualized as hearts. A Mayan book depicts gods showering their own sacred blood (from piercing their ears with obsidian blades) over cacao pods (figure 1.10).[69]

That chocolate was seen as a blood surrogate accounts for its prominence in fertility celebrations. One of the most important feast days in the central Mexican ritual calendar at the end of April brought together Mexica, as well as representatives from neighboring cities, to propitiate Tlaloc in his capacity as a rainmaker, the god of thunderbolts and storms. "The purpose of the feast was that of asking of a good year, since all the maize which had been sown had now sprouted," explained the friar Durán.[70] Cacao featured among the offerings. And even after the Spanish conquest and nominal Christian evangelization, Mayans in the Yucatán town of Petú continued to make offerings of a sacred cacao-maize beverage to traditional deities "who give life and water and sustenance" during the time of maize planting. Chocolate-laden rites tied to the agricultural cycle spanned Mesoamerica, from pre-Columbian times until the present.[71]

It seems the Classic Maya believed that cacao pods, shooting off directly from tree trunks, were imbued with *k'ik'*, the same essence that coursed through plants (as sap) and humans (as blood).[72] The divine forces immanent in godly blood are transferred to cacao and chocolate, which then invigorates its human consumers, who return the gift with blood and chocolate offerings of their own. For the Zapotec of Oaxaca, the requisite foam on chocolate evoked *pi*, or the life force.[73] The conviction of these associations must have related to the aggregation of transitive connections—if blood gave life to people and chocolate's redness suggested blood, then chocolate too was a life-giving force. This was supported by the physiological effects of chocolate, understood as invigorating, stimulating, and, so, life giving.

Figure 1.10. *Codex Madrid*, plate 95 (detail). One of four surviving Mayan codices, this one was either created shortly before or after the Spanish conquest. It contains descriptions of the rituals and divinities associated with each day of the 260-day Mesoamerican sacred calendar. In this detail gods perform ritual sacrificial bloodletting on their ears and bleed onto cacao. Hand-painted manuscript, 12.5×23 cm. Reproduced courtesy of the Museo de América, Madrid.

THE GENERATIVE POWER OF TOBACCO

In Mesoamerican cosmogony the pulverized tobacco was identified with the act of creation itself. A Dominican friar, seeking to compare native American cosmologies with Biblical Genesis, was pleased to find in the small town of Cuilapa one of the pre-Columbian screen-fold books that the Mixtec used as sacred almanacs and genealogies, one that was "written with those pictures, like the Indians of that Mixtec Kingdom had in their Books or rolled Manuscripts . . . in which contained the Origin, Creation of the World."[74] Before the Spanish conquest, such books served as a kind of a storyboard for those charged with remembering and telling history and commemorating and upholding the religious requirements of the sacred calendar. The local vicar found someone to interpret the stylized scenes, painted in red and black, for him.[75] He discovered the following account of the beginning of the world:

> In the beginning there was darkness. All was confusion and chaos and there was no god or even time. The earth was covered in water and slime. Then there appeared a divine couple—the Mother and Father. They begot other gods, and on a rocky outcropping on the top of a high mountain they erected a sumptuous palace and this was their seat and abode on the earth. The gods

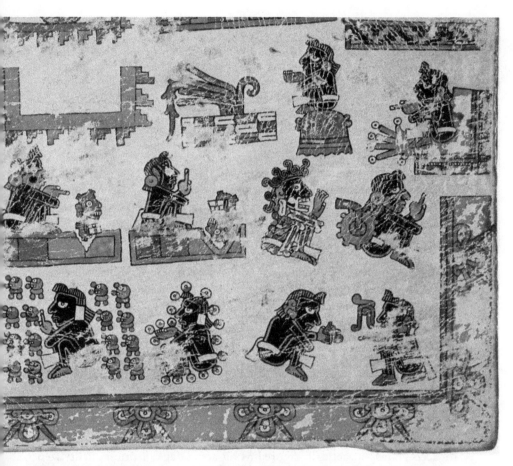

Figure 1.11. *Codex Vindobonensis Mexicanus I*, fol. 52 reverse (detail). This is the very first scene in a pictorial account of the creation of the world. Tobacco features prominently. The activities begin in the bottom right (and move left and zig zag), where two beings initiate creation through offering tobacco and copal. One of the other beings wears the sacred tobacco gourd (far right, middle row). Hand-painted manuscript, 26.5 × 22 cm. Reproduced with permission of Österreichische Nationalbibliothek, Vienna.

lived many centuries in this delightful spot with great contentment and tranquility, all the while the world was in total obscurity.

Then the divine Mother of all the gods bore two male sons, both handsome, gracious, and wise, and raised them in great luxury. The older one entertained himself by transforming into an eagle and he swooped among the mountain summits. His younger brother, taking on the shape of winged serpent, flew through skies with such agility and subtlety that he seemed invisible as he ducked among the peaks and cliffs.

Grateful for all this, the brothers decided to make an offering and sacrifice to the gods, their parents. They took some clay incense braziers, and sprinkled some ground tobacco upon them. Having made this sacrifice, the two brothers created a garden where they grew many kinds of flowering, fragrant, and fruit-bearing trees. They begged their parents, insisting that because of the sacrifices they had made of tobacco, and the gifts that followed, they were obliged to create. They supplicated their parents to form the skies, and bring the world into lightness, and make the waters congregate together to reveal dry tracts of land, so that they could have something other than that small garden for their enjoyment. And so the earth became habitable for humans.[76]

In this story tobacco is the only suitable gift or sacrifice that the quasi-mortal children could make to their divine parents. This was because in the tobacco itself inhered divine properties;[77] it had the power to require the parents to instigate further acts of creation. The friar in Cuilapa added that Indians considered tobacco "the first offering that was in the World."[78] Most screen-fold books, such as the one glossed by the friar, were destroyed after the Spanish conquest by nervous missionaries who worried they were works of the devil. Fortunately, one has survived that corroborates the friar's second-hand account (figure 1.11). In fact, in this version of the story, the tobacco offering itself generated creation, bringing into being supernatural creatures and physical features of the earth, including serpents, smoke, and volcanic eruptions.[79] In the painted books of central Mexico that delve into the origins of the cosmos, powerful deities—and even the primordial couple who started the world—wear the tobacco gourd (figure 1.12).[80]

The power attributed to *picietl* accounts for why the "tobacco gourd" was a standard accoutrement for Mesoamerican priests. The *yetecomatl*—tobacco gourd—practically figured as an appendage of priests in stylized representations. It could be strapped on as a kind of backpack for ritual garments or hooked around the waist. "All the offering priests," wrote Sahagún, "each carried their tobacco bags on their backs, and had their cord necklets, each one his cord necklet from which hanging their little tobacco bags, each of which went filled with dyed, powdered tobacco."[81]

Juan de Tovar, a Jesuit missionary who collected information about preconquest religion in New Spain, offered a thorough description of how the priests composed and used powdered tobacco during their rites. According to Tovar, the Mexica priests used a special unction when "they were going to make sacrifices and light incense in the dense woods and mountain peaks and hidden caves"; they used this "to lose fear and find great courage." First they made an "unguent" by burning to ash "diverse venomous reptiles and animals," such as spiders, centipedes, and snakes, which had been collected by the "dexterous" boys who studied in the priest schools. After placing these ashes in a mortar, they placed into it "much tobacco,

Figure 1.12. *Codex Borbonicus,* fol. 21 (detail). Based on a preconquest prototype, this page from a central Mexican book depicts the origin of the world. The primordial man and woman each wear a *yetecomatl* (tobacco gourd) on their backs. It is possible that the powder they are sprinkling to inaugurate creation is also tobacco. Hand-painted manuscript. Bibliothèque de l'Assemblée Nationale-Paris. Photograph by Irène Andréani.

which these people use to deaden the flesh and not feel travails." They ground into the mixture *ololiuhqui* [morning glory seeds] ("that the Indians consume ground in a drink to see visions") and black worms.[82] The unguent, largely made up of powdered tobacco along with crushed insects, assisted priests in achieving an entranced and divinely altered state in which they could communicate with gods, ward off animals, and feel an empowering fearlessness. The use of tobacco mixed with hallucinogenic seeds to instill fearlessness and to induce visions is consistent with the physical effects attributed to tobacco, especially in high doses and mixed with lime—the dizziness and intoxication described by so many. The use of tobacco to provoke visions, understood as a medium to access divine wisdom, was ubiquitous across the Americas.

In making offerings of *picietl*, Mesoamericans commemorated the first act of creation and also supplicated the creative forces to endure. Diego Muñoz Camargo, a mestizo chronicler who appears to have relied on now-lost accounts as well as oral testimony that circulated in his milieu, described how ground tobacco served as an offering in order to "see if the devil would be placated or concede to their wishes." The priests

> made an offering of *picietl*, . . . which they ground and made into a powder, . . . and because this herb is so prized for its medical virtues they offered it to [the devil]. . . . And placed in large vessels, they put it on the altars and pedestals of the temple along with other offerings, though they particularly watched over those of *picietl*, for if any miracle was to occur, here more than any other place they would see it.[83]

It is likely that the "devil" was Xiuhtecutli, the deity associated with fire, who was conventionally depicted wearing the tobacco gourd. The missionary Diego Durán likewise described how priests, out of devotion, fulfillment of a vow, or "for one's health or for search of prosperity or for the sake of one's children—for a thousand superstitions," made offerings of food to fire and its god, Xiuhtecutli, represented in "the crackling of fire, the creaking of the embers, the leaping of sparks, the smoking [of the fire]." They consecrated these offerings by sprinkling pulque, copal, and *piciete*, which he explained "is a type of plant with which the Indians deaden the flesh so as not to feel bodily fatigue," thereby connecting the spiritual efficacy with the physiological effects.[84] Priests were not the only ones who deployed *picietl*. The painted books of the Mixtec show offerings of powdered tobacco during betrothals, before births, at bird sacrifices, and for agricultural offerings.[85]

Mesoamericans did not distinguish between religious and functional uses of tobacco. To the contrary, the multiple useful qualities attributed to pulverized tobacco reinforced its sacred status, while even the most seemingly quotidian uses of the tobacco were inscribed with ritual. As travelers called upon the divine power of tobacco before leaving on journeys, so did woodcutters before felling trees with dangerous axes, hunters before setting snares, fishermen before placing their weirs and "conjuring fish," and farmers before transplanting tender maguey plants.[86] Farmers employed *picietl* to stave off animal pests and insect infestations. Having sown a field, they placed a boundary line of tobacco and copal "as if they were erecting a fence or wall" to deter coatis (raccoonlike creatures).[87] In doing battle with crop-threatening ants, the farmers used pulverized tobacco to beseech them to keep away from fields. But in case the ants "overstepped, not showing they had understood, in that case [the farmer] carried out his threat, going ahead with the destruction of their house, which he also did by conjuring a certain quantity of water and throwing it on the anthill and sprinkling the outer edge and circumference of the anthill with his so-venerated *pisiete* [*picietl*]." As he destroyed the anthills, he summoned the divine tobacco: "Come on now, green possessed one of wide leaves. What persistence is this? Go immediately. Throw out and run off the ants from where they are."[88] *Picietl* empowered those from the highest castes as well as humble farmers. The power associated with *picietl* was such that it was integral to the installation rites for inaugurating a new Aztec or Mix-tec ruler; brought to the temple of the god Huitzilopochtli, the incoming *tlatoani* was presented naked to the councilor-lords, thus ready for his transformation into ruler: "He went bare. They put on him a green, sleeve-less jacket. And they had him carry upon his back his tobacco gourd with green tassels" (figure 1.13).[89]

In all of these cases it is impossible to separate tobacco's utility in assist-ing people in activities requiring physical exertion and concentration or its potency as an insecticide from the belief in its divine power to help fortune ensure a favorable outcome. This duality was perhaps most manifest in the medicinal uses of tobacco. The Jesuit Juan de Tovar explained that *picietl* healed the sick, particularly by alleviating pain when applied as a plaster, for which it was known among the Nahuas as "divine medicine."[90] Often healers possessed sacred powers and performed divination rites to discover the cause of illness, so that the healer himself or herself could use tobacco in that quest, as well as apply it to the patient. The interwoven "religious" and "medical" nature of powdered tobacco comes through most explicitly in the seventeenth-century idolatry investigation, in which healers would apply tobacco to the body of the ill person while summoning its sacred forces as a divine entity. Female healers who were the protagonists during the pre-Hispanic festival of Toci, "Mother of the Gods and Heart of the Earth," adorned themselves with tobacco gourds.[91] (Women in childbirth appealed to the earth mother goddess, Toci, "Our Grandmother.")[92] The tobacco was a pain-alleviating substance, but it was also more than that—in it resided divine healing powers. Like Indians throughout the Americas, Mesoamericans used tobacco for these and many other cures, including treatments for eye and ear aliments, toothaches, throat and chest pains, open wounds, skin rashes, snakebites, and parasites.[93] The sacrality of

Figure 1.13. *Codex Tudela*, fol. 55r. The artist combined European and pre-Hispanic central Mexican iconographic elements to depict this scene of the initiation rites of the ruler (*tlatoani*). Central to the rite is the donning of the *yetecomatl*. Reproduced with permission of the Museo de América, Madrid.

tobacco reinforced its therapeutic value and vice versa: the sacred power assigned to tobacco explained its healing properties, just as its healing properties must have been attributed to its divinity. Part of the Mesoamerican explanation for tobacco's healing power was its connection to *tonalli*, meaning "to irradiate or make warmth," also connected to notions of solar heat and an individual's soul and spirit. Accordingly, it was indicated in "cold" illnesses, such as the swelling of the belly and gout.[94]

FOR people throughout Mesoamerica, the experience of tobacco or chocolate engendered a concatenation of physical sensations, including but going well beyond the alteration to brain chemistry effected by nicotine, theobromine, or caffeine. The substances provoked multiple sensory responses: olfactory (acrid tobacco smoke mingling with pine resin), gustatory (intense cacao flavors tempered with sweet wild bee honey and flowery vanilla), visual (the eagle painted on the pipe and shiny green gourd containing

red chocolate), tactile (the foamy softness of chocolate froth), and kinesthetic (the left hand cradling and then lifting the arm-length pipe to the
lips). The heightened, intense, enjoyable, and/or mind-altering sensations
afforded by tobacco and chocolate enriched and defined particular rituals.
They helped affect the moods of occasions—the sublime opulence of
courtly rituals, the festive and competitive conviviality of baptismal feasts,
the awkward relief and greedy curiosity of homecoming reunions, the "I'm
the man" bravado of warriors' victory parties, the reverential munificence
of thanksgiving ceremonies, the ecstatic frenzy of hallucinogenic dancing
rites, the entranced mortification of priests' solitary wilderness forays. In
turn, their use in these settings intensified and inflected the experience of
their consumption, imbuing the goods with the memories, associations,
and moods evoked. Without tobacco and chocolate, few important rites
could be celebrated in Mesoamerican societies. Priests could not perform
sacral duties, nor could rulers be installed unless gourds filled with tobacco
powder were strapped to their backs. Healers would be hard-pressed to
treat those suffering from headaches or hemorrhages, and midwives would
not be able to adequately assist women in childbirth. Members of the elite
could not uphold the respect of their peers if they did not lavish well-made
tobacco pipes and foamy chocolate upon their guests. Betrothal agree-
ments could not be validated without servings of chocolate. Nor could relatives prepare their deceased kin for their journey to the underworlds
without it. Victorious warriors and visiting dignitaries would feel slighted
if not feted with smoking tobacco and luxurious chocolate. Chocolate for
the Mexica was a delicious, "invigorating" drink that connoted social distinction, sacred aesthetics, a product of female skill, suggestions of blood,
and the ultimate gift, whose bestowal created an aura embracing the giver
and the recipient. Tobacco pipes, too, had the connective capacity to bond
the offering and receiving parties. Products of male skill, the tobacco tubes
also brought a lazy, refined peaceful quality. Powdered tobacco, applied to
the skin or held in the mouth, could ease pain and cure ills or produce a
dizzy, inebriated, even hallucinogenic state of mind desirable in priests
seeking divine knowledge or performing penitential rites. Its capacity to
connect the human to the divine mind made it a fitting symbol for ruling
authority as well as for the mediating power of priests and the healing
power of midwives.

2

Encountering Novelties

On October 11, 1492, ninety tired, hungry, and lost men were delighted to see solid ground after spending over four weeks at sea aboard their three ships. Nearing the shore the following day, they saw people unlike any they had ever come across before, even though among the well-traveled sailors there were those who had reconnoitered the coast of Africa and participated in the conquests of Muslim Granada. The resident strangers were the most unabashedly naked people they had ever seen, their tawny skin anointed with red, white, and black pigments; their thick, black coarse hair was worn with strange bangs and a long hank in the back. These men and women were likewise shocked, first by the strange sailing vessels, bearing tree poles hung with coarse white fabric, constructed very differently than their swift canoes. The men aboard were weird looking, too, seemingly unashamed of the hair that covered their faces, their bodies encumbered by heavy cloth, and their heads oddly covered by stiff black boards.

The leader of the three ships, the Genoese-born admiral Christopher Columbus, decided it was reasonably safe to go ashore in a launch; after all, these people looked vulnerable in their nakedness and did not display weapons. Columbus and a few other officials armed themselves and rowed to the shore. They brought with them flags bearing a green cross marked with an "F" on one arm for Ferdinand and a "Y" on the other for Isabella (Ysabel), the king and queen of Spain who were the official sponsors of the voyagers. In Columbus's abbreviated telling, the first thing he did was "take possession of the said island for the king and for the queen his lords," an act made official and legal, in his mind, by the presence of signing witnesses and notaries. The second thing he did was distribute goods—red caps, glass beads, and "other things of small value"—to the assembling people, in hope that they "would be friendly to us." His calculation seems to have been correct for later the people swam out to their boats and presented Columbus and the others with "parrots and cotton thread in balls and javelins and many other things," and the Bahamians happily accepted the glass beads and bells given in return. What to him seemed an asymmetrical exchange—baubles in return for valuable items—reinforced his belief that these near-naked folk were guileless and would be easy to subjugate. The first encounter between peoples of Europe and America pivoted around symbolic conquest and the exchange of goods. Among the goods was in all likelihood tobacco.[1]

Tobacco is suspected to be among the goods exchanged—as well as the "other little things that it would be tiresome to write down" that Columbus received the following day—because several days later (October 15), as the Europeans sailed toward a larger island, they sighted a man "passing alone in a dugout from this island of Santa Maria to Fernandina," as Columbus had named two islands in the Bahamas, "who was bringing a small amount of their bread, which was about the size of a fist, and a calabash of water and piece of red earth made into dust and then kneaded and some dry leaves." He added that the leaves "must be something highly esteemed among them, because earlier, in San Salvador," as he christened the first island, "they brought some of them to me as a present."[2] These nameless "dry leaves" were likely tobacco, and their repeated appearance and status as a gift forced him to take note.

Tobacco, in another guise, sneaked into the admiral's consciousness a few weeks later. By October 28, the European voyagers were off the shore of a large island—Cuba—that thrilled Columbus, who declared it "the most beautiful that eyes have ever seen: full of good harbors and deep rivers . . . full of beautiful mountains."[3] Columbus dispatched two of his men to investigate, providing them with guides, one a kidnapped man from the Bahamas and the other a willing participant from Cuba. The emissaries had brought with them samples of "gold and cinnamon and other spices" to find out if the inhabitants possessed any of these or if they knew where they could be found. They took off into the interior and returned several days later. They brought back no cinnamon or shiny metal or tales of splendid oriental cities, but they spoke of large villages, with as many as one thousand inhabitants, well-swept plazas, and nice huts, comparable to "very large Moorish campaign tents." They were well received, treated as dignitaries, and given stools on which to sit, while their hosts surrounded them on the ground. And the men informed Columbus of "the many people going back and forth between their village, men and women with a firebrand of weeds in their hands to take in the fragrant smoke to which they are accustomed."[4] They had seen smokers. It seems plausible that they had been offered these "firebrands" and perhaps even puffed on them as their hosts demonstrated.

Such was the Europeans' first contact with tobacco. Other than their retrospectively symbolic value, these first encounters had no special significance in terms of the European response to and assimilation of tobacco. Their significance lies in demonstrating the subtle, barely perceptible way that Europeans were made aware of things they were not looking for. There was no "Eureka" moment in that there was no sense of having "discovered" tobacco. Rather, the dried weeds initially registered only as a faint impression, hardly detectable amid the focus on those things that seemed to promise fulfillment of the aspirations and fantasies of the explorers.

The first sightings of tobacco were crowded out by the projections and expectations of the European voyagers. Columbus and his men came to the Caribbean conditioned by their experiences of trading in the Mediterranean and African Atlantic and their fantasies of the riches and opportunities awaiting them in a mythologized Orient. They saw wealth in exotic spices and gold, the most valuable goods in the late medieval economic system to which they were accustomed. Columbus also came loaded with the expectations and aspirations of his royal sponsors, King Ferdinand and Queen Isabella, of the recently united crowns of Aragon and Castile (he also received funding from Florentine investors). For the so-called Catholic Kings, the timing—1492—was no accident. Their decision to sponsor the Genoese merchant's wacky scheme to find a westward passage to the Orient was directly linked to their crusading fervor and belief in providential destiny, already manifested in the final stage of the Reconquista, the usurpation of the Muslim kingdom of Granada and the expulsion of the Crowns' Jewish population in the name of religious purification. His captain's log attests that during the first months—hours in fact—in the Americas, Columbus anticipated conquest and colonization. He wrote that the natives were ripe for conversion to Christianity and, even more ominously, for slavery, as they were "fit to be ordered about and made to work, plant, and do everything else that may be needed, and build towns and be taught our customs, and to go about clothed."[5] The beautiful coastlines dazzled him, but above all, they suggested harbors, such as the one where "there would be room in it for all the ships in the world."[6] In pine groves he saw "vast quantities of planking and masts for the greatest ships of Spain." A river "shining" with "some stones with gold-colored spots on them" persuaded him of the presence of valuable gold reserves.[7] The bundles of dried green leaves and the firebrands did not appear to have any relevance to these colonial aspirations and so received no mention in the "Letter to the Sovereigns" that Columbus wrote to Ferdinand and Isabella, which was pro translated, printed, and distributed throughout Europe.[8]

The slow dawning and seemingly irrelevant notice Columbus took of tobacco reveals that even as bound and blinkered as he and his cohorts were by their desires and expectations, unforeseen reality made a clearing in his consciousness. This was because Columbus—like all successful subsequent conquistadors—was at least partially adept at accommodating himself to unfamiliar vicissitudes. As single-minded and stubborn as Columbus was about clinging to the notion that he had found Asia, he was vulnerable to the impingement of unexpected facts. The recognition of tobacco—its transformation from being barely visible as dried up cellulose to being leaves "esteemed" by the local inhabitants—was predicated on opening up a space that could exist between prior assumptions and future hopes. It was because of this space that Europeans first came to "see" tobacco, but also came to consume tobacco, and chocolate as well. The success of military leaders and commercial traders—like all negotiators—depends at least in part on their ability to remain present minded, to react spontaneously to the circumstances in front of them. Columbus had to have possessed this ability to at least a degree for him to have achieved the earlier successes that made his uncharted expedition to the West possible. I think that this aspect of the American intercultural encounter has been obscured by the model in which Europeans solely view the New World through their filters or grids and hence see little more than a distorted reflection of themselves, a fabricated "other."[9] The very same present-mindedness that allowed Columbus to see what lay before him and, at least momentarily, to eclipse what he expected and wanted to see was the same state of mind that led other adventurers to eventually *try* tobacco and chocolate.

TOBACCO ON THE FRONTIER

This ability to see the reality, to respond in the present, was not the result of a disinterested curiosity but was actually an outgrowth of skills necessary for survival and, beyond that, success in commercial and military exploits. For Europeans to achieve conquest and domination, as well as trade, they could not solely pursue a slash-and-burn policy. In frontier zones, Europeans encountered Amerindians living on their own terms. This does not mean that they were untouched by their European interactions, for the native Americans quickly became desirous of European trade goods, coveting the exotic sparkle of glass and the enduring utility of metal tools, and they were all too willing to convert traditional raiding and slaving practices to meet the Europeans' insatiable demand for slaves to labor in mines and pearl fisheries. Most of all, Amerindians suffered the effects of Old World diseases. But while the interactions had significant effects on native political economy and demography, there was no reason for native groups to question their fundamental beliefs and practices concerning society and cosmology, nor did they. As Europeans sought and received native assistance and alliances, they had to immerse themselves—however temporarily—in roles constructed for them by those whose help they wanted. Frontiers necessitated role playing and mimesis; as conquistadors took on the role of "ally" or "dependent," they did not so much "view" Amerindian culture through a preconceived classificatory scheme as take on the roles foisted on them by their native hosts and guides. They did first and thought second, and in this way they learned about tobacco and chocolate from the inside out.

Initial European experience of tobacco and chocolate habits was an unexpected by-product of survival on the frontier. In general, Spanish sources do not often reveal instances in which Europeans had to take on native customs, temporarily or permanently, for the fact of Europeans conforming to customs of pagan and barbarous peoples undermined an ideology of the civilized dominating the barbarous, of the Christians converting the pagan "savages." In scattered asides, in the accounts of discovery and conquest voyages, however, one can catch glimpses of mariners, soldiers, settlers, and slaves learning from their native hosts in the New World. These views of inaugural experiences percolate through the sources and must serve to illustrate countless other stories and situations lost to recorded memory. In this "middle ground" that required negotiation and accommodation rather than unilateral conquest, Europeans, in pursuit of diplomacy, trade, and physical relief, accepted tobacco and cacao offerings from American Indians.[10]

The first documented account of a European tobacco initiation was in 1518.[11] That year the governor of Cuba commissioned Juan de Grijalva (1490–1527) to explore—and hopefully "possess"—the recently discovered lands of the Yucatán Peninsula where there were excited reports of stone towers and fine cotton dress, as well as golden jewelry festooning the local Mayans.[12] Grijalva's first attempts to meet and trade with local populations failed: the hostile Indians refused them water and, or worse, rained down arrows on them, doubtless aware of the Europeans' recent and ongoing depredations in the Caribbean.[13]

By the third month of the expedition, in mid-June, the Spanish had rounded the Yucatán Peninsula and began to investigate the coast of the Gulf of Mexico. They anchored in a bay separating the coast and a small island. There they entered a tall building, found vestiges of recent human sacrifice, and decided to return to the ships. Before long they were invited by some natives to come ashore, who promised them "much gold" according to their translator. The following morning they awoke to see the shore decorated with white cloths and the locals calling them to come visit. Grijalva and his men eagerly accepted the peaceful overtures; the prospect of potential trading partners and allies mattered more than the misgivings they had about the habit of human sacrifice. Awaiting them was a ceremonial meal. Cut tree branches provided shade and a cloth was set out on the ground, on which was placed dishes with some fowl spiced with a yellow broth, tortillas, and corn on the cob. The Spaniards declined to eat the stew ("as it was Friday [i.e., fish only] none of the Christians ate of it"). But, piety withstanding, they seemed not to hesitate before "black smoking tubes which they consumed like *tabacos*." (Nor did they refuse the gifts of dyed-cotton cloaks.)[14] They fully understood that such offerings indicated good will and amicable intentions, no doubt all the more appreciated because of the linguistic barriers. Perhaps the ceremony convinced Grijalva that he could now go after what he really wanted, for thereafter he indicated "with signs . . . for them not to leave but to bring him gold and other things." His signs correctly understood and heeded, the captain got what he desired, for which he exchanged some European textiles, bonnets, green glass beads, as well as "three combs and a mirror."

The following day, a neighboring chief across the inlet also made friendly overtures, perhaps not wanting to lose to a rival the opportunity to make a useful ally or desirable trading partner. Once again tobacco figured at the center of a ceremony, a reciprocally understood act of communication in the midst of mutual miscomprehension. These Indian leaders "embraced captain Grijalva and showed him and the other Christians much love, as if they had known them previously and had a friendship with them," but they "lost time in the many words they said without one understanding the others" (which explains why the Christians got away with "taking possession"). After the opaque exchange of "words," the chief initiated the ceremony by commanding some of his men to set up a seating area by laying down palm branches; other men were ordered to hold branches upright to create a shady arbor. The chief then motioned for Grijalva, along with "those Christians who seemed to him to be the most principal ones," to sit down on the seating area, and then indicated that all of the surrounding people were to sit as well (he also ensured there were guards to fend against ambush). Then this "principal Indian" gave to Grijalva and those seated with him "tubes, lit by him at one end, which are made so that when they are burning, they are spent little by little and are entirely consumed until they are finished without ever going up in flames, like the *pivetes* of Valencia [burning sticks made of aromatic paste], and they smell very good as does the smoke that leaves them."[15] The Indian hosts, perhaps seeing the Spaniards as novice smokers, "made gestures to the Christians to indicate that they were not to let that smoke be lost or escape, as do those who take tobacco." The ceremony concluded when the two of the Indian leaders "put both of their palms on the ground, kissed them in a sign of peace or salutation, but because they did not speak the language nor did the ones understand the others, it was very difficult and impossible to understand each other, and even though, as I have said, they spoke many words, by no way or intelligence was it possible to understand."[16]

In this scene, the Spanish received a smoking lesson that included the instruction that tobacco was associated with diplomacy, hospitality, and choreographed social ritual. Smoking tobacco was a ritual, ordered by a material grammar and requiring a fixed seating order and certain furniture, that substituted for language and that signaled peace. It is telling that the smoking rite appeared as a transparently comprehended act bracketed by frustrated attempts to communicate with verbal language. In this episode, one sees the formerly thwarted, somewhat desperate "Christians" not only enjoying the fragrant smoke but also finding solace in the clarity of meaning and intention as an alleviating counterpoint to the failures of language. The Spaniards knew from almost three decades of experience in the Americas that success was predicated on making friends, and they were thus highly motivated to become keen observers and apprentices of local diplomatic protocol. In this way they encountered and, at least some of them, learned to like tobacco.

Grijalva's expedition ultimately failed to establish a settlement, as it was routed by hostile Indians who thought them dangerous enemies rather than intriguing strangers. The successes he did achieve were based not on military prowess but rather on securing the goodwill of the native inhabitants. To do so, he and his men had to participate in local ceremonies, and this included smoking tobacco together.

During the initial stage of American expansion, the Spanish knew what they wanted from their New World trading ventures: first and foremost, gold; second, other precious metals and stones, such as silver and pearls, and also the chattel they could enslave to extract further riches from the earth; and third, the valuable spices, medicinals, and dye goods that could be sold for high prices in Europe. With the exception of exotic medicines, they were not looking for new goods but rather more for the Old World goods for which there was already European demand. To obtain their objectives—allies and trade goods—they filled the role given to them by their Indian hosts, one which included accepting offerings of tobacco. Though the assumption of the role might have lasted for a few hours or a day, it left its mark. They tried tobacco, yes. But more than that they learned what tobacco was in that way. The New World was not only a screen on which to project categories, it was also a mold into which they stepped, changing not only their bodies but also their minds.

CHOCOLATE ON THE FRONTIER

The European initiation into chocolate use likewise took place on the frontier. The failure of Grijalva's expedition to Mesoamerica did not dampen enthusiasm for plans of conquest and subjugation of these lands that seemed to possess prosperous peoples and abundant resources that promised wealth to the successful colonizers. The following year, in 1519, the governor of Cuba reluctantly granted permission to the swashbuckling conquistador named Hernán Cortés to return to the Yucatán peninsula. The governor later changed his mind, but it was too late, for Cortés had already departed with a force of six hundred men. Cortés's military genius stemmed not only from his ability to harness fractious and mutinous troops to his quest and effectively deploy the Spaniards' tactical advantages (metal weaponry, fearsome animals, and brazen arrogance) but also from his development of critical alliances with indigenous groups hostile to the Mexica.[17] In pursuit of the latter strategy, Cortés had to operate as a skilled diplomat. Though the famed accounts of the conquest portray Cortés as an idol toppler, temple destroyer, and outspoken objector to human sacrifice, they also reveal him as expert in cross-cultural negotiations. In order to win the favor he desperately needed of Cempolans, Tlaxcalans, and other groups, he sought not to offend and so to understand foreign customs and cooperate within their confines.[18] In this context, he and his men tasted chocolate in the context of diplomacy.

In an account at least partially based on native American perspectives of Cortés's march, the Spaniards appear as fearful but ultimately as players in the rites of Aztec diplomacy.[19] Moctezuma, on finally being persuaded that the tales of strange men arriving off the coast of Veracruz ("white men" with "very long and hairy beards" and "clothes of many colors" and who wore on their heads "round coverings") were not apocryphal, ordered an emissary to greet them with gifts and the lord of his coastal tributary of Cuetlaxtlan to provide the strangers with "all of the kinds of good that can be made, not only fowl but grilled and cooked meats, and to provide all types of bread and fruit, and many gourd cups [*jícaras*] of cacao."[20] On board the Spaniards' ship ("a house on the water"), the trilingual (Nahuatl-, Maya-, and Spanish-speaking) slave woman Doña Marina (Malinche) interpreted for the two parties—while Moctezuma's two envoys presented the Spaniards' leader with jewels, precious stones, and feather works, as well as the abundant dishes of food. The Spaniards delighted in the durable goods, "staring at them with great happiness and contentment," but through their interpreter, Marina, they expressed hesitation about the foodstuffs. She explained that the white strangers "are not accustomed to eat such foods and would like for [the Indians] to taste them first." The missionary Durán wrote:

The two Aztecs tasted the different foods, and when the Spaniards saw them eating they too began to eat chicken, stew, and maize cakes and to enjoy the food, with much laughing and sporting. But when the time came to drink the chocolate that had been brought to them, that most highly prized drink of the Indians, they were filled with fear. When the Indians saw that they dared not drink, they tasted from all the gourds and the Spaniards refreshed themselves with chocolate, because, in truth, it is a refreshing beverage.[21]

Durán is a far from a perfect transmitter of Indian accounts, but that some such encounter over food took place seems likely, particularly given that many subsequent European first encounters with cacao often began in a similar fashion, with a relative reluctance to try the exotic concoction.[22]

The conquistadores' experiences in the Mexica capital of Tenochtitlan further impressed on them the noble, even regal, valences of chocolate. Welcomed by Moctezuma on November 8, 1519, the Spaniards had taken their host prisoner in less than a week. They stayed on in the court in rather fantastic circumstances until the death of Moctezuma at the end of June 1520. In their seven months in the palace, neither the Mexica rulers nor the Spanish guests/captives/hostage takers had absolute control, until the Spanish aided by native and European reinforcements inflicted a lethal siege in August 1521. In the long days of uncertain waiting, the Spanish saw up close the centrality of chocolate to Aztec court society. As the prominence the veteran soldier Bernal Díaz del Castillo gave to chocolate in his *True History of the Conquest of Mexico* indicates, it did not take long for honor- and status-obsessed Spanish conquistadors to seize on cacao's special place in Moctezuma's court. The Spanish quickly learned that in Aztec society chocolate connoted, if not conferred, high social rank.[23] For Europeans, survival and success on the frontier depended on native cooperation; they relied on Indians for food, guides, military assistance, and trade goods (precious metals and slaves above all). The episode described by Durán explained how such conditions created an imperative that forced the Europeans to overcome their initial resistance to the alien substance.[24] Even the brief encounters that transpired between the Spanish and Indians during reconnaissance expeditions afforded opportunities for exposure to Indian consumption practices.

CONQUEST AND CLASSIFICATION

The first representations of tobacco and chocolate that circulated in the publications that informed Europeans about the New World discoveries did not accord with explorers and conquistadores' actual experiences on the frontier. While the frontier often immersed explorers in the cultural order of native hosts and induced them to behave like the local people, the emerging colonial discourse made the goods quintessential symbols of Amerindian otherness. The goods—tobacco in particular—became ensnared in efforts to reassure European states of the moral, ethical, and legal basis of conquest in the Indies, hinging on the existence of hard lines dividing the civilized from the savage and Christian from heathen. Alternatively, in the case of chocolate and cacao, they became symbols of a lost Edenic civilization, to be studied with nostalgia and idealized as a critique of the European dystopia. In published chronicles of explorations, official histories, and travelers' accounts, tobacco and chocolate went from having no dedicated signifiers to being symbolic of the cultural divides separating *"indios"* and *"cristianos."*

Peter Martyr d'Anghera (or Pietro Martire d'Anghiera, 1457–1526), who wrote *De orbe novo decades* (Of the new world), arguably the most influential text about the initial phase of European colonization in the Americas (the first edition appeared in 1516), himself never left Europe's shores.[25] Born in Lombardy, Italy, in 1457, Martyr came to Spain in 1487, where he prospered at court as a soldier, priest, chaplain, and, ultimately, as first official chronicler of the New World to Emperor Charles V. His prestigious position allowed him unparalleled access to manuscript reports of New World expeditions and personal interviews with returnees.[26] Martyr saw in America a mirror that reflected Europe's flaws, among them short-sighted materialism, decay, and corruption.[27] The Antilles that rise from his pages is a lost Eden, peopled by noble savages, deprived of the light of Christianity but blessed with pure souls ripe for conversion.

For his descriptions of the indigenous people of the Greater Antilles Martyr relied on a source written by Ramón Pané, a Catalonian friar who accompanied Columbus (and 1,500 soldiers and settlers) on his second voyage in the autumn of 1493. At Columbus's request, Pané spent two years living in the lands of the cacique Guarionex, in what is now the northwest Dominican Republic, in order to report on the "ceremonies and antiquities" of the natives, so as to assist evangelization efforts and to satisfy the growing curiosity of those in Europe.[28] Martyr framed his discussion by comparing Amerindians with the pagans of antiquity:

> You shall now therfore understand the illusions wherewith the people of the Island have been seduced after the errours of the old gentilitie, and wandered in the ignorance and blindnesse of humane nature, corrupted of the disobedience of our first parents, which hath remayned in all nations upon the face of the earth, except where it hath pleased God by the light of his spirite by his worde, to power upon his elect the face of renovation.[29]

Martyr appraised the cultural and religious condition of the New World peoples optimistically. Just as the pagans of antiquity left darkness and found the light of Christianity, the pagans of these lands would follow in due course.

What most captured Martyr's imagination in Pané's account was his description of *cohoba*—a substance subsequently identified as tobacco or a tobacco amalgam—particularly as it was used by their shamans to communicate with their "idols," the native term translated as *cemi* by the Spaniards.[30] Their temporal and spiritual leaders were culpable for the idolatrous "superstitions" of their innocent flocks. To perform their counterfeit rituals, their "kings" and *boitios* (shamans) relied on an indispensable aid, "a powder of marveylous effect" (as it is referred to in the margin of Richard Eden's 1612 translation). By "snuffing up into their nostrels the pouder of the herbe called *Cohobba* (wherewith the Boitii are dryven into a furie) they say that immediately they see the houses turned topsie turvie, and men to walke with their heeles upward, of such force is this pouder, utterly to take away all sence."[31] Only in this trance state could they communicate with supernatural spirits, "at which time (as they say) they learne many things by revelation of the Zemes [*cemis*]."[32] Zemes were their "idols"— some purloined examples of which he sent back to Spain—described as "certain images of Gossampine cotton, folded or wreathed after their manner, and hard stopped within . . . made to the likeness of young devilles" (they were also fashioned out of wood and stone).[33] He also related how the shamans performed healing rites under the influence of *cohoba*. Martyr inaugurated an enduring tradition that made *cohoba* the synecdoche of pagan idolatry ("their whole religion is none other thing then idolatry").

If *cohoba* symbolized all that was wrong with native life, cacao and chocolate signaled the opposite. The 1530 edition of *De novo orbe* (published posthumously) updated the story of the European invasion of America by telling of the conquest of Mexico.[34] Viewing the discoveries through the lens of fifteenth-century Italian humanism, Martyr found Mexico reminiscent of an overdeveloped, sophisticated Rome inhabited by decadent pagans, with cultural achievements that superseded Europe's though handicapped by its idolatrous ways. Martyr introduced chocolate in the context of the almost incomprehensible luxuries of Moctezuma's court—flowing gold and "1,500 garments of Gossampine cotton." He reported that in the ruler's court, food, like clothes, could be classified according to that which ordinary people consume and that intended for nobility. He referred to their chocolate as the "wine" that "Kinges and noble men delight in, differing from that which the people use . . . the ordinaire and common sort of Maizium."[35] Chocolate, here known only as a "wonderful drink" composed of "certain almonds," is identified as the exclusive prerogative of royalty. Yet it is better still. Not only is this drink "fitte for a king" but it yields a cure to avarice.

For Martyr, gold represented Europeans' unquenchable desire and destructive greed; cacao was its antithesis. It was the basis for a "profitable drinke for mankinde," and it "supplieth the use of monie." He exclaimed, "O blessed money, which yeeldeth sweete, and profitable drinke for mankinde, and preserveth the possessors therefor free from the *hellish pestilence of avarice, because it cannot be long kept, or hid under grounde.*"[36] Later in the book, Martyr returned to the subject of this "happie money," throwing into relief the contrast between Mexican chocolate and European gold.

> They have money, which I call happy, because for the greedie desire and gaping to attaine the same, the bowelles of the earth are not rent a sunder, nor through the ravenning greedinesse of covetous men, nor terrour of warres assyaling, it returneth to the dennes and caves of the mother earth, as golden, or silver money doth. For this groweth upon trees . . . [and from which a] drinke is made of them for rich, and noble menne.[37]

If he didn't invent the now-familiar noble savage, Martyr contributed greatly to the vision of "naked men" uncorrupted by insatiable greed and desire for vain luxuries, the perfect negative of degenerate, overdressed civilized men with their useless "heaps of gold."[38]

In Martyr's books *cohoba* and cacao figure at opposite poles of Europeans' spectrum of American Indians: the former belonged to the simple savages of the Antilles, while chocolate exemplified the highly evolved civilization of Mexico. *Cohoba* aligned with native depravity, contrasting with Europeans' Christianity, while cacao served as a reminder of Europeans' debauched decadence. But they shared the quality of representing Amerindian otherness. Despite the admiring tone Martyr uses to discuss chocolate, he never suggests that the conquering Europeans are or should be interested in the American drink for themselves. The Mexica of America are like the Greeks of antiquity for Martyr; they exist as a remote ideal, a convenient projection for dissatisfactions with Europe. Martyr did not anticipate that Europeans might be tempted by either the fury-inducing herb of Antillian shamans or the precious beverage of Aztec kings. There is never any suggestion that the boundaries between Europeans and Indians could become blurry.

In 1535, tobacco—or rather "*tabaco*"—first appeared in print in *La historia general de las Indias* (The general history of the Indies) by Gonzalo Fernández de Oviedo y Valdés (1478–1557), the royal chronicler of the Indies.[39] Martyr described Indian culture from the comfort, safety, and security of his position in Madrid, a distant vantage point from which it was easy to relay exotic detail of foreign peoples within a story intended to comment on European shortcomings and excite pride in the new discoveries. Oviedo, on the other hand, had a greater personal stake in the colonial project, and part of his motivation in writing was to defend the activities of conquistadores whose depredations were being lambasted by critics with the monarch's ear. Oviedo arrived in America to participate in the conquest of Darién (Panama) in 1514 and spent several years as a colonial official there and in Cartagena. He later settled in Santo Domingo, where he received royal subsidies to write histories of the Indies.[40]

Oviedo wrote amid a heated debate about the legitimacy of the Spanish conquest and the Crown's dominion in America. He was involved in an ongoing polemic with Bartolomé de las Casas, the famous "defender of the Indians" who revealed Amerindians as innocent victims of cruel and avaricious plunderers. Las Casas and others laid bare the contradiction of the Spaniards' vicious treatment of native Americans and the fact that the legitimacy of conquest was predicated on bringing salvation to American souls. Faced with such a challenge, propagandists and apologists for empire scrambled to come up with persuasive, internally consistent arguments for Spanish conquest in the decade preceding Oviedo's *Historia general*. Deploying Aristotle's definitions of "barbarians" and "natural slaves," theologians and jurists maintained that Indians' alleged cannibalism, sodomy, bestiality, and even their penchant for eating insects was evidence of their barbarism and thereby legitimated the Spanish invasion and dominion.[41] In this tradition, Oviedo's account of tobacco provided proof that Indians could never escape the condition of pagan barbarism.

Tobacco appeared in book 5 of *La historia general de las Indias*, which was devoted to the "crimes and abominable customs and rites" of the indigenous people of Hispaniola. (It is worth noting that tobacco did not appear in the book that enumerated native "plants and herbs" with medicinal value.) In the preface to book 5, he blamed the catastrophic death toll of the Caribbean on its victims, claiming it was a consequence of "their culpability and punishment." Where Martyr wrote optimistically about the impending success of conversion efforts, Oviedo complained that though for forty-three years the local population had been exposed to Christianity and "that there has been and there is no lack of preachers and zealous clerics," their teachings quickly faded in the Indians' minds. He declared the native population so innately perverse that they would never embrace the Catholic faith. Oviedo asserted that the indigenous inhabitants' unusually "thick" skulls were proof of their "bestial understanding."[42]

So it says a lot that perhaps more than any other object introduced in the *Historia general*, tobacco was the material embodiment of "bad" Indian culture. Oviedo introduced the section on tobacco with the statement,

bozes muy grãdes:yẽotras menozes z hue
cos y ẽcozados cõ vn cuero õ cieruo/o õ otro
animal:pero como enestas yslas no auia a/
nimales para los encozar/vsauan los atam
bozes que he dicho/y dellos mismos z de/
los otros se vsan oy enla tierra firme/como
se dira enla parte que conuenga.

¶Capitu.ij.delos taba-
cos o ahumadas que los indios acostũbzã
enesta ysla española:z la manera delas ca/
mas en que duermen.

Sauan los indios desta isla en
tre otros sus vicios vno muy
malo/que es tomar vnas ahu/
madas que ellos llamã tabaco
para salir de sentido:y esto ha/
zian con el humo de cierta yerua/ã alo ã yo
he podido entender es de calidad del vele/
ño:pero no de aquella hechura o forma ala
vista:porque esta yerua es vn tallo como ã
tro o cinco palmos/poco mas o menos õ al
to/y con vnas hojas ãchas z gruessas z blã
das z vellosas:y el verdoz tira algo ala co/
loz delas hojas dela lengua de buey/o Bu/
glosa:que llaman los erbolarios z medicos
Esta yerua que digo enel genero es muy se
mejante al Seleño. La qual toman de a/
questa manera. Los Caciques z honbzes
principales tenian vnos pali/
llos huecos: del tamaño de
vn xeme o menos/dela gros/
seza del dedo menoz dela ma/
no. y estos cañutos tenian
dos cañones respondiêtes a
vno/como aqui esta pintado
z todo en vna pieça. y los
dos ponian enlas ventanas delas narizes/
y el otro enel humo z yerua que ardia. y
estauan muy lisos z bien labzados: z que/
mauan las hojas de aquella yerua arrebu/
jadas o embueltas dela manera que los pa
jes cortesanos suelen echar se ahumadas: z
ponian la otra parte del cañuto senzillo en
la yerua que ardia: z tomauan el aliento z
humo para si/vna z dos z tres/z mas vezes

quanto lo podian pozfiar/hasta que que/
dauan sin sentido grande espacio tendidos
en tierra beodos o adozmidos de vn gra/
ue z muy pesado sueño. Elos Indios que
no alcançauan aquellos palillos/tomauan
aquel humo cõ vnos Calamos o Cañue
las de carrizos. E aquel tal instrumento cõ
que toma el humo/o alas Cañuelas que es
dicho/llaman los Indios Tabaco:z no a/
la yerua o sueño que les toma(como pensa/
uan algunos.) Esta yerua tenian los Indi
os poz cosa muy pzeciada / y la criauan en
sus huertos z labzanças para el efecto que
es dicho/dando se a entender / que este to/
mar de aquella yerua z sahumerio/no tan
solo les era sana:pero muy sancta cosa. y
assi como cae el Cacique o pzincipal en tier
ra/tomanle sus mugeres(que son muchas)
y echan le en su cama/si el antes selo ha mã
dado. Pero si no lo dizo z pzoueyo pzime/
ro no quiere sino que lo dezẽ assi/fasta que
sele passe el vino z aquel adozmescimiento.
Yo no puedo pensar que plazer se saca õ tal
acto/sino es la gula de beuer hasta dar de es
paldas:pero se que ya algunos chzistianos
lo vsauan:en especial los que estauan toca/
dos del mal delas Buas:porque dizen los
tales que en aquel tiempo que estan assi tra
poztados/no sienten los dolozes de su enfer
medad. y no me parece ques esto otra cosa/
sino estar muerto en vida el que tal haze: lo
qual tengo poz peoz que el doloz de que se
escusan/pues no sanan poz esso. Al pzesen
te muchos Negros delos que estan enesta
ciudad y enla ysla toda han tomado la mis/
ma costumbze:z crian enlas haziendas y e/
reoamientos de sus amos esta yerua para
lo que es dicho. y ellos toman las mesmas
ahumadas/porque dizen que quando pa/
ran del trabajo z hazen estos Tabacos les
quitan el cansancio. Aqui me paresce que
quadra vna costumbze viciosa z mala que
la gente de Tracia vsa entre otros sus vici/
os/segun el Abulensis escriue libzo tercero
capitulo ciento y sessenta y ocho sobre Eu
sebio õlos tpos. Dõde dize ã tiene poz costũ
bze todos/ varões z mugeres õ comer alrre

Figure 2.1. Gonzalo Fernández de Oviedo y Valdés, *Historia general de las Indias* (1535). fol. 47r. This marks the first printed reference to *tabaco*, one that categorized it as a "very bad vice" of the Indians. The accompanying image of the Y-shaped device emphasized the exoticism of the custom. Oviedo stated that native inhabitants of Hispaniola used it to smoke, but more likely it was a snuffing device. Reproduced courtesy of the John Carter Brown Library at Brown University.

"The Indians of this island have among other vices one that is very bad, which is taking smokeable things which they call *tabaco* in order to leave their senses." Like Martyr, he described how Indian caciques and other men of rank would use tobacco until they were left "without sense, remaining for a long period stupefied on the ground in a profound and heavy sleep," but referred to them taking "smoke" through their noses out of a "Y"-shaped device, or through the mouth in reed pipes, rather than by sniffing powder (figure 2.1).[43] He explained that the Caribbean "Indians hold this herb as precious, and cultivate it in their gardens and fields, so it is said that they take this herb and smokeable not only because they find it healthful, but also a holy thing," revealing the inextricability of healing and religious rites.

Oviedo's account of tobacco also illustrates how European notions concerning diabolism as well as witchcraft influenced their understanding of tobacco. The chronicler explained that many Europeans mistook tobacco for henbane (in Latin *Hyoscyamus*), which is in fact a close botanical relative of the former, as both belong to the nightshade family. "This herb of which I speak," wrote Oviedo, "is of a species that is very similar to henbane."[44] For Europeans, henbane evoked sorcery and witchcraft, further implicating tobacco as an important agent in insidious rites. Experts on witches and magic in the sixteenth and seventeenth centuries specified the pernicious herbs employed in their potions; in the recipes documented by witch authorities, henbane and other plants of the nightshade family appeared with frequency.[45] The association with witchcraft suggested the devil lurked nearby.

In the second part of the *Historia general* (never published), Oviedo made the devil a centerpiece of Indian rituals surrounding tobacco. In his damning ethnography of the Caquetio of Venezuela, he recounted how shamans (*boratio*) smoked "things that are called tabacos" when they wanted to "consult with the devil." Likewise, tobacco loomed large in condemnatory ethnographies of the Cueva of Panama, Chorotega of Costa Rica, and the Pemones of Venezuela.[46] For Martyr, tobacco lay at the core of specious Indian idolatry, but Oviedo went further by introducing the specter of diabolical agency.

There is yet one more way that Oviedo's take on tobacco—and the New World more generally—diverged from that of Martyr. He knew firsthand that Indian culture was not so easily containable. Oviedo concluded his entry on tobacco with "I know that now some Christians use it: particularly those who suffer from the *mal de bubas* (syphilis) and so transformed [by the tobacco] that they do not feel the pains of their sickness."[47] It hardly needs saying that the conquistador and chronicler adamantly disapproved of "Christian" adoption of the Indian tobacco habit.

Oviedo's treatment of cacao and chocolate puts into relief the special scorn and ideological weight freighted upon tobacco. Rather than fore-grounding cacao in the context of "customs and rites" of "barbarians" as he did with tobacco, Oviedo left out cacao and its blood-red beverage in his published version of the *Historia general*. It was not for lack of experi-ence; he was well acquainted with the plant and its beverage from his time among the Nicoya in Costa Rica, and he wrote extensively about them in a revised, expanded version that never saw print.[48] Perhaps its absence in his first edition was a result of the fact that chocolate, rather than fitting neatly into a taxonomy that divided the civilized from the barbarian, rather demonstrated the blurriness of such categories. He planned to ap-pend the chapter on cacao to his book 8 devoted to "fruit trees." Though he devoted ample space to describing the growing conditions (particularly admiring the taller tree specimen that "sprouts gorgeous flowers" and grows next to cacao trees to "defend from the sun by making shade with their branches and trees"), Oviedo did not skimp on ethnographic and culinary detail.[49] Based on his extensive time among Indian groups in Nicaragua and Costa Rica, he covered such aspects as cacao's use as money (ten "almonds" would buy one a rabbit or one "run" with a prosti-tute) and the concomitant phenomena of the circulation of fraudulent ca-cao, the method Indian women used to prepare chocolate, the way rank deemed the order in which chocolate was consumed by chiefs and their attendants, and the prophylactic use of the drink to immunize against snake venom.[50] Unlike the chapter on tobacco, characterized by unam-biguous scorn, Oviedo's treatment of chocolate waffled between firm dec-larations of chocolate and cacao's otherness and its actual appropriation by "Christians." He fixated on Indians' penchant for making it appear like blood: "And because those people are friends of drinking human blood, they add a little *bixa* (achiote) so this drink looks like blood." Later, when describing how remnants of the foam would stain the mouth, he wrote, "[It is] a horrific thing, because it appears like their own blood."[51] The chapter on chocolate suggests a failed effort to maintain the firm di-vide between "Indian" and "Christian" practices. While for the Central American Indians chocolate "is the best thing in the world," for him, watching the drinking of chocolate makes for a "disgusting view." But then he quickly acknowledged that "Christians have found it very benefi-cial." While never quite revealing whether he had been one of these, he did not hesitate to recommend other, less culturally dangerous uses of cacao. The conquistador recounted how he had suffered a deep cut in his foot while jumping out of danger from a wayward wave and how he was suc-cored by a "black slave woman of mine who told me that the Indians say that the cacao fat was good for wounds." Her ministrations, based on medical knowledge acquired from the native inhabitants, allowed him to resume his expedition.[52] This is a revealing aside, not only illuminating the role African slaves sometimes assumed as cultural go-betweens with the indigenous population and European conquerors, but also showing how the "medicinal" categorization allowed Oviedo to see cacao as acceptable. Another acceptable use of cacao was as a cooking fat, illustrated by a nostalgic memory of "an Italian, a good friend and companion named Nicolá" who made him an excellent meal of fish and eggs fried in cacao fat.[53] In this case, the Europeans were using a local substance in a quintessentially European way, utterly independent of Indian cultural forms—what went unsaid was that "that black slave woman of mine" who knew so well how to render the cacao fat no doubt had acquired that knowledge from the same Indians who informed her about the fat's healing properties.

ENDURING LEGACIES

It was the bold caricatures—tobacco as a diabolical sacrament, chocolate as the luxurious wine of a fallen civilization, or chocolate as the disgusting drink of barbarians—not the waffling confusion about where to draw the lines of appropriation that persisted in the subsequent chronicles of conquest in the Americas. The images of tobacco and chocolate as the apotheoses, respectively, of depraved barbarism and civilized luxury proved enduring. The works of Martyr and Oviedo circulated in numerous editions, and their renditions influenced and shaped how subsequent chroniclers wrote about the goods. For instance, the royal chronicler Francisco López de Gómara synthesized Martyr's and Oviedo's accounts for his representation of tobacco in his influential *Historia general de las Indias* (General history of the Indies), first published in 1552.[54] In his section on "the religion of the isla Española" he explained that "priests of the devil" either "eat an herb called Cohoba" or "take in the smoke through their noses" in order to "leave their senses and see a thousand visions" and so prophesize to the idolaters.[55] Similarly, Oviedo's description of Taíno tobacco use was adopted by Girolamo Benzoni, a Milanese adventurer who traveled to the Indies and published his influential *Historia del mondo nuovo* (History of the New World) in 1565. Following Oviedo and Martyr, Benzoni placed his discussion of tobacco in his chapter on "The Religion of the Indians of Hispaniola" and offered similar details (figure 2.2).[56] Even after Spaniards—and Europeans generally—began to ideologically domesticate tobacco, the diabolical and barbaric associations endured. Likewise the trope of chocolate as symbol of noble savage (or savage noble) persisted.

MONDO NVOVO. 55

Modo che tengono i medici nel
medicare gl'infermi.

Figure 2.2. Girolamo Benzoni, *Historia del mondo nuovo* (Venice, 1565), fol. 55r. Following in the tradition of Oviedo, Benzoni depicted the strangeness of shamanic tobacco healing ceremonies. Reproduced courtesy of the John Carter Brown Library at Brown University.

In the wake of conquest, ideology and pragmatism diverged dramatically where tobacco and chocolate were concerned. In published chronicles and histories, the former was an emblem of Amerindian otherness, epitomizing diabolically inspired paganism, while the latter suggested an idealized lost epoch of "noble savagery." Yet these ideologically motivated constructions did not prevent Europeans from becoming habituated to tobacco and chocolate; rather, social relations in colonial settings made them susceptible to native influence. Colonial frontiers required cultural improvisation on the part of would-be conquistadores—the willingness to observe and adopt the customs of local populations—most commonly for the short duration of a trade or military negotiation, but sometimes for a period of months or years or even for life, when explorers found themselves lost or captive in Indian-controlled territory. In these settings, Europeans did not and could not dominate but rather depended on the goodwill of the natives.

3

Adapting under Colonialism

❖ ❖

On August 13, 1521, the three-month Spanish siege of Tenochtitlan came to an end, after inhabitants decimated by smallpox could no longer resist the invaders nor bear the devastating famine that led them to eat ground-up adobe bricks and "chew at wood, glue flowers, plaster, leather, and deerskin."[1] So began Spanish rule in Mesoamerica. Soon after the fall of the Mexica, the conquistadores fanned out to neighboring communities and through entreaties, threats, and violence brought them to accept their rule. By 1524 Spanish domination extended throughout central Mexico, in what they called New Spain. Elsewhere in Mesoamerica conquest did not come for several decades and, in some places, even centuries.[2]

After military victory, the conquerors built a colonial regime. Their plans were guided by the twofold objective of reaping riches and saving souls. Both goals led them to focus their efforts on the indigenous population. The Spanish victors overlay colonial institutions onto existing social, political, and economic structures. They demanded tribute as the lords of the Aztec empire had done, copying Moctezuma's tribute lists and relying on local elites to serve as collectors. They based political and ecclesiastical jurisdictions on indigenous political units. They built churches on the sites of demolished temples. The Spanish Crown and colonists wanted to maintain those institutions and practices that did not strike them as dangerously pagan but that would make their goals of wealth and Christianization easier to achieve. Tobacco and chocolate survived the conquest in large part because the new colonizers erected their regime on top of the substratum of native society. Much of Mesoamerica remained Indian enclaves in the decades and even centuries after the Spanish conquest.[3]

For Mesoamerican Indians living under Spanish rule, tobacco and chocolate provided a link to past traditions that were under attack by the colonial regime or subject to atrophy with the disintegration of pre-Hispanic social structures. The goods themselves, like other features of the material environment, served as mnemonic reminders of traditional deities, worship styles, and social protocol. Yet, in the effort to preserve traditional practices, Mesoamericans also forcibly modified old customs, making necessary adjustments to escape persecution by colonial authorities or take advantage of new opportunities. So, in certain contexts, they took on greater importance, as other forms of traditional practice—such as human sacrifice and processions with monumental idols—became nearly impossible to execute. Not all Mesoamericans resisted colonial rule all of the time, particularly as the generation with preconquest memories succumbed to disease and old age. Tobacco and chocolate not only kept pre-Hispanic traditions alive, they also provided a means for Indian subjects to adapt to new circumstances. Indians were not merely passive subjects of Christian conversion campaigns but also remade Christianity with Mesoamerican elements and created hybrid forms of religion and culture that incorporated tobacco and chocolate. With tobacco they could discover how they had displeased saints, and they could offer them chocolate to show their gratitude, in the same way they deployed the goods with pre-Hispanic deities. Mesoamericans sustained and transformed traditional uses of tobacco and chocolate in the wake of the Spanish invaders.

Even taking into account ever-accelerating Spanish consumption, it appears that collectively, if not individually, Indians throughout Mesoamerica drank more chocolate after than before the conquest. The conquerors usurped and maintained much of the tribute system organized by the Aztec rulers, so they not only tolerated but encouraged the cultivation of cacao by their native subjects. Cacao and cacao beverages were readily available in Indian marketplaces.[4] Mesoamericans continued to drink the same array of cacao-based beverages they did before the Spanish arrived—cacao spiced with floral extracts, reddened with achiote, and/or mixed with maize. They served these chocolate drinks in crafted gourds and ceramic vessels that even the Spaniards knew by their Nahuatl names, *xicalli* (hispanized to *xícara* [*jícara*]) and *tecomate*, and frothed the beverage with turtle-shell serving sticks. Cacao beans still offered fungible wealth, competing with precious metals as panregional currency.[5] Tobacco did not present itself as a particularly lucrative trade good, so the colonizers mostly ignored it in the years after the conquest. Free of interference, Mesoamericans continued to cultivate tobacco in garden plots, to use green and fresh or to dry and cure it. They rolled it into cigars and put it in pipes with sweet-smelling liquidambar. They mashed up green tobacco for topical unguents, or they added lime to make a stupefying chew. Sellers purveyed all of these tobacco products in local markets. Indigenous nomenclature remained in place, for the colonizers had no vocabulary for these novelties.[6]

For the *encomenderos* (colonists with rights to Indian lands and tribute) and missionaries, tobacco and chocolate were not attention grabbing in the same way as human sacrifice, ritual bloodletting, or what they saw as diabolical idolatry. Yet their ubiquity and distinctive features meant that neither were they ignored. For Church authorities, tobacco and chocolate could be signs or accessories of heresy and apostasy, or of less damning but still pernicious superstitions. Alternatively, they could be indigenous material redeployed for the true and holy faith, or healthful and curative, or commendable, delectable luxuries.

In the Mesoamericans' innumerably varied and infinitesimally shaded responses to Spanish dominion, tobacco and chocolate figured in strategies that encompassed resistance, indifference, and acceptance, and everything in between. Those who defied or ignored Church authorities' demands to abandon their religion continued to use tobacco and chocolate to properly propitiate their gods. Those who embraced Christian baptism showed their respect to missionaries with offerings of chocolate and venerated saints by burning tobacco in incense braziers. Throughout the land, Indian elites and commoners continued to identify foamy chocolate served in fine lacquered gourds and well-made pipes filled with tobacco and liquidamber with luxury and refinement. Men burdened with the hard labor required by Spanish overlords chewed tobacco mixed with lime to lessen fatigue and discomfort. Healers used cacao and tobacco in a myriad of remedies, mingling sacred incantations and practical applications. Everywhere cacao served as currency. There was no single coherent colonial understanding of tobacco or chocolate, but rather there were many—all products of the unexpected outcome of colonial policies, divergent cultural memories, and unanticipated adaptations.

AUDACIOUS AND QUIET RESISTANCE

In the first decades after conquest—and sometimes beyond—a number of Indians mounted an active resistance to Spanish colonial rule. Indian communities throughout Mesoamerica sheltered men and women who would not give up their preconquest rites, refusing to turn in idols to be crushed into shards or their books to be burned. They did not stop piercing their ears and thighs or beheading quail and chicken or even sacrificing human victims to make the blood offerings their gods commanded. Nor did they cease to propitiate the sacred providers with the wafting copal, burning tobacco, and foamy chocolate. Many who practiced these rites belonged to the preconquest elite—the ruling, priestly, and merchant classes—who suffered a precipitous fall in status after the conquest. For them, tobacco and chocolate still belonged to a panoply of goods required for veneration of beneficent deities and fulfillment of ceremonial rites.

For hard-line Christian authorities, the stubborn loyalty to traditional rites was heresy, apostasy, idolatry, and devil worship. The first bishop of Mexico, Juan de Zumárraga, decided that these practices needed eradication and that the tool for the job was the Inquisition, which had proved so effective in quashing Judaism in Spain. In the 1530s and 1540s, the Inquisition interviewed and put on trial numerous witnesses who described how Indians upheld the rites of the Mesoamerican calendar, praying to traditional deities, venerating sacred objects, making blood sacrifices.[7] The investigators focused on attention-grabbing practices such as human (and bird) sacrifice and idol worship, yet they also frequently documented tobacco and chocolate as accessories to these crimes.

Fourteen leagues north of Mexico City, situated on a plateau between hills in a dry, rocky landscape of prickly pear cacti and proliferating sheep, was the town of Tlanocopan. Tlanocopan belonged to the *encomienda* of Lorenzo Suárez, a Portuguese conquistador who helped fell Tenochtitlan.[8] Though the Franciscan friars in nearby Tula oversaw evangelization, the traditional rulers of Tlanocopan were not willing to forsake their gods (or give up multiple wives) despite the orders of their new overlords. Two of the town's leading men, Tacatetl and Tanixtetl, defiantly orchestrated the continued, though clandestine, worship of the traditional deities according to the Mesoamerican calendar. They brought followers to hidden caverns to make sacrifices to stowed-away idols on altars. And, like traditional Mesoamerican shamans, Tacatetl and Tanixtetl were shape-shifters who could transform themselves into jaguars, coyotes, or wild boars. The preaching of the local missionaries did nothing to deter them. Even when Tanixetetl's own son—who had been kidnapped and raised by Franciscans in Mexico City—pleaded with his father to stop making sacrifices and burned some of his idols and altars, they did not desist. Instead, they tried to disassemble the town's church.[9] Faced with the betrayal of Tanixtetl's son, they apprenticed other local youths for induction into the native priesthood (who would later become key witnesses against them).

The *encomendero* Suárez—later notorious himself for murdering his wife—made a formal denunciation to the Inquisition in June 1536. He testified that two days earlier he had been in Tlanocopan "instructing the Indians in the things of our holy Catholic faith," though it is more probable he was checking on his tribute. He found the accused and "many others missing from the village." After making inquiries, one of the Indians expressed surprise at the *encomendero*'s ignorance, exclaiming, "Why do you bother looking for them, for they are now preparing for the celebrations of tomorrow . . . every twenty days they sacrifice to their gods and now it is time to fulfill the obligation of the said twenty days." The Indian informant reluctantly led Suárez, another Spaniard, and some Indian servants to the worshippers' secret cave in the middle of the night. Startled, Tanixtetl, Tacatetl, and their followers—more than thirteen according to the denunciation—quickly fled, but they left behind the incriminating evidence. Suárez and his companions

> found there many sticks, paper, maguey barbs, copal, knifes and clothing of idols, and feathers, and an herb called *yautle* [marigold seed used as incense and medicine], and *sahumerios* [tobacco pipes; literally, "that which makes smoke"], and incense braziers, all put in and around an altar, and vessels of pulque, and food, and cacao, and other kinds of cacao, and various kinds of beverages, and many provisions around the said altar, recently made, and much spilled blood on the said altar.[10]

Likely, the "cacao" referred to a chocolate drink as well as or instead of cacao beans, for "chocolate" had not yet entered the Spanish vocabulary, and so the drink was referred to as the "beverage of cacao," and sometimes just as "cacao."[11] (It is telling that Suárez could quickly identify different kinds of chocolate in the middle of the night; it suggests he was no stranger to the beverage.) It is likely that the *sahumerios* were tobacco pipes; powdered tobacco, too, could have belonged among the "great quantity of herbs that they offered to their idols."[12]

Along with the offerings of food and drink, Suárez and the others discovered two frightened teenagers, immobilized because of the wounds on their legs from bloodletting. They later provided the most damning testimony, swearing they had seen Tacatetl and Tanixtetl turn into various wild animals with the assistance of "herbs and potions" and, worst of all, plunge knives into ten victims to retrieve their hearts. It is impossible to know whether they did indeed oversee human sacrifice—it was certainly consistent with bloody Aztec festivals, but the testimony of scared, conflicted, and possibly tortured teenagers is weak evidence. Less ambiguous is that tobacco and chocolate ranked among ritual accessories that could be deployed more safely than blood, since they belonged to the more prosaic categories of food, beverage, and suspicious but tolerable herbs in the eyes of anti-idolaters. Tacatetl and Tanixetetl believed that the earth's sacred forces required sacrifices of sacred substances—human life-giving blood, tobacco and copal, whose fragrant smoke could penetrate celestial barriers, and foamy chocolate or precious cacao beans, which almost matched blood as a red and vital substance.[13] It may be that the importance of such goods even grew as other kinds of ritual offerings—such as human sacrifice—became increasingly difficult to carry out. The Mesoamerican loyalists paid a price for their loyalty to old gods and rites: the Inquisition sentenced Tacatetl and Tanixtetl to a public flogging in the marketplace of Mexico City and confinement in a monastery for several years, and ordered their idols incinerated in a showy bonfire.[14]

THERE were other kinds of idolaters, who were not so audacious as to attempt human sacrifice or try to take down the village church stone by stone. They were ready to comply with at least some of the Christians' demands while keeping up their rites in secretive ceremonies in private quarters under the safety of night. Cristobal, the cacique of Ocuituco, and his wife Catalina were this other kind of idolater. Before the conquest the lords of Ocuituco (not too far from modern-day Cuernavaca) paid the Aztecs tribute—including the prized flowers cultivated in the fertile lands from which they demanded tribute. They also amassed considerable wealth by ruling over a number of neighboring communities.[15] Even after the conquest, Cristobal and Catalina still lived prosperously. Their household included six slaves and numerous expensive objects: the Inquisition confiscated a set of black and green rosary beads, a golden crucifix, jade-encrusted jewelry (traditional earrings and lip plugs), woolens from Castile, "twenty-eight *xicaras* which are used for serving chocolate with eleven stirring-sticks," and three hundred cacao beans. The confiscated goods also reveal how the couple readily combined new and old cultural elements. Just as they mixed Castilian textiles with native feather headdresses, they possessed rosary beads, a crucifix, an idol, and "sixteen heads of goats and pigs and other trinkets the Indians wear when they dance." While they continued to worship their old gods, they made at least nominal efforts to abide by Christians' demands. When tested by the investigators, Catalina could ably recite the Ave Maria and Nicene Creed. Cristobal did not perform as well, and he had a poor attendance record at confession—only once in ten years. (This he blamed on the *encomendero*: his "job to collect tributes of the said village to give to his masters. . . . had impeded him and he had no opportunity to confess.")[16]

Whatever nominal Christian activities they consented to, Cristobal and Catalina's principal loyalties remained with their old gods. Yet, properly intimidated by the colonizers, they did not risk recruiting followers and apprentices, as did Tacatetl and Tanixtetl. For the most part, their rituals stayed under the cover of their household and the safety of the midnight hour. Their secrets were shared only with a few close friends, relatives, and trusted slaves. They worshipped gods weekly (every seven days) and monthly (every twenty days). For the monthly sacrifices, they relied on Cristobal's brother Martin, who was trained before the conquest as a "counter of the sun and of the holidays of the devils." Catalina recounted that "he came to tell them which devil was for which festival . . . telling her [if her husband was absent] 'you know today is the day of such-and-such devil.' "[17]

Catalina admitted that they worshipped "as they did in their heathendom." Typically, the rites began at midnight. Cristobal attended to the hearth fire, throwing copal into it and watching it sizzle. He then cut off the head of a live chicken or turkey, letting the blood flow over the copal. In a secret room in the house, he and Catalina set up an altar of sorts, putting a special mat (*petate*) on the ground. The household veneration hardly deviated from the rituals in the preconquest era that propitiated the fire god who brought the sun's warmth to the domestic hearth. The main elements were the same as those in the preconquest era—the sacrificial bird, savory tamales, foamy chocolate, sweet tobacco—offered to the fire god in a cloudy copal haze. They did not neglect the gendered aspect of the ritual, with the men and women consuming the ritual victuals in their separate quarters, signifying the differential male and female aspects of existence. The inquisitors were disturbed by idol worship, not by the use of tobacco or chocolate per se. But for the participants and witnesses, tobacco and chocolate were indispensable to the rites.

For the most part, Cristobal and Catalina did not want to antagonize the local priests. However, a few times when Cristobal was utterly inebriated, he and his friends took to the streets singing and even taunting the local priest, charging him with drinking the blood of Xhu Xho (Jesus Christ). These improprieties made their straddling of two religions no longer feasible. By 1539 the Inquisition elicited damning testimony from the household slaves and a confession from Catalina, leading to a sentence of public flogging for Cristobal, Catalina, and Martin and hard labor in the mines for the two men.

THE Church's campaign to evangelize and persuade Mesoamericans to give up their native religion was even more difficult in those areas farther removed from the central valley. Yanhuitlán lay in one of the many high-altitude valleys in the Mixteca Alta region (Oaxaca). The Mixtec shared many cultural attributes with the Aztecs, who conquered much of the region, including a fondness for tobacco and chocolate, but they spoke a language linguistically remote from Nahuatl. Before the Spanish arrived, Yanhuitlán was one of the most populous and prosperous towns in the region, a hub in the expansive market network. Yanhuitlán was politically dominant in the vicinity with seventeen or eighteen towns owing it trib-ute.[18]

Shortly after the fall of Tenochtitlan, the Spanish conquistadores sought to extend their conquests to the Mixtec region—attractive because of its obvious prosperity and local importance. In 1527 Francisco de las Casas (a cousin of Cortés) received Yanhuitlán as an *encomienda*.[19] Two years later the Dominican friars arrived, also lured by the town's regional dominance and wealth. The native ruling oligarchs of Yanhuitlán did not welcome new rulers, though they were not strangers to the practice of military vic-tors requiring tribute from subject communities. But the Dominicans were another matter altogether. These black-clad men with mostly shorn heads had very unusual and upsetting requirements. They insisted on wrecking the remaining temples and putting the villagers quickly to work on build-ing one of their own. They called for the region's inhabitants to turn in their clay god statues—which they labeled "idols"—so they could destroy them. They sought to put the traditional priests out of business. They preached for them to turn their backs on their ancestors' gods, to not make them offerings, not of copal nor food nor precious stones.

So—with the support of their *encomenderos*, who viewed the Domini-cans as meddlesome and a hindrance to maximizing the labor and tribute they wanted from their subjects—Yanhuitlán's indigenous leaders, Don Francisco and Don Juan, obstructed the friars and maintained their rites for well over a decade after the conquest. In secret rooms and on remote hilltops, priests made proper offerings—including human sacrifices—to various divinities: the gods of water, of the heart, of the merchants, and the god of gods, Tatuan. They regularly harassed the other local villagers and chieftains who cooperated with the Spaniards, demanding they leave their markets and jeering, "There go the chickens of the Christians of Castile." They succeeded in intimidating one of the local chiefs into not obeying the Christians' orders that they give up their idols. The "apostasizers"—as the friars saw them—sometimes tempered their audacious defiance with cau-tion. Their spies alerted them when the friars were going to make rounds searching for the illicit idols, so they took care to move them around to dif-ferent hiding spots in caves and hilltops on a regular basis. And they made regular, if disrespectful, appearances in the Christian church, enduring the unwelcome Mass delivered by the determined Dominicans.[20]

The rulers of Yanhuitlán made many enemies—insulted rival chiefs, be-reaved relatives of sacrifice victims, not to mention the outraged Dominicans—which led to denunciations and subsequently an idolatry trial in 1544 and 1545. As in the other idolatry cases, tobacco appeared as an important accessory to the illicit rites and ceremonies, but in this case it became a focus of the investigation, as it appears the chiefs of Yanhuitlán chewed tobacco as a tactic to undermine their coerced attendance at Mass. Numerous witnesses for the prosecution—and some for the defense—described how Don Francisco and Don Juan would prepare for Christian Mass when their attendance was required. The Indian governor of nearby Etlatongo said that "it is public and notorious that the above said [Don Francisco and Don Juan] burn copal as a sacrifice to the devil and chew tobacco, so as not to listen to the clerics and friars preach doctrine when they go to the church." Another local chief confirmed that "he had heard it said publicly that on all of the holidays, before they go to Mass, the don Francisco and don Juan offer copal to the devil and chew *picietl* and keep it in their mouths all the while they are in Mass."[21] A long-time slave of Don Francisco confirmed that his master had chewed tobacco in order to "not listen to the things of God," as a way to avoid "adoring the sacrament of the altar" and to stay faithful to "the demons that used to be in their temples." He also spoke of another ceremony that almost certainly involved tobacco. "As it didn't rain," he testified, "the said don Francisco ordered that the priests go into the woods and pulverize charcoal, grinding it to make a dye, and the said don Francisco disrobed and painted himself so he was covered in the soot and said 'now I am no longer a Christian but how I was before,' and then he made a sacrifice, bleeding his ears, and burned copal and ordered that quail be brought and sacrificed them." This bore great resemblance to the priestly sanctifications of the past. In preparation for holy rites, the Aztec priests used to go into the wilderness and cover themselves with an "unction" made of charcoal, hallucinogenic herbs and mushrooms, and tobacco. In all likelihood, the charcoal with which Don Francisco painted himself included these ingredients as well. Of course, in past times there would have been no need to chew tobacco in order to be inured to the contaminating words of preaching friars. Priests and those undergoing holy rites would ritually chew tobacco to defend and steel themselves against fear and cowardice when entering the dangerous wilderness to perform painful penitential rites. The chiefs and priests of Yanhuitlán adapted the old ceremonies to new circumstances; it made sense to use the strong chewing tobacco—bought from the vendors who still knew how to prepare it in the traditional way—as a way to keep the genuine commitments of faith and religious loyalty in mind, as well as mouth, in the face of the dangers presented by enemy priests. The buzz and even hallucinatory effects provided by the lime-enhanced tobacco assisted in blocking out the desecrating words of the Christian priests.[22]

TOBACCO and cacao are fleeting presences in these idolatry cases. Generally, these things were mentioned in passing by witnesses describing the crime scene, but tobacco and chocolate were not themselves targets of inquisitorial interrogation. Only in the Yanhuitlán case did the interrogators themselves ask about the use of tobacco, and only after one of the witnesses testified that he had seen the suspects chew tobacco so as "not to listen in church to what the clerics and friars preach."[23] The limited appearances of tobacco and chocolate reflect the preoccupations of the persecuting Christians, not the priorities of the worshipping Mesoamericans. In these early years of evangelization and idolatry extirpation, the authorities focused their efforts on activities they found most outrageous and diabolical—blood sacrifice, idol worship, shape-shifting, and intentional desecration of Christian holy places and blasphemy against Christian divinities.[24]

The cursory attention to tobacco and chocolate in the trial records does not mean that they were absent or unimportant to Indian worshippers, just that they did not (yet) warrant alarm. In some locales, such as Tlaxcala, authorities countenanced or resigned themselves to considerable continuity in preconquest practices.[25] Moreover, the Inquisition targeted high-profile idolaters, the Indian elite and rulers, so that the unorthodox activities of commoners often went unnoticed and, so, undocumented. Hints also come through the testimony that these practices were more widespread than the individual cases. Though the ritual use of lime-enhanced chewing tobacco was an explicit charge in only one of the idolatry cases, the lament of an offended witness ("the Indian merchants of Yanhuitlán commonly go about selling kneaded tobacco and feathers and stones and other things relating to sacrifices") suggests these "idolaters" were far from alone.[26]

In fact, that tobacco and chocolate appear at all in the testimony is indicative of their continued importance in traditional rites. The testimony of scared and pressured witnesses trying to stay out of trouble, and the outraged or vindictive testimony of those trying to avenge rivals or quash troublemakers, is not most conducive to dilatory storytelling. Yet their fragmented recollections provide evocative glimpses. The descriptions of the hastily abandoned or spied-upon altar places reveal not thoughtlessly thrown together offerings but rather the work of worshippers who had carefully gathered and assembled precious, symbolically redolent goods with the care of an artist setting up a tableau vivant. Passing asides show how particular material goods summoned or celebrated the aspect of the divine whose day it was, the staff and cloak instantiating male divine forces, and women's garments realizing the female. The poetry of assembled things persisted from pre-Hispanic times.

The defiant and aggressive resistance to Christianity undertaken by angry lords such as Tacatetl, Tanixtetl, and Don Francisco disappeared in central Mexico by the middle of the sixteenth century. Several of the Inquisition's

idolatry cases ended with the execution of prominent Indian nobles—
Zumarrága's zealotry had the desired deterrent effect. The disappearance
of institutions that had ensured the transmission of esoteric skills—such as
the special schools for priests where they learned the skills of reading skies
and sacred books—led to the loss of specialized knowledge necessary for
some of the elaborate rites. Other preconquest practices were casualties of
fading memories and dying elders. Moreover, the friars' ardent efforts to
evangelize took hold among some groups, particularly the children of native elite instructed in their schools and monasteries, and so growing numbers firmly identified themselves as Christians.

Elsewhere in Mesoamerica active resistance to Christianity persisted for
many decades, and even centuries. In the Yucatán Peninsula, the Spanish
did not have military control until the 1540s, and even then some of the
interior and southeastern regions remained independent until the eighteenth century.[27] The Spanish colonists were fewer in the Yucatán than in
the heart of New Spain, and so they relied to an even greater degree on
preexisting economic and political structures to extract wealth from the
colony. They collected the same tribute items that their Maya predecessors
had and relied on traditional elites to serve as mediators between themselves and the rest of the population. The colonizers were physically remote
from most of the Maya subjects, living in the Spanish towns of Mérida and
Valladolid and rarely visiting the tribute-providing communities. A dearth
of friars hindered evangelization; some towns saw a Christian priest no
more than once a week; others, once a year. Nonetheless, the Church remained the most consistent Spanish presence in Indian enclaves.[28] Missionaries were still combating widespread traditional worship in the 1560s,
including probable cases of human sacrifice.[29] And even in 1598 there were
Indians who continued to worship pre-Hispanic deities and vehemently
denounce Christian coercion and Spanish rule.

Despite half a century of nominal Spanish rule and the imposition of a
new spiritual order, in the spring of 1598 it was an open secret in the Maya
town of Petú that a cell of prominent residents sustained pre-Hispanic religious rites, rites in which chocolate appeared prominently.[30] Baltasar de
Herrera arrived in Petú in 1597 as the new parish priest, responsible for
ministering to the residents of that town and many of the surrounding
ones. Possibly he was the only Spaniard for miles; even one hundred years
later, only ten Spanish families resided in the vicinity of Petú.[31] It quickly
came to his attention that a group of villagers "many times and very often
gather and form assemblies of Indians in the house of Francisco Pech at
midnight until two hours before dawn and that they organize banquets
and celebrate, secretly eating and drinking at those hours, which many
people have seen," in the words of one reluctant witness.[32] Francisco Pech,

a native noblemen and the "head of the assembly," assumed the role of "head priest," fulfilling the role of the Mayan *ah kin*.[33] Pech elicited fear and respect from his followers—and also donations, ranging from thirty to fifty cacao beans. He doubtlessly derived status from his noble lineage and his age—at fifty he was at least ten years older than most of the other congregants, many of whom were in their twenties. In these rituals, Pech also worked to establish himself as a rightful noble in the Maya tradition. The expression of this power came through the other congregants' "gifts" of cacao beans.

At the heart of the ceremonies were "*xícaras* of cacao," which Pech and a select few "take to a room and are with it a good while the rest are outside, and then they return to their congregation and drink it, this they do for each *xícara* of *pozol* . . . and it is suspected that for these reasons they gather to worship idols and that the first *xícara* of cacao that they take to the room is a sacrifice that they make to the devil by way of some idols."[34] Testimony from Pech's inner circle leaves no doubt that Pech—and a number of others before him—repudiated the Christian teachings foisted on the villagers of Petú by the Spanish conquerors. Pech summoned his followers, eight or nine stalwarts, sometimes joined by a few others, often in the safety of nighttime darkness, but sometimes secretly during the day.[35] At the center of the group's rituals was the sacrifice of a sacred cacao beverage to divine forces who assured sufficient rain, abundant maize, and wild game.[36] At the assemblies, a woman—frequently Ana Quime, sometimes her daughter Catalina, who was also Pech's daughter-in-law and who did so under coercion, unhappy to be woken from a deep slumber to engage in illicit activities—prepared the cacao beverage, grinding maize and one hundred cacao beans.[37] The woman also procured "four new *xícaras* and they needed to be this way, so that they were never before used for drinking or serving." The chocolate drink was the paramount offering, known as *puyulcha*, which translated means "sacrifice." According to the confessants, "This was how the idolaters of old called it, being a sacrifice sent to the heavens."

After the *puyulcha* was prepared, Pech and another of the worshippers retreated to a small room where they made sacrifices to the gods. There Pech would offer the four deities copal and the *puyulcha*, and sometimes also corn tortillas and venison. When Pech emerged to join his congregants again, he brought the chocolate, stirring it and frothing it.[38] He sipped first from the *xícara*. Then each congregant drank the thick liquid from the gourd cup, as it was passed around in order of the rank of the assembled. (For the ritual was not only a way to satisfy providence but also to affirm social hierarchy.) Pech concluded the ceremony with a "benediction," during which the divine forces spoke through him. "I receive [the *puyulcha*] in the name of god," Pech would say, moving his arms in choreographed gestures. And, continuing on behalf of the divine forces, he added, "Have strength and consolation that it will rain in your cornfield." Or, as another recalled his words: "Lords, this sacrifice we offer you and I prostrate myself before your feet and trust myself to your hand—please send us the waters that we need." Pech continued to pray, now muttering words "between his teeth" that the other congregants could not and did not understand, perhaps deploying the esoteric knowledge only held by priests.[39] This ritual was repeated four times, corresponding to the four *xícaras* and four deities.

Along with Pech, Ana Quime emerges as another important leader and highlights the role of women in perpetuating preconquest rites and beliefs. One participant declared that she "was in charge of preparing and organizing the sacrifices." Evidence of her honored position emerges from her sharing in the rite of the *puyulcha*.[40] Like her daughter's father-in-law, Pech, she too was in her fifties and so could remember a time when the Christian presence was still too minimal to have had much effect on curtailing traditional rites. The art of preparing *puyulcha* (concocting a fine cacao drink, serving it in designated gourds) was passed down from mothers to daughters. One of the accused declared that it was Ana Quime who "had the duty to prepare and put in order the sacrifices." It was she who remembered that only new *xícaras* would serve for the offerings and ensured that they were available for the rites. Another worshipper credited (or blamed) his deceased wife for knowing and remembering "the rites and ancient ceremonies."[41] The rites could not have happened without the willing participation of women, who possessed the skills required to make *cacao pozol* and memories of the rites that accompanied its consumption.

Pech's ability to recruit participants was strengthened by the ongoing drought, which persuaded some of the villagers that rains did not fall as a punishment for their having forsaken their ancestors' ways for those of the Spanish. Pech also sought to instill traditional beliefs and practices into young men like his godson, who lived with him. However, the younger generation had more exposure to Christian teachings and often exhibited discomfort with the secretive and dangerous rituals of their elders. His godson told Herrera that "twice he had drunk the *pozol* called *puyulcha*, but afterwards separated himself from the others because it did not seem good . . . and he warned them not to do such things because they were not good."[42] Likewise, Catalina Que, Ana Quime's daughter, was reluctant to grind cacao in the middle of the night because the illicit activities discomforted her (and she coveted her sleep). Yet others gravitated to the traditional teachings and practices in spite of, or because of, their prohibition by Spanish authorities.

Some of the participants may have seen their activities as a supplement to the Christian devotion demanded of them, rather than as a repudiation of the Spaniards' doctrine. But there is no doubt that Pech took a stance of defiant opposition to Christianity and the Spanish colonizers. Juan Na described how Pech felt about Christian art, particularly the "image of San Juan to incite devotion" that Na had in his house. "It inspires great fear in me to come to your house," Pech told Na one day. When Na asked him the cause of his fear, Pech told him, "You have this image here that scares me—you know that you are cursed by god for having that here because it does not belong to us but to the Spaniards." And so under Pech's instruction, Juan Na removed the painting from his house and returned it to the church, and "from there on, he followed Francisco Pech in idolatrous rites and ceremonies."[43]

Herrera found the suspected idolaters guilty. As fomenter and "head priest" of the rites, Pech received the harshest sentence: flogging with fifty lashes "given publicly" and exiled for three years from Petú, during which time he was required to labor on the cathedral in Mérida. The others received lesser versions of this sentence—fewer lashes, no exile, but church penance and a work sentence in the local church.[44] Perhaps the crackdown and public humiliation (Herrera fulfilled his superiors' demands that the indicted be made an example of so as to deter others from such nefarious deeds) quelled the performance of pagan rites for awhile.[45] But they far from disappeared in the Yucatán Peninsula. In fact, Herrera himself was dismissed from a later post after it became known that idolatry continued to flourish in his jurisdiction.[46] A few years later, a cleric reported ascending a purportedly abandoned Mayan temple and finding there "cacao offerings and vestiges of copal burned not too long before, that was of some superstition or idolatry recently committed."[47]

The case of Francisco Pech and his followers offers a wonderful demonstration of the dynamics of cultural transmission. It helps to explain how and why chocolate survived with many of its pre-Hispanic associations intact. The confession of Agustín Que, one of the accused idolaters and a prominent villager, shows how beliefs and material practices were intertwined. Que confessed to owning idols, explaining that he received them "as an inheritance and under his guard."[48] For Que to have refused these idols would have been to renounce a fundamental family legacy. With the bequest of the idols came the responsibility to care for them and, concomitantly, the sacred forces they represented. And an essential aspect to caring for the idols and related divinities was to offer them sacrifices, exemplified by the sacred cacao beverage. Likewise for Pech, filial respect, family loyalty, and traditional rites were indivisible. He clearly tried to ensure that venerable traditions would not die with him by apprenticing his godson.

Traditional practices passed along family lines and attached themselves to the physical artifacts of veneration. There is no reason to think that composition of *puyulcha* had changed since the conquest, nor did the gendered division of its preparation. It was still synonymous with sacrifice, suggestive of blood and life.

Tobacco and chocolate rituals survived as a result of collective memories cherished, nurtured, and imparted. These goods—like other material artifacts—were themselves memory devices. As opportunities for open instruction and festivities disappeared, the challenge of preserving traditions, skills, and stories grew. So things like tobacco and chocolate, linked to forbidden rites yet themselves free from condemnation by the colonial authorities, worked in a special way. The smells, flavors, and textures evoked memories of arts, crafts, and knowledge and stimulated a chain of patterned habits that was a legacy of past generations. It is even possible that they assumed a greater importance in the clandestine colonial context than they had in the old days.

SYNCRETIC ADAPTATIONS

Tobacco and chocolate did not only accompany and encourage resistance to the spiritual conquest. They also figured in Mesoamericans' adaptations to Christianity. Among the early colonizers and missionaries, in fact, there was a common view that Indian material culture could be reconfigured in the service of Christianity. Toribio de Benavente (d. 1569)—known by his Nahuatl nickname Motolinia, or "the humble one"—was one of the twelve Franciscan friars who inaugurated conversion efforts in New Spain, roaming throughout central Mexico and beyond and baptizing thousands of Indians a day. He spoke admiringly of the devoted reverence manifested in the dress, movement, and song of his native flock. The beauty of the gleaming white cotton shirts, the cloaks "fashioned with feathers," the bouquets of flowers, and the dances and "songs in their languages"—all of these were important elements in preconquest religious festivals.[49] Native finery could show reverence to the Christian god just as it had for the old deities, and Mesoamerican instruments and melodies could become vessels for Christian prayers, as well as they had for pagan ones. The early friars not only tolerated but encouraged the rehabilitation of traditional rites in service of Christian devotion.

Chocolate rites, too, seemed like they might work in service of Christian devotion. Motolinia was enthusiastic about how the neophytes celebrated All Souls' Day, on which Christians commemorated the deceased and helped them to escape purgatory for heaven. He wrote, "On All Souls' day, in almost all the Indian towns, they give offerings for their dead. Some bring corn, others blankets, others food: bread, poultry, and in place of wine, [the drink of] cacao."[50] Thus, abundant precious chocolate could work in lieu of sacred but scarce wine. Motolinia was willing to countenance the substitution of one sacred liquid for another.

There may have been more equivalents than even Motolinia could, or would, recognize in the rites of All Souls' Day. In preconquest funerary rites it was customary to both propitiate the lord of the underworld (Mictlan) with offerings, such as the corn and blankets indicated by the friar, and to succor the deceased with goods to soften their journey to the hereafter. Chocolate figured supremely as one of those goods, at least for lords and wealthy merchants. Nahuas also celebrated an annual holy day in the winter months; in addition to rites of human sacrifice and ritual dancing, mourners served chocolate to the effigies of their recently departed kin.[51] In the fleeting image created by Motolinia's words, one glimpses Mesoamericans accommodating themselves to the cultural requirements of the foreign rulers by inserting their funerary rituals into the Christians' celebration of the dead. Such parallels helped make the new faith palatable. Chocolate escaped the condemnation of the friars—or at least this particular friar—as it fell under the label of benign, neutral, material culture that could be absorbed into Christian practices, functioning as a geographically appropriate substitute for wine. Yet for the Indian celebrants, the smell, taste, and feel of the foamy chocolate must have provided a visceral link to the feel of life and religion in a past era.

Cortés himself, in fact, was confident that pre-Hispanic traditions could be remade to serve the new rulers and new divinities. He ordered that the Indians welcome missionaries with chocolate, knowing well that that was how they formerly showed reverence to their priests under Aztec rule. Motolinia, however, was also aware of the hidden dangers of such substitutions. Though he appreciated the offerings of chocolate—he considered it a good drink when it was well made—he and his colleagues hesitated about the implied meaning. He knew well that the "reverence" and "welcome" the Indians demonstrated through their chocolate offerings was the same "they used to have for the ministers of their idols." The implicit equivalence between Christian priests and men whom they viewed as minions of the devil led some friars to forbid the chocolate welcome, though Motolinia conceded, "This was not sufficient to stop it everywhere."[52]

Despite the friars' scrutiny and debate over proper methods of evangelization, Indian reception of Christianity was largely outside of their control, as later generations of clerics bitterly lamented. The Mesoamericans' decision to make chocolate offerings on All Souls' Day reveals how they interpreted it and connected it to preconquest kinds of mourning and commemorative rites. Similarly, tobacco rites helped link the worship of old deities and Catholic saints. At the end of the sixteenth century, Indians burned tobacco, along with other sacred substances, in incense burners in the form of saints, as their ancestors had done for Mesoamerican deities. In 1598 the Inquisition prohibited the production of these braziers, displeased with the unseemly mixing of pagan and Christian practices.[53]

Tobacco and saint worship mingled in other ways as well. Hernando Ruiz de Alarcón was one of several clerics in the early seventeenth century who obsessed about enduring "idolatry" among supposedly Christian Indians. Assigned the remote curate of Atenango (in the region of Cuernavaca) in the early seventeenth century, Alarcón saw idolatry where his predecessors did not. Where earlier friars may have been ready to overlook vestiges of pre-Hispanic rites they did not see as directly challenging Christian faith and identity, Alarcón saw these remnants of the pagan past as insidious. Where the early friars may have seen admirable native culture reconfigured for Christian devotion, Alarcón saw the devil persuading Indians to desecrate Christianity by contaminating it with heathen customs. Part of the change in attitude may have been due to Alarcón's greater knowledge; he could see and hear nuances that his predecessors could not. Unlike the earlier generation of friars, he was born in Mexico, raised in the Taxco mining region and fluent in Nahuatl. Alarcón became a sort of vigilante idolatry extirpator, sniffing out alleged misdeeds and punishing offenders with floggings and public humiliation. The officers of the Inquisition in Mexico City got wind of his activities and were not pleased, for he had overstepped his powers. Yet when they examined his case further, they decided he had acted out of ignorance rather than malice, and so they appointed him an "ecclesiastical judge" around 1617. In this capacity, he officially ferreted out dangerous idolatry and misguided superstitions. He culled from his decades of experience, as well as others' reports, and documented the offenses in his 1629 *Tratado de las supersticiones y costumbres gentílicas que oy viven entre los indios desta Nueva España* (Treatise on the Heathen Superstitions and Customs that Today Live among the Indians Native to this New Spain). He not only described the practices he deemed idolatrous but also recorded the summonses and prayers in the original Nahuatl.[54]

Alarcón documented many traditional remedies. One of the responsibilities of the native healer was to determine the cause of illness in order to effectively cure it. Sometimes the cause was angered spirits. It led the healer, Alarcón lamented, "to put blame of illnesses on the saints and even on the Virgin, Our Lady, giving as a reason that they have angered her or another saint because of having done some discourtesy to their images. . . . or not having celebrated their holy day." It then fell to the healer to "immediately seek to find out through fortune-telling about the means of placating the angered saint, because that will be the cure of the illness." In order to discover the identity of the offended divinity, the healer had recourse to tobacco. Alarcón described the ritual. The healer would listen intently to the patient's problems and surrounding circumstances. Then, reported the investigator, "he [got] ready with the *piciete*." He took the tobacco in his right hand, then placed it in his left palm, crumbling it with his thumb. After "adjust[ing] his clothes like a person who is preparing for some business of importance," he carefully sat down and began to rub the tobacco between his palms. Then began the invocation. The healer summoned the tobacco, commanding, "Let it be soon! Come priest, Nine-times-rock-slapped-one, Nine-times-crumbled-in-the-hands-one, Green Priest, my mother, my father . . ." Continuing with the incantation, the healer studied the patient's arm in order to discover what divine force had been offended: "Let us find out who you are, you saint who are angry. Are you perchance Our Lady? Or perhaps you are the Saint Gaspar or perhaps Saint John?" For good measure, the healer investigated the possibility the patient may have upset a pagan spirit, asking, "Let us find out if the angry ones are the forest gods and he fell into their hands, or if he is One Rabbit face-up (for the earth)?" Once the angry saint or spirit was identified, the healer would recommend placating it by presenting it with "some clothing or a veil," or by holding a feast in its honor.[55]

The results of Alarcón's investigations show Mesoamericans' creative fusions of pre-Hispanic and Christian practice and point, again, to the ways that material and symbolic culture were entangled. Tobacco was a reminder that misfortune could be caused when supernatural entities were displeased. Just as healing practices were also spiritual practices before the conquest, so were they in the wake of Christianity. For pre-Columbian Mesoamericans, deities merged and morphed into one another; such ways of thinking and acting made it easy for the "Green Priest" and "One Rabbit" to participate next to the Virgin Mary and Saint John. For Alarcón this may have constituted heresy and blasphemy and idolatry, but for the men and women he observed it was a logical amalgamation of beliefs and practices.

A most striking instance of a pre-Hispanic belief about cacao folded into Christianity emerges from the pages of what is, at first glance, the utterly orthodox *Rhetorica christiana* (Christian rhetoric), a guide for the evangelization of Indians of Central Mexico.[56] Its author was a Franciscan missionary named Diego Valadés. Born in 1533, he seems to have been the son of an Indian noblewoman from Tlaxcala and a Spanish conquistador, though he passed as pure "Spanish," a professional and spiritual necessity for his chosen vocation, since only those of pure "Old Christian" ancestry were allowed admission into the Franciscan order. Valadés probably learned the Latin in which he composed *Rhetorica christiana* while attending the

Figure 3.1. Diego Valadés, *Rhetorica christiana* (Perugia, 1579). On the plate between between fols. 220–221. Valadés depicted a heaven (and a hell) with Mesoamerican and Christian elements. The Mesoamerican elements include the depiction of the universe as a series
of suspended disks and the presence of cacao (center, on the tree plane) in celestial realms.
Shelfmark: BV4209.V34.R5 1579. Reproduced courtesy of the Bancroft Library, University
of California, Berkeley.

school for native elites founded by Franciscans. As a missionary he evangelized the Nahua, Tarascans, and Otomi. In the 1570s he traveled to Rome to represent his order.[57]

In *Rhetorica christiana*, Valadés synthesized Renaissance "arts of memory" and his familiarity with traditional central Mexican cultures.[58] The pages reveal its author as deeply committed to the project of Christian evangelization and also sympathetic toward the native brethren (not surprising given his own lineage), lauding them for accepting the dictates of the preachers as if "they had come from God (as they have, in truth)" and defending "los indios" against the charges that they were "no more Christian then the Moors of Granada."[59] Valadés, who acquired spectacular engraving skills from Renaissance artists during his sojourn in Rome, generously illustrated his text in order to illustrate the workings of memory and suggest tactics for converting the illiterate.[60] In one of these engravings, whose purpose in relation to the text is not explained, Valadés revealed a syncretic, chocolate-inflected view of the cosmos (figure 3.1).[61] In some respects it is a conventional Christian cosmology. At top, the identifiably Christian heaven features a Father/God/King, seated on a throne, who embraces his fallen Son/Christ; Mary kneels at their side, and the heavenly family is surrounded by angels kneeling on puffy clouds. At bottom, there is a familiar Renaissance hell, replete with lapping flames, damned souls writhing in cauldrons, and demons taking sadistic pleasure as they met out tortures to deserving sinners. Yet Valadés's heaven incorporates distinctly Mesoamerican beliefs, for it depicts the celestial realm as a series of suspended disks above the flat surface of the earth, constant with the cosmological conceptions of Aztecs and other Mesoamerican groups.[62] Notably, throughout his book Valadés took care to explicate many of his illustrations, but he did not gloss this heterodox image (the only possible allusion to this image is the line "here it concerns how to inculcate Christian doctrine by means of representations and illustrations"), suggesting, perhaps, that it would have been challenging to explain how this depiction accorded with more conventional Christian imagery of heaven.[63] Valadés's cosmos is neither purely Christian nor Mesoamerican but a creative amalgam of the two. On one of his heavenly levels there are good Catholic saints, perhaps interceding on behalf of the souls below, residing in what may be a kind of purgatory, and thus hoping for admittance to true heaven. The celestial levels populated by trees and birds, however, suggest an atavistic familiarity with the pre-Hispanic central Mexican belief in sacred pairings of birds and trees associated with the four cardinal directions (as can be seen in figure 1.9). And, at the very center of the arboreal realm, and, so, symbolically of the utmost importance, Valadés depicted a cacao tree, along with its protective, shade-giving "mother tree." (Peter Martyr wrote of how the cacao was "carefully looked unto under the shadow of another great tree to cherish it.")[64] In this image one sees the enduring power of the symbolism of cacao as a sacred, godly tree, like the one painted on the pre-Hispanic sacred almanac known as the *Codex Fejérváry-Mayer* and evoked in the songs about the celestial realms fragrant with blooming cacao blossoms. This subtle though symbolically potent placement of a cacao tree in a Christian celestial realm hints at a childhood in which coexisted Latin grammar, New Testament stories, and verses that insisted the "place where the lords command" was one where "the flowering chocolate drink is foaming, the one which intoxicates men with its flowers." Nor was Valadés the only one to imagine a Christian paradise that sprouted cacao trees. In Malinalco (located eighty miles southwest of Mexico City), on the walls of an Augustinian monastery, indigenous artists painted a "paradise garden" of the afterlife. The main element is cacao trees, festooned with ripe pods and spider monkeys snacking on them.[65]

Tobacco and chocolate provided a set of tastes, smells, and sights, evoking familiar meanings like mnemonic devices of all five senses. As a string around the finger jogs the memory, their material presence reminded those who no longer had access to sacred books or the teachings of astronomers that the traditional deities could not be forgotten, that the birth of a child required certain kinds of festivities, that the divine was at hand when illness flared. And, just as material objects could be passed down from generation to generation, so too could the beliefs and rites that accompanied them. As the Spanish cleric Alarcón lamented, "superstitions" accompany the objects that are "inherited by the children and descendants."[66]

4

Going Native

The previous chapter's stories of adjustments and accommodations in Indian enclaves concern more than indigenous Mesoamericans. These stories are also about the experiences of the first generations of Spanish émigrés and Creoles (such as the *encomendero* Lorenzo Suárez, who had no difficulty distinguishing between varieties of chocolate in the middle of the night), as well as mestizos, Africans, and mulattos. In Mesoamerica and the Andes, non-Indians had frequent occasion to visit native enclaves. *Encomenderos*, accompanied by their retainers and servants, came to collect tribute and demand laborers for their agricultural and building enterprises; friars, clerics, and their assistants built churches and convents in and near pueblos to spread their faith and enforce orthodoxy; humble colonists and slaves perused Indian marketplaces. In colonial settings outside of the imperial centers, where Spanish control was more tenuous than secure, Europeans and Africans were even more susceptible to native influence. In such contexts, non-Indians continued their education in tobacco and chocolate, along with other facets of native culture, perhaps learning more than they wanted to know about how the tasty drink and powerful herb related to a non-Christian universe.[1]

The fifteenth- and sixteenth-century Spanish invasions of the Americas produced a wide array of colonial situations. These ranged from the Greater Antilles (the large Caribbean islands of Cuba, Dominican Republic/Haiti, Jamaica, and Puerto Rico), where the native presence diminished quickly, to the imperial centers in Mesoamerica and the Andes, where indigenous elements remained strong and influential despite the firm colonial grip, to the borderland regions that could be found throughout the Americas and particularly in the Lesser Antilles of the eastern Caribbean and northern South America, where European settlements coexisted with autonomous Indian communities, oscillating between peaceful dependence and violent acrimony.[2] Though diverse in their arrangements, the conditions in all of these colonial settings resulted in European acculturation to native ways, in particular acquiring a taste for tobacco and chocolate.

Following Columbus's discoveries, Spain established its first enduring colonies in the Caribbean. The brutality of the Spanish conquests in the Americas, particularly on Hispaniola (Dominican Republic/Haiti) and neighboring islands, is legendary, as is the precipitous collapse of indigenous cultures and populations. On his second voyage in 1493, Columbus established the first European settlement on the largest, most populous island that became known as Hispaniola, and the subjugation of the native Arawak quickly ensued.[3] By 1504 Spanish forces had eliminated all of the major caciques of Hispaniola. It was not long before Spanish conquistadores soon set their sights on neighboring islands and brought their firearms, man-eating dogs, and fearsome horses to Jamaica (1509), Cuba (1511), and Puerto Rico (1508–11), and the aboriginal population on those islands largely suffered the same fate as those of Hispaniola.[4]

Brutality did not cease when domination was secured. Those natives who did not escape, or succumb to disease, were forced to labor in gold mines and sugar plantations and could not tend the crops necessary for survival.[5] The consequences of war, exploitation, and, most of all, disease were cataclysmic for the islanders. Not only did autonomous polities perish in the Greater Antilles but so did most of the population and their cultures, victims of a brutal regime of virtual slavery and harsh tribute requirements but, most of all, of lethal Old World microbes to which they had no immunity. Of an estimated precontact population range of one million, only thirty thousand remained in 1514, according to one Spanish census.[6] Officials of the Crown and colonists decided to replace the native labor force with enslaved Africans; by the middle of the century Bartolomé de las Casas estimated that there were as many as thirty thousand African slaves on Hispaniola.[7]

IMPERIAL CENTERS

The precipitous and horrendous collapse of the aboriginal society of the Greater Antilles has often obscured the significant impact Arawak culture had on the ensuing colonial society that transplanted it. (A present-day legacy includes the words *hurricane* and *hammock*, as well as *tobacco*, that derive from the Taíno language.) Though the numbers who died are proportionally shocking, enough Arawak individuals survived to have cultural influence. In particular, black slaves and Indians forged a syncretic culture under their shared experience of oppression. A *cemi*—one of the traditional Arawak figures representing divine beings—manifesting both Caribbean and African elements bears witness to this mingling.[8] Consumption of tobacco was also an outcome of these circumstances, as testified by the (disapproving) conquistador and chronicler of the Indies, Gonzalo Fernández de Oviedo, who wrote in the early 1530s:

> Presently, many black slaves who live in this city and the island have adopted the same custom of growing this herb on the plantations and estates of their masters. And they take the same smokables because they say that when they stop working and take these *Tabacos* it relieves their fatigue.[9]

Oviedo was not alone. Throughout the sixteenth century, observers declared those of African descent to be among the most precocious of non-Indians to adopt the tobacco habit. Oviedo also sounded the alarm that in addition to being a "very bad" vice of the barbaric Indians of the Caribbean and slaves who emulated them, tobacco was used by "some Christians," who claimed it alleviated their suffering. Even Oviedo's perennial ideological foe, Las Casas, concurred that Spaniards had become enamored of smoking. "I met Spaniards on this island of Hispaniola who got used to taking it," he lamented. They persisted even when "reprimanded for it, told that this was a vice," with the European tobacco habitués responding "that it was not within their hands to stop taking it." "I do not know what pleasure or benefit they derive from it," he added.[10]

In another section of his work Oviedo provided more clues to the contexts in which European settlers in the Greater Antilles learned about tobacco—soliciting natives for their medical expertise. Even while denigrating Indian "barbarism," the chronicler believed that the Americas offered "innumerable plants and trees appropriate for the pains and wounds of humans." And he grudgingly acknowledged that their usefulness depended on direct education by natives when he lamented that in the large islands of the Caribbean "the old Indians are now dead and so with them the knowledge of these properties and secrets of nature."[11] Oviedo, never one to mind inconsistency or even hypocrisy, failed to appreciate that some settlers learned to use tobacco in exactly such a context. European colonists—outnumbered in the early sixteenth century by Indians, Africans, and their descendants—adopted the indigenous custom, mitigating the social stigma by asserting medical need, though in all likelihood motivated by a complex mix of reasons.

Settlers who moved from the Caribbean and those who came directly from Europe to the new imperial centers in Mesoamerica continued to have their habits reinforced or experienced situations in which to inaugurate them. Despite the dramatic reversal in power relations, Spanish colonists in sixteenth-century New Spain were enveloped within an Indian cultural milieu and experienced many spaces in which they were susceptible to native acculturation.[12] Even with Indians' catastrophic mortality in the face of Old World pathogens and increasing European emigration, Spaniards still were only a small minority in their most densely settled areas.[13] In mid-sixteenth century Mexico City, for instance, Indians vastly outnumbered Spaniards, and people of African descent almost equaled the Spanish in number. In 1570 Spaniards and their "pure" descendants made up only 5 percent of the population in Mexico City, and they were still only 10 percent by the middle of the seventeenth century.[14]

Spaniards learned to like chocolate because of their continued material dependence on Indians. Cross-cultural contacts flourished in intimate settings, some voluntary, others coerced. Both a drastic shortage of Spanish women and a conscious and explicit strategy of appropriation and conquest through matrimony led to many marriages, as well as less formal domestic unions, between Indians and Europeans in the early sixteenth century. Historian Pedro Carrasco has calculated that of sixty-five married men in Puebla in 1534, twenty were married to Indian women.[15] The role of women as cultural intermediaries has particular salience for the history of chocolate, since numerous sources disclose that women were charged with its preparation in pre-Columbian and colonial Mesoamerica (figures 0.3, 1.2, and 1.5).[16] As emigration increased the pool of Spanish women, elite Spaniards no longer married Indian women (though commoners continued to do so), but Indian women still dominated the domestic sphere.[17] In the Yucatán, for example, Maya domestics created a culturally indigenous milieu for Creoles. Writes the historian Nancy Farriss, "Creole children spent their infancy, literally from birth and their early childhood in almost the sole company of Maya women, suckled by Maya wet nurses commandeered from the villages, reared by Maya nurses, and surrounded by Maya servants."[18]

Another important site for early Spanish-Indian contacts were Indian villages. Maintained as political units by the Spanish colonial regime, these Indian enclaves were constantly penetrated by non-Indians.[19] During visitations, colonists and missionaries continued their education in chocolate, along with other facets of native culture. Mesoamerican tributaries and parishioners, following traditional pre-Hispanic practice, welcomed the Spanish lords and priests with chocolate, something encouraged by Cortés.[20] Despite—or because of—the colonial relations of subordination,

Indians' cultural practices infiltrated the colonists' milieu. Similar receptions of friars and colonists continued into the seventeenth century.[21]

The ubiquitous *tianguis*, the Indian marketplaces that still formed the center of the local economy well after the conquest, also lured Old World settlers and sojourners with their exciting bustle and dazzling array of regional products. One Spaniard who spent time in New Spain during the 1570s clearly viewed the marketplace as an Indian space, but one where Europeans and others moved freely, and found chocolate:

> In all of the neighborhoods there is a plaza where every fifth day or with greater frequency are celebrated markets not only in Mexico City but in all of the cities and villages in New Spain . . . in which congregate a numerous multitude of men and women. . . . The varieties of fresh and dried fruits, indigenous and from our land [i.e., Spain], sold there cannot be enumerated, and that which is held in higher appreciation than all of the others is the *cacaotl* [cacao].[22]

Another sojourner from the Old World left no doubt that the clientele encompassed whites as well as native folk. He denigrated "the Indians" as "great impostors, giving to their plants Indian names, which renders them in high repute. We can say that of the Chocolate sold in the marketplace and stands."[23]

Among the market vendors were *picicenamacac* (chewing tobacco sellers), *acaquauhchiuhqui* (smoking-tube and pipe sellers), and *pocquiyenamaca* (cigar sellers), ensuring that colonists, as well as native subjects, could buy the full array of tobacco products that existed prior to the Spanish invasion.[24] The naturalist Francisco Hernández, whose peregrinations in central Mexico took place in the 1570s, likewise commented that tobacco prepared with lime was "so desired among the Indians that the markets are filled with it, sold wrapped in corn husks."[25] According to a witness in the trial of the Yanhuitlán idolaters, "*Picietl* is a common herb in this land that many Indians and some Spaniards and blacks carry in the mouth and they say that it numbs the flesh and gives them energy, and it eliminates hunger and headaches and is for other sicknesses and that this is common knowledge and well known."[26]

Though colonists' initiations into native ways often took place unwittingly, such as when they learned from nursemaids or wandered into markets, in some cases colonists and slaves in established settlements in Mesoamerica, as in the Greater Antilles, actively sought native expertise in the guise of healers, sorcerers, shamans or spiritual leaders, the designation often a matter of one's perspective.[27] The Sevillan physician and proponent of American materia medica, Nicolás Monardes, explained that the purga-

tive called *mechoacan* (*Convolvulus mechoacan*, also known as *jalapa*) became known to Europeans because of a "close friendship" between a local
Indian cacique and the head of the Franciscan monastery; the former sent
over "an Indian of his who was a doctor," and the "latter consented to the
visit, seeing the insufficiencies he had in the way of doctors and resources
there."[28] Observers more rooted in the New World (Monardes was well
connected to colonists and sojourners in the New World but never visited
himself) understood that cures often blurred into the realm of what Europeans would consider "superstition." Indigenous or mixed-race practitioners with a variety of occupational titles—midwives, diviners, healers, or
the Nahuatl *tlicitl*, glossed by a Spaniard as a combination of "doctor,
soothsayer, sager and sorcerer"—assisted whomever needed his or her fortune divined, illness cured, or love requited.[29]

The results of a survey issued by the Crown in 1579 suggest that colonists learned of tobacco in contexts such as these. In response to a question
about "the herbs and aromatic plants with which the Indians cure themselves, and the medicinal and poisonous properties of these," tobacco appeared with insistent frequency, and several of the responses volunteered
that Spaniards as well as native subjects benefited.[30] A Spanish official in
Tabasco recorded that tobacco "taken in smoke is beneficial for phlegmat-
ics and asthmatics and chest coughs."[31] In a town in central Mexico, local
inhabitants suffering from congestion put "piciete water into their noses,"
the source explaining that these "were leaves also known as tobacco." It
also mentioned that they drank cacao pulp for hemorrhages of blood. Near
the mines of Zumpango, another reported that "natives and blacks and
even some Spaniards take [*picietl*] crushed in the mouth to put to sleep the
pains they feel and take the juice in the nostrils for headaches."[32]

By the late sixteenth century and beyond, the contexts in which new European arrivals learned about tobacco and chocolate—if not before—were
no longer only Indian. A growing number of people were designated as
castas—mestizos, mulattos, and more obscure combinations such as *casti-
zos* and *zambos*.[33] One should not imagine a Spanish America in which
people belonging to fixed racial or ethnic groups lived side by side but a
society in constant remaking, in which differences were broad within
groups as well as between them. Cross-cultural encounters were not just
between Spaniards and Indians but also between Hispanicized Indians and
Indians recently arrived from a remote village, and between Spaniards
born in the Americas and off-the-boat European émigrés or wayfarers. As
the demographic and social composition of colonial society changed during the sixteenth century, creole and mestizo spaces became important for
chocolate socialization as well. A Spanish physician's autobiographical
aside in his treatise on chocolate affords a quick peek at transmission in

creole spaces. He described his initiation into chocolate consumption when "arriving hot [in the Indies], visiting sick people and requesting a little bit of water to refresh" him, he was instead "persuaded to drink a *jícara* of chocolate . . . which placated [his] thirst."[34] Likewise, Thomas Gage, remembering disembarking in Veracruz as a young clerical recruit to the Dominican order, recollected how he and other novitiates participated in a procession to the cathedral and then how their supervisor, "Friar Calvo presented his Dominicans to the Prior of the Cloister of St. Dominic who entertained us very lovingly with some sweetmeats, and every one with a Cup of the Indian drink called chocolate."[35] When Europeans arrived in the Americas, they became integrated into social networks—organized around family, occupation, or religious order—that exerted considerable pressure on them to conform to local customs. The aggregation of countless such encounters led to the suffusion of tobacco and chocolate into the mestizo society of Mesoamerica.

BORDERLANDS

In regions such as the Greater Antilles, the Aztec domains of central Mexico, and the Incan-controlled territory in the Andes, the frontier gave way fairly rapidly to colonial rule. Yet in the eastern Caribbean and northern South America, European settlers struggled and often failed to maintain precarious holdings throughout the sixteenth century and even beyond. Beginning with Columbus's exploratory voyages, the Spanish were attracted to the Central American isthmus and northern coasts of South America that connected to inland South America through riverine waterways—today's Panama, Colombia, Venezuela, Guyana, and even parts of Brazil and Peru. There, they raided for slaves to replace the dwindling native labor force on the Greater Antilles; and soon the beautiful pearls adorning the Indians of coastal Venezuela and the intricate gold jewelry worn by the inhabitants of Panama motivated the Spanish to found settlements on the "Pearl Coast" (c. 1514) and the isthmus of "Tierra Firme" (1511).[36] The inhabitants of these regions, as well as those of the Lesser Antilles, shared many cultural traits with the native population of the Greater Antilles—love of tobacco being one of them. Though anthropologists and archaeologists once made much of an ethnic Carib/Arawak divide, recent scholarship has shown that much of this split was an ideological artifact of the conquest period, so that the Arawak designation was reserved for allies and the Carib one for enemies.[37] Collectively, the indigenous inhabitants of the eastern Caribbean fared much better in the face of Spanish invasions than did their cousins to the west. Many tribes in the eastern Caribbean eluded Spanish conquest. And many European settlements

foundered and even disappeared in the sixteenth century. They fell victim
to the internecine conflict among violent, competitive conquistadores; they
suffered from Indian attacks, compounded by incursions from rival Europeans; settlers abandoned them when they ran out of pearls or when they
joined the latest expedition that promised to capture El Dorado. Native
inhabitants in these regions cunningly played off European rivals. Autonomous Indian communities incorporated Amerindian refugees from Spanish
settlements and even the runaway slaves known as *cimarrones*. Much of
northern South America remained out of Spanish grasp until the middle of
the seventeenth century, and groups in the Lesser Antilles retained autonomy until the eighteenth century.[38]

Europeans who lived in these borderland settlements experienced conditions similar to the circumstances of initial exploratory voyages, particularly in their relations with Amerindians. To accomplish their objectives,
sometimes merely to survive, Europeans interacted with Indians in what
Richard White has conceptualized as a "middle ground,"

> [characterized by the inability] of both sides to gain their ends through force.
> The middle ground grew according to the need of people to find a means,
> other than force, to gain the cooperation or consent of foreigners. To suc-
> ceed, those who operated on the middle ground had, of necessity, to attempt
> to understand the world and the reasoning of others and to assimilate enough
> of that reasoning to put it to their own purposes.[39]

Colonists in these tenuous settlements depended on Indians for food,
guides, military assistance, and trade goods (precious metals and slaves
above all). For Indians, alliances with Europeans allowed access to attractive goods, provided a preemptive strategy against European attack, and
offered support for struggles with traditional foes. Borderlands tied Indians and Europeans together in vital, if frequently fleeting, webs of mutual
dependence. (This, however, does not in the least imply that conquistadores relinquished violence and terror as tactical strategies or conditioned
reactions. Astonishing brutality coexisted with diplomatic approaches.)

These borderland settings were conducive to Europeans' exposure to tobacco. Wherever soldiers and settlers went in these regions, they found tobacco in their allies' huts, during ceremonies, and on expeditions. "It
would be impossible to take away their rites and tobacco," noted a colonist
on the early Venezuelan settlement of Margarita Island of the Arawak
Guayqueri, an Indian group on whom the Spanish depended in that settlement as well as neighboring Cubagua.[40] The Guayqueri provided the colonists with water, food, and slaves (from their Carib enemies) and served as
guides and interpreters for their forays down the Orinoco in order to

obtain introductions to local caciques. In return for their favors, these Arawak avoided enslavement, received support for their ongoing struggles with Caribs, and acquired prestige within Amerindian trading circles because of their hold over European goods, particularly coveted metal tools. The Spanish settlers even forged alliances with certain Island Carib groups so that they could "put in there for refreshments . . . sometimes left their sick there to be look'd by the Caribbians with whom they had made a peace upon those terms."[41]

Nascent European settlements and expeditions along the coast and interior of western Venezuela relied on Caquetio tribes for food and geographic and political information. The Caquetio were a conglomeration of Arawak-speaking, ethnically related aboriginal communities whose territories encompassed the coastal region from Coro to the Gulf of Venezuela, south through the watercourse in the savannahs of western Venezuela, and into the sub-Andean valley of Barquisimeto. (The Indians' assistance to the Europeans did not protect them from subsequent savage attacks and atrocities committed by their erstwhile allies, which predictably soured relations.)[42] Galeotto Cey, an Italian trader and soldier who lived in Coro for nine years between 1534 and 1544, complained about having to endure Caquetio guides who insisted on conducting a tobacco ceremony before they would venture on an expedition:

> If you arrive at the home of an Indian and want him to take you to some place, beforehand with five or six others, he wants to take tobacco, no matter how much hurry you are in, and if you say yes, he will come very happily, and if not, only if you take him by force, and if you don't guard him well, he will flee from the path. If he comes and the thing does not succeed, he will attribute it to the evil tobacco, and if it does work out, he will be astonished and insist that they do not understand or that they were drunk.[43]

Cey's recollection suggests that he felt some complicity in the rite that he disapproved of. While viewing it with scornful condescension, he also acknowledged that in order to get needed assistance, he had little choice but to sanction the ceremony. One of Oviedo's informants who likewise had experience living in close proximity to the Caquetio confirmed that they used tobacco if they wanted to "know if they should go on a journey, or go to fish, or to sow, or whether to go hunting, or whether their wives loved them."[44] The informant also described shamanistic rites in which those "who are like their priests" used tobacco to facilitate communication with the spirit world or, in Spanish understanding, "the devil."

For much of the sixteenth century tobacco use was not something that Spanish colonists would readily admit to because of its Indian stigma, so surviving texts from the first part of the century tend to offer observations about Amerindian allies' use of tobacco along with obligatory expressions of disdain for the practice, showing either the influence of the chronicler Oviedo or sharing in the culture that produced his prejudice. Juan de Castellanos, another conquistador-turned-chronicler, who participated in an expedition into the Orinoco Valley in the 1530s, referred to tobacco as the property of "sorcerers and diviners."[45] Pedro de Aguado, a Franciscan missionary who lived in Bogotá between 1562 and 1575, submitted that Indians throughout the kingdom of New Granada (Colombia) used tobacco and another hallucinogen (*yopa*, the seed pods of *Anadenanthera peregrina*):

> They smoke, sometimes by mouth or sometimes through the nose, until it intoxicates them and deprives them of their sense, and thus they become drowsy while the Devil, in their dreams, shows them all the vanities and corruptions he wished them to see, and which they take to be true revelations in which they believe even if told they will die.[46]

Yet when examined closely some of the observations of the explorer-chroniclers provide evidence of how the frontier settings immersed Spanish soldiers and settlers in the milieu of tobacco-consuming Indians.

Pronounced in the memory of Oviedo was a night in August 1529, when he was still an ordinary conquistador and not yet a chronicler, that he and other soldiers spent in a Chorotega community on the Nicoya Peninsula (Costa Rica). They were the guests of a prominent chief, Alonso, known to Indians and Spaniards alike by his native nickname, Nambi (meaning "dog," Oviedo explained).[47] Nambi claimed to recognize Spanish sovereignty and had undergone Christian baptism, and the charismatic leader enjoyed making a big show of his enthusiasm for Spanish "friendship." Despite Nambi's record of assistance and proclamations of friendship, Oviedo and his companions were nervous in this place, remote from the "succor and help of Christians," wishing that they "were distant" from the Indians. They watched, feeling scared and powerless, as their hosts prepared for a feast and celebration that showed the emptiness of their ally's baptism to Christianity. Oviedo and his compatriots huddled in the shadows around a village square as they watched Nambi and his villagers, skin glistening with tattoos and preening in feathered finery, drum, sing, dance, and became inebriated on yolk-yellow *chicha* (fermented maize beverage), some passing out, one weeping, while others "lurched like madmen." The festivities lasted all night (with the assistance of chocolate), until the wives and children of the stupefied celebrants arrived to put them to bed. Between bouts of energetic dancing, the revelers enjoyed cigars. The picture of Nambi smoking lodged firmly in Oviedo's consciousness, allowing him, many years later, to write about the ritual for a European audience, who he still assumed to be ignorant of the outlandish practice:

> And just as they began to drink [the *chicha*], the chief took a roll of tobacco, spanning a *xeme* (the span between a thumb and index finger), and thin like a finger. . . . And so from time to time they put it in the mouth, the end that is not lit, and they suck inside some smoke, and removing it, they keep the mouth closed, holding the breath for a bit, and afterwards they exhale and that smoke leaves through the mouth and nostrils. And each of these Indians I've described had one of these corded leaves, which they call *yapoquete*, and in the language of Haiti or Hispaniola, it is called *tabaco*.[48]

Oviedo and his fellow travelers were profoundly unnerved by the spectacle. He confessed to finding it a "fearful" thing to see the Indians crying and yelling, and even more to see them inebriated. "We thought that the dance and drunkenness had to be a danger for the six or seven Spaniards who found ourselves there," remembered Oviedo. They saw the rites as a prelude to an attack. So Oviedo and his fellow Europeans spent the night wide awake "arms in hand, even though we were too few to defend ourselves against so many adversaries, but at least we thought to sell our lives dearly and to make sure to kill the chief and as many as the nobles as we could." The fearful guests survived the night without violence, but it left Oviedo rattled, making him feel that the Indians were in control and the Spanish at their mercy: "In truth I believe there is no contentment for the Christians, for the servants [Indians] have become the masters [of the Christians]." He pestered Nambi about the rites the following day, when the drunkenness had worn off and daylight returned a sense of control and confidence to the Spanish. The Chorotega chief placated his uppity guest, acknowledging that perhaps his customs were "bad," but as he explained, "this was the custom and that of his ancestors and if he did not do it then his people would not love him well and they would hold him as poor company and cheap, and leave him."

In borderlands, Europeans sometimes became much more enmeshed in the host society than they had anticipated. A variety of circumstances led Europeans to become integrated into native American groups for shorter and longer periods of time.[49] In some cases, Europeans became battle captives; rather than killing them, their Indian captors adopted them, often using them as slaves, but sometimes allowing them to become integrated into the community with significant status if they proved their usefulness in some way. Other times, Europeans found themselves lost, injured, and abandoned by their companions as a result of shipwreck or an expedition gone awry because of exhaustion of provisions, injuries, or the loss of bear-ings. Oftentimes, in such cases, their only chance of survival rested with local Indians taking mercy on them, feeding and nursing them to health and then requiring or allowing them to stay on as members of the commu-nity. In other instances, Europeans voluntarily lived in native communities for a period of time, perhaps to escape local authorities or to better ac-quaint themselves with an unknown region.

The case of Francisco Martín illustrates an extreme example of the blur-ring of Christian and Indian identities forced by the frontier. If Francisco Martín's transformation into a tobacco-healing shaman among the Pemeno of Lake Maracaibo (Venezuela) was unusual, the circumstances that led to his odyssey were not. Ambrosio Alfinger (a member of the Welser German banking clan to whom the Habsburg emperor and Spanish king, Charles V, was literally indebted) received a grant from the emperor to settle the is-lands and mainland of western Venezuela. In June 1531 Alfinger left the settlement of Coro with a company of 270 soldiers, including Martín, to search for a water strait leading to the Pacific Ocean, perhaps also spurred on by rumors of an Indian civilization possessed of staggering mineral wealth, the infamous and eternally elusive El Dorado.[50] They traversed the grassy savannahs, known as *llanos*, of Venezuela and Colombia and as-cended the eastern Andean front of the Magdalena Valley. Six months later, on the edge of the famously gold-rich Chibcha chiefdoms, they had amassed a great quantity of gold (through trade and more often plunder). Alfinger decided that a group should return to Coro with the gold and then come back with reinforcements before they continued to trek through the Andes in search of the Pacific strait.[51] Francisco Martín was one of the twenty-four soldiers (and an undetermined number of enslaved or auxil-iary Indians) led by the lieutenant Iñigo de Vascuña who left for Coro on January 6, 1532, carrying gold booty. Martín was the only one to survive. He later recounted his story to royal officials in Seville, and Oviedo and subsequent chroniclers used the soldier's recorded testimony as the basis for their accounts.[52]

The expedition was doomed almost immediately, for Captain Vascuña decided they would hazard a shortcut through the dense vegetation and confusing river network of the savannahs. They quickly got lost and began to succumb to predictable perils of the frontier. They did not have adequate food provisions, so they were forced to subsist on palm nuts, which soon dwindled. A few men lost their lives to Indian attacks. Others became in-jured or crippled and were abandoned by their companions and left to starve. Desperate, the still mobile resorted to cannibalism. In the first in-stance, a few of the soldiers slaughtered and ate one of their Indian serv-ants. Several weeks into their lost wanderings, another group committed an even more outrageous act of cannibalism when they repaid an Indian who offered help by eating him.

After the second instance of cannibalism, more days of lost wandering passed. Now Francisco Martín himself could no longer walk; pustules on the bottom of his feet forced him to crawl. His companions abandoned him to the jungle. Martín slept eight more nights on the river bank, eating nothing, too weak to cut down any more of the bitter palm nuts. He saw only one way to avoid sure death. Vowing to serve "Our Lady, with many tears" he heaved himself onto a log and let the river carry him away. The Virgin Mary answered his prayers in a surprising fashion. Floating downstream on his log, Martín saw some abandoned huts on the river bank and further inland, some rising smoke. He manipulated his raft to the bank, pulled himself ashore, and crawled his way toward the smoke on a small path, "and arriving there, the Indians saw him, came running toward him and picked him up and carried him to one their new huts, where were their wives and children, put him in a hammock and gave him food to eat and shared all they had. And he stayed there for three months during which time his foot healed."[53] Indian rescuers allowed him to survive the abandonment of his cannibalizing companions, his immobility, and near starvation.

Eventually, he ended up as a slave to another group, the Pemeno who lived in the mountains around Lake Maracaibo, who bought him in exchange for an eagle-shaped piece of gold. Despite his initial slave status, he became fully integrated into the Pemeno community, a testament to his adaptability.[54] He was eventually married to a chief's daughter. Oviedo wrote that Martín "lived for a year among these Indians, living as they did, and doing the same ceremonies and rites as them, because he did not dare to do anything else, because this was how they commanded him and taught him." During this time he was apprenticed as a shaman, "a physician and expert of their art." Though he claimed it was done only under duress, he succeeded in learning "the vocation of that medicine, in such a way that they held him as great teacher, and no Indian dared to cure, without first coming to him and consulting with him."[55] Martín testified that as a healer his "medicines were to bellow and blow, and to emit tobacco, and with his mouth full of salt and herbs, he blew smoke with that tobacco."[56] And Oviedo made Martín's induction as a tobacco healer into the climax of the tale:

> And so he was the chief physician, medical overseer and examiner of those physicians that the devil had in that province, and of his herbalists, occultists and bone-setters. His medicines were bellowing, blowing, and breathing tobacco; with this vocation he lived among them and was much esteemed.[57]

Martín's incarnation as a shaman came to an end when he was rescued—or kidnapped—by his European compatriots. In July 1532, some of the soldiers who remained with Alfinger were still trying to make it back to the Spanish settlements and were in the southern reaches of Lake Maracaibo, not far from Martín's new home. They discovered from a group of Indians with whom they skirmished that "near there was a Christian like ourselves."[58] Shortly thereafter a scout "stumbled across a Christian, naked in the flesh, as he was born with his shameful parts on the outside, and his body was painted, and his beard shorn like an Indian with a bow and arrows and a dart in his hand, and his mouth filled with *hayo* [coca]."[59]

For both Martín and Oviedo, Martín's use of tobacco exemplified his transformation into an Indian. When Oviedo spun the tale of Martín's remorse and redemption on encountering his fellow Christians, he wrote that Martín "gave infinite thanks to God and soon dressed like a Christian and left behind his old habitat with those evil customs that until then he shared with the Indians, and asked to confess, as a Catholic and as a man who had been forced against his will and with the fear of death, for having used that diabolical medicine and art," in other words, tobacco.[60] In Oviedo's words, Martín had been "made an Indian." And the quintessential manifestation of this conversion was his intimacy with the healing art of tobacco.

Oviedo insisted that Martín only became an "official" of the diabolical arts—that is, a tobacco-blowing shaman—because he feared he "would die of hunger and because of the fear he had of the Indians." He also suggested that Martín sought rescue by purposely going out into the forest when he heard that Christians were nearby, hoping to be discovered.[61] But other information suggests that Martín had more ambiguous—at the very least—feelings about rejoining the Christians. Once in the conquistadores' custody, Martín had little choice but to act as if he welcomed his return to their society. He might have been willing to cast certain activities in a light that would favor his story of wanting return; for instance, what he described as a forced captivity and food deprivation inflicted on him when he objected to learning Indian healing techniques could be another way of describing the ritual isolation and fasting demanded of a shaman undergoing purification and initiation rites.[62] His attachment to his Christian identity is further thrown into doubt by the fact that after his rescue, he fled the Spanish settlement in Coro and returned to the Pemeno. In due course he was captured by the Spanish, but he escaped a second time (and captured again, this time sent back to Spain for sentencing). Though he finished his life as a "good Christian" in New Granada, his vacillation suggests that his identity fluidly moved between "Christian" and "Pemeno."[63] In his recounting of Martín's story, Oviedo struggled to reconcile the ideological framework of conquest with the realities of borderlands. Martín's experiences inverted all of the tenets of conquest ideology. The insatiable cannibals were Europeans; the innocent, hapless victims were Indians. The treacherous, unreliable behavior was that of Martín's fellow conquistadores; the selfless aid came from Indian saviors. And the Europeans did not bring Indians Christianity and civilization, but rather the surviving European experienced conversion to an Indian mode of living. It is significant that Martín—and Oviedo—chose to single out tobacco among the Indian healer's arts. Tobacco occupies such a prominent place in Oviedo's telling of the tale (as it seemed to do in Martín's) because it exemplified Indian barbarism as a conduit to demonic forces, even as it became the handmaiden of the surviving "Christian." Martín's account and its retelling by Oviedo also demonstrate that those living in borderland situations understood that it was not easy to separate out physical practices—smoking tobacco—from cultural practices, that is, engaging in idolatry.

One could understand Martín's tale and Oviedo's decision to include it in his history as an extreme parable in which the "normal" is illustrated through its radical transgression. However, another more illuminating perspective is that Martín's odyssey is not so much an opposite of the conventional conquistador trajectory, but rather at an extreme end of a continuum of frontier experiences. At its essence, the key to Martín's survival was to let go of his Christian and European identity, to allow his Indian rescuers to save him by improvising and by filling the role that they imagined for him.

More commonly, the situations that led to Europeans' initiation into tobacco were less radical and resembled more closely the circumstances of Grijalva's expedition to the Yucatán Peninsula. A French missionary, Charles de Rochefort, who lived among the Island Caribs of the Lesser Antilles, discussed the tactics they used to sustain their autonomy on the island of Dominica, including adapting a tobacco rite traditionally used to contract trading alliances among indigenous groups of the circum-Caribbean region in order to incorporate friendly and useful Europeans in their network.

Since the earliest days of Spanish colonization, ships from rival European states preyed on and pillaged Spanish colonies and ships. Fueled by dynastic and religious conflicts, they terrorized the nascent colonies with pirate attacks and disrupted the monopoly system through contraband trade. First it was French pirates—with the sanction of the Valois kings at war with the Habsburgs—who menaced Spanish colonies and treasure-laden ships, particularly in the second quarter of the sixteenth century. The late sixteenth century saw an increase of privateers and corsairs, particularly those from England and the Netherlands, as geopolitical conflicts precipitated by the Reformation and Dutch Wars of Independence legitimated attacks on the Spanish enemy.[64] Those circum-Caribbean groups not blessed with Spanish alliances but rather victimized by slave raids and other depredations—who fell under the general designation of "Carib"—welcomed these incursions and conspired with Spain's European enemies to sabotage Spanish settlements and settle scores with Arawak.[65] The resistance of the Island Caribs in the Lesser Antilles, particularly on the island of Dominica, exemplifies this kind of successful opposition.[66] While it appears that Columbus was able to stop on Dominica for water on his fourth voyage without any trouble (or any contact) from the natives, before long the Dominica Caribs made clear that visits from Spanish ships were not welcome.[67] Conquistadores lost their campaign to the Island Caribs in 1524 and again in 1538, when Spanish forces failed in another war against the natives of Dominica and Martinique. After that there was no attempt at occupation for many years, but Spanish ships continued to call; in fact, the Casa de Contratación (the institution created by the government to oversee trade between Spain and overseas colonies) designated Dominica as a provisioning station for wood and water in the 1530s. Sometimes the Island Caribs greeted the Spanish wayfarers hospitably, but other times they chased them away. The Spanish maritime traffic provided an opportunity for the Caribs of Dominica to plunder shipwrecks, or even help cause them. The Indians sometimes feigned hospitality by offering provisions to the crew and then secretly cut the ships' cables so that the vessels battered against the shore.[68]

In addition to protecting enclaves from Spanish occupation, Island Caribs attacked and endangered Spanish colonies to the east (Puerto Rico) and west (Trinidad, Margarita, Cubagua), as well as maritime traffic. In the words of historian Joseph Borome, "Not only did the Caribs plunder plantations, fire buildings, rob churches, slay cattle and horses, haul away gold, silver, cassava, maize, hogs, arms and clothing, and abduct Negroes and Spaniards for slaves. They boldly fell upon laden vessels coming into the vicinity during their visits."[69] Carib raids, compounded by the attacks of French pirates, had destroyed parts of southern and eastern Puerto Rico by 1580; two large sugar mills were deserted by their owners, as were many fertile settlements along the coast. Even when settlements rebounded, some colonists and their slaves did not, becoming battle victims or slaves.[70] Island Caribs also posed a formidable challenge to the Spanish colonies to their west. The Spanish settlement on Cubagua, first established between 1512 and 1525, disappeared by the early 1540s, in part because of Island Carib attacks (it was recovered again in the late sixteenth century).[71] Island Caribs also imperiled Spanish colonies by conspiring with Spain's European enemies—first the French and later the English and Dutch. Florida-bound French settlers stopped at Dominica in 1567, and Francis

Drake obtained provisions there in 1572. However, if these Europeans overstepped their bounds or otherwise misbehaved, they quickly became the targets for poison-tipped arrows.[72]

Rochefort recounted how the "Island Caribs" of Dominica had perfected an elaborate system to assess and evaluate the relative threat posed by European visitors. They followed strict protocols for dealing with foreign embarkations, posting "sentinels all along the Sea-side in most of those Islands whereof they are solely possessed." On sighting European ships, several ("three men at most") of the Island Caribs set out in canoes "to discover what they are, and call to them at a distance to declare themselves." They knew better than to trust the flag flying "as having been often deceived thereby," but they could judge "by their voices whether they be French, Spaniards, English or Dutch." (Rochefort added that "some affirm, that the Brasilians and the Peruvians are so exact in their smelling, that they will discern a French-man from a Spaniard by the scent.") Once the Europeans were deemed to be the good kind, they were warmly received. The Indians' "excellent memories" were so sure that "ten years after such a meeting they will remember the names of their friends, and relate some circumstance of what has passed at the former interview."[73]

But the friendship and alliance were not cemented, according to the practices of the Island Caribs, until tobacco had been offered and accepted. Rochefort first explained how the Indians native to the Lesser Antilles, as well those of the nearby mainland, used tobacco to initiate trading—or even conversation—with Indians from beyond their community, until in "odd fashion" they engaged in "kinds of entertainment" or this tobacco rite. The cacique of the community brought the leader of the visiting delegation to "Publick-house, without speaking at all to him." Rochefort explained that "then he is presented with a stool and some Tobacco, and so they leave him for a time, without speaking a word to him, till he hath rested himself and taken his Tobacco: Then the Cacick comes and asks him, whether he be come? The other answering yes, he sits down with him and falls into discourse."[74] Before trading could begin, the outsider had to be incorporated into the community as a friend or ally. The somatic changes induced by tobacco were accompanied by the symbolic meanings attached to tobacco as gift, as a way of manifesting and paying honor to another. And the trader, by accepting the tobacco, manifested his good will and intentions toward the community. Only after his body and mind had been led into the community space by his physical location on the host's stool in his hut and under the spell of tobacco could "discourse" and then trading or diplomacy or visiting begin.

In dealing with the Europeans, the Island Caribs continued to use tobacco to consecrate allies and trading partners. They did, however, modify the tobacco ceremony to make it "more rational" in the eyes of Europeans like the missionary Rochefort, who considered that "our Caribbians triumph over all other savages in point of civility, for they receive strangers, who come to their Islands to visit them, with all manner of kindness and testimonies of affection."[75] The Island Caribs understood, according to Rochefort, that while their fellow native Caribbeans were comfortable with the silence that preceded the offering of tobacco, the garrulous "French and other Europeans . . . would be loath to keep silence so long." So, in "entertaining" these visitors, the hosts "speak to them, and fall immediately into discourse." The Island Caribs were thus "accommodating," in Rochefort's words, to the "humor" of the French and others in their willingness to dispense with the silence. After sealing bonds of alliance in such a way, trade could begin. Europeans offered such things as "crystal, fishing hooks, needles, pins, or little knives" in return for fish, sea turtles, and cotton. The missionary's account demonstrates that the core of this Caribbean rite—tobacco—was not negotiable; while the residents of Dominica might "[cross] the rules of their own Ceremonies" by eliminating the period of solitary silence, they viewed the tobacco offering as utterly indispensable for contracting alliances, ensuring that Europeans interested in their assistance would have no choice but to inhale.[76]

It is not an accident that this illuminatingly detailed description comes from a French, rather than Spanish, source. Such tobacco consecrations almost certainly cemented the Spaniards' alliances with their Caribbean allies; Rochefort himself attested that the tobacco ceremony he described was shared by Caribs of the maritime littoral as well as the island inhabits, suggesting its regional compass, and the Island Caribs themselves were historically culturally closer to the mainland Arawak who were befriended by the Spanish. But tobacco—and the larger specter of "going native"—remained more stigmatized among the Spanish than among other Europeans frequenting Caribbean waters, in part because of the longer period of colonial immersion and in part because imperial hatreds made the Spanish more of the enemy than the Indians for these northern Europeans.[77] The stigmatizing of tobacco was no barrier to consuming tobacco, or at least not an unbridgeable one, but it may well account for the reticence of Spanish sources.

The fact that this description comes from a French observer also points to the fact that the Spanish were not the only ones to live in borderland settlements in the sixteenth and seventeenth centuries. Similar episodes of tobacco initiation characterized the frontier experiences of people who were not Spanish Iberians. In 1555, in a French settlement among the Tupinamba on what is today the coast of Brazil, the Franciscan friar André Thevet observed that the Tupinamba fashioned large cigars with a palm leaf encasement, smoking them "to drive forth and consume the superfluous moisture in the head" and "to endure hunger and thirst for some time." He noted that "the Christians there today have become very attached to this plant and perfume."[78] The Portuguese too adopted this habit of the natives: a skeptical friar, describing the settlement at Colegio de Baya in the late sixteenth century, wrote that "a great many of the Portuguese had come to drink [the tobacco smoke], and have taken it for a vice or for idlenesse, imitating the Indians to spend days and nights about it."[79] Nor did the French in their doomed, short-lived colony near present-day Jacksonville, Florida, abstain. A member of an English expedition that made a stop at the settlement in 1565 took note of the odd habits of the local inhabitants, Indian and European alike. The Floridians have "a kinde of herbe dried" that they put in "a cane and an earthen cup in the end" and light "with fire" and do "sucke thorow the cane the smoke." He explained this "smoke satiffeth their hunger, and whereeith they live foure or five days without meat or drinke" and concluded that, in addition to the natives, "this all the Frenchmen used for this purpose."[80]

BRIDGING THE ATLANTIC

In borderlands and imperial centers alike, Indians passed along practices and beliefs concerning tobacco and chocolate not only to their progeny but also to the growing black, mestizo, and European population. If colonists and slaves from the Old World became habituated to tobacco and chocolate while living among indigenous inhabitants of the New World, when did these goods cross the Atlantic? In some respects the answer is right away, for the ocean was not an unbridgeable barrier to those acculturated to American customs. The habituated—merchants, sailors, galley slaves, returned sojourners, delegations of visiting Indians—arrived in Europe with stashes of tobacco, cartons of chocolate, gourd vessels, and their bodies' cravings.

By the middle of the sixteenth century, tobacco appeared in European herbals, albeit not under that name, but in the words of the Italian naturalist Pietro Mattioli as a "new variety of *Hyoscyamus*." In a later edition, Mattioli noted of tobacco—still under the above alias—that "some people have brought a certain new plant into Italy, really very beautiful to look at."[81] In 1571 Nicolás Monardes, a physician in Seville, reported that black slaves in that city, like their counterparts in the New World, smoke themselves into a "stupefied trance, they find themselves very relaxed, and that they find a reprieve from having been that way."[82] He also noted in his 1574 edition, at the other end of the social scale, a "gentleman" smoking in the Mesoamerican fashion. Monardes explained, "They bring from New

Spain . . . canes covered within and without by a sort of gum and it seems that it is mixed with juice of tobacco."[83] That same year the Dutch herbalist Matthias de l'Obel included an entry on tobacco, in which he wrote that "many sailors, all of whom have returned from [the Indies] carrying small tubes . . . [that] they light with fire."[84] The illustration depicted what he apparently assumed was an unknown practice to his readers—smoking—by featuring a disembodied head with African features inhaling smoke from an enormous cigar; that he expected contemporaries to view this custom as outlandish is evidenced by the fact that while the other entries' illustrations are of botanical specimens, only this one illustrates a substance in use (figure 4.1).

Likewise, chocolate and cacao made sporadic entries into Spain in the first part of the sixteenth century. Their presence is only detectable when someone bothered to make note of it, and one of the earliest traces appears in a lawsuit filed by the Indians of Tepetlaoztoc against their abusive *encomendero*, Gonzalo de Salazaar, during the late 1520s and 1530s.[85] The plaintiffs noted that among more egregious abuses, Salazaar ordered his native tributaries to prepare a thousand pounds of "ground cacao ready to drink" and "40 painted *jicáras*" (as well as "hundreds of natives to carry these and other goods—turkeys, sandals, clay pitchers—and serve him during his overland voyage to Veracruz," many of whom died during the journey) for a trip to Spain in 1531.[86] Another trace comes from the account of a visit made to Prince Philip by a retinue of Indians, who brought the future king a gift of chocolate in 1544.[87] It is interesting to note that the first author to reference cacao in print in a work intended for and about European consumers was the female physician Oliva Sabuco de Nantes Barrera.[88] Her 1588 *Coloquios de la naturaleza del hombre* (Colloquies on the nature of man) described her theories about human physiology and offered health advice. She wrote that "some fruits of white marrow have a similitude with the brain" and so "are advantageous to the medulla of the brain, and expand and revitalize it . . . these are very beneficial during convalescence and for the marrow of bones." For the same reason, she counseled that breast-feeding women should eat those foods "of white marrow," including "cacaos," along with almonds, hazelnuts, and pine nuts "because these strengthen the [baby's] brain."[89] Later male authors took pleasure in impugning her views and proclaiming her ignorance. Given women's specialization as producers of chocolate, it makes perfect sense that a female author was responsible for Europeanized cacao's inaugural appearance in print. She also anticipated later European authors' celebration of chocolate for "comforting the brain."[90]

All of this evidence supports the predictable: that some of those who became aficionados of the goods in the Americas sustained their habits

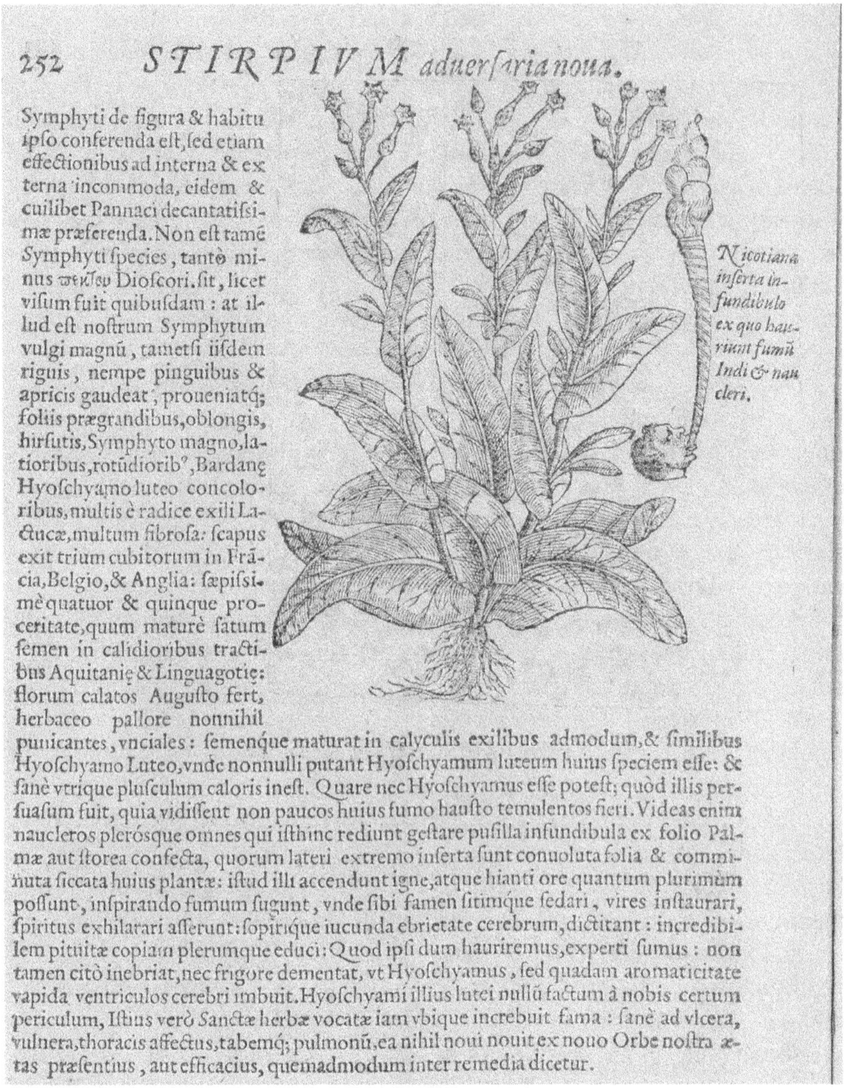

Symphyti de figura & habitu ipfo conferenda eft, fed etiam effectionibus ad interna & externa 'incommoda, eidem & cuilibet Pannaci decantatifsimæ præferenda. Non eft tamē Symphyti fpecies, tantò minus σπίσυ Diofcori. fit, licet vifum fuit quibufdam : at illud eft noftrum Symphytum vulgi magnū, tametfi iifdem riguis, nempe pinguibus & apricis gaudeat', proueniatq; foliis prægrandibus, oblongis, hirfutis, Symphyto magno, latioribus, rotūdiorib', Bardanę Hyofchyamo luteo concoloribus, multis è radice exili Lactucæ, multum fibrofa: fcapus exit trium cubitorum in Frācia, Belgio, & Anglia: fæpifsimè quatuor & quinque proceritate, quum maturè fatum femen in calidioribus tractibus Aquitanię & Linguagotię: florum calatos Augufto fert, herbaceo pallore nonnihil

Nicotiana inferta infundibulo ex quo haurium fumū Indi & naucleri.

punicantes, vnciales : femenque maturat in calyculis exilibus admodum, & fimilibus Hyofchyamo Luteo, vnde nonnulli putant Hyofchyamum luteum huius fpeciem effe: & fanè vtrique plufculum caloris ineft. Quare nec Hyofchyamus effe poteft; quòd illis perfuafum fuit, quia vidiffent non paucos huius fumo haufto temulentos fieri. Videas enim naucleros plerófque omnes qui ifthinc rediunt geftare pufilla infundibula ex folio Pálmæ aut ftorea confecta, quorum lateri extremo inferta funt conuoluta folia & comminuta ficeata huius plantæ: iftud illi accendunt igne, atque hianti ore quantum plurimùm poffunt, infpirando fumum fugunt, vnde fibi famen fitimque fedari, vires inftaurari, fpiritus exhilarari afferunt: fopiríque iucunda ebrietate cerebrum, dictitant : incredibilem pituitæ copiam plerumque educi: Quod ipfi dum hauriremus, experti fumus : non tamen citò inebriat, nec frigore dementat, vt Hyofchyamus, fed quadam aromaticitate vapida ventriculos cerebri imbuit. Hyofchyami illius lutei nullū factum à nobis certum periculum, Iftius verò Sanctæ herbæ vocatæ iam vbique increbuit fama : fanè ad vlcera, vulnera, thoracis affectus, tabemq; pulmonū, ea nihil noui nouit ex nouo Orbe noftra ætas præfentius, aut efficacius, quemadmodum inter remedia dicetur.

Figure 4.1. Matthias de L'Obel and Pierre Peña, *Stirpium adversaria nova* (London, 1571), p. 252 (detail). The novelty of smoking is apparent because this is the only illustration in the herbal that depicts usage as well as the botanical specimen. The engraver's decision to endow the smoker with African features was in the enduring tradition of representing blacks as the first non-Indians to consume tobacco. Reproduced courtesy of the John Carter Brown Library at Brown University.

when they crossed the Atlantic. Nonetheless, until the last decade of the sixteenth century, tobacco and chocolate remained Indian goods that some Europeans consumed. Prior to the 1590s, there is no evidence that Europeans viewed tobacco as a saleable commodity. Tobacco is completely absent in a report on settler economies in the Spanish colonies at the beginning of the 1570s.[91] Colonists in Coro, Venezuela, which would become a major tobacco center by the end of the century, did not cultivate tobacco for trade; a contemporary report ascertained that "the commodities and trade of the region are very little, other than some horses, chickens, and some produce traded in the Rio de el Hacha."[92] Even though officials in Caracas reported that "the Spaniards and natives take [tobacco] in smoke by the mouth and in powder by the nose," tobacco made no appearance in the response to a question about "the trade and principal commerce of this region."[93] There was no clue in this period that the colonies in present-day Venezuela and Trinidad would become organized around tobacco within twenty years.

No different than the pre-Hispanic past, during the early colonial period tobacco production and consumption belonged to the village or even household economies, rather than interregional markets. Native producers, traders, and settlers were largely able to maintain such local economies even after the Spanish conquest, ensuring indigenous people as well as increasing numbers of colonizers easy access to tobacco. Europeans consumed tobacco products because they procured them directly from Indians, either those still living independently or those under colonial rule who maintained traditional forms of production and distribution. Mesoamericans grew tobacco in garden plots and sold it in local markets to European as well as native consumers; slaves produced it the margins of their masters' estates; South American tribes continued to harvest tobacco along with other traditional crops; perhaps some settlers grew their own tobacco in garden plots where they cultivated vegetables for household consumption, but they did not see it as a potential livelihood.

On the other hand, colonists viewed cacao as a valuable commodity, but not for European markets. In contrast to tobacco, cacao immediately became a colonial—as opposed to a local—commodity because it was a long-distance trade good valued by rulers *before* the Spanish conquest. Even prior to the toppling of Tenochtitlan conquistadores recognized cacao as a lucrative sales good. Once they achieved the conquest of Mexico, it required no imagination on the part of colonial officials and settlers in New Spain and Guatemala to take over existing production and trade networks, and little imagination to set up new cacao plantations when over-exploitation and Indian deaths led to the demise of earlier ones. The colonizers' immediate ability to profit from the conquest depended on their usurpation and maintenance of the tribute system organized by the Aztec rulers. Thus it was to their advantage to maintain the existing commodity production, and, in fact, cacao production expanded under Spanish rule.[94] The way that the colonial trajectories of tobacco and chocolate diverged reflected precolonial conditions: Europeans maintained cacao as a commodity, but they did not commodify tobacco, because it was primarily a local, not a long-distance, good in native America. Before Europeans viewed tobacco or chocolate as Atlantic commodities, a few of them began to investigate their medicinal properties.

5

Learning from Indians

In 1571 Nicolás Monardes, successful author, well-established physician, and prosperous trader of transatlantic commodities in Seville, published *Segunda parte del libro, de las cosas que se traen de nuestras Indias Occidentales, que sirven al uso de medicina: Do[nde] se trata del Tabaco, y de la Sassafras* (The second part of the book of the things brought from our Occidental Indies, which are used as medicine: in which Tobacco and Sassafras are discussed). A reader who thumbed through the tome would have his or her attention directed first to tobacco.[1] A full-page engraving immediately following the title page and dedication to His Majesty depicted *El Tabaco*, an elegant sprig, stylized with tapered leaves and delicate blossoms (figure 5.1). Tobacco became the emblem of New World regenerative riches. In the prefatory poem to the 1574 publication, "a gracious wreath / of precious Tobacco / of Emerald color" is "more lovely than that of Apollo or Bacchus." The New World's immanent triumph over the Old World was symbolized by tobacco's ousting of the spices of Asia, the beloved laurel of antiquity, and even the olive branch of the Bible.[2] That tobacco was chosen of all the New World drugs to represent the West Indies' eclipse of the East Indies indicates its exemplary status. In promoting tobacco as a medicine in the 1571 edition of the herbal, Monardes dramatically revised earlier chroniclers' assessments of the glossy green plant. Tobacco's appearance under the rubric of "those things that serve medicine" startlingly diverged from its previous inclusion among the "abominable rites" practiced by Indians in Gonzalo Fernández de Oviedo's *Historia general*.

Monardes's publications did not precipitate the introduction of tobacco or chocolate into Europe—for they already had a presence, albeit a minor

SEGVNDA
PARTE DEL LIBRO, DE
las cofas que fe traen de nueftras Indias Occidentales, que firuê al vfo de medicina. Do fe trata del
Tabaco, y dela Saffafras, y del Carlo fancto, y de
otras muchas Yeruas y Plantas, Simientes y Lico
res, que nueuamente han venido de aquellas
partes, de grandes virtudes, y ma-
rauillofos effectos.
¶Hecho por el Doctor Monardes Medico de Seuilla.

DEL TA   BACO.

Figure 5.1. Nicolás Monardes, *Historia medicinal: de las cosas que se traen de nuestras Indias Occidentales, que se sirven en medicina* (1574), title page. The identical engraving appeared first as the title page of the 1571 edition. Reproduced courtesy of the John Carter Brown Library at Brown University.

one, and it took another twenty years before they were systematically imported—but his works mark a pivotal moment in the histories of these goods, nonetheless. This Spaniard and his emulator Francisco Hernández, who discussed cacao and chocolate (Monardes did not), struggled to reconcile tobacco and chocolate's pre-Hispanic origins and enduring functions as elements in rites that official imperial ideology deemed as "idolatry." Monardes was the first to develop a framework for exorcizing, sanitizing, and civilizing tobacco by depicting how it could be transferred from a context of pagan idolatry to one of European medicine. Paradoxically, the works of Monardes and Hernández also served as vessels for the diffusion of Amerindian knowledge. These investigators derived their understanding of American goods by hybridizing Indian knowledge—gleaned directly or indirectly from indigenous informants—with the neoclassical paradigm that dominated elite medicine and natural history in Europe. The successors of Monardes depended on and deployed his medical framework, yet they also could not but recognize the goods' powerful social, recreational, and consoling uses.

EUROPEAN MEDICAL TRADITIONS
AND THE NEW WORLD

Iberian medical consumers were quick to embrace New World remedies. "Balsam" was imported from Santo Domingo. *Cassia fistula* (*cañafistola*), used to "benignly purge" choleric and phlegmatic humors (particularly useful "in maladies of the kidneys"), had been imported no later than 1529 from the Antilles. A faint but steady stream of the purgative *mechoacan* and sarsaparilla (used to induce sweats) entered Spain in the second half of the sixteenth century. Trade records also indicate significant imports of guaiacum wood to cure syphilis, "china root" to treat gout, and the "balsam of Peru" to dress wounds.[3] Also in slight but commercially perceptible use were liquidambar and copal (burned as an incense).[4] One reason that New World medicines were assimilated quickly into Spain was a tradition of medical pluralism: Iberian consumers were accustomed to patronizing a variety of healers and receptive to trying new cures that promised relief from pain and misery. The panoply of healers included the elite university-trained physicians, but also those without degrees: blood-letting barbers, apothecaries, bonesetters and hernia setters, stone pullers and tooth pullers, midwives, and *morisco* (converts from Islam) practitioners. Philip II himself insisted on having a smorgasbord of medical experts from distinct traditions. For instance, he paid an "empiric"—the derogatory term foisted on healers without university credentials—as much as royal physicians to treat his family for disorders such as hernias, and the king's medical team included a *morisco* healer, despite the rise in laws barring *moriscos* and *conversos* (those of Jewish ancestry) from admittance into universities and medical guilds.[5]

Though the market still supported healers from many traditions, the sixteenth century in Spain, as elsewhere in Europe, saw the ascendance of university-educated physicians.[6] These men, steeped in the newly recovered medical texts of antiquity, paid slight or invidious attention to New World medicaments. Academic medicine in Renaissance Europe was transformed with the humanist recuperation of ancient authors, preeminently Hippocrates (460–370 BCE), Galen (131–201 CE), and Pedanius Dioscorides of Anazarbus (c. 40–c. 90 CE). While Muslim scholars, principally Avicenna (980–1035 CE), were responsible for preserving the Greco-Roman heritage during the Middle Ages, zealous Renaissance

scholars desired to recover the integrity of the original texts.[7] The veneration for the "original" texts partly explains why humanist medical authorities were not inclined toward the materia medica of the New World.
As the objective was to recover the uncorrupted version of the classical
texts, there was a push to purge Arab influence in both theory and practice. Medical authorities affected by these currents thought it better to
dispense with medicines and spices of East Indian provenance and rely on
native European materia medica.[8]

Both the conservative and dynamic aspects of Renaissance medicine led
to American plant material receiving a frigid reception from humanist
medical authorities. The conservative tendency meant that American medicaments would not appeal to those who thought that there was nothing of
importance that was not already in Hippocrates, Galen, and Dioscorides.
For this reason, the first humanist physician-herbalists classified tobacco as
a long-lost variety of henbane (*Hyoscyamus*). The innovating aspect meant
that the older, eclectic approach to multicultural medicine was under attack. Accordingly, it was healers outside the humanist medical establishment who promoted guaiacum to treat syphilis, while those inside reacted
with hostility.[9] When considering the reception of New World natural
products by the first generation of humanist botanists and doctors, it is
easy to concur with historian J. H. Elliott that "in some respects the Renaissance involved . . . a closing rather than an opening of the mind. The
veneration of antiquity became more slavish; authority staked fresh claims
against experiences."[10] Before 1571 the humanist tradition of medicine
embraced tobacco only under an alias, and cacao not at all.

MONARDES: HUMANISM AND THE
ATLANTIC TRADE

It was, then, a pivotal moment in 1565 when Nicolás Monardes published
*Dos libros. El uno trata de todas las cosas que traen de nuestras Indias
Occidentales que sirven al uso de medicina* (Two Books. Book one concerns those things brought from our West Indies that are useful in
medicine).[11] He was the first humanist-trained university doctor to systematically consider American materia medica, a dramatic reversal of the hostility humanist-inclined botanists and physicians had shown to New World
substances until that point. Going further, Monardes advanced the claim
that the West Indies had usurped the role of the East Indies as the world's
singular source of pharmacopoeia. The city official, nobleman, and humanist Gonzalo Argote de Molina trumpeted this claim in a verse gracing
a later edition of the work by Monardes: "How much of the world / Our
Spain provisions and / Makes envious all of the Orient."[12] The Far East, for

many centuries the supplier of Europe's most valued spices and luxury imports, the poem declared, had lost is place to the New World.

To understand what made possible the startling originality of Monardes requires situating him in his intellectual and social milieu. Monardes's immersion in two overlapping worlds—that of pan-European humanism and that of an Atlantic network bustling with mobile people, information, and goods—made him especially sensitive to the many channels by which tobacco arrived in Europe. If Monardes had inhabited solely one of these, it is unlikely that he would have written or published his writings about the New World. The medical profession provided him with a conceptual framework and vocabulary based on classical authors, yet the dominant intellectual currents of his field resisted the incorporation of American species into European apothecaries. The mercantile community guaranteed his exposure to goods and people disembarking in Seville, yet immersion in it alone would not have supplied him with the intellectual equipment he deployed or the yearning to write medical books.[13]

Neither Monardes's classical education nor his prestigious credentials impelled him toward his interest in New World goods. Educated first at the University of Alcalá de Henares, Monardes studied liberal arts and medicine and read the works of the classical authorities Hippocrates, Galen, and Dioscorides via the translations and commentaries of medieval and humanist scholars. Two great humanist luminaries of Alcalá de Henares who shaped Monardes' intellectual formation were Antonio de Nebrija and Andrés Laguna; perhaps the most important legacy that Nebrija and Laguna bequeathed to Monardes was their scholarship on Dioscorides of Anazarbus, the Roman author of the medical compendium, *De Materia Medica*.[14] Monardes graduated with his bachelor of arts and philosophy degree in 1530 and got his medical degree in 1533. Later he received a doctorate in medicine from the University of Seville.[15] Monardes's involvement in the world of humanist medicine disposed him toward a particular way of seeing New World goods and technologies, one that was overwhelmingly negative.

So what happened in the intervening years to inspire him to publish his 1565 book that "concerns those things brought from our West Indies that are useful in medicine" and inaugurate a new genre, the Indies herbal? His intellectual conversion was not precipitated by changes internal to the academic medical profession but came from his immersion in dynamic, mercantile Seville.[16] Between 1536 and 1565 Monardes became enmeshed personally and professionally in a web of strands connecting to the Indies. Just as he typified the university doctor, he also embodied the quintessential Sevillan trader. The cliché bandied about sixteenth-century Seville was that there was no one who was not somehow involved in the Atlantic trade.[17] Seville's cultural and economic links to the Indies allowed Monardes entrée to the world of the transatlantic trader. No doubt his interest (beginning about 1551) was provoked by the rapid growth in the American trade in the 1540s.[18] The physician sold slaves from Africa to the Caribbean, and he imported cochineal, hides, and mineral riches from the Caribbean and Mexico into Spain. Notarial documents reveal Monardes's hands-on management of his Indies' business ventures, leading him to be in constant contact with correspondents and associates in the New World;[19] his main business partner was based in the Caribbean, and four of his seven children spent extensive time in the Indies. He was a familiar face at the Casa de Contratación, where he picked up regularly appearing shipments of American medicinal goods. He had many successes. His involvement in the slave trade is one marker that he was able to mobilize significant capital (and makes his observations about slaves' customs credible). In 1566 he and his son-in-law Alonso de Carrión shipped slaves worth forty thousand ducats to New Spain. By 1554 he had done well enough to move to a gracious home with sufficient room for his collection of curiosities and a botanical garden. He ranked as one of the most powerful merchants based in Seville.[20]

Moreover, he lived in sixteenth-century Seville, a singular place. As a "port and gateway to all of the Occidental Indies," he wrote (by which he meant all of the Americas), it had privileged access to the "future" before any other region in Spain or Europe. In a sense, Seville itself is a central protagonist in this story. Monardes was profoundly shaped by living in this valve that controlled the intercontinental flow of things and people. He was affected by his experiences and expectations of trade, and by his constant contact with those embarking on journeys to the New World and those returning from their sojourns in the Indies. Seville itself was an Atlantic community, where the enriched *indianos*—as the returned New World émigrés were know—were a conspicuous presence.

The competing prerogatives of Monardes's two professional fields—medicine and transatlantic commerce—inspired his innovative project. The tension that came from straddling these fields catapulted him to intellectually break with his medical peers. The result was that Monardes styled himself as the compiler of materia medica for the Spanish empire as Dioscorides had been for the Roman Empire. Dioscorides, a Greek doctor who served in the Roman army during Nero's reign (54–68 CE), dedicated himself to collecting and classifying things with therapeutic value, resulting in the compendium *De materia medica* that included some five hundred plants, animals, and minerals, most of which were native to the eastern Mediterranean.[21] In his 1574 work Monardes made explicit his admiration for the Greek botanist who traveled with weaponry, in the armies of Anthony and Cleopatra, and wherever he went, he sought herbs, trees, plants, animals, and minerals and many other things; from which he made those six books, which are so celebrated all over the world; which brought him glory and fame that we see he has, this writing has brought him more fame than if he had conquered many cities with his military arms.[22]

Following Dioscorides, Monardes allotted a chapter to each medicinal in which he described its place of origin, recounted how he came to hear about the medicine, and evaluated it according to the medical conceptual framework of his time. He considered twenty-four different medicinals in this first edition, including copal, liquidambar, balsam, guaiacum, "china root," sarsaparilla, chili peppers, *Cassia fistula*, and *mechoacan*—to which he gave the most emphasis.[23] In explicating these, Monardes devoted the bulk of this work to those medicinals that already had penetrated European apothecaries.

If Dioscorides' example influenced the shape of the project, Galen's humoral paradigm permeated Europeans' understanding of the body and its environment and offered Monardes criteria for considering the properties of each substance. From Galen, his medieval interpreters, and Renaissance commentators and translators Monardes received a particular way of viewing the body and notions of health and sickness. Galen followed Aristotle and Hippocrates in viewing the world and its elements as classifiable according to four essential properties: hot, cold, wet, and dry. In the human body, these corresponded to four humors: blood, yellow bile, black bile, and phlegm. In the view of Galen and his Renaissance disciples, health depended on obtaining an optimal balance of the humors in the body. Conversely, sickness followed when one had an excess of a particular humor. Different temperaments corresponded to the dominance of a particular humor in a body. The humoral balance of men and women were affected by their personal profile (occupation, sex, age), their environment (geographic, seasonal, and diurnal conditions), and, of course, their consumption habits (the food, drink, and medicines they ingested). This understanding of physiology underlay the practice of bloodletting and the prominent use of purgatives, laxatives, and emetics. A major component of Renaissance medicine, then, involved classifying food, drink, and medicine according to the four essential properties. Degrees denoted the intensity of the given property. Since both food and medicines affected the balance of humors, the boundary between food and drugs was not fixed or essential.[24]

While celebrating classical precedent, Monardes did not eschew empirical investigations. In fact, he made clear that Europeans were indebted to indigenous expertise for their knowledge about useful medicaments. The physician described the social context in which Europeans learned about American remedies. In one instance he recounted how "a lady who had returned from Peru" told him that after receiving unsuccessful treatments from Spanish doctors for many years, she finally "went to an Indian, who was in possession of knowledge about many herbs with which Indians were cured." The Indian healer gave her a medicine made from an herb, after which she "evacuated a worm—she said it was a snake—hairy and two palms long and very thick, and it had a split tail, and after having purged it she was well and healthy."[25] In the framework elaborated in the 1565 work, Monardes, rather than denying Indian origins of medicinals, drew attention to them and called for the systematic interrogation of native informants.

Monardes wrote herbals of American materia medica not only to guide apothecaries and educated readers but also to spur systematic investigation of substances and technologies indigenous to the New World. He implied that Spaniards had only scraped the surface of collective Indian knowledge and excoriated colonists for their lack of curiosity and laziness. He sorrowfully complained that Europeans underexploited the potential of indigenous medical knowledge:

> Certainly we all deserve great blame, seeing that there are in New Spain so many herbs and plants and other medicinal things, which are of such importance, yet there is no one to write of them, or understand their properties, and the forms they have, to compare them with our plants. If someone had the motivation to investigate and experiment with all of the kinds of the medicines such are sold by the Indians in their markets, it would be a thing of great utility and benefit.[26]

In effect, Monardes wanted to systematize what was already happening informally between colonists and colonized. But where did that leave tobacco, since Europeans already knew *a lot* about how tobacco was used by native Americans, and not all of those uses related to "medicine"?

THE TOBACCO PARADOX

The word "tabaco" appears nowhere in the first volume of Monardes's work on New World materia medica, published first in 1565. Yet, in the second volume published six years later, tobacco received pride of place. What propelled the Sevillan physician to celebrate tobacco in the 1571 sequel?

In 1567 a French publication appeared entitled *L'agriculture et maison rustique* (Agriculture and the country home).[27] In that hefty book—a cross between an almanac and an herbal—Jean Liebault provided entries for different agricultural products, medicinals, and methods of cultivation. Most of these were of Old World provenance, but he also included sections on tobacco and *mechoacan*.[28] (Liebault's source of information on the purgative *mechoacan* appears to have been Monardes's 1565 book on "things brought from our West Indies," offering further evidence for the pan-European, intertextual world both scholars inhabited.) Liebault began the chapter on tobacco by stating of "*Nicotiane*":

> Although it has only been known in France for a short time, it holds the first place among medicinal plants, because of its singular and almost divine virtues, such as you will later learn. Because none of those, ancient or modern, who have written about plants have made mention of it, I wished to know its whole history, which I have heard from a gentleman, the first author, discoverer and importer of this herb into France.

He proceeded to tell the origins' account by which the French ambassador to Portugal began growing a "gift" of a plant from Florida and then discovered its anticancerous properties.[29]

Some credit Jean Liebault with having alerted Monardes (and many others) to tobacco's existence.[30] However, a more likely case is that Monardes already knew of tobacco in various guises but Liebault prompted Monardes to reconsider the plant as a meritorious medicinal and rehabilitate its notorious reputation.[31] Perhaps the Spanish physician was annoyed that credit for tobacco's introduction to Europe should go to the French rather than Spanish. Monardes read Liebault's tendentious account of the "holy herb"—as it was also known—as a chauvinistic challenge that demanded a patriotic rebuttal.[32]

In terms of pages and prominence, tobacco occupied an exceptional position in the 1571 *Segunda parte del libro, de las cosas que se traen de nuestras Indias Occidentales*, but in other ways Monardes's treatment typified his method throughout; the chapter mingled in ramshackle fashion botanical, etymological, ethnographic, and medical information, interspersing piquant anecdotes and seeming digressions.[33] Most importantly, the entry on tobacco exemplified the syncretism that resulted from the encounter between two long-autonomous traditions concerning the relationship between human bodies and their environment, health, sickness, and healing. Monardes employed the Dioscoridian framework of *De materia medica* and the language of Galenism for discussing the body and environment *and* he incorporated therapeutic discoveries, ethnographic information, and even elements of a classificatory system from different parts of the American hemisphere, particularly Mesoamerica.

Monardes presented two kinds of medicinal information about the substances he examined: their physiological properties (including therapeutic and adverse effects) and explanations for the basis of such effects. The medicinal uses Monardes ascribed to tobacco far surpassed those in Liebault's discussion. Where the latter only discussed tobacco as a topical treatment and for chest congestion when ingested as an elixir, Monardes outlined twenty curative uses of tobacco.[34] For headaches, "especially those originating from the cold cause," he recommended the application of leaves directly on the site of the pain "multiplying [the number of leaves] as necessary until the pain subsides." For those suffering chest pains, Monardes enthused that "this herb does marvelous work" and prescribed a preparation of tobacco distilled with sugar. For asthmatics, "taken in smoke by mouth, [tobacco] expels chest material."[35] Tobacco was prescribed as a surgical preparation: "For recent wounds, such as knifings, beatings, punctures and whatever wound, our tobacco works marvelous effects, because it cures them by coagulation."[36] Tobacco figured in cures for stomachaches, gas, children's breathing problems, parasites, rheumatism, swelling, bloating, toothaches, poisonings, various skin diseases, and uterine ailments. Monardes also devoted a section to the "cure of animals with tobacco."

On what basis did Monardes "know" about the twenty curative uses of tobacco? Scholars have long considered Monardes's tobacco therapies as informed by European traditions. For instance, Sarah Augusta Dickson, an erudite scholar on the history of tobacco, argued that the entry of Monardes on tobacco was based on Dioscorides' entry for henbane, which, as has been seen, was in fact the plant for which tobacco was first mistaken.[37]However, this hypothesis founders, for there remain aliments for which Monardes prescribed tobacco (e.g., stomach pains, gout, snake bites, asthma) that are absent in Dioscorides' entry on henbane. Rather than being a transposition of Dioscorides' Old World henbane, Monardes's understanding of tobacco's physiological effects largely derived from Amerindian knowledge that migrated through colonial and Atlantic information networks and that were confirmed and tested through direct experimentation by Monardes and others in his milieu.

In the first place, all of the therapeutic uses Monardes claimed for tobacco are ones for which there are independent native sources.[38] Moreover, Monardes himself described a process of information transfer that originated with native Americans, spread to Spanish colonizers, and migrated to the denizens of the Old World. He noted, for instance, that Spaniards learned from native allies in the West Indies how tobacco could heal wounds caused by the poison-tipped arrows of hostile Caribs. It seems likely that after Liebault perturbed Monardes and piqued his interest, the Sevillan doctor mobilized his transatlantic network to discover more about indigenous uses of this herb. His 1571 and 1574 publications suggest that the fame he acquired from his first volume increased his capacity to attract information. These books reveal constant contact—personal and epistolary—between himself and Spaniards in and returning from the Americas.[39]

It could still be argued that Monardes and other Europeans independently arrived at their findings concerning tobacco's properties through their own empirical research. This, of course, is a process Monardes described particularly in his tobacco chapter. Though he made no mention of experiments conducted by Portuguese botanists or visiting Frenchmen, he wrote proudly of research undertaken in the court of the Spanish king Phillip II: "His majesty, wanting to investigate . . . the virtue of this herb against *ballestero* [a poison used by hunters]," ordered his chamber doctor to experiment on a small dog.[40] But it also seems that the initial knowledge came from direct experience in the Americas.

Monardes did more, however, than describe tobacco's properties when ingested or applied to the body. He also gave an explanation for why tobacco did what it did. At first glance this theoretical discussion appears to be a purely European artifact, as it is presented in the humoral terms associated with Galen's framework. Tobacco, according to the doctor, was hot and dry in the second degree. He described its main properties as "providing heat, dissolving with astringency, and invigorating."[41] He explained that the therapies worked because the heat of tobacco would dissolve the surplus cold humors that caused congestion and discomfort in the head and chest. Though Monardes gave no hint that the conceptual frame in which tobacco was placed built on native American knowledge, the origins of the designation of tobacco as "hot" very likely was based in Mesoamerican principles that predated the Spanish invasion. First, consider the counterargument: What if tobacco naturally lent itself to a "hot" classification in the Galenist framework—in other words, Monardes inducted Galenist principles according to experience, finding substances with "known" humoral designations and deducing that these resembled tobacco? That this was not the case is proven by earlier European botanists' classification of tobacco as a type of henbane (based on its similar appearance and psychoactive effects). Henbane and other Old World solanaceous psychotropics were classified as "cold."[42] In other words, European precedent should have led Monardes and his emulators to classify tobacco as cold, as were the other plants in the nightshade family. Rather, Mesoamerican etiology of diseases hinged on the idea of a balance between hot and cold (thus independently sharing features with the European medical model) and Mesoamericans classified tobacco as hot.[43] Monardes assimilated and followed Mesoamerican precedent.

EXORCIZING THE DEVIL

That tobacco was the focal point of Monardes's 1571 work reflects its centrality in pre-Columbian societies throughout the Americas, where its special prominence in overlapping and interlinked rites of healing, spirituality, and sociability meant that alien visitors were bound to take notice of it. And since tobacco was a common denominator among diverse Amerindian groups, European and Africans were going to run into it wherever they sojourned or settled in the Western Hemisphere. But there is another, related, reason that tobacco was at the heart of Monardes's 1571 book. Lurking just below the surface of Monardes's discussion of tobacco was the question of whether Europeans who embraced the American herb became the pagan, potentially diabolically inspired, idolaters whom they emulated. In addition to whatever details his informants offered Monardes about tobacco's role in American societies, the Sevillan also had to contend with the legacy bequeathed by Oviedo and his chronicling successors—Benzoni and López Gomara, in particular—that had made notorious tobacco's haunting origins.

Monardes employed a variety of strategies to reconcile his unbridled enthusiasm for tobacco's therapeutic potential with its well-imprinted suspect associations. First of all, the physician directly confronted the question of tobacco's alleged diabolical origins. Following Oviedo and Benzoni, Monardes described how native "priests" employed tobacco in order to advise on "matters of great importance" or to "learn of future enterprises and events." Almost directly paraphrasing the chroniclers who preceded him (though never citing them directly), he wrote that in order to prophesize and advise, a priest

> took some leaves of tobacco, threw them in the fire, and received the smoke
> of the leaves through his mouth and nose with a tube: and upon taking it, he
> fell on the ground as if dead—his condition reflecting the amount of smoke
> which he had taken. And when the herb had done its work, he remembered
> and gave them his answers according to the fantasies and illusions that he
> had seen in that state.[44]

Monardes distinguished himself from earlier appraisers, however, when he made clear that tobacco itself was innocent in these dubious rites. He acquitted tobacco from diabolical culpability by adducing a triangular relationship between the devil, tobacco, and New World Indians. He offered a new origins' account for tobacco: "As the devil is a deceiver, and has knowledge of the properties of herbs, he showed them the virtue of this one, so that with it he could see those imagined things and the fantasies they represented, and through them he deceived them."[45]

In this passage Monardes reconciled tobacco's legacy with his earlier unhesitating celebration of it. In this scheme, tobacco itself did not cause demonic delusions but rather put its users into a drunken state of altered consciousness that allowed the devil to place "fantasies and illusions" in their minds. The devil did not invent tobacco or even invest it with its mind-altering properties; rather he is portrayed as a keen observer of the natural world. Knowing about its hallucinogenic effects, the devil introduced tobacco to the Indians so that he could then slyly intervene as a deceiving illusionist. The devil was not the creator of tobacco but its discoverer, so that in essence tobacco was still good, or at least neutral. In this way, tobacco may have abetted the transferal of demonic powers but was not itself an agent of it.

With this explanation of tobacco's psychotropic effects, he appropriated and intervened in a contemporary debate about the balance of natural and supernatural forces and the power of the devil.[46] In the sixteenth century there was a growing belief among theologians that denied the devil direct agency in the world. Prominent sixteenth-century Spanish religious authorities argued against the notion that the devil and demons possessed the power to directly intervene in situations or control the actions of individuals. But these theologians did subscribe to the efficacy of Satan to affect the "subtle workings in the imagination," to intrude and create phantasms. Those who overindulged in food and alcohol made vulnerable their imaginations, allowing Satan to plant them with delusions, which the glutton or alcoholic might then mistake for divine rather than demonic apparitions. In a similar vein, Monardes argued that the devil was incapable of investing natural substances with supernatural properties, but he could encourage people to imbibe substances that would induce hallucinations, incapacitating them from distinguishing between the real and the imaginary. For contemporary audiences, Monardes was attempting to counter the earlier representations of tobacco that linked it to diabolical inversion.

But even if he had shown tobacco was not the cause of Satanic interventions but rather a powerful agent that could make those who misused it vulnerable to demonic delusions, there still remained a broader question about whether the appropriation of material goods from a foreign culture entailed the migration of cultural meanings.

This question could be asked of almost any of the novelties discovered in the Americas and brought to Europe, but it was particularly pertinent in the case of tobacco, whose centrality to native rites was all too known. Monardes sought to sanitize tobacco—reconcile European use of it with its pagan, idolatrous associations—by demonstrating tobacco used medically was properly European, and tobacco used for other purposes was not.

Monardes designated the medical consumption of tobacco as civilized and the social consumption of tobacco as barbarian. He did this by comparing tobacco's place in Indian rites to the use of other mind-altering substances among various pagan or "barbarian" cultures. By ensconcing his discussion of the nonmedical uses of tobacco within a comparative framework—permitting him to lengthily digress to discuss marijuana, opium, and hallucinogens of antiquity—Monardes demonstrated that the problem lay not with the substance but in the inferiority of the culture that used it in this manner. His chapter on tobacco was bifurcated accordingly. In the first part of the tobacco chapter, the doctor advocated tobacco as a panacea, assuring readers of its effectiveness in curing or alleviating aliments ranging from parasites to asthma to epilepsy. He made the second part, marked by the title heading "The Way the Priests of the Indians Use Tobacco," the repository for all of tobacco's possible "social" uses.[47]

He also digressed into comparative ethnopharmacology to make his point. The section "How the East Indians Use Opium" illustrates how Monardes made the medical, as opposed to social, use of tobacco become a marker of a Christian, European identity, distinguished from a pagan, Turkish, Asian, or African one.[48] Opium, its raw materials, and derivatives had a secure place on the shelves of Spanish apothecaries, used as an ingredient in sedatives and soporifics.[49] In contrast, he recounted two transactions he witnessed in apothecaries in Seville that demonstrated the very different manner of consumption employed by "an Indian from the same East Indies." Ever nosy, the physician inquired why the foreigners were buying the opium, and both times he was told that it was "to allow [them] to relax from work." He concluded the subsection on opium by remarking that "it is a thing worthy of great consideration that 5 *granos* of opium kill us and 60 provide them with health and rest."[50] He explained:

> Barbarians use similar things to relieve fatigue not only in our West Indies, but also very commonly in the East Indies. And also in the India of Portugal, for this effect opium is sold in stores—the way sweets are here—which the Indians use to relax from work and to make themselves happy and to not feel pain from those trying things that come to the body and mind.[51]

In this passage the words "barbarians" and "Indians" apply both to the Indians of the Americas and Asia. This discussion of opium served to illuminate tobacco by analogy. Readers were meant to understand the discrepancy between the uses Monardes recommended for tobacco with the uses he attributed to Indians by the parallel example of opium. Whether tobacco or opium, what was an ingredient in therapeutic concoctions for Europeans was a leisure drug for Indians of the West and East. Monardes was explicit about his concept of the relationship between consumption and identity in this section: "It is certainly a thing to marvel seeing that these barbarous people consume such medicines in such quantities and that they do not kill them."[52] Similarly, the "barbarians" of the "East Indies" indulged in *bague* (cannabis) in order to "leave their senses" and "receive pleasure and contentment." And Africans were emulating Indians, as he noted in the subsection entitled "blacks use [tobacco] in the manner of Indians."[53]

At the same time that he recognized, and in fact promoted, the Spanish dependence on native knowledge, Monardes also found a way to present the medicines as safely European. In his model, European pharmacopoeia could effectively accommodate the New World drugs with the assistance of classically trained authorities such as himself. If a humanist formation did not stimulate Monardes to initially write about New World materia medica, once he decided to devote himself to its study, it largely determined his approach.

FRANCISCO HERNÁNDEZ

And chocolate? Despite its accelerating use among colonists in Mesoamerica, chocolate did not make an appearance in Monardes's work. Chocolate may have visited his household, since one of his sons, something of a black sheep, returned to his father's house after a lengthy sojourn in New Spain. But, if it did, the strange foamy drink failed to pique the Sevillan's interest. Yet Monardes laid the foundation for future writers who did contend with chocolate and further investigated tobacco.

It seems that Monardes's plea for proactive investigation reached a sympathetic and powerful audience: it is hard to see no correlation between Monardes's call to action and the initiatives Phillip II sponsored during the 1570s.[54] These projects included the appointment of a "general cosmographer-chronicler" to describe the resources of the Indies and a massive survey known as the "Geographic Reports" (*Relaciones geográficas*) sent to localities through the American possessions that asked officials to report on local resources. Most significant in terms of the history of tobacco and chocolate was the project commissioned by Philip II in 1569 to collect native medical information in New Spain. Its principal, a physician named Francisco Hernández, was to interview "physicians, surgeons, herbalists, Indians and others who appear to you knowledgeable on these matters."[55]

Born around 1517 near Toledo, Francisco Hernández shared an alma mater with Monardes: he received his medical degree from Alcalá de Henares in 1536. Afterward he practiced as a physician and researcher throughout the peninsula (Seville, Toledo, and Guadalupe). Initially, his interests did not veer toward the New World; one of his early academic works was a translation of works by the classical geographer Pliny. Likely, his turn toward the New World was related to his stay during the 1550s in Seville. In the early 1560s, Hernández moved to Toledo, perhaps to benefit from proximity to the court; if so, he succeeded in that he was appointed as a chamber doctor to Philip II in 1567. A royal decree from December 1569 allocated funds for Hernández to "go to the Indies as its *protomédico general* and to make a history of those natural things . . . for the period of five years that it will take."[56] Arriving in Veracruz in 1571, he traveled to numerous localities throughout New Spain, including central Mexico, Oaxaca, and Michoacán. Hernández and his entourage (including painters, an interpreter, a botanist, scribes, attendants, and Indian doctors, as well as two mules) collected specimens and interviewed "old Indians" and healers. He also became enmeshed in the small world of the local Spanish and creole medical elite.[57] From March 1574 until he returned to Spain in 1577, the doctor lived in Mexico City, organizing his data, experimenting with his materia medica, and also attending to patients in the Hospital Real de Indios. Already an accomplished classicist (see his work on Pliny), he learned Nahuatl and even translated some of his work into that language so that native Mexicans could also enjoy the fruits of his labor. He also undertook archeological and historical investigations into pre-Columbian Mexico.[58] Francisco Hernández more than achieved the objective articulated by Monardes of combing the Indies and interrogating natives about their local products in order "to discover and understand their properties and experiment with their varieties . . . which the Indians proclaim and manifest with the great experience that they have among themselves."[59] His seven-year research project far surpassed that of his predecessor (and successors) in the scope and intensity of research, culminating in a manuscript featuring over three thousand entries on plants, minerals, and animals of central Mexico.[60] Hernández provided the king with thirty-eight volumes filled with text and drawings accompanied by specimens—live and dried plants, hides, feathers, dissected animals, and minerals. Though Hernández's original manuscripts perished and his work was not published during his lifetime, surviving fragments and copies reveal that his output included an eight hundred–page "Natural History of New Spain" in the Dioscoridian model organized by plant, mineral, or animal substance, and a text organized by aliment that Hernández referred to as "Table of the Aliments and Remedies of this New Spain."[61]

Francisco Hernández is a protagonist in this history of tobacco and chocolate for several reasons.[62] First, even though his works were not published until much after his death, Hernández's treatment of cacao and chocolate became the *locus classicus* for the European medical under-standing of chocolate that lasted until Linnaeus's time (much as Mon-ardes's was for tobacco).[63] And like Monardes, Hernández folded together European and Mesoamerican elements in a thoroughly syncretic fashion. Hernández also grappled with the same knotty ideological issues that chal-lenged Monardes concerning the relationship between material and sym-bolic appropriation that stemmed from Spanish colonizers adapting Mesoamerican practices.

That the chapter dedicated to cacao occupied a place of particular sig-nificance even in the context of his enormous work is made patently clear by the introductory sentences. He opened by borrowing (unattributed) Pe-ter Martyr's riff that made cacao the synecdoche for pre-Columbian Mes-oamerica as gold was for Europe. "In discussing *cacahoaquáhuitl*," Hernández wrote, "the great phases of human history come to mind."[64] Hernández followed the philosophical musing with precise botanical infor-mation, classifying four varieties of cacao trees, explaining how and where they grew and describing the appearance of the plant and its fruit (see fig-ure 5.2). The investigator mentioned the practice of eating the toasted nibs "like almonds" and enumerated the various beverages (*cacahoatl*), ranging from the simplest preparation of ground cacao and water to more elaborate concoctions in which toasted ground corn, barley, various spices (such as the floral trilogy of vanilla, *mecaxóchitl*, and *xochinacaztli*, as well as achiote), and chilies were added.

Just as Monardes imported Amerindian knowledge about tobacco into a European idiom, so did Hernández for chocolate. Offering a humoral pro-file, he wrote that cacao was "formed of a blackish substance divided into imbalanced components but very well adjusted as a whole, tender, of much nourishment, somewhat bitter, a little sweet, and of a temperate or slightly wet and cold complexion."[65] Many of the other ingredients in the cacao drink, he explained, were hot (with the exception of achiote) and thus tem-pered the coldness of cacao. And in a similar vein he described most cacao beverages as "cooling" and "refreshing." In contrast to tobacco, chocolate was more a neutral substance—bespeaking its status as a beverage rather than a medicine—though it could be customized toward hot or cold, de-pending on the humoral needs of the individual consumer.

Hernández's professed methodology made it clear that his information was based on Indian knowledge gleaned through systematic interrogation of local informants.[66] Moreover, the fact of his multiyear residence also meant that ambient knowledge that circulated in New Spain filtered into his consciousness. So it is hardly surprising that several aspects of his chocolate (and tobacco) descriptions betray indigenous origins. His humoral classifications of chocolate and cacao suggest Mesoamerican influence. As

De CACAVA QVAHVITL, seu arbore CACARI Cacauifera. *Cap. XLVI.*

AT in *Cacaua Quahuitl*, magna deteguntur humanæ fortis volumina. in veteri fiquidem Orbe, perq. prifca illa tempora, quæ vitæ hominum erant neceffaria, atque adeo apud alios cum deeffent quærenda, non rependebantur ære. nondum aureus argenteufuè nummus circumferebatur, aut pecudum, Regumue, aut Principum fimulacra metallis cernebantur infculpta. rerum viuebatur permutatione, vt olim factum cecinit Homerus, & fructuum quos recondebant facta alijs copia, mutuum ferebatur auxilium. tandem æra percuffa, atque fignata funt, & mille rerum effigies numifmatis impreffæ confpiciebantur. at in nouum hunc mundum nunquam auaritiæ figna penetrauerant, aut caput erexerat ambitio, donec noftri, velis ventouè deuecti, impetum fecere. non vfque adeo fplendebant illis argentum atque aurum quibus præcipuè abundabant; auium pulcherrimarum plumæ, lintea quædam goffippina, & gemmæ, quæ ea fert affatim fua fponte tellus, erat diuitiarum, & copiarum fumma. nondum Armillæ, torques, aut brachialia, nifi fortaffis concinnata è floribus, plebi innotuerant, aut Margaritæ erant illis in pretio. nudi penè incedebant, vitam degebant hilarem. neque vaftos congerendi thefauros, aut rei familiaris augendæ, veluti de futuro parum follicitos, cura euigilabat. in diem viuebatur, indulgebatur genio, humili forte, fed tranquilla & felici, & potifsimis naturæ bonis magna cum iucunditate potiebantur. Semen *Cacauatl* erat illis pro nummo, & eo præcipua vitæ præmio, cum opus erat, comparabantur. duratq. in hodiernum vfque diem

non

Figure 5.2. Francisco Hernández, *Rerum medicarum Novae Hispaniae thesaurus* (Rome, 1651), p. 79 (detail). Hernández's original manuscript was never published, but several abridged versions appeared in the seventeenth century. Reproduced courtesy of the John Carter Brown Library at Brown University.

with tobacco, one can test this hypothesis. The Sevillan physician and medical professor Santiago Valverde Turices, who was the first Spaniard in Spain to write a book devoted to chocolate, explained exactly how one would come up with a humoral profile for cacao—"with much speculation (*especulación*) and extensive experience, which is even more necessary for cacao and chocolate." He made clear, however, citing Galen, that the latter trumped the former, for "it is absurd to believe in reason while ignoring experience." Experience, he asserted, "tells us that [cacao] is cold." This "experience" came directly from the Indies and Indians, for he explained that it was from "an erudite physician" who visited his medical school who informed him and his colleagues that "in the Indies an emollient of only cacao is applied to happy success in hot illnesses."[67] The notion being, of course, that cacao must be cold in order for it to work as an antidote to an excess of heat. And this treatment does, in fact, reflect pre-Hispanic traditions of using cacao against heat-based illnesses, such as in treating fevers. Valverde's discussion suggests that there was nothing obvious about a cold humoral designation for cacao; rather he relied on precedent, Mesoamerican precedent to be exact.

Though Hernández must be viewed as an emulator of Monardes, he also diverged from his predecessor in significant ways. The fact Hernández undertook his investigation in the New World and received state sponsorship allowed him to directly retrieve information from native informants who served not only as interogees but also as collaborators, in that indigenous men conducted many of the interviews, wrote the responses, and synthesized them as well as made the illustrations. His Mesoamerican surroundings also led Hernández to experience directly many of the substances within their creole or native contexts. The result was that his work was an even more effective vector for syncretic knowledge than was that of Monardes. Hernández's New World experiences also led him to somewhat different conclusions about the conundrum of whether the use of New World resources could be extricated from Amerindian cultures.

Whereas Monardes found solace in drawing a clear boundary between medicinal and cultural uses in his consideration of tobacco, Hernández recognized the inextricability of "natural histories" from cultural histories. In the introduction of an unpublished treatise entitled *Antigüedades de la Nueva España* (Antiquities of New Spain), he explained to Philip II "that although you commissioned me only for a natural history of this world, Most Sanctified King, and although one could consider that the charge of writing about antiquities does not belong to me, nonetheless, I judge that customs and rites of these people is not too distant from [the natural history]."[68] His time in Mexico left Hernández convinced that it was impossible to separate the medicinal uses of American resources from the cultures that had discovered them. This stance left him with a profoundly ambivalent attitude toward native Americans.

On the one hand, the Spanish physician's debt to indigenous collaborators and informants marked him as an ideological heir to Peter Martyr. Hernández drew from, indeed plagiarized, Martyr with his opening that made cacao the synecdoche for pre-Columbian Mesoamerica as gold was for Europe. And, as in his predecessor's work, the contrast between cacao and gold stood in for the opposition of the pure and simple savages of the prelapsarian New World and the corrupted and cunning conquerors of the decadent Old World.[69] Cacao—plucked off trees—could serve as currency in a society where people were driven by basic wants. A society motored by insatiable desires demanded gold plundered from the earth. Though admiring, the effect was a distancing one, for he used it as a basis of an evolutionary scheme of human development, suggesting that prior to the gold, or even bronze or iron age—though perhaps after a stone age—there was a "cacao age." In this, Hernández was one of the first of New World Spaniards to claim an indigenous "classical antiquity," a phenomena that historian Anthony Pagden has described for the late seventeenth century.[70]

While invoking the more noble and less avaricious indigenes of the past, such a romantic perspective was not brought to bear on the Indians of the present on whom he so depended, making him more heir to Gonzalo Fernández de Oviedo than Martyr. Hernández disparaged the indigenous healers who helped him,[71] and in a poem to a Spanish patron dramatized his hardships by complaining of Indian informants' reluctance to share their knowledge and of perfidious conspiracies and malicious falsehoods, "the perverse lies with which they heedlessly mocked me, speaking with great deceit . . . the barbaric condition of the Indians who are not the least truthful and unwilling to tell the truth about their herbs."[72]

Hernández diverged notably from Monardes, finally, in that he left no doubt about the social as well as medicinal character of tobacco and chocolate. Though Hernández dutifully attended to chocolate's physiological effects and cacao's use in treatments for fevers and dysentery, his discussion exposed the essentially social and hedonic character of chocolate (and tobacco) consumption. Chocolate beverages promised sensory pleasure, increased vitality, alleviation of melancholy, and enhancement of the libido (or the "veneral appetite" in the terms of the day). Such properties made it understandable that overindulgence could be a problem, and he cautioned that the "excessive use of the drink of *cacahoatl* obstructs the organs, drains color, and induces cachexia and other incurable illnesses."[73] This understanding of the effects of chocolate consumption also bears the imprint of the Mesoamerican milieu in which Hernández encountered the substances.

Monardes's presentation of tobacco reflected his location in the imperial gateway of Seville where he was a recipient of information flowing from the persons and missives that emanated from far-flung and numerous locales in the Americas. Hernández's offerings concerning chocolate and tobacco, by comparison, reflected his immersion in Mesoamerica. Hernández was somewhat cagey about whether he had personally acquired a taste for the cacao beverage during his years in the New World: though he never explicitly announced his conversion, his occasional expressions of taste—judging a fragrance "agreeable," or referring to the "pleasure" of chocolate removed of its foam—betray first-hand experience. In terms of tobacco, it is hard to avoid the conclusion that Hernández himself was a convert to the Amerindian custom, given his reference to effects "borne out by daily experience" and his exalted language in enumerating the effects of smoking, which he gleefully claimed, "invigorates the head, brings sleep, lessens pain; it allows the stomach to recover its strength, cures migraines, dulls the sensations of pain and work, and completely fills the spirit with a tranquility affecting of all the faculties that could almost be called inebriation." Likewise, Hernández's discussion of different modes of tobacco consumption also suggests that he internalized the social biases of his Mesoamerican milieu. Chewing tobacco was associated with Indians and exertions of physical labor. And the preference for smoking reflects the pre-Hispanic tradition that associated smoking as a form of elegant refinement of high status, as well as inducement of ethereal pleasure. This recognition and adoption of tobacco as a social custom might explain why Hernández omitted any mention of religious or "idolatrous" uses of tobacco, despite widespread knowledge of these associations, and his discussion of such associations in the context of other substances, such as the hallucinogenic morning glory seeds.

THERE is no evidence that Monardes's publications or the works of his successors caused an immediate surge in the numbers of European tobacco and chocolate consumers or in imports. Tobacco and chocolate did not come to Europe because of medical publicity but because of consumers who had adopted the habit in the New World. Yet the naturalists' representations of tobacco and chocolate had an enduring legacy throughout the seventeenth and eighteenth centuries. The scientists had little impact on how Europeans used the New World substances, but they contributed greatly to how they thought about them. Monardes did succeed in providing a model of the doctor who, armed with classical medical erudition, could channel the newfound Indian knowledge and translate it into a Galenist and Dioscoridian idiom.

From a European perspective, tobacco and chocolate were transformed in the last third of the sixteenth century. Once synonymous with the alien qualities of Amerindian culture, they were now reimagined as outstanding members of the European apothecary. Monardes's *Historia medicinal* depicts one version of this transformation, offering stories of energetic Sevillan humanists applying Galenist theory to American pharmacopeia and ingenious court doctors testing new substances on animals. Given what is known about epistemological circumstances that conditioned their representations, one can argue that most everything Monardes and Hernández "understood" about tobacco and cacao beverages derived from a Mesoamerican system of taste and medicine strained through a Dioscoridian and Galenist framework. Indian knowledge reached Monardes and Hernández and their successors via a variety of conduits—through the systematic interrogations of local informants, through dispersed ambient knowledge that circulated in America and then the Atlantic world, and through direct experience that was itself predicated on exposure to Mesoamerican cultural practices. The process of incorporation was dialectical rather than one-sided. On the one hand, they brought their Galenist apparatus when evaluating and describing the composition and physiological effects of cacao and the other ingredients in chocolate. On the other hand, their view of the New World drink could not but be mediated by Indian interlocutors. In translation this Indian medical knowledge was irrevocably transformed, but, while their lens distorted, original qualities of the Indian interpretation survived the transfiguration. Their works were vehicles for the transmission of the syncretic formations that assembled around tobacco and chocolate in the culturally mestizo environment of the New World.

6

Enduring Idolatry

❖ ❖

The 1570s witnessed a dramatic shift in colonial policies and attitudes toward Amerindian culture. While the early part of the decade saw an enthusiastic response to Monardes's call for systematic investigation of Amerindian knowledge and the state's commissioning of Hernández's ambitious ethnobotanical project, by the end of the decade, Philip II did not deign to publish the results of Hernández's Herculean labors and missionaries viewed Indian conversion to Christianity as superficial at best and as a veneer for enduring pagan beliefs at worst. Moreover, Creoles were increasingly suspected—by themselves as well as snooty Spaniards of the metropole—of having "gone native" or, in sixteenth-century terms, of having degenerated due to the environmental conditions of the Americas and their proximity to obstinately pagan Indians. Tobacco and chocolate were often the flashpoints for cultural authorities in the New World and the Old World who sought to define the boundaries separating Christian and idolatrous, European and Amerindian, and civilized and barbarian. The goods' recurring presence had everything to do with the unresolved conundrum articulated by Monardes and Hernández about how much meaning adhered to materiality in cross-cultural appropriation. Furthermore, detailed works such as Hernández's opus were themselves seen as dangerously memorializing the pagan practices.

Missionaries' earlier paternalistic stance toward Indians shifted to a "more fundamental preoccupation with the demonic nature of their persistent idolatrous practices" at the end of the 1570s.[1] In this milieu, the ubiquitous pre-Hispanic elements—in landscapes, artistic tropes, texts—were seen as troublesome reminders or even catalysts for pagan backsliding. Where missionaries such as Motolinia once believed that Indian material culture could help native neophytes adapt Christianity to their milieu, colonial religious authorities now believed that vestiges of pre-Hispanic practices were evidence that Indian Christianity was merely a superficial veneer disguising a pagan substratum. Accordingly, the Mexican ecclesiastical council of 1585 banned the depiction of animals and devils next to saints so as to ensure that Indians not "adore them like they used to."[2] Such preoccupations also help explain why Franciscan superiors suppressed Bernardino de Sahagún's monumental treatise on Indian culture and why, in 1577, Philip II decreed an end to all further investigation of native Indian religion. Whereas the stated goal of Sahagún's *Historia general* was to assist missionaries in distinguishing between those practices that indicated genuine conversion to Christianity and those that indicated pre-Columbian paganism dressed in Christian guise, many religious authorities now feared that such a work, especially when printed, threatened to "memorialize" paganism and so contribute to its preservation. Church authorities deemed the ethnographic precision of Sahagún's work an affront to God.[3] Likewise, this tidal shift in religious views may well account for Phillip's decision to not have Hernández's manuscript published in its original form.[4] The rationale for this censorship was clearly articulated by a Dominican cleric who warned in the early seventeenth century that the character of the Indian, more than any other people in the world, is inclined toward "idolatry" and "seeing [it] in print and brought to the memory, one can fear the facility with which they would return to [idolatry]."[5]

Authorities fretted about enduring, even revitalized, "idolatry" among native subjects, but, even more worrisome, they contended with the specter of reverse acculturation as idolatrous practices seemed to be contagious, affecting European, as well as black and mestizo, populations in the New World. Historian Solange Alberro writes that zealous priests "sounded the alarm . . . that not only the Indians continued to remain idolaters they were before the Spanish arrived" but had spread idolatrous practices to those "who lived among them."[6] The (re-)implementation of the Inquisition was one of the tools used to uproot the growing influence of Indian culture on European colonial society. "The ruling class," argued the historian Gonzalo Aguirre Beltrán, "felt the imminent danger of seeing themselves conquered by Indians and blacks. To defend the social and cultural forms they had established, they put into violent implementation the counter-acculturation instruments directed by the Holy Office."[7]

It is in this context that the earliest theological directives targeting European use of tobacco and chocolate in the Americas must be understood. Around the time Monardes and Hernández wrote warm letters of introduction for tobacco and chocolate, Spanish colonists publicly came to terms with the fact that the goods' had thoroughly infiltrated creole society. In 1577 a Dominican friar in Chiapas beseeched the Vatican for a papal opinion on whether chocolate qualified as potable or comestible, so as to decide whether it could be consumed during the Church's fast days that permitted beverages but not solid foods. This query about a narrow doctrinal issue articulated a broader concern about how one could maintain a Christian and European identity in the colonial milieu. The reaction of the pope and cardinals could not have assuaged the worried Dominican: the pope did not deign to give the quandary a written response; rather, reported one in attendance, he found the request trivial and so amusing that it prompted laughter from him and his cardinals. The laughter and refusal to officially respond to the petition must have underscored the geographic and cultural distance between Rome and the domains of this controversy (though the pope apparently rendered an oral verdict that drinking chocolate would not break the ecclesiastical fast).[8]

The sight of clergymen (as well as parishioners) throughout the Spanish colonies in the Americas smoking, sniffing, and chewing tobacco on Church precincts led to some consternation, particularly when consumption took place dangerously close to the rite of Holy Communion. A troubled friar in the Yucatán reported to officials of the Inquisition that "in this province there is the custom among clergy to consume the smoke of tobacco, [who give] pleas of necessity, [claiming] that just like laborers they need to exert themselves, and among them there are those . . . who shortly before arriving at the saintliest sacrament at the altar use this smoke."[9] Such concerns led to the 1583 ruling in Lima (Peru) that priests could not consume tobacco before administering Communion: "It is forbidden under the penalty of eternal damnation for priests to take tobacco before administering Mass whether taking tobacco or *sayre* [the Andean term] in smoke or snuff, by way of the mouth, or the nostrils, even under the guise of medicine."[10] In 1585 a provincial meeting in Mexico forbade tobacco not only to the consecrating priests but also to those receiving the host "because of the reverence that should be shown in the taking of Communion."[11] As with chocolate, the explicit terms of the discussion revolved around a closely defined theological quandary—here ensuring the sanctity of the Eucharist. But the phenomenon of priests ingesting the odiferous, notably pagan substance in such proximity, corporal as well as temporal, to one of the holiest rites, which was likewise based around the ingestion of substances, indicated broader issues concerning the contagious effects of Indian idolatry. While narrow doctrinal issues were the immediate impetus for these theological inspections, the larger context in which these questions surfaced was the efforts of creole elites to define colonial identities during a period in which anxieties mounted concerning the persistence of Indian "idolatry" and the specter of reverse acculturation among colonists.

The creole identity crisis was exacerbated by peninsular Spaniards' scornful derision of their New World counterparts. "The greater part," asserted one such denigrator of Creoles, "take the nature and customs of the Indians, since they are born in the same climate and reared among them."[12] For the Jesuit José de Acosta, author of 1590's best-selling *Historia natural y moral de las Indias* (Natural and moral history of the Indies), chocolate was a measure of the distance that divided Creoles and metropolitans.[13] His year in New Spain—he spent more time in Peru—left him astonished at how the foamy drink was "a crazy thing prized in that land, and Spanish women born in that land would die for the black chocolate." He added that it "disgusts" those "not of the land," that "those who had not grown up" with chocolate "could not have a taste for it," and that the "scumlike" foam that capped the drink resembled feces.[14] Spaniards, such as Acosta, noted emerging cultural divergences between *criollos* and *peninsulares*—exemplified in bizarre habits like smoking tobacco and drinking chocolate—and alleged creole degeneration. Not only did Creoles in Mexico worry about contaminating effects of Indian culture but they also needed to defend themselves against scorn emanating from the metropole.

CREOLE SCIENCE

These challenges to creole identity spurred a flurry of writings about American materia medica around the turn of the sixteenth century. Born in the early 1560s, in Colmenar Viejo of the bishopric of Toledo, Spain, Juan de Barrios shared his birthplace with Francisco Hernández. And like Monardes and Hernández, though a generation later, Barrios attended Alcalá de Henares, probably graduating before 1581. He arrived in the New World in 1589, disembarking for stints in Santiago de Cuba and Havana before installing himself in Mexico that same year, still a young man at about twenty-six. Juan de Barrios's 1607 *Verdadera medicina, cirugía y astrología* (True medicine, surgery, and astrology) included a "fourth treatise of all the herbs applicable to illnesses and how and in what quantity that by order of His Majesty, the *Protomédico* Francisco Hernández discovered in this New Spain . . . and then examined and seen by the Doctor Nardo Recco in Madrid."[15] More significantly for the history of chocolate, Barrios published in 1609 *Libro en el cual se trata del chocolate* (A book that discusses chocolate).[16] Born in 1563 in Constantina near Seville, Juan de Cárdenas was an exact contemporary of Barrios. However, unlike the latter physician, he lived most of his adult life in the Americas and acquired his medical education in Mexico.[17] He was the first to *publish* a work—*Problemas y secretos maravillosos de las Indias* (Problems and marvelous secrets of the Indies), in 1591—that discussed chocolate use among Spaniards in the New World.[18]

Creole elites such as physicians Juan de Cardénas and Juan de Barrios (they were born in Spain but came to identify as Creole) were all too aware of enduring Indian "superstition," and even "idolatry," that permeated their milieu and the attraction that these heretical practices had for some of their compatriots. At the same time, they were acutely aware of the peninsular denigration such as Acosta's that considered the American environment a cause for degeneration. In addition to being vehicles for the transmission of Mesoamerican knowledge, their works can also be read as efforts to define what it meant to be "Spanish" while living far away from Spain, amid a majority of non-Spaniards. Tobacco and chocolate lay at the seams of these sometimes overlapping, sometimes clashing influences and anxieties. This explains why Cárdenas devoted a chapter to "declaring in particular the properties and qualities of *piciete* and how to use its smoke" and assured his readers they would soon understand his reasons for "lingering over the qualities and effects of cacao and chocolate,"[19] and why Barrios wrote the first book devoted solely to chocolate. For these physicians, defending tobacco and chocolate became tantamount to defending creole identity. They were paradigmatic of substances that had crossed over from Indian to creole society but not yet Spanish society, making them potential agents of both reverse acculturation and targets of peninsular scorn.

In part Cárdenas wrote to chastise fellow colonists who struck him as dangerously undiscriminating in their adoption of the customs of the natives of the land. He worried about marking the line between Creoles and Indians. The need for this demarcation is demonstrated by his concern about Spaniards' recourse to Indian healers. He complained of

> listen[ing] every day to 2,000 tales and so many other stories, fables, and nonsense concerning those who cast spells, or another who expelled a bag of worms because of a potion or *patle* they gave, and this business does not stop here but they want you to believe that there are herbs, powders, and roots that have properties to make two people fall in love, or hate each other . . . and not only are the ignorant multitude [*vulgo*] persuaded to believe this but also to believe and imagine (mostly barbarous and stupid people) that herbs and potions can be taken that predict the future (a matter reserved only for God).[20]

Like his creole contemporaries, Cárdenas fretted that the "multitudes" (Indian, black, and whites) believed in the theories of non-Spanish healers and consumed their mind-altering "potions." The shadowy characters to whom Cárdenas alluded—those who dispensed cures to the "multitudes"—included "a certain black slave" and "these Indians who are great dissimulators and clamorers."[21] This phenomenon disturbed the doctor for several reasons. First, it contradicted what he considered to be infallible scientific and theological truths concerning the boundaries between the natural and supernatural. Second, it disrupted the natural social order, since it made those at the bottom of the social echelon—black slaves and Indians—into sought-out authorities and it blurred the lines between different groups who were linked as clients of the potion pushers. Finally, it indicated that pagan "idolatry" persisted after years of evangelical efforts.

But Cárdenas, as well as Barrios, also sought to bolster Creoles' status in the face of mainland derision, as well as harnessing it before it ran wild into Indian territory. Cárdenas rejected the idea of innate American inferiority advanced by his condescending peninsular contemporaries and repudiated unflattering stereotypes that circulated about the "properties and qualities of the men and animals born in the Indies." Cárdenas, like other "creole patriots," did not so much reject the environmental explanation as invert it to claim creole superiority, rather than inferiority. He declared that it was "an absolutely certain and infallible conclusion that all of those born in the Indies were much longer-living than those of Spain." Not only did Spanish in the Indies last longer but they also spoke better than their Spanish-born siblings. He insisted that "all those born in the Indies were possessed with sharp, sensitive, and agile wits," more so than those of the Old World.[22]

In particular, the physicians flinched before the criticisms of chocolate that emanated from Iberia. Cárdenas complained, for instance, about "those doctors in Spain, without understanding and inquiring what it is condemn everything about it." (These same doctors may have sponsored the unfriendly attitudes toward a spice commonly added to chocolate; Cárdenas similarly lamented the "claim that achiote is a bad and suspicious spice for this drink.")[23] Though Barrios could speak of the "many aficionados of this valuable beverage," he shared with Cárdenas a defensiveness toward critics of chocolate. He was irked by "those in my profession who, without having given the sufficient study demanded by such a grave matter, condemn and prohibit" chocolate.[24] Barrios singled out "Father Acosta" (José de Acosta) for irresponsibly and ignorantly imputing to cacao "malice."[25]

Cárdenas posed the problem presented by chocolate, revealing that it caused consternation, not just for himself but for many of his compatriots. "Everyone," he complained, has "his own opinion" about the "harms and benefits" of the beverage:

Some despise chocolate, considering it the inventor of numerous sicknesses; others say that there is nothing comparable in the world, that it fattens, elicits appetite, imbues the face with good color, makes the sterile woman pregnant, and [drunk with *atole*] makes the new mother overflow with milk; so there is no one who does not present their judgment to the populace.[26]

While unhappy with those who "despised" and "condemned" chocolate, the physicians also worried about those who used it indiscriminatingly. Cárdenas particularly identified women as guilty of improper chocolate consumption practices—"for using [cacao] that is very worm-eaten and decayed"[27] and accused "women and ladies of the Indies, particularly in New Spain, of eating earth and cacao . . . many doing it purely out of vice, completely insisting that by doing this they restore lost color."[28] This habit, Cárdenas wrote, led to "bloating, obstructions, coldness, and the abundance of thick humors in the womb that are the cause of the terrible pains that come during the period," which afflicted "the women of the Indies more commonly than those of other provinces." Though highlighting the popular controversy surrounding chocolate's health effects, the medical here is also an idiom for social issues that it presents. The disarray in opinion (that just as some were in love with its salubrious effects, others distrusted chocolate and considered it damaging) was dangerous because it damaged the facade of a single-minded authority before the "multitude."

For Cárdenas the solution to these excesses and abuses was to promote proper use according to European medical principles in the classical tradition. He wrote, "Only the divine Hippocrates can deliver us from this confusion with that much-cited sentence that says: 'Not all for everything, but each thing for what it is,' which is a way of saying that we do not want to give one single thing to all subjects, to all complexions, to all illnesses."[29] While even more indebted to the Mesoamerican milieu for his knowledge about the use of these substances, Cárdenas went further than either Monardes or Hernández in using the Galenist humoral framework to prescribe proper use of the "Indian and appetizing" drink as "so important and necessary for the health of man in the Indies, if one knows how to use it appropriately." Following Galenist principles, he matched different types of chocolate preparations to individuals' humoral needs based on temperament, age, hour, and geography. The dilemma articulated by Cárdenas and the solution he proposed thus encapsulated the issues that propelled his whole book—defending and controlling the acculturation of Europeans in the Indies. Like Monardes he offered himself as a valve that could open up useful information about New World resources while obstructing the flow of wrong-headed beliefs and practices by demystifying and revealing their impotence. His tools were European erudition based on classical authorities.

Invoking European ideas about proper consumption could quell oblique anxieties that, in smoking tobacco or drinking chocolate, Europeans blindly imitated Indians.[30]

Though responding to the same pressures as Cárdenas, Barrios pursued a different strategy for defending not only chocolate but creole identity; unlike Cárdenas but in line with Hernández, he made a virtue of chocolate's Indian past. Barrios argued that "it is necessary first to observe that this drink Chocolate is *not new* but rather very ancient among the natives of this New Spain. And it was brought from the province of Guatemala, where it had its beginning and origins and where it was first used, and there it was always very common."[31] Barrios's tactic suggests that he viewed novelty as the most persuasive argument deployed by chocolate's deriders, so the best response was to challenge that premise by demonstrating that chocolate had deep roots in the Americas, that its origins and long use among Indians bespoke desirable effects. In linking the history of chocolate to the history of Mayans and Nahuas, his favorable view of chocolate attached itself to the people who developed it.

> And it is important to note that as all regions have their particular drinks, made of those things that their regions produce, so Flanders and Viscaya have cider, and Asia and China have coconut wine, and the Mexicans have Pulque and other varieties of wine. The province of Guatemala is the same way—from their Cacaos are made various drinks that are so good and healthful, that they have not stayed within the limits of their province. Rather, with others seeing the benefits of such a drink, little by little [these drinks] spread. So this drink has conquered the entire kingdom, which exports Cacao from Guatemala, where it is grown, which is no small argument for its goodness, the way that our wine runs all over the world. And from Spain cacao is taken to other regions where it is not grown. This is what has happened with Sir Chocolate, so that those in Spain are no longer content with their wine.[32]

Though somewhat reminiscent of Monardes's urge to analyze native Americans' tobacco in the context of psychotropics used by other "barbarians," Barrios compared Guatemalans and Mexicans to European societies via a juxtaposition of their beverages. Chocolate's imperialism even suggested that the Mesoamerican cultures surpassed those of Europe (though he also claimed that the Spanish conquerors had improved on the pre-Columbian concoctions with the additions of new ingredients).[33] Barrios's manner of celebrating chocolate as quintessentially native American was a far stretch from Cárdenas's defense that bound chocolate most tightly to Hippocrates and Galen.

Tobacco remained a knottier problem. Cárdenas did not try to hide the fact that it was "from the natives of this land whom blacks, many Spaniards, and even women had learned" to take "*piciete*, the strangest kind of medicine among all medical arts." He acknowledged that "many contend—mostly Indians, blacks, and ignorant and stupid people" that if they consumed "*peyot, poyomate* [possibly *Quararibea funebris*], *hololisque* [morning glory, *Rivea corymbosa*], and even *piciete* . . . the devil appears before them and tells them their future."[34] He mused that when "I put myself to speculating who was the inventor of sucking on this smoke of *piciete* . . . I suspect that it was either some angel or some devil." On the one hand, tobacco "liberates us from so many illnesses that it truly appears to be the medicine of angels." On the other hand, Cárdenas conceded, "it appears to be a remedy of devils . . . because when we begin to look at what one is sucking, we see emitting from the mouth and nose blasts of awful, foul smoke that appears like a volcano or the mouth of hell."[35] Addressing this issue in the last chapter of *Problemas y secretos maravillosos de las Indias*, he imported the solution of Monardes—as always, without attribution—and maintained that it was erroneous to ascribe magical properties to herbs; rather "in nature there is nothing more than medicine that heals, poison that kills, or food that sustains."[36] And, like Monardes, he sought to depict tobacco as thoroughly therapeutic if used correctly, singling it out for alleviating pain and treating "illnesses caused by coldness" and excessive phlegm, such as tooth infections, asthma, cholera, and stomach pains. Answering his own question about whether it was invented by an angel or devil, the creole physician offered that it was of "no matter who invented it," what mattered was that "knowing how to use it well" made it a "remedy from heaven" and if used "without order or measure or distretion" then it was "dangerous, pernicious, and pestilential."[37] For Cárdenas, the efforts of European medical and theological authorities to draw clear boundaries between the natural and supernatural had a particular salience with respect to the preoccupations of his own colonial, pluralistic society.

The representations of Cárdenas and Barrios of tobacco and chocolate emerged from a moment in which there was a dawning realization about the porousness of "Spanish" culture and the ascendance of mestizo forms of culture. Cárdenas's insistence on a European framework for his beloved chocolate stemmed from his desire to distance himself from these syncretic forms that he, and many others in his position, found so discomfiting even as they (literally) incorporated them.

Cárdenas and Barrios articulated anxieties about the implications tobacco and chocolate had for colonial identities but hardly dissolved them. Concern about persistent or revitalized paganism among Amerindian and European subjects alike led to prosecutions for heresy and idolatry extirpation campaigns in the late sixteenth and seventeenth centuries in Spanish America. There was, of course, Baltasar de Herrera, the cleric who confronted chocolate-laden idolatry in the Yucatán town of Petú in the last years of the sixteenth century. Another extirpator in the Yucatán, Sánchez de Aguilar, reported that "in this city of Mérida . . . Indian women put certain spells in chocolate that bewitch their husbands."[38] The Spanish were attuned and often concerned about Mesoamericans' use of chocolate as a magical potion to mend disaffections. And Hernando Ruiz de Alarcón devoted the second chapter of his *Tratado de las supersticiones y costumbres gentilicas* (Treatise on the Heathen Superstitions and Customs) to "the idolatry and abuses and observations of things to which are attributed divinity, especially *ololiuhqui, piciete* [tobacco], and peyote." With his fluency in Nahuatl and obsessive personality, Ruiz de Alarcón found vestiges of heathendom lurking wherever tobacco appeared, in quotidian as well as special occasions: in the rites used by midwives to deliver babies, doctors to cure illness, farmers to rid growing fields of anthills, theft victims to recover stolen goods, fishermen and hunters to catch fish and birds, woodcutters to fell trees, travelers for protection on long journeys, and householders to ward off misfortune from newly constructed houses. In all of these, he always found tobacco, omnipresent, as he put it, like "the little dog at weddings."[39]

Meanwhile, the Inquisition targeted blacks, mestizos, and Creoles suspected of heretical behavior.[40] The idolatry investigator Jacinto de la Serna wrote that "it is worthy to note that blacks, mulattos, and some Spaniards, having left the hand of God . . . search out Indians to whom they pay" for services with various drugs.[41] The prominence of tobacco and chocolate indicates that authorities tied these substances to "superstitious" rites that had contaminated the larger creole population. For instance, in Tlaxcala a creole woman, Juana de Sossa, used chocolate to ensure success in her carnal pursuits. When she wanted to have sex with either Francisco Sanchez Cortés, a butcher's apprentice, or another man named Nicolás Cavallero, Sossa would ply them with specially doctored chocolate, according to the denunciation of the jealous daughter of the butcher's apprentice. The "famous sorceress" María de Rivera, a mulatta in Puebla, to ensure that one of her paying customers would capture the affection of a man, instructed her client to grind cacao in the *metate* and add "certain powders and give the said chocolate to the said man to drink."[42] The roster of cases of "superstition" or even "sorcery" brought before the Inquisition in the seventeenth century that involved women of all ethnicities doctoring chocolate in order to rein in philandering husbands or induce crushes to requite their love is lengthy.[43]

THE clash of paradigms that vexed seventeenth-century Spaniards' understanding of tobacco and chocolate did not stay confined to the New World. Published in 1618, not only was the *Diálogo del uso de tabaco, los daños*

que cause, etc. y de chocolate y otras bebidas (Dialogue concerning the use of tobacco, chocolate, and other beverages and the harms they cause) the first publication about these goods directed at consumers in both the Old World and the New World, but it also was the first to explicitly unite these transcultural substances as similarly problematic.[44] Taking the form of an imaginary conversation between a "Physician," an "Indian," and a "Townsman," the treatise dramatized the collision between medical and idolatrous frameworks. The treatise reflected tobacco and chocolate's changing status from strictly Indian and creole goods to ones with a detectable European following. Its author, Bartolomé Marradón, a native of Andalusia and a medical professional (either a physician or apothecarist), exemplified the kind of person who would have been in the vanguard of tobacco and chocolate users in the metropole; he traveled to the Indies—New Spain, Guatemala, or perhaps both—several times and had family who sojourned or even migrated there (his son-in-law and perhaps daughter as well).[45]

In introducing the Physician personage and giving him as his first words the declaration that chocolate "is considered medicinal" and that "it is fitting to learn of its properties," Marradón deployed the medical framework refined by his sixteenth-century predecessors. Despite his misgivings, the Physician acknowledges that a "doctor of name and reputation" "found benefit in the composition of this beverage." The information voiced by the interlocutors concerning the natural history, humoral properties, therapeutic benefits, and adverse consequences of misusing cacao and chocolate reveal that their creator had read and synthesized the works of Francisco Hernández and Juan de Cárdenas, as well as those of Girolamo Benzoni and José de Acosta.[46] Without naming Cárdenas, Marradón's Physician then renders (and somewhat distorts) the Mexican physician's opinion of the humoral properties of cacao and his advice concerning its preparation.[47] Later in the conversation, the Physician delineates the varieties of cacao-based beverages that match almost exactly those described by Cárdenas.[48]

Yet the conversation then moves away from medicine and natural history to anecdotes concerning chocolate's culpability in sacrilege and sorcery, reflecting its Indians origins and revealing the insufficiency of the medical paradigm. Marradón demonstrates that chocolate had infiltrated Christianity's holiest sacrament, the "divine office" of Communion. The Indian conversant recounts how he witnessed a Spanish priest—who was supposed to be proselytizing to Indians—so dependent on chocolate that he was compelled to interrupt his Mass to guzzle chocolate: "I once saw in a port town, where we disembarked to purify water, a priest saying Mass who was obliged by necessity—being exhausted—to sit on a bench and drink a *tecomate* full of chocolate, and then God gave him the energy to complete the Mass."[49] In addition to this unseemly trespass, the Townsman notes that clerics had taken to drinking chocolate inside churches, a practice that quickly migrated from the New World to the Old World. The suggestion here was not only that clerics' dependence on chocolate violated the sanctity of a holy ritual and hallowed spaces but that chocolate competed with the consecrated wafer and wine as a source of divine power.

The last words of the "Dialogue," which belonged to the Indian, made explicit chocolate's connection not only to Indian culture but to diabolic sorcery, mediated by women, both Indian and Spanish.

> But in terms of the way that Ladies have used this beverage, it has given them the occasion to avenge their jealousies, learning and making use for themselves the sorcery of the Indian women who are the great Instructors, as they have been shown by the Devil: it is why wise people should avoid the company of Indian women, if only for the suspicion of sorcery, and I will not dare to say, in order not to scandalize anyone, the number of deaths and homicides that came about by this sole means, according to a Priest in the Company of Jesus, who preached in a church in Mexico City: so that if only for this, without taking into account the other objections, it would be very good to abstain from chocolate, in order to avoid familiarity and the company of a people so suspect of Sorcery.[50]

This passage draws a striking set of relationships: the devil teaches Indian women; Indian women deploy their diabolical knowledge through chocolate; finding common cause with "Indians" in their female deviousness, Spanish women learn how to bewitch and poison with chocolate from their Indian counterparts. The Indian, not averse to self-implication, ends his warning by advising that total abstinence may be the best relation to have with chocolate, since its Indian origins are part of its essence and diabolic enchantment goes hand in hand with Indian practices. Through his fictional dialogue, Marradón captured exactly the underlying worries afflicting creole—and now metropolitan—elites about the tenuousness of Spanish identity in the New World, and the fragility of Christian orthodoxy in the face of potent American goods: Could they be used without implicating a person in native idolatry? Marradón's "fictitious" Indian women of the marketplace who apprenticed Spanish and mixed-race women into magical uses of chocolate had their real-life counterparts in the women prosecuted by the Inquisition in New Spain and Guatemala. In committing such depictions to print, Marradón ensured that such associations would arrive and endure in Europe beyond the original context. He underscored the ironies inherent in Spanish adoption of Indian habits in a world where ostensibly they were sowers of civilization, not the apprentices to Indian culture.

7

Commodifying across
the Atlantic

❖ ❖

Herbals and fleeting asides in lawsuits attest to the fact that tobacco and chocolate infiltrated Europe in the belongings of returned colonists and scruffy sailors, in the gardens of botanical collectors, and in the arsenal of more adventurous healers. But documents' silence can reveal as much as their noise. For most of the sixteenth century neither tobacco nor chocolate appeared as systematic imports, not registered in trade records in even modest quantities. Nor do they figure in a collection of letters between correspondents in Iberia and Latin America (though several mention sarsaparilla, indigo, and *mechoacan*).[1] For almost a century after Columbus's first voyages, tobacco and chocolate in Europe remained foreign oddities, accoutrements to the strange behaviors acquired by *indianos* or *peruleros*—as were nicknamed New World returnees—from their experiences among savages in Americas, despite Monardes's promotion, in the case of tobacco, of it as a miraculous panacea. In the collective imagination of Europeans, even those who were among the aficionados, tobacco and chocolate still belonged to the Americas. An Atlantic trading infrastructure was in place by the early sixteenth century for the importation of exotic medicaments as well as precious metals, dyes, and other American staples. Such an infrastructure could have accommodated these goods but did not. This all changed at the end of the century.

The period between 1590 and 1610 corresponds to the transitional period in which both tobacco and chocolate went from having a negligible presence in Iberia to having a firm social and commercial foothold on the peninsula. In order to find evidence of a moment or period in which a

discernable market for tobacco and chocolate appeared, I relied on the research of Huguette and Pierre Chaunu and searched through lists of
shipping cargo maintained for a tax (*avería*) on goods shipped across the
Atlantic.[2] My search yielded 1591 and 1598 as the first years in which
chocolate or cacao and tobacco imports were, respectively, registered.[3] It
should be kept in mind that earlier shipments could have escaped notice if
they were generically declared to be "things of the Indies." Others are hidden from our view because passengers and sailors were allowed a certain
quantity of personal goods that did not require registration. So the significance of these records is not that they prove that these were in fact the first
years the goods were imported—that was definitely not the case as previously seen—but rather they mark, more or less, the beginning of a period
in which trade officials would no longer let them pass as oddities but rather
were compelled to register them as regular imports. The figures yielded by
these records do not reflect the actual quantities of goods entering Spain,
since some lists are incomplete, others are lost, and it is well known that
fraud was endemic; it is safe to assume these figures grossly underestimate
imports. Nonetheless, the data gleaned from these cargo lists are useful as
indicators for the timing and patterns of market growth. Whereas in the
1590s, a handful of individuals were arranging for modest shipments (one
hundred pounds or less), by the 1620s large buyers purchased thousands of
pounds of cacao, and ships returned from Venezuela filled entirely with
tobacco (tables 7.1 and 7.2).

The timing of tobacco and chocolate's systemic entrance into European
markets is one of the main planks *against* the story that is so often told
about their integration into Europe: that the inhabitants of Old World societies first accepted tobacco and chocolate as medicines and later learned
to appreciate them as recreational substances.[4] In general Spaniards were
quick to embrace New World substances that purported to heal; since the
Middle Ages Europeans believed that exotic realms—first the East, now
the Americas—were home to miraculous medicaments, and humanist skepticism of medicines of foreign provenance did little to interfere with actual
importations. The time lag of tobacco and chocolate's entrance is even
more striking if one considers that a number of New World substances had
made a significant entry into Old World pharmacopoeia from the earliest
days of colonization. A sampling of apothecary inventories show a variety
of American materia medica—*mechoacan*, sarsaparilla, and *Cassia fistula*
above all—as a standard part of Iberian apothecaries in the late sixteenth
and seventeenth centuries, but, with one exception, tobacco and chocolate
do not appear.[5]

Other kinds of evidence do suggest that tobacco was used medicinally,
but, consistent with the main thrust of Monardes's recommendations, it

TABLE 7.1. Recorded Tobacco Imports into
Seville, 1598–1613 (in pounds)

Year	Norton	Chaunu and Chaunu
1598	2,675	
1602	14,127	
1608	70,065	
1609		15,010
1610		63,410
1611		183,526
1612		327,218
1613		404,554

Sources: Huguette Chaunu and Pierre Chaunu,
Séville et l'Atlantique, 1504–1650, (Paris:
S.E.V.P.E.N), vol. 6, bk. 2: 1033. Their figures are
based on the "Relación del tabaco que ha venido
de diferentes partes de las Indias de 1609 a 1613,"
AGI Contrat., leg. 4434. My figures come from
tobacco shipments recorded in *avería* (fleet tax)
records. The extant *avería* records for 1598 listed
shipments from eight ships (AGI Contrat., legs.
2411, 2155), for 1602 sixty-one ships (ibid., legs.
4412, 4413), and for 1608 twenty-five ships (ibid.,
leg. 4424).

TABLE 7.2. Recorded Imports of Cacao and Chocolate from *Avería* Records, 1595–1635

Year	Number of ships tallied	Number of ships tallied with cacao or chocolate shipments	Pounds of chocolate and cacao
1595	14	4	250
1602	32	9	990
1608	6	4	545
1625	8	5	1730
1634–35	16	16	12348

Sources: AGI Contrat., legs. 4389, 4412, 4413, 4424, 4452, 4462. The figures for pounds
are rough estimates: oftentimes the data referred to one or several *cajones* (boxes) rather than
specifying pounds. Based on known conversion factors and other evidence (such as price when
available), I estimated a *cajón* at one hundred pounds, but in fact they could vary between fifty
and two hundred pounds.

was mainly as a topical treatment that relied on homegrown green tobacco,
not the dried, cured varieties shipped from the Indies. A 1592 Spanish
manual for apothecarists attested that tobacco "is nowadays contained in
gardens throughout all of these kingdoms," and featured it prominently in
its chapter on "unguents." It was lauded for mitigating pain and eliminating scrofulous matter and commended as a medicine "for the benefit of the
poor."[6] Since the tobacco intended for topical uses came from fresh uncured

plants, it was not that which arrived in Spain from the Indies, for that "instead of having green leaves . . . is of a putrefying color."[7] In other words, Europeans' demand for imported tobacco to snuff, smoke, or chew did not flow from their use of tobacco cultivated in garden plots to make into plasters and unguents. What then explains the relative delay of tobacco and chocolate's integration into European markets and their astounding popularity after the initial takeoff, one that far surpassed the demand of any other American "medicine"?

On the demand side, the creation of a nascent market for tobacco and chocolate in Spain was predicated on the existence of a critical mass of consumers who associated as a community, who, in socializing together with the goods, deepened the grooves of habituation by reinforcing and legitimating one another's consumption. On the supply side, cacao was already a commodity produced for colonial consumers and there already existed an infrastructure for Atlantic trade; so once there was perception of demand, little adjustment was needed to turn it into a staple of the transatlantic trade. However, tobacco did not become a long-distance, much less transatlantic, commodity until the end of the sixteenth century, and its commodification was the result of burgeoning European demand and transformations in the political economy of the Caribbean involving the interplay of Indian, Spanish, Portuguese, Dutch, English, and French parties.

One way to understand the reasons when and why these distinctly American goods entered the Atlantic trade is to investigate the individuals involved in this transformation. In 1591 Pedro de Mendoza arranged for one hundred pounds of cacao to be shipped from Guatemala via the port in Honduras.[8] Four years later he shipped another crate of cacao, along with a dozen Mesoamerican chocolate-drinking vessels—lacquered gourds ("*xícaras* of Mechoacan") and a ceramic *tecomate* embedded with amethysts.[9] A resident of a prestigious neighborhood in Seville, Mendoza belonged to a select coterie of merchants who trafficked in massive quantities of the most valuable commodities of the Indies—bullion (silver and gold) and dye goods (red-hued *cochineal* and blue indigo).[10] He had contacts and agents in Guatemala and New Spain. By 1596 he had amassed over four million *maravedís*, making him one "one of the wealthiest Indies traders."[11]

Ambrosio de Sofia—one of the first names to appear as a tobacco shipper—was also enmeshed in an Atlantic network, but one quite distinct from that of Mendoza. Where Mendoza's trade route connected Seville to Mesoamerica, Sofia's connected to the Caribbean. In 1602 he returned from Santo Domingo with 300 sheaves of tobacco (between 300 and 450 pounds), a modest shipment, even in comparison with his other cargo—1,100 cowhides and 800 pounds of guaiac wood, favored for treating syphilis.[12] While Mendoza was at the apex of Seville's merchant oligarchy, Sofia was on the fringes of the established mercantile community: he was a foreigner (a native of Genoa), and in 1607 trade authorities busted him for illegal activity. According to the suit, he was guilty of sailing directly between Santo Domingo and Veracruz without permission, smuggling goods into Spain by shipping them offshore of Cadiz, and bringing foreign passengers without licenses. (Many merchants were involved in different forms of contraband and fraud, but those better connected, such as men like Mendoza, tended to avoid prosecution.) Details of the case link Sofia to a Portuguese Atlantic commercial network: the prosecutor alleged that "without having licence nor permission he brought in his ship the passengers Antonio de Silva and many other Portuguese." Silva had arrived in the Caribbean via Angola—part of the semilegal slave trade—and Sofia's ship also carried Miguel Rodrigo, a Portuguese resident of Caracas, a center of burgeoning tobacco cultivation.[13]

The nodes of Mendoza's Atlantic circuit were a privileged ambit in Seville and the centers of Spain's mercantile empire centered in New Spain (Mexico City and the port of Veracruz), while the nodes of Sofia's were the plebeian quarters of lower-class mariners in Seville and the Caribbean, particularly the lawless outskirts of its eastern regions. Mendoza's orbit was closely tied to Spanish officialdom and effectively protected from foreign, and even domestic, competitors, while Sofia's Atlantic was multinational, like Sofia himself, engaging English, Dutch, French, Portuguese, and Amerindians who flouted Spain's monopoly, with the complicity and collusion of local Spanish officials and settlers in places like Trinidad, Caracas, and Maracaibo. The entrance of tobacco and chocolate into European markets flowed through both circuits.

THE ELITE SPANISH ATLANTIC

The community in which Mendoza belonged was that of elite Andalusia, comprising wealthy merchants, municipal oligarchs, professionals, clergy, and aristocrats, all of whom shared in direct and indirect connections to Spanish America. Wealthy merchants such as Mendoza, who appear in shipping tax records as the earliest and most frequent buyers of chocolate, were perhaps the most important subset of this community in accounting for the creation of a Spanish market for the Mesoamerican beverage. Other precocious purchasers of chocolate included Antonio de Armijo in 1601, described as "one of the most powerful Sevillan merchants" at the end of the sixteenth century.[14] One who shipped three boxes of chocolate in 1625 was, in the words of a contemporary, of the "men who are already rich and no longer trade with the Indies but rather are retired and watch the bull fights from very high up and of those are Rodrigo de Vadillo who brings fifty thousand ducats into the city purely on interest and with other kinds of gains."[15] Among this cohort some also shipped tobacco, such as Jorge Reynoso and Francisco Marroquí, who registered shipments from Havana and Santo Domingo, respectively.[16]

This prosperous and powerful clique controlled the *consulado*—the merchant guild that sought to ensure their members' monopoly of the Indies trade.[17] In this capacity, they appointed one another to farm the import taxes, which both was another source of enrichment and no doubt facilitated their efforts to restrict fraudulent trading to themselves.[18] It stands to reason that the caste of elite merchants would be on the forefront of tobacco and chocolate consumers as they were in some sense culturally creole, having spent significant time in the Indies and in contact with their factors who resided there.[19] This is corroborated by a recent study that found merchants and clergy ranked first among groups who crossed the Atlantic in both directions most frequently.[20]

Clergy, who vied with merchants as the subgroup making the greatest number of transatlantic trips, likewise appear among the vanguard of tobacco and chocolate consumers in shipping records.[21] Church canons appear as plaintiffs in some of the earliest lawsuits (1612) concerning tobacco shipments gone awry.[22] A lawsuit brought against a ship's captain by a Jesuit in Seville for lost containers of chocolate illustrates how the Church's transatlantic—or rather global—network also facilitated the diffusion of these American habits.[23] Father Andrés Gonzáles, rector of the Jesuit house in Veracruz arranged a shipment of chocolate (five boxes), cacao (two *petacas* and one box), and the chocolate spices *orejuelas* ("a bundle") and *mecasuchil* ("a chest") "in the name of Hernando Toribio Gómez, *procurador general* of the said order in New Spain," to reach Father Fabian López, the *procurador general* of the "company of Jesus of the West Indies." López was the designated recipient, perhaps because the *procurador* (representative of a religious order) was generally in charge of disbursing the chocolate as diplomatic gifts, but one box was designated to "brother Antonio Robles of the Company of Jesus who lives in Rome," and a "box, smaller, for our *padre general*." López's duties appear to have included arranging for American shipments of chocolate, since he also appears as buyer for twenty boxes of chocolate that same year in the fleet tax records.[24] The reminiscences of the former friar Thomas Gage illustrate how chocolate came to grease the wheels of the Church hierarchy. Clerics who adopted the habit in the Americas transported it to Europe. Gage explained that when *procuradores* from the Americas attended the general meeting of their order in Europe, they made sure to "carry with them great wealth, and gifts to the Generalls, to the Popes and Cardinals and Nobles in Spain, as bribes to facilitate whatsoever just or unjust, right or wrong they are to demand." Among these "gifts" were "a little wedge of Gold, a box of Pearls, some Rubies or Diamonds, a Chest of Cochineal, or Sugar, with some boxes of curious Chocolate, or some feather works of Mechoacan."[25]

Titled aristocrats, families of local and colonial officials, and professionals filled out the ranks of the Sevillan elite. The fleet tax records of 1595 indicate that the Marqués of Villamanrique purchased a set of chocolate drinking vessels—fourteen *"xicaras de mechoacan"* in 1595.[26] In 1615 a shipment of five "boxes of chocolate and gifts" were registered to the Marqués de Salinas, perhaps a prototypical chocolate disseminator among the aristocracy, as he was the son of a Mexican viceroy.[27] Shipping tax records from 1598 show a municipal notary receiving one hundred pounds of tobacco from a relative in Hispaniola, a councilman in Santo Domingo sending some of the stuff to associates in Seville, and Doctor Juan Quesada de Figueroa, a councilor on the highest legislative and judicial institution in the Americas (the Real Audiencia), registering sixty pounds for "the provisionment of his household" in Spain.[28] This roster of buyers represents the vanguard of European tobacco and chocolate consumers. They were bound together by the common experience of residing on both sides of the ocean—in the New World immersed in the thoroughly mestizo culture of Creoles, which they could not and did not completely leave behind when they returned to the Old World.

These buyers belonged to overlapping and interlocking communities within Spain that allowed them to reinforce their mestizo habits. For instance, as was common among the merchant class of early modern Europe, the elite traders sought to consolidate their wealth and improve their status by marrying and buying membership within the nobility. They set up entailed landed estates known as *mayorazgos* for their heirs. They became part of Seville's ruling oligarchy, serving as council members and mayor. In other words, they were connected and married to other elite networks of Spanish society. Their connections included the aristocratic grandees and links to the royal court itself.[29] A lawsuit will reveal how chocolate lubricated social relations among different groups of elite Andalusia. In 1633 the treasurer of the Casa de Contratación, Diego Jiménez de Enciso, made a gift of seventy-five pounds of chocolate to the Marquesa of Alcanizas. When the ship captain failed to turn in the shipment, the treasurer sued the captain for the waylaid chocolate gift, only to discover it had been destroyed by seeping salt water. (The incident led to the captain's imprisonment, suggesting the gravity of diverted chocolate presents.)[30] The importance of communities of consumers—rather than solitary consumers—helps to explain why a Spanish market for tobacco and chocolate did not exist before the late sixteenth century, even though there is evidence of assorted *individuals* consuming both goods in Europe during the earlier period.

Even though merchants were among the first to import chocolate, they did so more in the capacity of consumers than as sellers. Merchants such as Mendoza trafficked in massive quantities of bullion and dye goods, so the single entry for a box of cacao jumps out on the ledger as an anomaly.[31] All of the initial imports of chocolate and tobacco were modest: in 1595 each shipment of chocolate contained a maximum of fifty pounds, an amount that would supply a household of regular consumers and their guests for no more than a few months.[32] And they were often accompanied by no more than four or eight *jícaras*, suggesting again the anticipation of a restricted number of consumers.[33] Similarly, the shipments of tobacco in 1598 seem intended for the personal consumption of the consignees rather than for sale to a broader market. Here too the quantities were parsimonious and there was the atypical explication next to the colonial official Figueroa's entry that the shipment was for his "provisionment of his household." As telling is the cargo arranged in 1612 by the Carmona brothers, prominent merchants, who included among a ship full of indigo two chests of tobacco.[34] Even taking into account the high probability of underreporting, imports of tobacco and chocolate were insignificant in comparison with the quantities and value of other goods they imported. As Mendoza, the Carmonas, and their associates were perched on the top tier of the merchant echelon with large quantities of capital and Atlantic connections at their disposal, economic constraints do not explain their slowness to import more chocolate. The personal rather than entrepreneurial interest in the goods likely reflected the merchants' culturally bound categorizations that parceled tobacco and chocolate into the category of *indiano* habits, not commodities that would interest a broader market. By the second decade of the seventeenth century, members of the merchant oligarchy shifted to actively enter the market as traders as well as consumers. Chocolate and cacao could be easily assimilated into a transatlantic mercantile system, for it was already a colonial good with an extensive trading infrastructure in colonial Mesoamerica; so, while assimilating chocolate into Europe-bound cargo required a conceptual shift, logistically it was only a tiny step.[35] Tobacco is another story.

COMMODIFYING TOBACCO IN THE
MULTINATIONAL CARIBBEAN

Tobacco was primarily a household, local, or—at most—regional commodity in the Americas. Unlike cacao, it did not figure in the colonial imagination as a lucrative commodity. Tobacco's entrance into the European market necessitated supply-side changes. To understand this transformation requires understanding the orbit of Ambrosio de Sofia, one that was multinational, multiethnic, and organized around the Caribbean.[36]

A number of mutually dependent circumstances led the Caribbean to become the region in which tobacco was produced for European export. The social and economic situation in the Caribbean was very different than that in Spain's prized bullion-rich colonies of New Spain and Peru, where men like Mendoza participated in the Atlantic trade. For one, in the second half of the sixteenth century it was economically depressed. Though colonists forced native subjects to extract gold from Hispaniola and to dive for pearls in the islands and mainland of the eastern Caribbean, in later decades, these treasures were exhausted; the Caribbean had become the impoverished outskirts of Spain's American empire.[37] The ports of these regions held little attraction for the ships in the Spanish fleets, because now their main products—hides and sugar—were greedy of cargo space and less profitable than the dye goods and silver offered by the mainland colonies. Nor were the Caribbean settlements inviting markets for expensive European manufactured goods, because the population, mostly slaves and poor settlers, could not afford them. Spanish settlers in the Lesser Antilles and on the coasts and islands of eastern Tierra Firme (Venezuela and Trinidad) complained that their neglect by licensed shippers threatened their ability to survive.[38] From the imperial vantage point, the Caribbean, particularly the eastern parts, not only languished economically but had been overrun by "enemy" traders and treacherous colonists. It had become a lawless backwater where Iberian settlers; traders and privateers of Dutch, English, and French provenance; runaway slaves and their descendents (*cimarrones*); and Amerindians brokered with one another for trade and survival in fragile alliances often punctuated by violence. This combination of mutually reinforcing factors—that Spanish settlers were cut off from the lucrative mainline trade, that Indian communities remained both independent and engaged in trading and diplomatic relationships with Europeans, and that Spain's European rivals established a foothold that imperial authorities could not dislodge—catalyzed a new phase in the commodification of tobacco.

Circumstantial evidence suggests that indigenous groups in the eastern Caribbean such as the Carib Kalima and Arawak Lokono of the mainland and the Island Caribs of the Lesser Antilles were the first to actively promote tobacco as an export crop; they are one of the links that connect tobacco's transformation from a household, local, or regional commodity in the Americas into a transatlantic one. These groups had successfully resisted European subjugation, in part through canny alliance building (turning the Europeans' divide-and-conquer tactics back on themselves). Their survival strategies included actively seeking trading and military alliances with Europeans; they were desirous of their metal tools and weapons, which were not only useful in themselves but facilitated trade with other native groups that had not established direct relations with the Europeans. In turn, Europeans relied on native allies for military assistance, food, and tobacco. Before there is any record of European-run tobacco plantations, Amerindians provisioned Europeans with tobacco in exchange for weapons and tools.[39] During Francis Drake's 1585–86 expedition to the West Indies (during which he sacked Santo Domingo), the crew stopped on Dominica to procure food and potable water, and also traded for tobacco with the Island Caribs.[40] In 1593 the Spanish governor of Trinidad complained "that English ships resort here very commonly . . . it was four months ago that two English ships were cruising here trading tobacco with the Indians," and two years later his lieutenant referred to "Englishmen who went there to trade for tobacco," taking natives to England to learn the language and bringing them back to further their trading and diplomatic relations.[41] A pamphlet published in England in 1615 still referred to "tobacco . . . which is brought from the coast of Guiana, from Saint Vincents, from Saint Lucia, from Dominica, and other places, where we buy all of it of the naturall people."[42] As seen, there was nothing unusual about indigenous groups supplying Europeans with tobacco in the sixteenth century; this was a phenomenon general to the Americas. But what set apart these transactions was the fact that these were groups of Indians who were simultaneously free of European rule and engaged with Europeans in market relations, both motivated to exchange commodities for which they could garner European trade goods and capable of producing those commodities without interference from exploitative *encomenderos*. These native groups in the eastern Caribbean were among the first to commodify tobacco for a transatlantic market.

Spanish settlers for most of the sixteenth century did not see tobacco as an export crop because of preconceived notions that precluded "new" commodities, the stigma attached to the Indian good, or both. But they were quick to emulate indigenous groups that cultivated tobacco to trade with Portuguese, Dutch, English, and French traders. Spain's "enemies" not only preyed on and pillaged her colonies and ships, they also established trading relationships with her settlers. Like the Amerindians, the Iberian settlers too were desperate—probably more so than their indigenous rivals—for the European manufactures offered by the "enemy" traders in return for goods like hides, sugar, *Cassia fistula*, and salt in the 1570s and 1580s.[43] In the 1590s these traders sought tobacco most of all. Sometime between 1588 and 1591, settlers in Trinidad, from Spain and

Portugal, organized free and unfree labor to cultivate tobacco; this is the earliest record so far discovered for European-initiated tobacco production.[44] Within a couple of decades tobacco plantations cropped up in Cuba, Santo Domingo, Honduras, and the Veracruz region of Mexico, but particularly proliferated along coastal Venezuela, from Caracas to Cumaná, around Maracaibo Lake and the fertile valleys of nearby Barinas. By the end of the sixteenth century somewhere between 150,000 and 200,000 pounds of tobacco came from this area alone (figure 7.1).[45] Cultivation of tobacco in northeast Brazil followed as well.[46]

Formally, the Spanish Crown pursued policies that would restrict the wealth generated by the Atlantic monopoly to itself. Accordingly, it restricted migration to Castilian subjects, established Seville as the only legal entrepot for goods coming to and from the Indies, organized the fleet system, and tried to keep navigational and other strategic information from general circulation.[47] Yet the reality, particularly in the Caribbean, was of a multinational milieu. In the last decade of the sixteenth century, the Venezuelan coast, in particular, supplied tobacco to French, Dutch, English, and Portuguese, as well as Spanish, ships.[48] The governor of Venezuela described how tobacco became incorporated into these *rescates*, as the illegal trades were known. Ships coming from the Netherlands, England, and France "search for tobacco in quantities since there are not hides, sarsaparilla, or other things that the foreigners search for in quantities in other parts of the Indies," and "they know who grows tobacco and in what amounts and where." Because "tobacco is the major trade along these coasts," declared the official, the coasts "are heavily frequented because of the great demand [for tobacco] and because [Spanish settlers] exchange it for manufactured goods that they get for much less than their sales price in Spain," since the goods came directly from their source rather than through the legal but costly route via Seville.[49] Though the governor of Venezuela who described these clandestine activities professed outrage at the treacherous conduct of desperate settlers, he and other local officials played a two-faced game. At least some, if not most, of the *rescates* were conducted with the collusion of local authorities.

If local colonial officials more than tolerated the penetration of foreigners into Spanish possessions, authorities in Santo Domingo and the metropole were outraged, and they held the growth in tobacco production and trade as largely culpable. In 1606 the Crown prohibited the cultivation of tobacco for ten years in Hispaniola, Cuba, Puerto Rico, Margarita, and the provinces of Venezuela, Cumaná, and New Andalusia (in eastern Venezuela and Guyana) after noting that "many ships of Dutch, English, and French rebels come frequently to *rescatar* tobacco of which there is an abundance for being the principal product these settlers have because of the

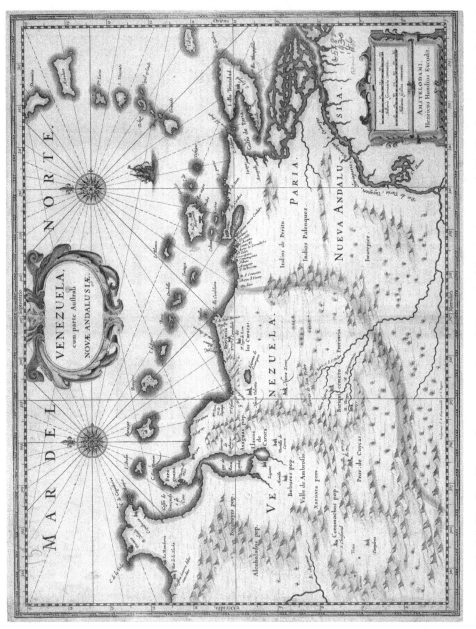

Figure 7.1. Hendrik Hondius, *Venezuela, cum parte Australi Novae Andalusiae* (n.p., 1630). The Dutch cartographer depicted the northern coasts of South America, which were already important producers of both tobacco and cacao. Though nominally under Spanish control, the Dutch used their base in Curaçao to trade with Spanish colonists and imported a majority of the region's

profit they derive from it being greatly esteemed and sought by the said nations." Furthermore, the Council of Indies—viewing the colonists in regions such as Cumanagotos (Venezuela) and the Islas de Barlovento as unwilling to desist from smuggling with foreign traders—proposed the evacuation and depopulation of those recalcitrant settlements.[50] The pleas from settlers that the ban was destroying their livelihood ("the principal trade that these settlers had was tobacco, and since they have not been able to benefit from it all of them have become very poor and needy") testify to how important tobacco had become to the local economy.[51] Yet the prohibitions did not put an end to tobacco cultivation or to contraband.[52] For one, independent Indian groups took up the slack, stepping up production of tobacco for the expanding export markets.[53] Nor did the colonial settlers desist: for instance, it came to light in 1612 that the governor of Venezuela had an arrangement with two English traders to provision them with eight thousand pesos worth of tobacco annually.[54] Another effect was to stimulate newer (or refounded) settlements, the focus again on Trinidad and farther east in the province of Guiana, along the Orinoco.[55] To the outrage of those in settlements complying with the tobacco ban edicts, Spanish authorities in Port of Prince (Trinidad) and the hamlet of San Tomé (on the south bank of the Orinoco, near the confluence with the Caroni) exploited the situation, organizing tobacco trades with English and Dutch ships. At the end of 1608, the governor of Cumaná complained that "now tobacco is cleared from all these provinces except San Tomé and the island of Trinidad where Don Fernando Berrío de la Hoz is governor. They tell me, on good security, that in Trinidad a great quantity of goods is smuggled and that English and Dutch ships are never lacking there."[56] An English captain estimated that between October 1608 and March 1609— the time when sailors could sail without risk of "outrageous gustes" and "contrarie winds"—twenty ships had docked at Trinidad for tobacco. Thirty ships arrived the following season. Planters in Trinidad and Orinoco harvested about 200,000 pounds of tobacco annually during these years.[57] Heeding the cries of distress from plaintive settlers in the Caribbean, or perhaps recognizing the futility of their efforts to outlaw tobacco cultivation, the Crown rescinded the ban in 1612.[58]

As so far seen, the genesis of tobacco as a transatlantic commodity was a truly multinational, multiethnic affair, involving Amerindian and Iberian producers, and English, Dutch, and French traders, Castillian mercantilist claims notwithstanding. Yet it must be underscored that a certain group played an especially vital role in the commodification of tobacco. As suggested by Captain Sofia's network, those of "Portuguese" extraction recur in the Caribbean and Atlantic in accounts of maritime and mercantile activities.[59] The protagonism of the Portuguese nation or mercantile community in the commodification of tobacco, in particular, and in the expansion of Atlantic trade, in general, has roots in several phenomena. First of all, Portuguese merchants had been in the forefront of overseas commerce since the late Middle Ages; they were the first Europeans to trade on the west coast of Africa, where they procured gold, pepper, and, later, slaves.[60] By the middle of the sixteenth century they had successfully penetrated the Castilian Indies, as traders, mariners, settlers, and laborers. Ten percent of all ship personnel involved in the Castilian-Atlantic routes identified themselves as Portuguese, suggesting the actual number was even higher, since there must have been others who tried to "pass" as Spanish.[61] Because of their primacy in the African slave trade, Portuguese shippers were able to gain special licenses from the Spanish Crown to travel directly to the Americas with their human cargo, deployed to work in the colonial mines, and, before long, in tobacco plantations. Over time, Portuguese merchants began to specialize as importers of American goods as well. Officially, Portuguese had no more right to trade and travel in the Indies than any other non-Castilian foreigners, but cultural proximity, Spain and Portugal's unification in 1580, and the demand for overseas mercantile experience, allowed Portuguese to become a significant presence in the Caribbean. (Many Portuguese still came illegally, as Sofia's case attests, but the mere fact of being Portuguese did not implicate someone in illegal trade as did the fact of being Dutch or English.) On the island of Margarita contemporary reports declared that Portuguese settlers numbered five hundred, more than three times the Spanish population; at the turn of the century the governor of Cuba complained that the island was controlled by Portuguese traders.[62] Portuguese were well-represented among the planters in burgeoning tobacco settlements, and they assumed the role of brokers between tobacco producers and foreign shippers.[63] One of the first, if not the first, European tobacco plantations on Trinidad was established by a Portuguese, Rodrigo Manuel Nuñes Lobo; and his nephew orchestrated the Spanish-English tobacco trade farther west along the Venezuelan coast. The role of the Portuguese as intermediaries with English shippers was partly a consequence of England and Portugal having had a sustained trading relationships since the Middle Ages. Likewise, the preponderance of New Christians among the Portuguese mercantile nation allowed them connections with Jewish and *converso* communities throughout Europe, inadvertently bolstered by the expulsion of Iberian Jews that similarly helped them forge trading relations with traders from the Netherlands. Portuguese traders facilitated the involvement of the Dutch and English in tobacco smuggling. For instance, when a Dutch merchant banker began to trade in the Caribbean at the end of the sixteenth century, he hired a Portuguese to serve as master on one vessel and employed others to accompany the expedition as interpreters.[64]

And when the *rescate* trade came to a close under increasing pressure from both Spanish and English authorities, Portuguese involvement in organizing the Atlantic tobacco trade became, if anything, more important, responsible for making shipments to Lisbon and London, as well as Spain. Jorge Fernandes Gramaxo, from his base in Cartagena de Indias, brokered significant trades from Maracaibo to London.[65] The names of buyers based in Seville suggest that the Portuguese network was no less important for tobacco brought to market in through the Castilian gateway of Seville.[66]

By the 1610s, the virtual monopoly held by Portuguese shippers on tobacco trade was widely acknowledged. This realization led the Spanish Crown to dramatically change tactics, deciding it was better to collude with Portuguese traders and benefit from the trade, rather than struggle against them. In 1620 a royal decree made tobacco importation a government-administered trading monopsony.[67] The Crown commissioned the Portuguese Diego Pinelo as "factor and administrator of the Tobacco that grows and is cultivated in the maritime places of the West Indies." Pinelo and his hired agents were responsible for buying all of the tobacco grown in the region and shipping it to the Spanish mainland. Accordingly, the residents of the Indies were forbidden to sell their tobacco for export to anyone but Pinelo and his representatives, though free sale for domestic consumption was still permitted. The royal decree specified that Pinelo's ships were to collect tobacco from ports along the Caracas coast, at Maracaibo, Cumaná, Margarita, Trinidad, and San Tomé. Officials in Cuba were responsible for shipping their tobacco to Cartagena. So, on "arriving at the Puerto de la Trinidad," the decree mandated that Pinelo go "where the governor resides, who will call the *cabildo* (city council), the town citizens, laborers of that city, and other people who seed and cultivate Tobacco in that region." Informed of local prices, Pinelo was to set a price, or various prices depending on the tobacco type, and then pay local cultivators, who were to bundle the tobacco "as is customary." The decree explained that thereby "Tobacco will be collected and brought to these Kingdoms [Spain] where it will be sold to foreigners and local people, thus removing the ability of the enemy corsairs."[68] Cultivators in Cumaná protested that the prices paid by Pinelo for tobacco were too low.[69] The plan lasted no more than two years, thwarted by the opposition of the plantation growers and continued contraband.[70] Portuguese traders continued to dominate the tobacco trade, particularly in Venezuela, and the state would find another way to cooperate with them.[71]

The multinational context of the Caribbean, despite the ruptures in formal diplomatic relations between Spain, and England and the Netherlands, helps to explain why the penetration of tobacco into these Atlantic-bordering European countries was more or less simultaneous. In 1611 more than one million pounds of tobacco arrived in London from Trinidad and Venezuela, some of it arriving through legal channels via Seville and more of it illegally shipped directly from the Caribbean. Officials in England reported in 1621 that they had been importing annually almost 150,000 pounds of tobacco from Spanish colonies since 1614.[72] The Caribbean origins of the commodification of tobacco link directly to the much more well-known story of the runaway success of Britain's tobacco colonies.[73]

The experiences of English and Dutch mariners in the Spanish Caribbean gave rise to the increasing demand for tobacco in northwestern Europe in the late sixteenth century. Given the famous success of Britain's tobacco colonies, it is particularly notable that it had its origins in the experiences of English traders and privateers in Spanish America.[74] That in late sixteenth-century England "Trinidado" meant tobacco in common parlance attests to the formative role of the Spanish-controlled Caribbean. The illegal (*rescate*) trade became increasingly impossible as Spanish and British authorities cracked down on it. In the words of a contemporary Englishman, "The Spaniards have now utterly banished our Merchants, and put all to the sword, or to a more cruell death."[75] These circumstances led English explorers to grow their own. The English settlers who founded short-lived colonies in Guiana in the first decade of the seventeenth century hoped that tobacco would become an important source of wealth.[76] After the settlements in South America expired, the English raised tobacco in the recently established colonies of Barbados and Virginia. The year 1607 marks the first time that English settlers grew tobacco in Virginia, though it was another six years before the first substantial load of tobacco grown there docked in London.[77] The imprint of Caribbean experiences continued to shape the development of tobacco cultivation in British America. When English settlers tried the native tobacco (*Nicotiana rustica*) grown by local Algonquian Indians in Virginia, they deemed it unsatisfactory— weak and "of a byting taste"—and decided to cultivate the kind to which they had come accustomed, tellingly known as "Orinoco," a variety of *Nicotiana tabacum*. "Spanish Caribbean tobacco," writes historian Philip Morgan, "was the basis for the English tobacco boom, first as a trade item, then as export crop in Bermuda, and only later in Virginia and in the fledgling British Caribbean islands."[78]

PLEBEIAN ATLANTIC

Ambrosio de Sofia embodies another factor that contributed to tobacco's systematic entrance into the European market—the role of mariners in creating nascent demand among Europeans and in inaugurating the marketing of tobacco to their cohort and beyond. Contemporary observers often identified mariners as the vanguard of consumers within Europe. An elite Cordoban author, wanting to explain the origins of tobacco in Spain, asserted in 1620 that sailors and "all of the people who travel by sea" inaugurated tobacco use in Spain, and that initially tobacco was "thought of as something vile and low, and a thing of slaves and tavern drinkers, and people of low consideration."[79] (And contemporaries viewed sailors as "people of low consideration.")[80] Rather than being incidental, the plebeian character of this Atlantic circuit was fundamental to the diffusion of tobacco. In the scornful phrase of the haughty Cordoban one catches a fleeting glimpse of the plebeian maritime world, an itinerant community whose shared experiences spilled over shipboard to the docks and into sailors' neighborhoods where old companions and workmates could find one another in familiar taverns. When sailors returned to the Old World they did not simply disperse but often continued to maintain links with one another. Sailors tended to live in certain neighborhoods, such as the Triana on the other side of the Guadalaquivir River from Seville. Those who came from elsewhere to Seville often stayed in inns or hung out in taverns that catered to sailors, in the Arenal, the area between the city walls and the riverbanks.[81] Introduced to tobacco in social settings in the New World settlements, sailors found tobacco a fortifier of bonds in their peripatetic lifestyle and likely, too, found it helped ease hunger, thirst, and fatigue, adversities integral to sailors' precarious existence. Europeans appreciated these effects as much as Amerindians; a poem "in praise of tobacco" published in 1644 included the lines: "a few balls of tobacco are enough / carrying them in the mouth / stays thirst and hunger."[82] That the maritime network was black as well as white deserves emphasis. Historian Pablo E. Pérez Mallaína has documented the considerable presence of black slaves and freedmen on the Indies' fleets, noting that "on some galleons there were veritable families of slaves or ex-slaves."[83] This may help to explain why the first depiction by a European artist of someone smoking—the image accompanying the entry on tobacco in a 1571 herbal—suggests that the smoker was of African descent (figure 4.1). This, too, lends credibility to Monardes's report of black slaves in Seville smoking to escape their exhaustion.

A critical aspect of mariners as a vector for the diffusion of tobacco lies in their role as a bridge between consumers and distributors. Sailors supplemented their pathetic incomes by bringing over small quantities of goods to sell that they could claim as part of their personal cargo.[84] Such cargo does not often leave archival traces, for goods carried for personal use were exempt from trade duties and thus not registered by custom officials.[85] However, contemporaries referred to "pilots, sailors, and passengers" who, returning from the Indies, sold meagre amounts of tobacco in order to pay off their boats fares.[86] The logical next stage in this early distribution system would be for those higher up the food chain—ship captains—to import larger quantities to sell to the maritime community. Sofia may well be such a figure. The record makes clear that the ship captain registered the relatively modest amount of tobacco on his own account, not that of another merchant, which indicates that he was personally responsible for its sale. While members of the merchant elite did not yet see tobacco as a marketable good, the immersion of ship captain Sofia in the plebeian Atlantic circuit prompted him to bring home tobacco in the cargo space left over from the more conventional shipments of cowhides and guaiac wood.

Though a plebeian mariner network belonged to the Atlantic world since its inception, it expanded significantly during the years in which tobacco entered the European market, which both bolsters the hypothesis that the plebeian circuit was a major cause of this transformation and helps to explain its timing. The rapid increase in transatlantic commerce in the second half of the sixteenth century meant that mariners became a more important segment of society. During one of the peak years, in 1594, at least 150 ships sailed between Seville and the Americas. The more than 7,000 men required to crew these ventures would have been a visible presence in Seville, which had a population of about 130,000 in those years.[87] When one adds to this the increasing number of mariners participating in the Atlantic trade from European regions outside of Iberia, then it stands to reason that the increasing demographic weight of sailors in the last decades of the sixteenth century meant that they, along with the Sevillan elite, formed a critical and visible mass of tobacco consumers, from which tobacco could penetrate the customs of the rest of society.

There may be another facet to the importance of the plebeian network in the origins of its European commodification. Those of a superior rank—like the Carmona brothers who imported two chests of tobacco in their ship filled with indigo—might have felt comfortable smoking tobacco, but to traffic in it might have been beneath them, compartmentalizing tobacco as part of a *criollo* culture but not as a commodity. Once back in Europe, and ready to parlay their *indiano* wealth into courtly palaces and dowries to procure upscale marriages, were they inhibited about flaunting a practice associated with New World "savagery," which might hinder efforts to reintegrate into conservative nobility? Were men of lower status, such as Sofia and his Portuguese associates—already outsiders by virtue of their foreign provenance and less likely to infiltrate Seville's upper echelons—less constrained by such status concerns?

❖ ❖ ❖

As in their migration from Indians to Europeans, and from Creoles to *peninsulares*, the spread of tobacco and chocolate from an Iberian vanguard to a wider market hinged on their entanglement in social rites. As much as requiring a site of sociability, tobacco created one. Its suitability to the moveable feast of street life is well illustrated by a Dutch engraving, picturing a group congregating around a barrel on which pipes and smoking embers rest (figure 7.2). Almost any odd corner could become a site of tobacco diffusion—the alleyway behind the tannery, under the shade of the oak tree next to the wheat field, even the private quarters of the cathedral, any place there was a gathering of folk desirous of a respite from their labors and enjoying the company of their peers.

Taverns and inns, in particular, served as a cultural relay that contributed to the migration of the tobacco habit from being the peculiar trait of mariners' subculture to its emergence as a national pastime by the 1630s (figure 7.3).[88] One of the few surviving *Spanish* paintings that depict smokers is entitled *The Tavern*. Not only were inns and taverns places where sailors could socialize with one another and maintain a sense of community despite their profession's demands of itinerancy, but they were also

Figure 7.2. Jan van de Velde, *The Quack* (n.d.) (detail). The easy sociability inspired by tobacco is represented here. Etching and engraving. Print Collection, Miriam and Ira D. Wallach Division of Art, Prints and Photographs, the New York Public Library, Astor, Lenox and Tilden Foundations. Reproduced with permission.

Figure 7.3. *La Taberna* (seventeenth century). One of the very few paintings that exist by artists in seventeenth-century Spain that depict smoking. As the title suggests, it shows the tavern as a central place of tobacco sociability. Tobacco is depicted as producing a meditative relaxation that links the two men in quiet camaraderie. Reproduced with permission of the Museo de Pontevedra, Pontevedra, Spain.

places where people from different regions, occupations, and classes mingled (though they were frequented by lower-class men and women, social custom dictated elite women restrict their socializing to the home).[89] Such a dynamic is visible in a revealing one-act play by Luis Quiñones de Benavente (1598–165?) that provides a glimpse of the microinteractions on which the diffusion of tobacco and chocolate depended. A character remarks that "passing through hostels and inns" left one at risk of an "*indiano* abusing you, making you drink chocolate, or some dirty rogue forcing you to sneeze tobacco."[90] The stanzas portray the hostels and inns as places where drunk, convivial patrons might be induced to experiment with novelties and where individuals of different social rank caroused together, where one could find everywhere the nouveau riche *indiano* merchant, the petty thug on the other side of respectability, and everyone in between.

As suggested by the stanza above, it seems one could also find chocolate in taverns, but this seems much less common.[91] Chocolate—among the elite—belonged to the domestic space of the household. Unlike coffee, which became so identified with the "public sphere" of the coffeehouse, chocolate belonged to the private—though not individual—sphere.[92]

BEYOND THE VANGUARD: SPREADING, SEGMENTING, AND DEMOCRATIZING THE MARKET

In the years between 1590 and 1610 tobacco and chocolate established a foothold in Iberian markets. For the rest of the seventeenth and eighteenth centuries the goods crossed over from the vanguard communities linked to Atlantic networks and spread far and wide, vertically and horizontally, approaching, if not quite obtaining, the status of mass commodities. Tobacco's rapid diffusion was worthy of notice:

> *Tobacco* is so fortunate—wouldn't we all have such charm—that in the little time it has been known, it has become almost sacred, insinuating itself in noble households with subtle methods, serving them assiduously for low wages, working diligently to gain their good will (unlike the servants they hire), so it has put down roots and been granted citizenship.

Attesting to tobacco's thorough insinuation among the Andalusian elite, this same author was the one who stated that tobacco had come to Spain among "people of low consideration."[93] He was correct in that tobacco entered Spain among both elite and humble communities of the Atlantic and expanded its market from there. Writing in 1634, a *madrileño* remarked on this egalitarianism: "This herb is so used among all sorts of persons—that from the soldier to the student, from the monk to the priest, from the city-dweller to the rustic, from the plebeian to the noble, from the youth to the old man, there is hardly anyone who has not at least tried it, and even more use it habitually."[94] He thought a significant factor in its diffusion was its low cost, writing "the reason that tobacco is used so much is that it is so cheap, because with four *quartos*, or *maravedís*, an entire household can be purged." He could have noted, as well, that it did not distinguish between the sexes. As in the Americas, women, of the highest as well as the lowest social classes, were habitual consumers. A 1722 memorandum to Seville's tobacco factory managers asked for a special batch of tobacco for the queen, noting "that our Queen is *aficionada* and uses tobacco like that of the enclosed sample." The queen's request for the special shipment specified that the "color and smell" match that of the sample.[95]

Nor did chocolate discriminate by gender, it being the perfect accompaniment for same-sex and coed gatherings among the elite. Yet chocolate, in contrast to tobacco's class blindness, was a trickle-down phenomenon. A poem published in Seville in 1640 asserted that "it is brought to kings in golden *jícaras*," but by 1690 an author, considering the merits of a proposed trading monopoly on cacao, wrote that in the years since its first introduction "into these kingdoms . . . time has turned it into nourishment that all working men (*hombres de ocupación*) use for breakfast in place of lunch having experienced that life is maintained more adequately by this [food] than by any other."[96]

It is not easy to corroborate with quantitative evidence these impressionistic sources about the diffusion of tobacco and chocolate among different social sectors. The quantities of imports tabulated from *official* trade records would not seem to support the assertions made by contemporaries that these had become mass commodities in the later seventeenth century. The total quantity of cacao registered in Seville mostly arriving from Venezuela and New Spain between 1650 and 1700 was 1,619,700 pounds (legal chocolate imports were 35,325 pounds). For the same period, the registered imports of tobacco—*much less expensive* per "serving"—were 1,333,400 pounds.[97]

First it is important to recognize that official trade figures cannot and do not reflect actual imports. While it is axiomatic that fraud, smuggling, and contraband was endemic in Europe of the ancien régime, tobacco and chocolate seemed to surpass almost all other commodities in inviting their share of the black market. One reason was the imposition of special excise taxes—and in the case of tobacco a state monopoly—that made the legal price much higher than the market price.[98] It was estimated, for instance, that one could buy tobacco on the black market for about one-third of the monopoly price in the late seventeenth century. The research of historian Wim Klooster offers some indication of the scale of smuggling through his investigation of the illegal trade that developed between Spanish colonists in Venezuela and Dutch traders in their colony of Curaçao. Tobacco, cacao, and sugar were the major goods produced. Comparing official Spanish records with Dutch records, Klooster found that almost 90 percent of the cacao produced in Venezuela (about 9 million pounds) between 1721 and 1725 was shipped illegally to the Netherlands. Much of this was re-exported to Spain.[99]

Given the preponderance of smuggling and fraud, it may be that the most reliable estimates for tobacco consumption in the seventeenth century come from those who operated the royal tobacco monopoly, implemented in Castile in 1636 (as discussed in chapter 9). In 1682, the monopoly concessionary declared that "these kingdoms that are encompassed by this Rent consume each year between 500,000 and 600,000 pounds of Havana tobacco and more than 400,000 of that of Virginia, and of these the *estancos* [tobacco monopolies] sell no more than 400,000 pounds, and the rest of the quantity is defrauded without any use to the Royal Treasury."[100] In other words, Castile consumed about one million pounds (at least .16 pounds per capita) of imported tobacco by the late seventeenth century, of which more than half was purchased on the black market. In 1739, *legal* tobacco purchases throughout all of the Spanish kingdoms amounted to 3,086,700 pounds (at least .386 pounds per capita); though actual consumption levels were higher since contraband remained endemic. However, total consumption was likely to be greater still, since, despite monopoly prohibitions, consumers and illegal sellers could and did grow tobacco in Spain, combining it with better-quality tobacco from the Indies.[101]

Net and per capita figures alone do not tell us what percentage of the population regularly consumed tobacco. It is estimated that two pounds of tobacco a year would allow an individual to smoke a daily pipe; however, significantly less tobacco was needed to fuel a snuff habit.[102] Taking, then, one and a half pounds a year as an amount that would fuel an "average" person's more or less daily tobacco consumption, these figures would lead to the conclusion that about 650,000 or about one tenth of the Castilian population regularly snuffed, smoked, or chewed *imported* tobacco in the late seventeenth century, and that more than 2 million, or one quarter of the population did so in the early eighteenth century (keeping in mind that this latter figure only reflects legal consumption). By comparison, Carole Shammas estimates that, between legal and illegal imports, people in England consumed one pound per capita by 1670, enough for half of the population to smoke a pipeful a day. Jordan Goodman estimates that western European consumption levels reached around one pound per capita by 1710.[103] It is impossible to know if Spain's comparatively lower figures reflect higher levels of undocumented consumption or, in fact, lower levels of total tobacco consumption, which could be a result of the monopoly's high prices and the population's lesser wealth.

The most concrete quantitative data I could find concerning chocolate consumption comes from Madrid. While Madrid consumption patterns are unlikely to be representative—the court-capital was infamous for its concentration of the richest and poorest subjects of the kingdom—the metropolis was Spain's largest population center, a trendsetter for the rest of the country and a motor for economic growth.[104] It is almost certainly an exaggeration to maintain that *all* workers regularly consumed chocolate, but it does appear that the beverage had penetrated a wide social swath by the early eighteenth century. In the spring of 1722, municipal tax officials found 704,071 pounds of cacao and 78,469 pounds of chocolate in the stocks of wholesalers and retailers throughout Madrid.[105] If the ratio between stock and annual sales of one of the largest wholesalers is typical, and the typical composition of chocolate is roughly two parts cacao to one part sugar (and miniscule amounts of spice), then these figures can be used to estimate an annual consumption figure of about 2 million pounds of chocolate for Madrid.[106] If one further invents an "average chocolate consumer" who consumed two ounces daily, then about 24,000, or 19 percent of Madrid's population, were regular chocolate consumers at the beginning of the second decade of the eighteenth century.[107] In February 1775, a member of the chocolate-makers guild declared that *madrileños* spent 50,000 *reales* every day on chocolate; if this was correct, they consumed about 2,281,250 pounds of chocolate a year, somewhat more than the estimate for 1721–22.[108]

Given the number of suppositions needed to arrive at these estimates, it is good that we possess other kinds of evidence to assess *who* in the population regularly used tobacco and chocolate. Sources that allow us to profile tobacco and chocolate retailers in Madrid indicate a range of purveyors, some who marketed their goods to the city's upper crust and others who appear to have sold to a non-elite clientele.[109] Surviving records from Madrid's notarial archives—contracts between the state monopoly and individual retailers "obligating" them to sell specified quantities of tobacco—reveal that there were at least 190 individuals licensed to sell tobacco in 1641.[110] The fact that Madrid, with a population of around 135,000 inhabitants, could support this number of *estanqueros*, as the tobacco vendors came to be known, supports the idea that tobacco habits extended across social strata. This impression is further supported by the social diversity of the retailers themselves.[111] The vendors included women as well as men; literate as well as illiterate; substantial shopkeepers as well as small-timers—the five largest contracts were for more than one hundred pounds, while the widow Isabel Mojica was only "obligated" for seven pounds.[112] Some of the retailers were high-end purveyors, reflected by the designation of *joyería*, which literally translates as "jeweler" but came to encompass sellers of all manner of luxury goods. These included a substantial vendor named María de Grados, designated as a "single female *joyería*," who was "obligated" to sell one of the largest quantities of tobacco of all the *estanqueros* (220 pounds, 110 of them of the pricier scented snuff).[113] Other high-end shopkeepers who sold tobacco were a spice-dealer (*especiero*), confectioner, and a retailer who described himself as "a merchant of things from the Indies."[114] But the contracts also imply that there were a significant number of *estanqueros* who marketed to less prosperous consumers. Forty-seven contracts referred to the retailers only as shopkeepers—the absence of a more specialized description indicates that they did not possess the status of the luxury retailers. Finally, the majority of contracts did not specify that the sellers owned a store, suggesting, along with the typically small quantities which they had agreed to sell, that they sold tobacco from their homes, or as itinerant peddlers. In this category were two soldiers, perhaps in charge of procuring tobacco for their companies.

Perhaps the strongest evidence that chocolate found a socially diversified market in Madrid by the end of the seventeenth century was the appearance of new kinds of selling practices. Chocolate spread beyond elite networks as it entered the public space of the city. In 1685 city officials lamented that "there was hardly to be found a street without one, two, or even three stands making and selling chocolate, and beyond this, there is hardly a confectioner, nor a store on the streets of Postas and Calle Mayor and others where it is not sold—before we know it will be sold in oil and vinegar shops. In addition to the men who are occupied in grinding and preparing it, there are many other women who walk from house to house, selling it."[115] The clamor for chocolate sold by the *jícara* and "ounce" in stands dotting many city streets suggests a clientele that did not have the income to lay out seven to ten *reales* for a pound of chocolate or have the equipment to prepare it—a copper *chocolatera* and fuel for fire—but who could now and then, during good times, indulge in a cup or a half-cup of the sweet stimulating drink. In 1655, the price for a "half" *jícara* containing one ounce of chocolate cost ten maravedís, less than a loaf of bread (about 34 maravedís) and about the same as three eggs.[116] In support of this interpretation, a chocolate guild member from the late eighteenth century said that only "the poor are the ones who buy" chocolate sold by the ounce.[117]

The size of Madrid's chocolate sector by the early eighteenth century attests that its trickle-down progress was well under way. An inventory of all vendors—retail and wholesale—of chocolate in Madrid in the spring of 1722 indicates that there were 290 retailers of cacao and chocolate that year for a population of 127,000. There were also clearly high-end stores—again the *joyerías*—and also confectioners and glassmakers (*vidrerías*). But 72 of them were the less vaunted, ordinary shops, under the anachronistic designation of *tiendas de aceite* (oil shops). Despite their name, such shops sold much more than oil; they were more like grocery stores, or simple stands selling sundry comestibles. The presence of chocolate in such establishments lends credence to those who said it had become a daily necessity for many. The seventeenth-century city official who worried that chocolate would soon be seen for sale in *tiendas de aceite y vinagre* was, indeed, prophetic. In 1757 a census recorded 125 individuals engaged in chocolate making (there would have been many more involved in its sale), almost half the number of tavern owners (254) recorded for that year.[118]

TABLE 7.3. Chocolate Retailers, 1721–1722

Type of establishment	Number of vendors
tienda de aceite (oil or oil and vinegar seller)	72
confitería (confectioner)	67
joyería (luxury goods)	90
vidrería (glass maker)	21
molendero (chocolate miller)	13
chocolatero	14
other	13
total	290

Source: AVM Sec. 3, leg. 277, exp. 78.

Like the availability of chocolate sold by the "cup" in stands dotting Madrid, segmentation in the market suggests the democratizing of chocolate. By the eighteenth century, chocolate was largely distinguished by the provenance of cacao, with that from Caracas costing the most, and the cheaper kinds from Guayaquil (Ecuador) and the Antilles, costing less. Chocolate aficionados also distinguished between classes of sugar and cinnamon.[119]

Beyond this sanctioned chocolate, there were also other preparations that authorities and chocolate specialists qualified as "adulterated." In 1685 the above-quoted municipal authorities bemoaned "that every day there are new methods found to defraud it by adding ingredients that augment the weight and diminish its goodness," such as adding bulk to it with "hidden bread crumbs, corn meal, dried orange peels that are ground up and much other garbage."[120] Such practices suggest an effort to more cheaply manufacture chocolate for humbler segments of the population. Of course, the practice of adding maize to cacao beverage had an ancient lineage, but in Europe it took on a class-tainted stigma.

Both goods moved from Andalusia to the Court-capital by the end of the 1620s. Investigation is still required to determine when they spread beyond Andalusia and Madrid, but a study of postmortem inventories suggests that Barcelona may have lagged behind the court by several decades in the general diffusion of chocolate, though by the late seventeenth century it was an integral part of elite society. Tobacco arrived more quickly and diffused throughout society in Barcelona: twenty-three artisans and agricultural workers who died between 1683 and 1690 possessed tobacco paraphernalia according to their postmortem inventories.[121]

LEARNING TO TASTE

The most important mechanism for the transmission of tobacco and chocolate was social. It was less the goods themselves that passed from Indians to Europeans, from Creoles to Iberians, from those belonging to an Atlantic network to those outside of it, but rather sets of practices, habits, and tastes. This explains the considerable continuity in material forms. Many—particularly in the case of chocolate—have assumed a radical rupture, asserting that Europeans found Amerindian forms distasteful and reinvented them to suit their palates. Like the view that Europeans first embraced tobacco as a medicine and then only later as recreational drug, the common belief that Europeans needed to "transform" chocolate in order to make it appetizing is false. Europeans who had grown up with the drink in the New World—or had been immersed in an Indian milieu for sufficient time—not only acquired a taste for the thick chocolate but consumed it in the manner that it had been long consumed in Mesoamerica. Likewise, colonists in the New World learned to consume tobacco in the manner of the Indians with whom they first interacted. Europeans assimilated the tobacco complex and chocolate complex in their entirety, attempting to maintain the sensory sensations even across the ocean divide.

Spaniards, Creoles, and mestizos immersed in an Indian milieu for sufficient time acquired a taste for chocolate in the manner that it had been long consumed in Mesoamerica, adopting the whole spectrum of cacao beverages that surrounded them; once initiated, colonizers assimilated their subjects' aesthetic sensibilities vis à vis chocolate.[122] Juan de Cárdenas gave pride of place to the flower-spiced cacao beverage, but he also recommended the other cacao drinks. He opined that of all the chocolate beverages, *atole* (a cacao and maize concoction) "is that which is most refreshing and most quenches the thirst and provides the most sustenance."[123] As described by Cárdenas, Europeans in the New World enjoyed all the various cacao preparations, selecting the ones that best fit their needs or temperament, choosing the more common *atole* chocolate when wanting something refreshing and sustaining, and favoring the spicier, more potent chocolate at other times. European acceptance of native forms is indicated by the Hispanicism of the Nahuatl terms—*atextli* became *atole*. The flower spices *gueynacaztle* ("great ear" in Nahuatl) and *xochinacaztli* ("flowery ear") became *orejuelas* ("little ears"). Colonists Hispanicized *mecaxóchitl* into *mecasuchil*, and baptized *tlixochitl* into vanilla ("en nuestra romance vainillas olorosas").[124] The Spanish appropriated the Nahuatl term *cacauaatl* ("the drink of cacao"), and *cacauatl* ("the grain of cacao"), Hispanicizing both as "cacao." (The separate term "chocolate" for a cacao beverage did not appear until the late sixteenth century.)[125]

This is not to suggest, however, that Europeans did not add their own "inventions" to chocolate. Change in the composition of chocolate did take place; there was no radical rupture but, rather, evolutionary and gradual tinkering and modifications. The most famous modification was the addition of sugar. Contrary to the popular view that the Spanish invented the idea of sweetening cacao, native Mexicans and Mayans already sweetened many of their cacao beverages with honey. Sugar can be seen as a substitute for honey, in which the intention is to approximate the taste of the original, not to radically change it. Cárdenas mentioned that some dissolved the cacao tablets in hot water with a "touch of sweetness, which makes it very pleasing," but notably, he did not indicate whether the addition was sugar or honey, suggesting their interchangeability. Another arena for Spanish "invention" was spices. Spanish colonists modified traditional Mesoamerican chocolate by adding or substituting spices esteemed in the Old World—cinnamon, black pepper, anise, rose, and sesame, among others—in place of the native flower spice complex, achiote, and chili peppers. Cárdenas, the creolized doctor, indicated that Spaniards innovated with the recipes by using Old World imports, yet he insisted that "the fragrant spices of the West Indies [the Americas]" were superior, since they "do not give us the excessive heat of those brought from the East Indies."[126] This statement also indicates that the Old World spices were thought to mimic the effect of New World additives: black pepper duplicating the heat of red chilies; cinnamon capturing the spicy tingle of *mecaxóchitl*, and the rose of Alexandria simulating the floral notes of vanilla and the rest of the floral triumvirate. He praised achiote for "giving sustenance to and fattening those who drink it," and he reprimanded those who "err by saying that achiote is a bad and suspicious spice for this beverage."[127]

In the early seventeenth century, all of the Amerindian-derived varieties of chocolate arrived in Spain. In the first place, during the early years of chocolate's diffusion in Spain, metropolitans more often imported chocolate than cacao.[128] In other words, chocolate consumed in Europe was manufactured in the American manner. It was not until the 1630s that chocolate artisans were noticed by Madrid's municipal authorities, though chocolate manufacturing began earlier in Seville.[129] This trajectory makes clear that European chocolate was not just similar to American chocolate but that it *was* American chocolate. When they started to systematically manufacture chocolate, the Spanish recipes followed those of Indians and Creoles in Mesoamerica. Royal legislation from 1632 hints at Spaniards' appreciation for the chocolate-flavoring agents vanilla and *mecasuchil*.

That year the Crown levied a special tax on chocolate consumption in Spain, and the levy singled out these two additives as essential raw ingredients of chocolate, and in 1691 vanilla and *mexacóchitl* were still being taxed as chocolate ingredients.[130] More evidence is provided by the Jesuit who brought a lawsuit against a ship captain in 1634 for a wayward shipment: the suit charged the captain with the loss of valuable chocolate and also various flavorings that formed the Mesoamerican flower-spice complex—not only the more common vanilla, but also *"orijuelas"* (*gueynacaztle*), *"mecasuchial"* (*mexacóchitl*), and "achiote."[131] Even the Sevillan physician Santiago Valverde Turices, who viewed American ingredients a bit suspiciously, grudgingly acknowledged the "truth" that achiote was necessary for giving a "better taste, color, and flavor to chocolate."[132] Recognizing that it was more difficult to come by American spices than those of the Old World, the Madrid physician and chocolate enthusiast Antonio Colmenero de Ledesma offered suitable Old World substitutions for those consumers who could not acquire the New World ingredients. Like Cárdenas, he suggested that the rose of Alexandria could replace *mecasuchil* because both substances possessed the "purgative" quality (perhaps he also noted that they were both flower blossoms).[133] Black pepper could be used instead of chilies and *mecasuchil*; cinnamon and cloves were found to be adequate substitutions for the *orejuelas*.

The sensory effects of chocolate the Spanish learned to anticipate were not restricted to the impact on the taste buds. Just as pre-Columbian iconography makes clear that foam was fundamental to chocolate consumption, so does the iconography of seventeenth-century Spanish art. The *molinillo* (the wooden beater) used to produce the froth became standard in representations of chocolate in seventeenth-century Spain (figure 7.4). And Iberians learned from Mexicans that chocolate must be sipped from a special vessel—the *tecomate* (Hispanicized from the Nahautl *tecomatl*), a cup fashioned from clay, or the *xícara* (or *jícara*), a lacquered calabash gourd (from the Nahuatl *xicalli*).[134] Ship manifests indicate that in the late sixteenth and early seventeenth century, Iberian-based chocolate consumers imported *tecomates* and *jícaras* along with chocolate and cacao, often in conjunction with other luxury novelties from the Americas—Indian-crafted feather work and magical gemstones, suggesting consumers well acquainted with creole ambits, nostalgically hankering for the regional specialties now at remove.[135] By the 1630s groupings of such goods became the subject of compositions of still lives.

By the eighteenth century, the chocolate recipe was pared down. Two (*mecasuchil* and *orejuelas*) of the three Mesoamerican floral spices rarely appeared, and no one seemed to add maize. In standard recipes, all that remained of the spice complex was cinnamon.[136] While the composition of

Figure 7.4. Antonio de Pereda, *Still Life with an Ebony Chest* (1652). This is one of the most sumptuous exemplars of the chocolate still life, a genre that was popular in the seventeenth and eighteenth centuries. It testifies to the enduring Mesoamerican sensory aesthetic. To the right are the central ingredients of chocolate—cacao and sugar. On the chest (a place to lock up valuable chocolate) is a large lacquered gourd (a *jícara* imported directly from Mexico); on the platter to the left are the porcelain versions of the *jícara*. Behind them is the *chocolatera* and the all-important *molinillo*, testifying to the continued desirability of foam. Oil on canvas, 80×94 cm. Reproduced courtesy of the State Hermitage Museum, St. Petersburg, Russia.

chocolate did change, it was a gradual, evolutionary process, rather than a radical disjunction based on essential taste differences dividing Amerindians and Europeans, or Creoles and *peninsulares*. For instance, the disappearance of maize might reflect the preservation of Mesoamerican ideals of luxury, since the spiced cacao beverage without maize seems to have been considered more special and *atole* more routine. Chocolate neophytes, whether Creole or Spanish, intended to approximate original tastes, rather than create new palate sensations. The same was true of tobacco.

Spanish colonists learned to consume tobacco in the manner of the local natives. In Mesoamerica tobacco was "consumed in reed pipes, wrapped with liquidambar, so that users of this method light one end and suck on the other . . . and this is now well diffused among Spaniards."[137] Others took to the clay pipes favored by indigenes in northwestern Mexico or the maize-wrapped cigars characteristic of the groups in Central America.[138] While pipes and cigars dominated among the elite (Indian, Creole, and mestizo alike), chewing the pulverized, lime-enhanced tobacco was associated with relieving fatigue, thirst, and hunger, and fortifying strength and was often used in contexts of manual labor, leading labor-averse elite Creoles and Europeans, as well as mestizos and acculturated Indians, to disdain it for its associations with commoners. "Few Indians who grew up among Spaniards use it this way," explained Juan Bautista de Pomar, a descendant of a Spanish conquistador and Nahua nobility, "nor do refined and urban people, but only rustic men and workers."[139] Colonists in the eastern Caribbean and South American highlands emulated indigenous allies, enemies, and subjects by adopting snuff as well as smoking tobacco. Local officials in Caracas noted in 1578 that "the Spaniards and natives take [tobacco] in smoke by the mouth and in powder by the nose."[140] In the Colombian highlands, settlers procured tobacco from Indians that was "admirable for this snuff (*polvo*) and not for smoke."[141] As with chocolate, the indigenous influence was also reflected in nomenclature—those in Mesoamerica adopted the Nahuatl term *picietl* (or the Hispanicized variant *piciete*) to refer to tobacco through most of the sixteenth century, until the Caribbean loan word, *tabaco*, took over. They knew tobacco pipes as *sahumerios* (that which makes smoke), but they also literally translated the Nahuatl term acayetl, as "reed that gives off smoke" (*caña de sahumerio*), or more simply, "tube" (*cañuto*).[142] Those in the Andes called tobacco *sayri* while French in Brazil adopted *petun*.

All of these forms of tobacco—smoke, snuff, and chew—arrived in Europe, reflecting the ubiquity and diversity of American provenance. Spain was like a funnel for the Americas, bringing together return migrants, Indians, and mestizos from diverse and far-flung locales in the Americas and with them their divergent preferences for tobacco consumption. Juan de Castro y Medinilla, the Cordoban apothecary who wrote a treatise on the properties of tobacco in 1620, asserted that there were two "factions" of tobacco partisans, those who "consume it in smoke with a hollowed tube like that used for containing gun powder in a musket" and those who take "that powder through the nostrils, the tobacco pricking sharply where they meet, and along the esophagus and windpipe."[143] In addition to pipes, Spaniards smoked cigars and cigarettes (known as *papeletes*).[144] Castro y Medinilla added that there was "another method, by way of the mouth," clarifying that it was "incognito for not being in use."[145] More likely Castro y Medinilla's dismissive appraisal of chewing tobacco and its neglect on the part of other elite authors reflected their social biases, for, as in Mesoamerica, chewing tobacco was associated with manual labor and life on the edge of survival, so disdained by the higher classes. The continuity in material forms of tobacco and chocolate from America to Europe is proof of the acquired and learned nature of tastes. Manufacturers delighted in innovating with all of these forms throughout the seventeenth and eighteenth centuries—particularly in the case of snuff—and by the eighteenth century consumers could choose from over seventy different varieties. And there was considerable change in fashions. At the very beginning elites seemed to prefer smoking, then in the 1620s opted for snuff, and then at the end of the eighteenth century gravitated toward cigars, yet throughout this whole period there were aficionados of all three modes of ingestion: smoking, sniffing, and chewing.[146] And Spain, it seems, dictated tobacco fashion for elites throughout Europe. Though Virginia tobacco had the market share, it was tobacco cultivated in Spanish America and manufactured in Spain (though Havana-processed tobacco was increasingly desirable by the end of the seventeenth century) that remained the most coveted among connoisseurs.[147]

All of these material practices had their origins in pre-Columbian America. And, as in pre-Columbian America, the powerful sensory experience induced by tobacco and chocolate grounded the symbolic associations associated with them.

8

Consuming Rituals

❖ ❖

On November 6, 1669, the king of Spain, Charles II, turned seven. In honor of the event, the viceroy of Valencia threw a party at his palace. The fête occasioned the consumption of tobacco and chocolate, and reflection on the meaning of that consumption. There is good reason to think that the illustrious guests (titled grandees aplenty) convened at a set moment to enjoy fine chocolate served in expensive *jícaras*. Tobacco was present too, but, unlike chocolate, it was probably not the case that its consumption was scheduled on the agenda; rather, somewhat on the sly, during moments stolen between gaming, feasting, and dancing, men and women might discreetly take out their fancy tobacco boxes (silver, gold plated, inscribed with "curious" designs) and offer some of their contents to a friend for smoking or snuffing. The festivities culminated with the awards ceremony of a poetry competition held in honor of the king. The competitors (noblemen, clergy, and lawyers among the group) had submitted verses on prescribed topics (e.g., write about a jovial dispute among the numbers 7, 6, and 9, representing, respectively, the age of Charles II, the day on which he was born, and the month in which he was born; describe a bullfight that took place on a rainy day). Topic number five was to "write in praise of chocolate and vituperation of tobacco," with the explanation that "we cannot neglect hospitality at this party." Two of the winning verses on this topic were published a few weeks later. A poet with a doctorate in law submitted that chocolate is "manna," while tobacco is a "mania." Chocolate prepares one for heaven, tobacco for hell. Tobacco is "garbage," chocolate a tasty medicine. Tobacco only feigns gallantry, while chocolate deserves its great acclaim. For his composition, a Carmelite friar offered that chocolate is "that inspirational Ambrosia," while tobacco turned an "astute" man into a "beast."[1] Yet, as even the poets duly recognized, tobacco was as much part of the habits of "grandees and lords" as was chocolate. As at the banquets held in Mesoamerica, aristocratic parties such as these ensured the reciprocal exchange between symbolic and material artifacts, the power of what was said about the goods enhancing the experience of their consumption, and the latter grounding the symbolic notions.

In their pre-Columbian context, tobacco and chocolate were ritual objects that connected the individual body to the social body, and humanity to divinity. As they migrated across cultures and oceans, these investments endured, accounting for how they became integrated into—and transformed—collective and solitary rites. Consumed collectively, tobacco and chocolate consecrated bonds of caste, trust, and intimacy, surpassing even food and drink as objects of commensality. Reflecting pre-Hispanic antecedents, chocolate in Spain came to be the focus of quintessential rites of civility, served during formal greetings, court parties, and occasions of alliance, invested with properties of sensual pleasure, social affinity, and noble refinement. Tobacco, too, could convey sumptuous refinement, but it also often was associated with transgression. Tobacco accompanied or even occasioned rites that celebrated the disruption of normative hierarchy, the florescence of the uncontrolled microcosmic body signaling the inversions of the uncontrolled macrocosmic body politic. Though integral to collective rites, the goods also organized profoundly private rites, allowing, as in pre-Columbian America, individuals to harness an external life force. One catches glimpses, for instance, of a depressed nobleman, an exhausted preacher, and an anxious nun seeking out chocolate to lift spirits, soothe agitated nerves, rouse a tired body, and summon creative energies. The scholar in his study, the woman heartbroken by a lost love, and the soldier surviving harsh landscapes all found succor in tobacco, which they credited with augmenting mental faculties, anesthetizing woes, and suppressing discomforts of cold, hunger, and exhaustion. The goods' appearance in heterogeneous contexts—collective and solitary—reinforced their potency in each. Their indispensability in rites of sociability validated the properties that made them so attractive during solitary occasions, and, reciprocally, the succor they offered the individual contributed to their efficacy in communal settings.

CHOCOLATE: REFINED COMMENSALITY

Chocolate in European society simultaneously served to fortify social bonds and underscore, or even confer, distinction, as illustrated by the fact that it came to exemplify the Spanish term *regalo*, with today's meaning of "gift" and, more specifically, of an object invested with properties of sensual pleasure, social affinity, and noble refinement.[2] In a poem purporting to simulate a contest between aficionados of wine and chocolate, the devotee of the latter made his refrain: "Chocolate is my *regalo*, all the rest are chimeras."[3] The author of a chocolate treatise, Antonio de León Pinelo, equated *regalo* and chocolate, writing that "it has been so well received, that it is already used as the common *regalo* in many cities and in no place more than this Court, where its use is now in competition with those places of its invention and origin." And he wrote of pre-Hispanic Mesoamerica that chocolate was "a beverage of *regalo* and such great and singular quality that it was not used nor permitted to all alike, but only to lords and principal men and commanders and brave men . . . and it came to be such a valued privilege to drink it that it was an act of ennoblement and the prize of heroic feats."[4] Though purportedly describing the practices of pre-Hispanic Mesoamericans, León Pinelo also indicated its similar ennobling status in the colonial Indies and Spain of his day.

A tile painting created in the early eighteenth century depicted how chocolate served as a *regalo* in a ritual context (figure 8.1). The tile painting, which once decorated a wall enclosing a courtyard of the aristocratic estate of the Marqués de Castelvell near Barcelona, depicts the activities that a hospitable aristocrat—such as the Marqués—might make available to his honored guests, the same kind of activities that accompanied the birthday celebration for Charles II. The festivities took place in a courtyard flanked with orange trees in terra-cotta pots, classical statuary, and a fountain in the center, likely evocative of the space in which the tiles were themselves installed. The noble revelers, women elegantly clad in long dresses and elaborate silk headdresses and men sporting velvet hats or curled manes, ruffled shirts, heeled shoes, and silk stockings, do a number of things in the featured scene: Guests arrive in a litter borne by servants. Wallflowers assemble and sit on benches around the perimeter. Couples stroll by the fountains (a gallant offers a rose to a lovely who sniffs appreciatively, a lady has her skirts pulled by a frisky pup on one side, as a suitor leans toward her—for a kiss?—on the other). Two ladies survey the scene, gossiping behind their fans. A solitary gentleman stands by his loyal dog; another refreshes himself in a flowing fountain. In the bottom row, the foreground, the most central and communal activities of the nobles appear. On the left, a group of women and men dance together in a circle. On the right, the group sits for a meal at a richly laden table, waited on by attentive servants.

These visual vignettes show nobles at play, but these activities are secondary to the most important rite of aristocratic sociability, that which fills the center bottom panel (figure 8.2). There, chocolate—its preparation,

Figure 8.1. *La Xocolatada*, (Barcelona, 1710). As the title suggests, the activity that defines the frolicking of upper-class men and women is chocolate drinking. Reproduced with permission of Museu de Ceràmica, Barcelona, Spain.

Figure 8.2. *La Xocolatada* (detail). The couple flirting over a *jícara* of chocolate marks the visual center of the scene.

service, and consumption—dominates the scene. (The special place of chocolate at noble festivities is further confirmed by one of the assigned topics for a poetry competition in honor of King Charles's twenty-ninth birthday: offer a reason why "chocolate is very conceited, because it seems it is only he who is chosen to celebrate the birthday of His Majesty.")[5] At the very center, a *jícara* of chocolate binds a couple: The man, on bended knee, offers a seated woman the vessel capped with dark foam; their symmetrically raised hands frame the cup, a plumb line down from cupid perched on top of the central fountain. To their right, a group of men—seemingly noble connoisseurs and not servants—are engaged in the preparation: one man rotates the *molinillo* to form the froth on the brass *chocolatera* above the brazier; another fills cups with the hot liquid from a second *chocolatera*; and two others prepare to serve the *jícaras* to the waiting ladies. To left of the central couple, two other pairs lean over the conjoining chocolate. And to their left, a woman, who should be looking at the man kneeling in front of her (the admirer shows his respect and courtesy by doffing his cap but fails to compel in the absence of chocolate), cannot help but look over her shoulder, longingly, at those behind her who are blessed with and by the desirable beverage.

This reconstruction of a noble gathering recalls the banquets of the merchants, warriors, and nobility described in the *Florentine Codex*. The most obvious parallel uniting the chocolate-inflected banquets was as an occasion for members of the elite to solidify their alliances and class position through shared ritualized consumption. More specific aspects of protocol also coincide—the chocolate service is clearly separate from other eating activities; emphasis is put on proper service (the usurping warrior host then, the gallant gentlemen here). Other commonalities are perhaps coincidence but deserve mention—the juxtaposition of flowers and chocolate, the linking of dance and chocolate, even the courtyard setting.

The Barcelona tile painting is a particularly rich source because it, like the *Florentine Codex*, depicts ritualized chocolate consumption within its broader social context. And, like the *Florentine Codex*, it insists on two aspects of chocolate use, the first of which is its singular capacity to consecrate social bonds. The painting shows sharing chocolate as an activity that surpasses promenading, flirting, gossiping, and even dancing and feasting as a powerful rite of sociability. This is an assessment that is echoed by a line in a seventeenth-century poem: "If the party lacks chocolate, then it is worthless."[6]

In seventeenth-century Spain, chocolate became the quintessential expression of hospitality, routinely "offered during visits and occasions of friendship," among those who could afford it.[7] It was conventionalized to the point that a scene in a 1666 play, set in an opulent household, had a lady of the house welcome her guests by commanding her maid to "bring chocolate to these two gentlemen."[8] It became so expected protocol in rich (or would-be rich) homes that some families preferred the spiritual services of nuns who belonged to the Order of Discalced Carmelites to the members of other orders because the Discalced Carmelites refused to drink chocolate (as it violated their vow of poverty, since it constituted a luxury) and thus saved the families the expense of the delicacy.[9] The emergence of special chocolate-drinking quarters in the grand residences of aristocrats also testifies to its unique social function. In the house of Don Pedro de Aragón, an inventory taker designated a chocolate room (*pieza de chocolate*); its suitability for receiving guests is suggested by the fact that it was ensconced between the large hall (*salón largo*) and a drawing room (*pieza de estrado*) where guests were received.[10]

In addition, like the long-distance merchants who attended trade councils in Mesoamerica, Iberian businessmen drank chocolate to accompany their negotiations,[11] as did elite women who socialized together in their *estrados* (a room with a dais festooned with tapestries and pillows), their activities centered around conversation and drinking chocolate.[12] A trial transcript from the Inquisition offers up a particularly poignant and powerful example of the way chocolate was used to consecrate feelings of trust in the most fraught situations. Manuel Fernández, whose father was under investigation for crypto-Judaizing, testified to the Inquisition in 1649 about an incident in which another member of the Portuguese *converso* community sought to induct him into the world of clandestine Jewish practice. The previous year, he visited Francisco Díaz, "who had a store of chocolate and luxuries on the plaza of Anton Martin"; the "said Francisco Díaz brought him into a room behind the store, and being alone, offered him a *xícara* of chocolate" and proceeded to explain to him how to follow the "rule of Moses."[13]

As playfully indicated in the Barcelona painting, chocolate also marked intimacy of an erotic nature. (The way that the couple at the center of the scene are conjoined by chocolate uncannily, but not accidentally, mirrors the Mixtec couples depicted marrying in the pre-Columbian codices.) Yet, whereas in pre-Columbian Mesoamerica the chocolate ritual was clearly tied to official betrothal and marriage ceremonies, after the conquest, in New and Old Spain, chocolate was more associated with libidinal relations not necessarily sanctified by legitimating authorities (the Church). Cases before the Inquisition from New Spain and Guatemala testify to the ubiquity of chocolate as the medium for love potions intended to acquire or repossess the affections of men. In seventeenth-century Spain, chocolate figured as a catalyst to libidinal desire and a requisite accoutrement to courtly love. The jurist Solórzano Pereira, when considering the nature of chocolate as it related to the ecclesiastical fast, invoked the report that Montezuma "was accustomed to drinking this drink of chocolate in cups of gold to be better equipped to turn himself over to his concubines."[14] The nobleman and courtier Antonio Hurtado de Mendoza, who was a regular attendant at the literary academies in Madrid sponsored by prominent grandees, wrote verses entitled "Stanza 115 to a Blonde Lady: Couplets of Chocolate."[15] These following stanzas entangle the corporal pleasures of the body and "this scarlet extravagance called by the bad name chocolate":

> Porcelain-traps hold the love of chocolate
> What is it that embraces at the boiling point
> So as to enjoy the perfect culmination?
> What is it that so softly bites? What is it that embraces the chest
> Leaving the appetite satisfied?
> What sustains? What dream is not indulged?
> What is it that hides with sugar its pepper?
> Where is its *molinillo*? And what of the *xicara* that is most
> Pleasing when it most bites?
> . . . .
> The definition of love is chocolate.[16]

It could be a flirtatious or even seductive act to send chocolate to the object of one's desires, as suggested by nun-poetess Sor Juana Inés de la Cruz's verses entitled "A Ballad to the same Lady, sending her a shoe embroidered in the Mexican style and a gift and message *(recado)* of Chocolate."[17] Thomas Gage, the former Dominican, reported that a "gentlewoman . . . of a very merry and pleasant disposition" sent him gifts of chocolate accompanied by a plantain carved with "two of blind Cupid's arrows sticking in it" to leave no doubt about her intentions.

The Barcelona tile painting indicates another aspect of chocolate consumption that stretched straight through the pre-Columbian period to early modern Spain: chocolate's association with social status and notions of honor. In addition to depicting activities that bind people together, the tiles represent the elite's self-legitimating ideas about refinement. The artist paid attention to markers of class in art and architecture (the presence of expensive statues and monumental fountains), dress (the high-heeled shoes of the men, the expensive ruffles, the elaborate lace headdresses), skills (knowledge of dancing and hunting), transportation (the carriage was the luxury car of the seventeenth century), and dining. But, again, chocolate surpasses all other forms in this depiction. In the 1666 play mentioned above, chocolate rivals "rich paintings," "walls that breathe amber," and "crystal trifles," as markers of opulence. The convention of writing poems in praise of chocolate at the aristocratic literary competitions reinforced the connection between chocolate and nobility. The 1640 *Panegírico al chocolate* (Panegyric to chocolate) asserted: "Lettered men are those who drink it; rich men are those who eat it; the ignorant and poor do not dare to allow these greatnesses to enter through their door; it is brought to kings in golden *jícaras*; princes consume it; noble courtiers also participate; it is denied to the wretched and commoners."[18]

In seventeenth-century Spain chocolate became routinized as a gift in many formal and ceremonial occasions, a testament to its power as a ritual object, since its properties were recognized even in absence of the ceremony of consumption. This investment, too, echoes the emphasis placed on the Aztec merchants' offerings of chocolate gifts to the demanding warrior and noble guests at their party. In 1691 chocolate was served after a public broker passed his guild exam, and boxes of chocolate were part of the award bestowed in literary competitions. In 1705 clients presented their lawyers with a gift of chocolate "as is the style in such cases." And by the same year it was customary to give a pound of chocolate when one received a knighthood (not a far cry from the Aztec warriors who were rewarded with chocolate).[19]

A gloss on the meaning of these offerings is provided by Jerónimo de Barrionuevo, a courtier who kept a detailed account of notable events that took place during the latter reign of Philip IV—the gossip, festivities, and political events.[20] In his entry for November 7, 1654, the chronicler wrote:

> I have seen the present of chocolate that the [Duke of Albuquerque] sent to the councilors and lords. There are 16,000 pounds ... not including the presents for the king, queen, the infanta, and Don Luis de Haro [the prime minister], which they say are another 8,000. He has paid for its transportation, which cost 4,000 ducats, though he was exempted from taxes. What majestic craziness for a lord to throw away 50,000 reales as if they were grains of sand! They all come in gold-coated, one-pound boxes, and I am certain that the leaf alone is worth more than 2,000 ducats.[21]

When Albuquerque made this lavish "crazy" gift, it was not only impulsive generosity that stirred him. In undertaking such an expansive and expensive gesture, the duke did not neglect the symbolic meaning of the gift itself. In the context of court society, where proximity to the king and peers' perceptions of one's rank were the most highly valued capital, his magnamity had enormous significance.[22] That Albuquerque chose chocolate on which to "throw away 50,000 reales as if they were grains of sand" indicates that the equation of chocolate with regality was as true for seventeenth-century Spaniards as it had been for Mesoamericans for millennia. That a titled aristocrat chose to give chocolate to the royal family in an ostentatiously public gesture is persuasive evidence that the connotations of honor and nobility had adhered to chocolate in its travels across cultural and oceanic divides. Chocolate figured as an exemplary gift, which could communicate and solidify the nature of the giver and receiver's social bonds (friendship, alliance, patronage, fealty, romance).

TOBACCO: COURTLY AND CARNIVALESQUE

One of tobacco's trajectories looks a lot like the one just described for chocolate. Elite Andalusians, like their counterparts in colonial New Spain, appeared to directly replicate the smoking practices of their noble Mesoamerican forbears. Writing in 1619, the Cordoban apothecary Juan de Castro y Medinilla explained that tobacco

> is today in such usage in those regions [the Indies] that people of merit (*gente de consideración*) enclose a great quantity of tobacco and keep it in aromatic, carefully guarded places, as they do in Spain with good wine. ... When it is time to sit down for a meal, they gather three or four leaves or more (depending on the number of people at the table) and, taking them with other aromatic ingredients, they twist them into a roll that they call a

Zigarillo and, beginning to eat, take swallows of smoke, as we do wine. It is considered so decorated and customary, that its smell is overlooked. And if anyone of importance comes to visit, they take some and toast them with Tobacco. Such usage is now introduced in our parts, such that it is not only for toasting, but such that one who is lacking Tobacco, goes out to request some, and with this, there is a feast.[23]

In the first instance, it is revealing the way the text moves in an almost happenstance way from the Indies to Spain and so mirrors the way individuals and their customs moved between these continents, reflecting the cultural integration of Andalusia and creole America and the way tobacco moved not only as a material artifact, or even something hankered after by an individual, but as a set of collective practices. The passage testifies that Andalusians inherited the Mesoamerican tobacco practices, in which smoking was integral to the reception of vaunted guests and displays of luxurious refinement. Again, the imprint of pre-Columbian antecedents is in evidence in subtle ways as well, such as the use of the *zigarillo*, which derived from the highland Mayan word *sikar* (cigar or tobacco), and the practice of smoking at the commencement of a "feast."[24]

The following passage, written just a few years later, in 1623, by another Andalusian informant, a Carmona physician named Fernando de Almirón Zayas, gives a rather different portrait of the social context of Spanish tobacco consumption:

[Clergy] smoke out their senses in their sacristies and choirs, while [laborers], with their alluring tobacco boxes, induce others to use it as well while they chitchat and gossip, the rustics leaving their workshops and jobs, so their masters don't see them, offering the excuse "I must go to relieve myself," carrying with them fire for that purpose. This leads the former to dishonor their habits and calling, and to deform their faces and beards full of smoke or snuff of this Tobacco, and the latter to cheat their masters and workshops, and all of them to risk their consciences and health.[25]

The settings and occasions evoked in this passage of casual, even slummy sociability differ dramatically from the elegant gathering around the sumptuous table described above. A transgressive quality is ascribed to the experience. In contrast to the open and opulent setting of the elite Andalusian household, now the setting is occluded and the pretext deceitful or sacrilegious, either because it is predicated on lies (scatological ones at that—the pretense of eliminating one's bodily waste as the justification for leaving one's workshop) or because it is implicated in profaning the hallowed spaces of the Church. The smokers and snuffers flout the normative expectations (piety and duty) of their occupations (clergy and laborers). Yet these

transgressions in no way lessen the camaraderie affected by sharing tobacco but, rather, they heighten it, because the consumers are conjoined
with one another in conspiracy as well as tobacco. As with the refined
consumption of cigars described by Castro y Medinilla, the intensely social
facet of shared smoking and snuffing remains; the boorish, even sacrilegious associations did nothing to diminish the capacity of tobacco to
consecrate social affinities.

All manner of historical sources confirms these authors' testimony
about tobacco as singularly convivial, surpassing all other substances, except, of course, chocolate. The language, verbs such as *brindar* (to toast)
and *convidar* (to invite), used to describe collective tobacco consumption
itself speaks to tobacco's capacity to consecrate social bonds. Tobacco advocate and medical school professor Cristóbal de Hayo explained that
people "in these and foreign kingdoms" would "toast one another gra-
ciously with it during feasts, conversations, and outside of these [occasions]
with feeling," noting that snuff tobacco was particularly "common and
suited" for this use and for "which effect there are fabricated boxes of different materials for bringing it always prepared for company." A tobacco
treatise related that creole women in the New World had taken to carrying
conch shells filled with snuff tobacco and would toast one another with
them as they passed by. A circulating complaint, addressed to Church authorities in Galicia and Toledo in the 1630s, decried that clergy were "not
content to drink smoke inside their houses before saying Mass, but go to
church to take snuff, meeting in gossip circles and inviting each other to
share it."[26] A satirical verse asserted that tobacco "serves conversation . . .
reconciling sometimes conflicting wills" and "confirming friendships."[27]

Another aspect of tobacco's social character was its (contested) capacity
to "incite" the "venereal and lasciviousness even in those who are well inclined."[28] There is the poem, "To a Lady, who, when she was asked for
tobacco, pulled out a snuff box with a heart painted on the cover with an
arrow that penetrated it."[29] The snuff box decoration both illustrates
cupid's arrow and evokes sexual penetration. In recounting being smitten
with love, the narrator invokes "an arrow with two wings and a quiver of
ivory" passing through him, alluding to the box containing the tobacco
that was the occasion for the smiting encounter. Similarly, Dutch artists
and writers connected tobacco to lasciviousness in a variety of ways (see
figure 8.5).[30] In other contexts, however, as will be seen, tobacco was seen
to impede erotic attraction or to assist efforts to maintain celibacy.

Visual sources also leave no doubt that Europeans viewed tobacco as a
uniquely social substance. In varied and nuanced ways, smoking and its
apparatuses (pipes, bowls of embers, tobacco pouches, tobacco itself) were
the focal point of sociability depicted in numerous canvasses, surpassing

even the mugs of ale and wine that also contributed to the escapist convivi-ality (figures 7.3, 8.3, 8.4, 8.5, 8.6). Flemish and Dutch artists, in particu-lar, seized on smokers and smoking as the quintessence of plebeian sociability. Because of the political linkages between Flanders and Spain, as well as the internationalization of the art market, Spanish patrons ac-tively sought out Flemish works for their collections, including those that featured tobacco as a subject.[31] Moreover, David Teniers the Younger, a most famous and prolific painter of lowlife scenes that prominently fea-tured smoking and smokers, had particularly strong ties to Spanish art patrons. A resident of Flanders (part of the territories belonging to the Spanish Habsburgs during this period), Teniers was a curator as well as painter in service to two successive governors of the Spanish Netherlands between 1646 and 1659, and he sent his painter son (David Teniers III) to serve as court painter for Philip IV between 1661 and 1663.[32] The Prado's considerable holdings from the Low Countries, including Teniers's *Monkeys Smoking and Drinking*, are a legacy of the interconnectedness of the Spanish and Flemish art markets.

The scenes of elegant Andalusians sharing cigars and that of clergy and laborers secretively sharing a smoke or snuff are united in that they both indicate the way that tobacco could bring people together in a powerful way. Tobacco was a moveable feast that consecrated community, whether around a tavern table, in a Church choir, on a promenade, or in a literary salon. The scenes diverge as well, for in the former, tobacco becomes an opportunity to display refinement, and in the latter, an opportunity for enticingly boorish provocations against social probity and propriety. Both of these associations characterized tobacco use in seventeenth-century Europe.

The men and women described by Castro y Medinilla, following in the footsteps of Mesoamerican and colonial forbears, associated luxury and status with elegant pipes. And these elite Andalusians, like their forbears, associated smoking with courtly refinement and chewing tobacco with ar-duous exertion. Castro y Medinilla thought snuffing, too, beneath the high born. Over time, however, upper-class men and women in Spain, while not entirely eschewing the practices described by Castro y Medinilla, increas-ingly made snuff, rather than pipes, the form of tobacco that connoted courtly pleasure. Other European elites followed suit.[33] What stayed the same was the desire among the elite to mark off their tobacco use from those of the lower classes to emphasize refinement; what changed was the coding of particular practices. In Spain, smoking tobacco increasingly brought to mind Indians and slaves: one upper-class observer commented that those who smoked did so "to relax from work, finding themselves fa-tigued like blacks, slaves, and laborers, and it serves them during disembar-

Figure 8.3. David Teniers the Younger, *Peasants Smoking in an Inn* (1640). This painting emphasizes the shared alteration to mood and consciousness that unifies the smokers, held together in their inward-looking languor. The man outside the physical circular space of the smokers seated around the barrel, and outside their altered consciousness, is eager, filling his pipe, to join them. Oil on wood, 37.2 cm × 26.3 cm. Reproduced courtesy of Cleveland Museum of Art, gift of Mr. and Mrs. J. H. Wade 1916.1046.

Figure 8.4. Adriaen Brouwer, *The Smokers* (c. 1636). The Flemish painter depicted a raucous group who bond around the impertinent puffs of smoke they blow at the viewer. The smoking clouds overhead unite them as if under an enchanted umbrella. The artist put himself in this portrait; he is blowing smoke rings. Oil on wood, 46.4×36.8 cm. The Metropolitan Museum of Art, the Friedsam Collection, bequest of Michael Friedsam, 1931 (32.100.21). Image © The Metropolitan Museum of Art.

Figure 8.5. Jan Steen, *The Dancing Couple* (1663). The joined hands of the eponymous pair frame a symbolically potent pipe behind them, an association underscored by the foregrounding of a more prominent pipe resting against a bowl of lighted embers. This image, like others painted by Steen and fellow artists, suggests that the nature of their tobacco-inflected communion was of a most intimate nature: the telling bulge of the young woman's belly, dissimulated under wraps, and the broken shells beneath their feet were iconographical testament to the couple's amorous activities. Oil on canvas, 102.5 × 142.5 cm. Widener Collection, National Gallery of Art, Washington, D.C. Image © Board of Trustees.

kations in the Indies and other parts."[34] Perhaps snuff, too, gained in popularity among clergy because it could be ingested with slightly less obvious sacrilege in Church and other sacred spaces. But even with the transposition from smoke to snuff there was fundamental continuity with one of the prized aesthetic qualities of tobacco refinement; just as Mesoamerican-style pipes mingled sweet and herbaceous fragrances, so did the same or proximate odiferous additives enhance snuff. Scented with jasmine, orange blossoms, clover, ambergris, and rose, among others, the snuff known as *polvo de olor* became the heir to the tobacco pipes delicately scented with liquidambar described by Castro y Medinilla and his smoking forbears in Mesoamerica. A pamphlet commissioned by the royal tobacco monopoly in 1656 described as a particular specialty of the Seville factory a snuff variety known as "polvillos de Ambar" that combined essences of rose, mint, clover, oak bark, and liquidambar. It was commended for "softening" the bitterness (*mordacidad*) of tobacco. The essential continuity was of the value placed on tobacco consumption as a form of fragrance ingestion, as native roses replaced Mesoamerican floral spices and liquidambar was retained as an essential ingredient.[35] The elite pipes of Mesoamerica, prized for their clever craftsmanship, gave way to other accoutrements: the *tabaqueras*—tobacco boxes for both smoking and snuffing tobacco—made of precious materials, and the Holland linens from which the necessary handkerchiefs were made.[36] The fact that silver tobacco boxes (sometimes decorated with gold plate) were among the prizes—along with silver spoons, perfumed gloves, silk stocking, imported fans, and, of course, chocolate—awarded to winning poets during aristocratic contests is indicative of their regality. And a verse published in 1644 had a fictitious sovereign pronounce "there is no *regalo* in the world like that of *tabaco de olor.*"[37]

In certain settings, such as before or after a formal banquet, tobacco could serve in displays of courtliness, but more often it was quintessentially ribald, a dirty pleasure, more pleasurable because it was dirty. Part of the attraction of tobacco consumption was its outré character. Tobacco consumption was a carnivalesque outlet, more specifically an opportunity to revel in the grotesque and flout normative social order, however unseriously and fleetingly.

Carnival, defined narrowly, refers to the late February and early March celebrations marked by communal spectacle and bodily excess (profligate indulgence in food, drink, sex, and violence) that took place before Lent. The latter, in contrast, was a period demanding renunciation and sobriety according to the Christian liturgical calendar. Christian tradition sanctioned such celebrations based on the valuation of commensality, primordially in the sharing of wine and bread, when the community of believers came together as one. This worldview, organized around the dialectic between feasting and fasting, flesh and spirit, and earth and heaven was enacted in the celebrations that marked the Christian calendar, paradigmatically during the Lenten Carnival, but similar celebrations of fleshly abundance marked almost all the celebrations of the liturgical calendar: the pageants, processions, and feasts occasioned by holy days. Of particular importance in Spain were the commemorations of the Eucharist (Corpus Christi), the Immaculate Conception, and the miracles of the Virgin

Mary and those of the multitudinous saints. Carnivalesque merrymaking also attended important secular events, such as royal weddings, births, and birthdays, as well as coronations.[38] And, in the seventeenth century, carnival elements appeared in theatrical spectacles that became mass entertainments in cities and large towns; burlesque performances marked the intermissions of tragedies and comedies. Tobacco easily infiltrated carnivalesque celebrations. For instance, when Cordoba staged its 1636 Corpus Christi celebration, the pagan god Bacchus—patron deity of profligate excess—was outfitted with a tobacco pipe.[39] And tobacco was a recurring theme in the comedic theater, appearing as props, habits, and even characters, performed on festive occasions. Even when tobacco was consumed and represented outside of these contexts, in literature, in paintings, it took on the elements that the eminent twentieth-century theorist Mikhail Bakhtin argued defined carnival: the celebration of the grotesque body and hierarchical inversions.

Early modern European representations of tobacco consumption depict the unbounded body with tobacco as a vector that turns the inside out, and the outside in. Certainly, critics of tobacco consumption marked it as symbolizing, or rather embodying, antirefinement, antiurbanity, and anticourtesy, or the grotesque. "Taking tobacco is contrary to good manners, urbanity . . . and against the politeness (*política*) and urbane life that instructs and requires maintaining modesty, conducting oneself with cleanliness," decried the physician Francisco de Leiva y Aguilar. He continued his rant:

> Notice that those who take tobacco go around so disagreeably, so nasty and gross, with so many sneezes, always accompanied by slovenliness and great noise. . . . Then is the spitting and nose blowing tidy or clean? Is it delightful or respectful for the person who is watching?[40]

"What delight do you find in something so foul smelling, even if you couch it up with musk or ambar?" clergyman Tomás Ramón asked of snuff devotees.[41] He continued:

> Is it politeness and rational civility to walk around all day long like monkeys, making gestures, faces, arching the eyebrows, wrinkling the brow, sucking in the cheeks, pushing the snuff with the finger into those sewer holes of the nose, turning it to one or another part, enlarging and taking them out of natural proportion? Oh, if only they would look in the mirror and see how bad they appear making such faces![42]

It would be wrong, however, to take these condemnations as evidence that elite men and women completely disowned these aspects of tobacco consumption.

For other sources suggest that for seventeenth-century elite Europeans these grotesque features were part of the appeal.

Elite artists and writers delighted in depicting tobacco scenes as paradigmatic of boorish behavior and plebeian sociability. In part, they did so because it reflected tobacco's actual accessibility and hence popularity among men and women of humble means, as well as its ubiquity in tavern and inn settings. But their works also reveal that elite Europeans found tobacco's carnivalesque qualities enticing. There is a striking contrast between the fixation of painters and authors (as well as their patrons) on their own noble status and the attention that they lavished on the base associations of tobacco. For instance, in stark counterpoint to the scenes of plebeian and peasant life that he depicted so lovingly in many paintings, Teniers the Younger in his own life worked diligently to acquire marks of nobility: he petitioned the Spanish monarchy for a noble title, made an upwardly mobile second marriage, and acquired a chateau.[43] Moreover, those who purchased Teniers's and similar canvasses filled with smokers—a genre for which there was considerable demand given the prolific output, not only of the paintings but of cheaper engravings they inspired—included members of the highest echelons, such eminent grandees as the Admiral of Castile (Duke of Medina de Ríoseco), who owned *A Maritime Scene with a Slave Taking Tobacco*, and the Count of Peñaranda, who owned a painting of *A Man Who Holds in One Hand a Tobacco Pipe, and in the Other Hand a Glass*. Likewise, the Spanish courtier Francisco de Quevedo, who devoted an *entremés* (short comic play) to tobacco and used it frequently as a burlesque and plebeian trope in his bawdy verses, lived his life in the Spanish court: his grandmother, aunt, and mother were royal attendants, his father a palace secretary. As his literary genius won acclaim, he moved in the entourage of some of the most powerful grandees of the age.[44]

What does it mean that these painters and authors traveled in elite circles but depicted tobacco as something base and low? It was not because the nobility rejected tobacco, as has been clearly demonstrated. Teniers and Brouwer went so far as to insert themselves in lowlife tobacco paintings (figure 8.3).[45] Francisco de Quevedo did not hide his affection for tobacco, nor for chocolate, for that matter. Quite to the contrary, he wrote in 1631 that he astounded an Italian diplomat visiting the Spanish court with his fondness for both goods. In February 1645, the last year of his life, he enthused several times about a gift of "four buns of very good chocolate and a very large paper full of *tabaco de olor muy excelentísimo*" that arrived from a Madrid printer.[46] This is in no way to suggest that Teniers and Quevedo had egalitarian impulses, but rather that there was something attractive about representing tobacco consumption as transgressive.

In scenes painted by Teniers and others that showed coarse plebeians smoking, tobacco occasioned the grotesque body: mouth opening to pipe, smoke flowing through nostrils, fingers digging in pipe bowl.[47] Teniers went so far as to transform profligate peasants into actual chimps that overindulge their appetites with food, drink, and tobacco. In *Monkeys Smoking and Drinking*, the animals are particularly enraptured by the process of smoking (figure 8.6). The association between tobacco and animality came from the gestures and expressions of snuffers and smokers, whose behavior struck some as "against all urbanity and human politeness," so anathema to polite society and hence closer to the animal kingdom.[48] The representational practices associated with chocolate put into relief the artists' decisions to make tobacco grotesque. No seventeenth-century painting—as far as I have discovered—shows anyone in the act of drinking chocolate; to do so would be to depict the grotesque body, the body that is open, the mouth connecting to the outside world, resonant with sex, food, and violence of the fleshy world. But Spanish artists in the seventeenth century did not ignore chocolate, they gave it to the still-life genre, which allowed them to depict clean, closed lines of gleaming vessels, pure colors, elegant compositions and so to evoke stately regality, gentility, decorum, and regulated bodies, the accoutrements proxies for the bounded, civilized body, or negations of the messy, unbounded body (see figure 7.4).[49]

Spanish burlesque texts reveled in the grotesqueness of the tobacco devotee. The sneezing and snot produced by snuff was fodder for showing how this very "gallant" activity interfered with the courtly flirtation of the gentleman or gentlewoman (which, by contrast, chocolate so usefully facilitated). Competing in a Madrid literary academy, Vicente Suárez submitted verses entitled "To a gallant who because of forgetfulness discarded his tobacco in a love letter that he had for his Lady." Elaborating on the storyline revealed by the title, the verses proclaim that "the vehicle of your love, for Laura, now is tobacco. The action that was noticed, and was quite obviously inadvertent because of the effect that it prompted, for having seen it, left poor Laura bewildered." The extended conceit of the poem is that the "gallant's" affection for tobacco undermined his courtly devotion to his lady. The author concluded by advising the thwarted lover that "if your snuff maddens her more, it's a thing to send you to the roll [of tobacco]."[50] A similar scenario, though with the sexes reversed, underlay verses entitled "To a Gallant who, while going to kiss his Lady, bit her nose." Blinded with love, this gallant "took the nostrils of his lady between his lips." As it happened, his lady had recently consumed snuff, for the narrator celebrated the "man who could without revulsion take in the mouth squirts of tobacco."[51] In both of these, lust for tobacco appears to trump

Figure 8.6. David Teniers the Younger, *Monkeys Smoking and Drinking* (mid-seventeenth century). Nothing expresses the animality of tobacco more than turning smokers into monkeys. In an attractive historical coincidence, the smoking monkeys also recall the Mayan vase with the same conceit. © Museo Nacional del Prado, Madrid.

the lust felt for the beloved and, at once, becomes messily combined with it, snotty snuff mingling with love letters and kisses, respectively.

In keeping with the material detritus that snuffing exacted, along with the medical characterization of tobacco's work as one of evacuation, snuffing was often likened to defecation, and the resultant snot, to shit. Comparing the ubiquity of "nostrils full of snuff" to that of gloves among gentlemen, a Valencian court poet added that "with tobacco, [they have] handkerchiefs, like diapers of babies." Even more crudely he wrote, "Thus the sodomite searches for filthy occasions, I imagine that he will walk among the nostrils where there is tobacco, lost." A humanist poet-scholar included the following lines in his Latin epigram "In Eos Qui Summut Naribus Tabacum": "It is a sweet thing to take tobacco, but . . . who can look at the nostrils dirtied with this mess and not imagine baby buttocks full of *caca*?"[52] We are more directly heir to the ideas of Victorians and Romantics than the Renaissance, so "grotesque" today is usually a negative appellation. But there was a different view of the grotesque in the Middle Ages through to the sixteenth and seventeenth centuries, one that was, according to Bakhtin, "deeply positive," related to celebrating life and renewal, overcoming fear, and subsuming the individual in the social and natural worlds.[53] The grotesque united life and death together in a cycle of decay and renewal. It subordinated the individual into a larger communal or natural whole. The very vivid way that tobacco use facilitated and demonstrated the porousness between body and environment also made people closer to the animal world than the divine spirit world. As with the other ways tobacco fostered the grotesque, part of its appeal was the play with corporeal boundaries.

Another defining element of the Lenten Carnival and carnival was symbolic inversion or, in Bahktin's words, "the suspension of all hierarchic differences, of all ranks and status; carnivalesque revelry is marked by absolute familiarity. Differences between superiors and inferiors disappear for a short time, and all draw close to each other." In carnivalesque festivities, the "world turned upside down"—beasts ruled over people, women over men, and peasants over kings.[54] Dressing up in costumes—and later masquerade balls for the elite—was essential to carnival celebrations. With these costumes and masks, people assumed alternate identities in street fairs and court spectacles. While carnival studies have greatly emphasized the significance of the Fool who becomes King for a day, it is also important that the King could become a Fool; a 1638 Carnival skit in Madrid saw the royal favorite dressed as a porter and one of the most powerful grandees dressed as a woman.[55] Hierarchical inversions allowed for temporary suspension of the social order, wherein people of different social levels commingled and where the transitoriness of identities was performed through the exchanging of them.

Like prime ministers who became porters in carnival skits, elite tobacco consumers saw themselves as playfully subverting conventional hierarchies. Christians copied pagans, elites emulated plebeians, and men mimicked beasts. Like Teniers's painting, comic verse (as well as moralists' diatribes) referred to tobacco consumers as "brutes," "beasts," and "monkeys." In the notion that tobacco consumers are like animals, the inversion as well as grotesque facet of the carnivalesque is at play. Satirical literature portrayed tobacco consumers as idolaters, appropriating pagan customs, sacrificing Christian devotion for pursuit of their appetites, and worshipping false gods (manifested both in their devotion to vice and the pagan gods with which the goods and correlated behaviors were associated).[56] In consuming tobacco, lords and gentlemen became low born; comic verses referred to tobacco having found a "fearsome" "fit" among grandees and lords, even while there no "rustic" ignorant of it.[57] In evoking the lowlife settings of Madrid, Quevedo wrote of "Tobacco, offered in smoke, among bad company."[58] The *Sátira contra el tabaco* (Satire against tobacco), anonymously published along with *Romance en alabanza del tabaco* (In praise of tobacco), declared that "Turks, blacks, and slaves take it in great excess in order to celebrate, dancing, the festivals of Bacchus and Venus." In fact, it envisioned a moment in which three worshippers of Bacchus—convening in a tavern, of course—decide that their god needs more acolytes. Accordingly, they succeed in bringing Philip IV, the rulers of France and Catalonia, and the "new" Portuguese king (a reference to the recently rebellious Portugal) under the pagan god's dominion. Their "government[s] . . . all came to halt in the paper wrapper of tobacco."[59] In other words, under tobacco's powerful sway, the civilized imitate the barbarian and the rulers of Europe forgo sovereignty. Like the comic literature, the paintings of lowlife made elites—however transitorily and jokingly—emulators of cultural practices associated with plebeians and idolaters, and even animals. The smokers who populate the canvasses of Teniers, Steen, and their fellow genre painters frequently come from the lowest classes; they appear as coarse ruffians in torn clothing who spend their leisure hours carousing in rustic, even squalid, interiors and indulging their base appetites for lecherous gropes and leers, card playing, and unruly drunkenness.

In consuming tobacco—and in thinking about and representing snuff and smoke in the way that they did—elites maintained some of the "uses" of the symbolic inversions during carnival but without it necessitating actual interclass mingling. If this is so, it also offers a contributing explanation for a cultural phenomenon that has somewhat mystified historians—why the intermingling of classes that characterized carnival in the seventeenth century and before gave way to increasing class stratification in celebration and leisure.[60] Perhaps some of the work of carnival, for elites at least, was now being done by tobacco—providing an opportunity for social communion marked by sensual, transgressive excess. The emphasis on the grotesque and symbolic inversions clashed with the honor-laden rites of civility.

The particular elevation of chocolate coincided, even accentuated, a phenomenon that Norbert Elias has called the "civilizing process"—elite Europeans' growing obsession with manners and etiquette centered around control of bodily processes (e.g., the triumph of the fork over eating with the hands and that of the napkin over wiping one's hands on the nearby dog; the exile of farting, spitting, belching, and other bodily processes to places and situations outside of public view).[61] Erasmus of Rotterdam, one of civility's most influential and articulate advocates, believed that the

Christian ideal of renunciation should not be expressed in dramatic cycles of extreme indulgence and extreme abstinence, but rather he encouraged constant moderation and regulation that he thought would allow for inward-directed spiritual attention and encourage bellicose princes to give up their hotheaded warfare.

Other analyses of the place of the "low" in the representational practices of the "high" have suggested a conservative function, by having the "low" part legitimate the "high" part of the binary or offering a "frame" that puts into relief the solidity of the normative values of courtliness. Perhaps the carnivalesque may have become even more desirable, as well as more fraught, with the ascendance of rites of civility. The restrictions and repressions required of Renaissance courtliness made the outlet afforded by Carnival and the carnivalesque even more necessary as an opportunity to rest from the demands of courtesy and urbanity—in Freudian terms, a legitimate venting of the id.

PRIVATE SUCCOR

To understand how these goods could have such a powerful effect on Iberian society requires looking at how they became woven into the fabric of everyday life, in solitary settings as well as those communal ones that have already been investigated. Private rites centered on the consumption of tobacco and chocolate eased the tribulations of daily life.

A day without chocolate came to be viewed as one of great suffering. By the late seventeenth century "in Spain it [was] held that the greatest misfortune that can befall a man is to be without Chocolate."[62] For those who could afford it, consuming chocolate two, three, or even four times a day was considered standard.[63] A serving with or as breakfast, in particular, was indispensable on both sides of the Atlantic.[64] A realist novel from the mid-seventeenth century illuminates the relationship a typical aficionado had with his chocolate. On waking, a "rich" and "powerful" man is saddened when his servant reports to him that the day is bleak, gray, and rainy. The narrator chides his protagonist:

> Powerful man, open your eyes of understanding and you will see how the time is over for spilling tears; order that the windows are closed and that you are brought some chocolate, get going ... already a servant awaits you, his hands busy with velvet slippers, putting them on your feet, and another servant placing a scarlet cape on your shoulders and a cap on your head; sit down near the bed, close to the lit brazier because you feel cold; but enough of what you've heard, because you are getting warm, in comes the chocolate, drink it, and finish getting dressed, call for the carriage.

In this passage, chocolate is even more central to the waking-up process than dressing. The request for chocolate is a natural response to the news that the weather is nasty and sad; implicit is its uplifting effect, as well as its capacity to banish sleepiness. It is the only thing consumed before the man leaves his house for Mass (which he endeavors to make as short as possible).[65] Proof that this was a fictionalized, but not fictional, description of Spaniards' dependence on chocolate to surpass moments of difficulty comes from the confessional autobiography of a devout Carmelite novice, Isabel de Jesús. Isabel avidly wanted to take religious vows, but her family and even Church superiors sought to deter her and to persuade her to enter an earthly marriage instead. On discovering that she was expected to attend a cousin's wedding, she was overcome by anxiety and fear. "Bothered by the most horrible thought about having to go to this wedding party," Isabel "asked [her] companion to give [her] a little bit of chocolate."[66] For this would-be nun, anxious and besieged by even her closest intimates, the solution was chocolate, which she found a source of resolve and support.

Numerous and various sources referred to chocolate as cheering, uplifting, and invigorating; it was an antidote to fatigue and melancholy. In both medical and popular discourse, the verb *confortar* was frequently used to describe chocolate's effects, which encompassed the English meaning of comfort, but also denoted giving "vigor, spirit, and strength," "fortifying," or "in a certain way to revive."[67] The *Panegírico al chocolate* pithily stated that chocolate "gladdens the heart."[68] With more hyperbole, it claimed that chocolate wards off death, slows time, and prevents suicide:

> To death and time, I challenge
> And to both I make a bet
> That there is no man in the world
> Who would kill himself
> If once he had drank chocolate.[69]

The life-giving properties of chocolate extended to endowing people with youthful vitality. The *Panegírico* featured an old man "whose expiring age overwhelms him" and a woman, "another Sarah who is facing ninety," until chocolate transforms them into youthful lovers.[70] In the early eighteenth century, a writer proclaimed that on drinking chocolate "a great quantity of preoccupations distance themselves from the heart, the corrosive disquiet flees. You [meaning chocolate] apportion afflicted men with the rest they crave, and ensure that the pangs of sadness get dispersed."[71]

People consumed chocolate to combat grogginess and keep sleep at bay not only in the morning but also when they needed to work into the night.[72] Beyond its rousing properties, chocolate appealed to scholars, artists, and preachers for summoning creative energies.[73] In the poem "Vituperation of Tobacco and Proper Praise of Chocolate," the narrator credited chocolate with "empowering [his] pen to lofty heights."[74] Another wrote that chocolate succors the scholar, the soldier, and the poet, who is provided with "sacred inspirations for his verses"; the enchanted beverage "increases the years of the one that wants to enlighten the world with his writings, and with continual attention tend to public affairs."[75]

Chocolate's capacity to release creative energies and invigorate the tired body and mind made it the particular friend of preachers and evangelizing priests, as Marradón had noted with disapproval during his sojourn in the New World. But before long, priests' reliance on chocolate became commonplace in Spain itself. In 1690, a chocolate aficionado noted without shock but, rather, approval that "preachers find much good in taking chocolate before and after preaching, taking it before relaxes and gives them better vigor for their task, and after, it repairs the exhausted spirits, and they ascertain that in addition it gives them ideas and fortifies the memory."[76]

Tobacco, in all its ingestible forms, was likewise cherished for offering succor. Though they disagreed on its effects on health, civility, and morality, both its proponents and foes acknowledged that it had become a quotidian, if not hourly, practice for many. The tobacco advocate Cordoban apothecarist Juan de Castro y Medinilla recommended it be used first thing in the morning and last thing before bed in order to "decongest and calm the body." The critic Bartolomé Jiménez Patón decried how people took tobacco "on an empty stomach in the morning, after having snacked, before the midday meal, as well as after it, all during the evening and at night."[77]

Even more than chocolate, tobacco was protean, offering whatever assistance was needed at the moment. Echoing the descriptions of its usefulness to laborers and travelers since the early colonial period, a chronicler of conquest of the Valle de Upar in northeastern Colombia recalled how during a difficult expedition (descending a mountain, navigating waterfalls), one of the soldiers, a certain Juan Hogaza, would "succor himself with tobacco in smoke." The chronicler added that in tobacco "the soldiers find more virtues than rosemary, so when they are full, they say it empties them, and when hungry, sustains them, when hot, refreshes them and when cold, warms them."[78] In keeping with its shape-shifting qualities, tobacco was appreciated for its mitigation of overindulgence as well as deprivations. Castro y Medinilla noted that "it helps the digestion, effecting in this case such wondrous work, that many times those who are so full they could vomit, and then taking the said smoke, within a half hour, they find themselves with greater hunger than ever, as if they had not eaten in two or three days," though he cautioned restraint, considering such uses appropriate in only "very urgent cases."[79]

Tobacco offered more than physical relief. Quevedo dramatized the psychic relief afforded by tobacco in his one-act play *El médico del tabaco* (The doctor of tobacco). When a patient complains, "I suffer from great melancholy," the eponymous physician prescribes tobacco and replies, "Then, make an oboe-sized cigar." His next patient, a woman suffering from heartbreak after losing her student lover, asks, "What remedy can I take for such an illness?" "Inhale tobacco priced at two reales," replies the physician. The woman asks, "So snuff tobacco helps one to forget?" The answer:

> To forget, the remedy is well known
> Sniff quickly with the hand pinching
> So that the senses are stirred up and sneezed
> And with that apprehension is then lost.[80]

Cristóbal de Hayo, a faculty member in the Seville school of medicine, favored tobacco as an antidote to feeling lonely: "One who is journeying alone, bringing tobacco, now and then snuffing some, will feel neither the loneliness nor the journey; likewise, a person being home alone, who has with him snuff and uses it, does not feel loneliness."[81]

It was a widely held belief, albeit disputed by critics of tobacco consumption, that tobacco sharpened cognitive faculties, particularly memory, which is still a matter of debate among scientists.[82] Accordingly, scholars and students sought out tobacco to help them with their intellectual labors. Hayo attested that "if someone is studying something and gets frustrated with not being able to understand it, and he snuffs a little tobacco, returns to the [subject], he is able to apprehend it with more facility." Tomás Hurtado, an author of a tobacco treatise, remarked on snuff being a mainstay of the lawyers and university graduates who staffed the state bureaucracy, who "on one side have their books, and on their other, a box with Tobacco. . . . It seems to them that it stimulates the wits, sharpens their logic." The physician Francisco Leiva y Aguilar thought that it was delusional to think tobacco had such effects, but in his despair makes clear that he was in the minority: "Many, such as businessmen and scholars and clerics take it for the memory." Clerics, he alleged, believed that by taking tobacco they would become

> erudite, in little time and without work, and, wise with grace, they will become heads of their orders. This too happens to new students and those lazy ones, who, seeing their teachers and others successful in learning, want to learn for free . . . believing that tobacco augments the memory and all their study is to take it and with each snuff they believe that they acquire a barrel of science, such that some believe that they only need to pass a course in tobacco in order to ascend to magistracies and prelacies.

To prove his point, he felt compelled to point out that great intellectuals of the caliber of St. Jerome, St. Augustine, St. Thomas, and Galen and "other doctor Theologians, Jurists, Physicians, and of other professions in whom we find such beneficial subjects and read such admirable writing" were "men who never took tobacco," unlike the many tobacco users of his day who "do not write things of importance." The common view that tobacco assisted intellectual and creative labors percolated into broadsheet satire, such as one spoofing the tobacco-inspired poet who writes verses "as stiff as rocks."[83]

Tobacco, it was agreed, had powerful effects on sexual desire and activities, though what those were was subject to considerable debate. It was a widely held belief among clerics that tobacco not only buttressed their intellects but also their vows of chastity. "It must be warned," wrote the Cordoban apothecarist Castro y Medinilla, that tobacco "*CONSUMES SPERM AND DIMINISHES MARKEDLY COITUS*" (the capitals are his own), adding in the margin that it was "excellent for ecclesiastics and a danger for the betrothed and soldiers." The *Sátira contra el tabaco* (Satire against tobacco) mocked the belief of religious novices that tobacco was "contrary to lust," but thereby indicates that it *was* a belief. In the next decade the medical school professor Hayo was compelled to defend tobacco against those who blamed it for an epidemic of sterility "in men as much as women."[84]

The prominence of tobacco and chocolate in situations of almost hyperbolic sociability *and* those of extreme, even paradigmatic, solitariness was not a paradox. Rather, they were mutually reinforcing. Those properties that made them so right for use alone—heightening alertness, calming agitation, creating well-being—allowed individuals to join together in a shared mood, creating a powerful experience of union. Conversely, the fact that the goods could create a sensory bridge, eliding the distance between individuals, influenced private episodes of consumption, but in these contexts the goods re-formed from bonding agent to desired other, becoming a surrogate companion, offering wholeness and relieving loneliness. The fact that tobacco and chocolate belonged to varying rites intensified the somatic and ritual power of their consumption. In this, early modern Europeans' use of the goods greatly resembled that of native American forbears.

TRADITIONS AND TRANSFORMATIONS

But do the similarities that marked pre-Columbian and European consumption of tobacco and chocolate reflect a causal or coincidental relationship? It seems unlikely one could ever "prove" one interpretation or the other, but there are compelling reasons to believe that the symbolic

attributions and ritual contexts that characterized European use of tobacco and chocolate, like their material preferences, reflected Amerindian
antecedents. Just as Europeans developed sensory proclivities for a spicy,
foamy cacao beverage, tobacco smoke brushing tracheal airways, and
scented snuff pricking nasal passages, they learned from others—in a
chain of transmission beginning with native Americans—that tobacco
and chocolate were singular substances to consecrate social bonds. One
rebuttal to the alternative argument that Europeans would have embraced
tobacco and chocolate as social lubricants even without these antecedents
because consumption of food and drink are "universally" social activities
is that today powerful psychotropic substances, some which work on the
brain in ways quite similar to tobacco, namely pharmaceutical antidepres-
sants that affect the presence of brain neurotransmitters such as serotonin,
are most often not consumed in collective settings.[85] Rather, their consumption is a medical, solitary ablution. Popping a pastel-colored pill out
of a orange-tinged plastic tube is culturally more proximate to inserting
eyedrops or flossing teeth, than sharing a cigarette on a door stoop, even
if the pharmacological effects have strong semblances. In other words, it is
worth considering that the intensely social character of European tobacco
and chocolate consumption was not a given but the result of learning. It is
perhaps most straightforward to see pre-Hispanic origins in the associations of chocolate with courtly refinement and erotic titillation. It is more
of a stretch, but still worthy of speculation, that even the grotesque and
transgressive objectives of European tobacco consumption relate to
pre-Columbian usage. Recall that Indian groups throughout the Americas, while valuing tobacco as a means to cement bonds and celebrate social cohesion, also deployed it in ways that temporarily disrupted
conventional order, that put into abeyance the quotidian rules. Shamans
in the Caribbean and South American consumed copious amount of tobacco to enter dramatically altered states that let them depart society in
order to communicate with spirits; priests and penitents in Mesoamerica
used tobacco when they set off on arduous pilgrimages and mortified their
flesh. Europeans who valued tobacco for precipitating a carnivalesque experience also pursued a temporary hiatus from normative society, wanting
to experience the body in its full beastliness, wanting, however fleetingly,
to experience social identity as transitory and mutable.

9

Monopolizing Vice

❖ ❖

In the first years of discovery and conquest the Spanish Crown had no use for tobacco. When Indians on the island of Hispaniola (probably) offered Columbus a bouquet of dried tobacco leaves, it did not stimulate great excitement. Columbus—like his royal sponsors—knew that precious metals and the desirable spices of the Orient generated riches. The initial indifference had paradoxical effects. Europeans' commodification of tobacco was integrally related to the Spanish Crown's efforts to maintain a monopoly on trade with its American possessions. Despite the state's initial apathy-turned-antipathy toward tobacco, this New World good not only turned out to be a fundamental staple of the Atlantic trade but the basis of substantial revenues for the Spanish state. In 1636 the Spanish Crown decreed a state monopoly on tobacco within Castile, and later other kingdoms followed suit, requiring its procurement, processing, and sale to be the exclusive prerogative of its chosen concessionaire. Tobacco, in fact, would generate more wealth for the Crown than metallic bullion by the end of the seventeenth century, becoming "the greatest and most considerable jewel of the Royal Treasury" by 1684.[1] But the significance of this institution—and the other fiscal impositions that preceded it—went beyond the revenue it produced for the impecunious treasury; it effectively increased the importance and the power of the state, legally, symbolically, and administratively. In this chapter I bring to the fore a set of connections that show the mutually determining effects of state, empire, and the community of diasporic Portuguese New Christians. This reveals how the state used empire to expand its juridical domain domestically, how private citizens fomented the growth of the state, and how imperial and fiscal policies inflected consumer culture.

My portrayal of the state in this chapter accords in some ways with the recent revisionist interpretations of Spanish state-building.[2] In the older view, Spain had long been accorded the role of precocious front-runner in the development of the absolutist state. The marriage of Ferdinand and Isabella in 1469 united the kingdoms of Castile and Aragon under one crown, and the sovereigns made feuding aristocrats submit to royal authority, particularly in Castile. In these narratives, Castilian absolutism reached its apotheosis under Philip II; in the seventeenth century the baton passed to France where the paradigmatic absolutist state developed under the reign of the "Sun King," Louis XIV (r. 1643–1715). But more recently, historians have "done much to modify the aging construct of Castilian absolutism." Where municipalities were once viewed as "chastened and inert pawns of the central government," they are now assigned considerable powers because of their "deep involvement in state administration and the collection of taxes at a local level." And where the emphasis was once on the "populace and resources being bled dry" for the sake of the Habsburgs' failed efforts at imperial hegemony, now we are shown that elites "profited from the creation and consolidation of the complex political, economic and social structures through which the empire was financed and managed."[3]

The "state" that we see in the following pages coincides with this revisionism, in that as much as it was the brainchild of government ministers and advisers, the monopoly was an invention of those who consistently "leased" the concession throughout the seventeenth century—primarily members of the Portuguese New Christian community, who, like the Mexica *pochteca*, or long-distance merchants, sustained strained relations of mutual dependence with the state. They developed one of the most far-reaching and powerful institutions of the state in the Spanish empire, one that inspired emulation throughout Europe and beyond.

But the history of the royal tobacco monopoly also shows that it would be premature to completely abandon the notion of absolutism, even if the state was a "confusing plethora of competing jurisdictions presided over by the figure—actually a legal fiction—of a monarch."[4] In the seventeenth century this "legal fiction" of a sovereign monarch expanded its authority and jurisdiction in ways that had powerful social and political consequences. More particularly, the New World—in the form of tobacco—became the basis for absolutist jurisprudence in Castile.

My view of that state accords with an understanding of the state as not only a series of social constituencies empowered by the "legal fiction" of a monarch but also as "new techniques of organization and articulation."[5] In Michel Foucault's account, these "techniques" or "disciplines" emerged to "enclose and partition space, systematize surveillance and inspection, break down complex tasks into carefully drilled movements, and coordinated separate functions into larger combinations." Such methods spread from "field to field in the eighteenth and nineteenth centuries," appeared simultaneously in the organization of "factories, schools, prisons, hospitals, commercial establishments and government offices," and "represented a new, localized yet enormously productive technology."[6] Many of these "disciplines," however, were precociously deployed by the inventors of the tobacco monopoly, as originated in Castile in the first half of the seventeenth century.

Finally, the story of the fiscal policies relating to tobacco and chocolate reveals a dialectical relationship between culture and state. Cultural understandings of tobacco and chocolate—regarding their New World provenance and their status as "luxuries"—were partially responsible for the state's ability to expand its power. These policies, in turn, influenced the cultural meanings of the goods themselves. But even as it justified imposing a monopoly on tobacco because it qualified as a "vice," the state sanctioned it, and "vice" more generally, by becoming the "guarantor" of its "provision" to subjects throughout the land.

TAXES ON VICE

The regime of Philip IV was desperate to come up with new ways to remedy its chronic fiscal woes caused by the demands of an overextended empire. The renewal of war with the Low Countries in 1621 quickly drained coffers. The Habsburg Crown found itself in dire fiscal straits in the early seventeenth century, culminating in a cessation of payments to creditors (i.e., bankruptcy) in 1627.[7] At the same time, rents, never sufficient to meet the costs of empire, were waning. Income from bullion flow dropped off sharply; in the first years of the seventeenth century, the Crown received 2 million ducats of silver annually, but by 1620 the amount diminished to 800,000.[8] And revenue from other rents was mortgaged to bondholders. The situation worsened when the government took the short-term expedient of minting new currency, adding almost 20 million ducats of copper coinage between 1620 and 1626. This not only added inflationary pressure but further decreased the worth of royal rents. This situation led to bankruptcy, so that on January 31, 1627, the Crown's Genoese bankers did not get payments but were involuntarily indemnified with bonds (*juros*). These disastrous years led the Crown and kingdom to experiment with new fiscal devices. The pressure was particularly acute on the Kingdom of Castile. When Castile and Aragon were united under one crown in 1469, and later when Navarre joined them, they were on the forefront of the centralizing trend among European states. However, this did not lead to either institutional or legal uniformity, or to economic integration. The terms of the union maintained the medieval constitutional arrangements in which the relationship between the sovereign and kingdom depended on charters that defined the limits of royal authority. By the seventeenth century this had led to a situation where Castile, not happily, bore the fiscal brunt of empire, along with, in the view of the other kingdoms, its benefit.[9] This largely explains why new levies that were transformative appeared first in Castile.

Central to the political context in which new imposts on tobacco and chocolate were decreed was a notorious and politically divisive subsidy that the Cortes (the parliamentary body of Castile that needed to assent to new taxes) conferred to the Crown for the first time in 1590. Implemented in the aftermath of the English defeat of the Spanish Armada, the *millones* (as the tax was known because its quantities were figured in millions of ducats rather than *maravedís*) was supposed to be a one-time contribution spanning six years, rather than a regular new tax. Phillip II was able to convince the Cortes to confer the *millones* only as an extraordinary, short-term measure and by appealing to the feelings of patriotism and military shame of the representatives (*procuradores*) of the Cortes. (The memorials to the king and the exhortations of the president of the Council of Castile, the Count of Barajas, underscored that the naval losses of the Armada put Spain and its empire in a situation of dangerous vulnerability.) But, through renewals, the *millones* quickly became a permanent feature of the fiscal landscape. The initial accords did not specify how the taxes were to be raised, but beginning with its 1603 renewal, the revenue for the *millones* came from imposts levied on "four species"—wine, meat, olive oil, and vinegar—all basic foodstuffs in the early modern Spanish diet.[10]

These were clearly desperate measures, because excise taxes on necessities contradicted one of the central tenets of early modern theories of political economy or the economic polity. A tax on basic foodstuffs jeopardized the general populace's already marginal level of subsistence. Many members of the elite perceived this not only as morally unconscionable but as politically untenable, increasing the potential for hazardous social instability in the form of hungry mobs. Taxing municipal granaries was considered an unacceptable way to raise money to service the *millones*, because these cereals "mattered to the well-being of the poor."[11]

The taxes on these provisions incited outrage at the other end of the social spectrum too, because they were applied to nobles and clergy, estates normally exempt from paying taxes. These privileged constituencies complained that the universal application of the *millones* effaced the line between commoners and their social betters. Nobles accused "the estate of tax-paying men" of "using the said taxes and expedients to hurt gentlemen and nobles, and to relieve and unburden themselves of payment." Similarly, the clergy strenuously objected to paying the imposts for which the Crown solicited and obtained a papal bull in 1591.[12] Throughout the seventeenth century, Church and Crown battled over whether or not clergy had to pay the *millones* on wine, oil, meat, and fish. They invoked the traditional medieval justification for clerical exemption, that it is "the right arm of the Monarchy," "as the Vicar of God," and as such, "exempt from all taxes." They contended that the vocation of the clergy is "to revere and praise good, to be the mediator between God and the People, interceding for them with Prayer and the Sacrifice: this is the tax that they must pay, this is their charter, and that of continually commending the life and health of His Majesty and the governance of his kingdom, and the conservation of the Monarchy, to God." Clerical advocates even proclaimed that declining Spanish fortunes were due to the unjust taxes imposed on the ecclesiastical state—that God was punishing the kingdom because of this injustice.[13]

In 1631, Philip IV's prime minister, the Count-Duke of Olivares, tried to allay the widespread discontent by abolishing the umbrella of the *millones* and, instead, hiking the price of salt, which was sold through a royal monopoly.[14] The cure proved worse than the disease, however. First, the income did not meet expectations, or even come close to matching the revenue raised by the *millones*. Again, clergy claimed exemption because of ecclesiastic immunity. Nor did it appease the populace. Given salt's importance as a basic commodity, the increased salt prices were even less popular with Castilian subjects than the *millones*. Fishermen used salt to preserve fish, salted fish being a fundamental foodstuff in a society that observed at least 150 Church-required meatless days a year; butchers used it to cure meats that would otherwise spoil in an age without refrigeration.[15] The repeal of the *millones* endured only one year; they were reinstituted and renegotiated in 1632.

Royal officials learned their lesson; the new taxes targeted goods not considered "essential to life." Before the disastrous salt price hike, Prime Minister Olivares convoked a special meeting of theologians and his advisers to consider a variety of "remedies" for the bankruptcy of two years earlier and the hot fronts in Italy, the Low Countries, and France.[16] The committee members recognized an important distinction between those taxes levied on products essential to life and those that are not.[17] Accordingly, they were eager to tax cacao, and so approved it "because it falls on a luxury good and is not necessary and is free of other taxes." At the meeting the rationale for vice taxes was fully articulated. For instance, one committee member recommended raising the price of playing cards—sold through a royal monopoly—for moral and pragmatic reasons. He explained that since the "idle and wasteful buy this commodity, and from their own estates pay for its malignant appeal, and lose many hours time," if the price increase did have a deterrent effect, it would be a good thing to "liberate" them from this huge waste, this "affliction." The proposal made good economic sense, he added, because card players would hardly be deterred from shelling out two or three times as much as they were currently accustomed to paying because of their dependency on the "entertainment," and so a price increase would not reduce the sale of cards.[18] He did not feel compelled to address the fact that the economic justification rendered moot the moral one. Similar rationales were put forth for proposals to increase taxes on theater tickets and the fee prostitutes were obligated to pay for wearing silk dresses. Concerning the requirement that prostitutes (*mujeres públicas*) pay for that privilege, he said, "if it makes them leave their evil vice (which it will not) it will have been a great service for Our Lord."[19] Vice taxes were then seen as particularly attractive because they were founded on the recognition that those partial to the vices had a dependency such that mere price increases would not deter their passion, and hence not risk sabotaging the economic success of the tax, but, in the impossible condition that it would, the effects would be salubrious for the vice-doing person and for the moral condition of the kingdom.

In the aftermath of the political upheaval unleashed by the salt tax disaster, royal officials were ready to try out one of the other "remedies" proposed at the 1629 meeting, new taxes on tobacco and chocolate.[20] In 1632 the Cortes approved the Crown's request for a renewal of the *millones* that levied new taxes on chocolate and tobacco, as well as sugar, conserves, paper, and fish.[21] It stipulated a rate of 3 *reales* per pound of tobacco, 1 *real* per pound of chocolate, and also taxed its ingredients (one-half *real* per pound for cacao and *mecaxóchitl* and 12 *reales* per pound for vanilla), to be paid in the customs house of Seville. The rhetoric that accompanied these new taxes emphasized their status as luxury goods, rather than essentials. A circular announcing the new taxes in 1634 claimed that these measures were "the least harsh and the most soft that could be discovered," and contrasted them to the older taxes that caused "harms, irritations, and vexations in the cities, towns, and villages of these Kingdoms."[22] In the discussions in the Cortes, one proponent of the increased taxes on paper, sugar, and tobacco explicated what was meant by "least harsh." In his elaboration of luxury taxes, he explained that since these goods were not necessities, increasing taxes on them would not affect the poor.[23]

This basis for "sin taxes" was hardly a new idea, but the *millones* agreement did more than tax tobacco and chocolate, it also included a provision that allowed the Crown to control the sale of tobacco throughout the kingdom through a royal monopoly. The willingness of the Cortes to agree to a kingdomwide monopoly was a political coup for the Crown, for contemporary jurists viewed royal monopolies as an illicit way for sovereigns to raise revenues, since they were consumption taxes in disguise (which required the consent of the Cortes) and, potentially, unfairly raised prices on basic necessities.[24] Furthermore, in consenting to the *millones* agreement, the Cortes had further stipulated a veto on any new monopolies. Even the commission convened by Olivares in 1629, desperate to find new measures to meet revenue shortfalls, recognized that "monopolies are prohibited by law and, also, in Castile as a condition of the *millones*."[25] The idea of a kingdomwide monopoly on tobacco was more than a decade old. It had been circulating at least since 1618, when Duarte Eustacio, likely a member of the Portuguese community, proposed such a fiscal device to the Treasury Council. Its members rejected it.[26] In the interim, however, municipal monopolies on tobacco appeared in the southern cities of Ecija and Antequera.[27] And in 1623 the king had imposed a tobacco monopoly on the sale of tobacco in the Spanish presidios of Oran and Mazalquivir in North Africa, much to the distress of the local inhabitants who used tobacco almost like currency in their exchanges with North African traders. (It appears part of the motivation had been to give the monopoly farm to the widow of a couple who had raised Olivares's bastard son.)[28]

Because of the political sensibilities surrounding monopolies, the legal and symbolic justification of the new rent on tobacco was of the utmost importance. The justification began with the widely held belief that certain goods were exempt from the ban on monopolies because they were deemed *regalía*—or under the possession of the sovereigns, part of the royal patrimony and thus subject to taxation and monopolies by the Crown without parliamentary assent. All mineral deposits found in the kingdom were *regalía*—this was the basis for the lucrative royal salt monopoly. Because kings and queens granted permission and support for overseas exploration, they also claimed a portion of all "treasures" discovered as a result of such endeavors. On the basis of its overseas provenance, black pepper constituted a *regalía*, and the same reasoning was applied to tobacco and chocolate; in fact, the legislation decreeing the tobacco monopoly specified that it was to be leased "with the conditions of the pepper monopoly."[29]

In addition to the obvious benefits to the royal coffers in imposing a monopoly on a *regalía*—and in contrast to the rationale accompanying "sin taxes"—the Crown also employed a paternalistic rhetoric, presenting the state as the purveyor of vital goods, clearly in evidence in the royal decree that reinvigorated the salt monopoly in 1564.[30] Uniform procedures would guarantee quality. Centralization would unite the kingdom, removing impediments to the free movement of salt and liberating consumers from "aggravations, annoyances, vexations, and harm" that resulted under the former salt regime. Finally, a royal monopoly ensured provision: "hence We must provision in a manner whereby there is sufficiency and abundance." The legitimacy of the royal monopoly on salt derived from the monarchical privilege of the *regalía* but also the notion that the Crown was the best, and sole, guarantor of uniform access to consumption in the royal domain. Similarly, the tobacco monopoly *arrendador* (lessee or concessionaire) was "*obligated to provision and supply* tobacco in powder, leaf, and roll of these Kingdoms."[31] While the apologists for the new taxes on tobacco and chocolate emphasized that they were more equitable than the previous taxes on basic foodstuffs because the poor presumably could opt not to consume these luxury goods, the rhetoric of royal monopoly paradoxically made tobacco a basic necessity whose provision was the king's obligation to his subjects.

Absolutist jurisprudence put into relief both the exotic origins and sinful qualities of the goods. An impecunious treasury catalyzed the search for new fiscal devices, but a significant reason that tobacco and chocolate became such attractive targets was not only accelerating demand but also their cultural attributes. They combined three characteristics heretofore not seen together: as items of widespread consumption (or potentially so in the case of chocolate), they promised a consistent and expanding source of revenue; as goods identified as a luxury or vice, rather than "essential," they hurdled political opposition; and as overseas imports, they could be defined as a New World *regalía* and so sidestep constitutional objections. "Inventing tradition" when they developed the legal basis for monopolies on tobacco and chocolate, royal jurists fused together the paternalism that justified monopolies on essential goods and the categorization of "vice" that justified taxes on luxuries. For their first years, the new imposts on tobacco and chocolate remained as taxes; tobacco consumption in Castile (excluding Seville, which was farmed separately) netted the treasury an estimated 12 million *maravedís* annually.[32] Then, in 1634, officials of the Crown decided to put into effect the *millones* decree that allowed the establishment of a state monopoly on tobacco, implementing it in 1636. (They also decreed a monopoly on chocolate, but did not seem to attempt its implementation, for reasons that remain obscure.) Castile was the first of Spain's kingdoms to impose a monopoly on tobacco. Its astounding success as a source of revenue led to its imitation in other Spanish kingdoms. The Kingdom of Navarre followed suit in 1642. In keeping with its tradition of greater local autonomy, the Crown of Aragon[33] saw the establishment of tobacco monopolies in individual polities—Mallorca in 1650, Aragon by 1686, the city of Barcelona in 1655—but not uniformly implemented throughout the entire Spanish kingdom until after the War of

Spanish Succession (1701–14).[34] It was one thing to decree a royal tobacco monopoly; it was another, however, to implement it. The dynastic state had assumed the legal and political clout necessary to invent such an institution as the tobacco monopoly. Yet it did not possess the means to develop it. Castile's monopoly on tobacco was born at the intersection of three trajectories: the royal treasury's chronic bankruptcies; tobacco's entrance into Spain as a good that was seen as at once exotic, viceful, and popular; and a community of diasporic Portuguese merchants and financiers trying to succeed commercially and socially.

THE ROYAL TOBACCO MONOPOLY: CREATING THE STATE FROM THE OUTSIDE IN

Jerónimo de Barrioneuvo, the courtier who chronicled the happenings that occurred in mid-century Madrid, recorded on September 15, 1655, the following: "Monday at midnight the Inquisition detained 14 Portuguese merchants, businessmen, in particular two tabaccists, one in the Puerta del Sol, and the other by the Palace. These people sprout like mushrooms." The following week he recorded that the Inquisition imprisoned another seventeen "Portuguese" families, commenting that "there is not a Portuguese in Madrid who does not Judaize." The next month, on the 23rd of October, Barrionuevo wrote to his friend: "No tobacco seller remains in Madrid who the Inquisition has not captured. In recent days, it apprehended two entire families, parents and children, and many others have fled to France."[35] This chronicler was wrong that all Portuguese in Spain were secret Jews or crypto-Jews, but he was right that Portuguese *conversos* or "New Christians" dominated the monopoly concession throughout the seventeenth century. The newsworthiness of these events also reveals the strong currents of xenophobia and anti-Semitism in the court around the monopoly and Portuguese merchant dominance.[36] The tobacco monopoly was the joint invention of government—narrowly defined as the monarch, parliamentary bodies, councilors, and their employees—and the *arrendadores* who "leased" it.

In making the tobacco monopoly a concession for lease, the Spanish Crown was following common practice: throughout Europe governments contracted out tax-collecting and royal monopolies to private individuals or syndicates who bid the highest. This way the state could reap the advantages of the monopoly without having to create a standing bureaucracy to administer it. The salt and pepper monopolies were the model used by the *millones* officials when they set forth the conditions for the lease of its tobacco monopoly. In return for payments to the royal treasury of a fixed yearly amount (generally paid twice a year at Christmas and in June) the Crown granted the *arrendador*—whose formal title was "treasurer" of the monopoly—the exclusive right to process, distribute, and sell tobacco within Castile for the period of the lease, generally arranged for ten years (though none ever lasted that long due to death, bankruptcy, and incarcerations by the Inquisition).[37] The lessee was empowered to subcontract and employ subordinates and employees as he saw fit. It was forbidden to all but the monopolist and those he designated to process or sell tobacco within Castile. At the time of the monopoly's implementation, or during its transfer, all who owned significant quantities of tobacco and tobacco-processing equipment were required to sell their tobacco to the monopolist. To ensure compliance and guard against smuggling and fraud, the state conceded ample coercive force to the monopolist and his subordinates. To this end, the *arrendador* and his subordinates could "carry offensive and defensive weapons." The contracts also mandated that the monopolists' representatives in maritime ports were responsible for registering all incoming tobacco so as to guard against contraband.[38]

The implementation began when the state administrators organized a public auction, announced throughout the kingdom by public criers. Bidding for the tobacco monopoly took place throughout the fall of 1636.[39] On December 10, the *millones* commission convened in a patio of His Majesty's palace and reviewed the bids and the fiscal accountability of the bidders. In its pursuit of maximizing its rents from the leased monopoly, the state wanted the highest bid, of course, but it also wanted a lessee who would effectively administer the monopoly and reliably make the promised payments, so it also considered the experience of the potential monopolists. One contender was rejected as too risky, deemed, in the words of an evaluating official, "neither a well-known nor wealthy man, nor does he possess property whatsoever."[40] During later negotiations, the commission rejected another suitor for the monopoly because of his fraudulent practices when he administered an earlier tobacco tax.[41] The state also required that potential *arrendadores* offer collateral for their bid, and suitors for the monopoly often also offered a signing "bonus" if they were selected.

A brief ceremony—a prayer, candle lighting—and a crier's proclamation in a "loud and intelligible" voice announced that the monopoly would rest for 28 million *maravedís* with Antonio de Soria, a Portuguese New Christian who was an established businessman and tax farmer for the *millones* in Murcia.[42] But even as Soria began to administer the monopoly in early in 1637, a short, thin, and precociously ambitious man—he farmed the *alcabála* (sales tax) for Cordoba before he was twenty—named Diego Gómez de Salazar set off from Antequera, in southern Spain, for Madrid, where he also entered a bid for the monopoly. It seems that thirty-one-year-old Gómez de Salazar was not actually pursuing the monopoly for himself but on behalf of Luis Méndez Enríquez, a resident of Seville. Counterbids escalated the price to 36 million. At this point, more monopoly suitors entered the fray, including the tax farmer for the earlier tobacco tax and a salt monopoly *arrendador*.[43] Finally, in 1638, Méndez Enríquez and Gómez de Salazar pushed the lease price to 55 million *maravedís*.

Though the new bids were allowed according to the auction rules, Soria nevertheless felt himself the victim of an injustice. He blamed his ouster on copycatting. It was he who saw the potential and the true value of the monopoly "without exaggeration" before anyone else "held it in esteem, or dared to make an offer for it." But then, by making himself "an exemplar by introducing himself into this rent" and by "giving order and form to its administration," others coveted the organization he had created. Soria charged that his rivals, so impressed by the institution he had set up, were led to overestimate the monopoly's worth and "tried to take it away from me . . . by means of a higher bid." The presiding official (*procurador general*), who supported Gómez de Salazar's takeover effort, claimed that it was Gómez de Salazar who "recognized" that Soria's bid for the rent "was not true to its value," while Antonio de Soria "maliciously . . . intended to defraud the rent."[44] Soria fought back with all of the legal means at his disposal, winning his first appeal, when the lower tribunal agreed to return the lease to him for 30 million *maravedís*. But when the case went to the next level of appeal, Méndez Enríquez was the victor. Soria waged a battle of public opinion as well. He printed his arguments for the illegality of Diego Gómez de Salazar's hostile takeover in a pamphlet that appears to have been for wider circulation than the deciding judge. The protracted monopoly intrigue did not remain a backroom or patio affair but spilled into published briefs, consumed, perhaps, by the inhabitants of the court the way today's newspaper readers follow stories about corporate sharks and leveraged buyouts in the business pages.[45]

Soria ultimately prevailed in his quest for the tobacco monopoly lease. Méndez Enríquez apparently *had* overestimated what he could provide to the Crown from the tobacco rent—willfully according to Soria—after obtaining the lease for 55 million *maravedís*. Thus, in a "short time" according to Soria, Méndez Enríquez negotiated a discount of 15 million. In 1642 Soria convinced the commission to reinstate him as the lessee of the monopoly on the basis that Méndez Enríquez did not meet the terms that he had negotiated and so the lease rightfully belonged to him instead. Soria resumed control of the monopoly in April 1642 with the agreement to pay annually 50 million *maravedís*. The price of the monopoly lease continued to escalate dramatically over the course of the seventeenth century (though some of the increase was due to spiraling inflation), so that by 1684 it was declared to be the "chief rent" of the treasury.

The Crown—and its *arrendadores*—profited from the monopoly through the substantial markup at which tobacco was sold to consumers from the price paid for it on the "open" market—the shipments arriving in Seville, as well as Málaga, Cadiz, and Bilbao, from the Spanish, Portuguese, and, increasingly, from the English colonies in the Americas. Prior to the monopoly, the wholesale cost of tobacco in Andalusia ranged between 5 *reales* per pound for "roll" and 11.5 *reales* for scented snuff, though generally prices ranged between 7 and 9 *reales*.[46] Under the new regime, retailers (*estanqueros*) were required to pay 20 *reales* per pound for the scented snuff and 14 *reales* per pound for the other varieties from the monopoly distributors.[47] These prices endured through most of the seventeenth century, and account records indicate that the monopoly concessionaire paid 7 *reales* per pound of roll tobacco and 8.5 *reales* for high-quality *monte* tobacco in 1658. Retailers then had some discretion as to how much to charge when they sold it in smaller quantities.[48]

While government officials drew up the legal contours of the new royal monopoly, its actual organization and operating processes were developed by its concessionaires, the *arrendadores*. It was true, as Soria asserted, that it was the *arrendadores* who "[gave] order and form" to the royal tobacco monopoly.

THE MONOPOLY AND MARRANISM

A common denominator of a vast majority of the monopoly lessees throughout the seventeenth century—including Méndez Enríquez, Soria, and Gómez de Salazar, who became the concessionaire himself in 1656—was their membership in "the Portuguese nation."[49] In fact, all but two or three of the thirteen tobacco monopoly *arrendadores* were either born in Portugal or of parents who had emigrated from there.[50] Moreover, in the words of historian Antonio Domínguez Ortiz, in the seventeenth century "tobacco monopolist came to be synonymous with Judaizing Portuguese."[51] (See table 9.1.)

In fact, the New Christian or *converso*—though not necessarily crypto-Jewish—identities of the so-called Portuguese nation are central to understanding the development of the tobacco monopoly. The Crown's expulsion of Jews from Spain in 1492 had the inadvertent consequence of reshaping the identity of the Portuguese mercantile community. First, it resulted in an influx of thousands of Spanish Sephardim, who, quite logically, found Portugal an attractive destination, given its proximity, cultural familiarity and, for some, even a place with kin. Yet the haven was

TABLE 9.1. Seventeenth-century *Arrendadores* for the Royal Tobacco Monopoly of Castile

Year	Arrendador	Value of annual contracts (millions of *maravedís*)	Portuguese New Christian
1637	Antonio de Soria	23	yes
1638	Luis Méndez Enríquez	55	yes
1642	Antonio de Soria	50	yes
1650	Juan de Rosales and heirs	57	yes
1656	Diego Gómez de Salazar	62	yes
1663	Jorge Bautista Carrafa	83–124	yes
1673	Francisco Centani	285	no
1673	Simón Ruiz de Pessoa	285	yes
1676	Francisco López Pereira	285	yes
	Manuel de Aguilar		yes
1677	Francisco Centani	unknown	no
1680	Pedro Parada	unknown	unknown
1680	Francisco Centani	380	no
1680	Luis Márquez Cardoso	unknown	yes
1682	Manuel de Cáceres	265–345	yes
	Luis Márquez Cardoso		yes
1683	Francisco López Pereira	240–300	yes
1684	direct administration	159	n.a.
1687	Simón Ruiz Pesoa	178.5	yes
1691	Pedro Parada	183	unknown
1701	direct administration	n.a.	n.a.

Sources: Manuel Garzón Pareja, "El tabaco y la real hacienda," in *Homenaje a Profesor Carriazo* (Seville: Universidad de Sevilla Facultad de Filosofía y Letras, 1972), 2: 235–67; José Manuel Rodríguez Gordillo, *Un archivo para la historia del tabaco*, ([Spain]: Tabacalera, 1984), 19; AGS DGT, inv. 4, leg. 29; BN VE sig. 252-110; AVM Sec. 3 leg. 462, exp. 9; BL Add. Mss. 10262, fols. 714r–716v; 86; Julio Caro Baroja, *Los Judios en la España moderna y contemporánea* ([Madrid]: Ediciones Arión ,1962), 2:81–86; Julio Caro Baroja, "La sociedad criptojudia en la corte de Felipe IV," in *Inquisición, brujas, y criptojudaismo* 2nd ed. (Barcelona: Ediciones Ariel, 1972), 108; Sabino Lizana Fernández, "Administración y administradores de la renta del tabaco en la segunda mitad del siglo XVII en Castilla," in *Tabaco y economía en el siglo XVIII*, ed. Agustín González Enciso, Rafael Torres Sánchez (Pamplona: Ediciones Universidad de Navarra, 1999); Lutgardo García Fuentes, *El comercio español con América, 1650–1700* (Seville: Escuela de Estudios Hispano-Americanos, 1980), 40. The *arrendamiento* values refer to the *bid* amount of the lease, but quite often the *arrendador* did not pay the full bid amount and negotiated reductions because of fraud or for other reasons.

short-lived, for the new king of Portugal, Dom Manuel I, succumbed to Castilian pressure to impose religious orthodoxy in his kingdom as well, but with an important twist—rather than expelling Jews (who now included as many displaced Spaniards as Portuguese natives), the Portuguese king decreed in 1497 that its Jewish population convert to Christianity, so as not to lose this important community. Unlike in Spain, in Portugal enforcement was relatively lenient for the first decades after the decree—the Inquisition was not immediately established—which led many *conversos* to continue to practice Judaism in relative safety. It also allowed *conversos* to dominate the Portuguese mercantile community, so that new Christian merchants outnumbered "Old Christian" merchants three to one by the end of the sixteenth century. Prior to 1492, Portuguese merchant houses were identifiable as Old Christian, New Christian, or Jewish, as endogamy prevailed; after 1492 and the influx of Castilian Jews, Portuguese *conversos* and Old Christians increasingly intermarried, which led to a general conflation of "Portuguese" and "New Christian," since the presence of *any* Jewish ancestry led to the designation of "New Christian," even if three out of four of an individual's grandparents were of "Old Christian" stock.[52]

There are several reasons why Portuguese New Christians came to control the royal tobacco monopoly. First, as has been seen, they were on the forefront of transatlantic trade, generally, and tobacco commodification, particularly. In the early seventeenth century, members of the Portuguese New Christian community came to forge a closer relationship with the Habsburg state. The transformation of Spain into a safe(r) haven for Portuguese New Christians was partially the result of the deliberate policy of the prime minister, the Count-Duke of Olivares, to court their richest as financiers. Throughout the sixteenth century Genoese bankers had extended credit to the Habsburgs, but they increasingly withdrew their services after repeated state bankruptcies and forced indemnities. Olivares, always ready to put *raison d'état* before all else, was enthusiastic about a new group that would supply credit, and even direct monetary contributions, in exchange for the Spanish Crown's willingness to overlook its Jewish and Judaizing past, and perhaps even present. In 1627 leaders of the Portuguese New Christian community and royal officials came to an accord known as the "pardon" (*indulto*): in return for a loan of 400,000 ducats to the royal treasury, the Portuguese New Christians wrangled important concessions from the Crown. Foremost among them, those under investigation by the Inquisition for "Judaizing" in Portugal would be pardoned, and they would be free to settle in Castile and participate in the New World trade.[53]

That members of the Portuguese mercantile community in Spain vigorously pursued the new monopoly is no surprise. "Trade, state finances, and monopolies," were, in the words of historian Daviken Studnicki-Gizbert, "the three pillars of [their] enterprise."[54] There were efficiencies—legal and illegal—to have an overlap of personnel in trade and tax farms. For instance, those who administered customs duties could facilitate smuggling, so even when Spain reimposed a trading embargo on the Netherlands in 1621, Dutch Sephardim and peninsular New Christians maintained commercial ties.[55] (This practice was by no means unique to this group; fraud among tax collectors and tax farmers was endemic in early modern Spain and throughout Europe.)[56] The first tobacco monopoly *arrendadores* had experience with other tax farms. Before obtaining the monopoly contract, Soria had farmed the *millones* for the Kingdom of Murcia; another future monopolist farmed the sales tax for Cordoba. Portuguese merchant tax farmers found in the tobacco monopoly a powerful mechanism to legally integrate their positions as the Crown's financiers and transatlantic merchants.

The religious identities of "Portuguese" *conversos* elude any simple characterization, encompassing those with genuine commitments to Christianity, others pledged to Judaism (survival in Iberia requiring a cloak of Christianity), and many who straddled and vacillated between the two identities.[57] Though originating as a derogatory term to tar *conversos* suspected of being secret Jews, *marrano* has been put to use to describe those individuals who desired to live as Jews but were unable to do so without risking their survival, and Marranism to signify those crypto-Jewish beliefs and practices. Historian Yosef Yerushalmi explains that crypto-Jews, or *marranos*, were "a part of the New Christian group but were not coextensive with it." One cannot even speak of *marrano* families, since it was common to find instances where, for instance, a father was clandestinely carrying on Jewish practices while his son was a true Christian, or to find wives ignorant of their husbands' Judaizing. There was also the phenomenon of creative hybrid religiosity, such as the apparent veneration of "Saint" Moses and the taking of communion with matzoh during Passover ceremonies.[58] As historian David Graizbord argues in his study, *Souls in Dispute*, the common glue among Portuguese *conversos* was, more than anything, a "cultural liminality," which meant that just as a *converso* could be regarded as a potential Jew, a reconverted Jew could be regarded as a potential Christian.[59] While keeping in mind the considerable range and instability of identities among Portuguese New Christians, there is convincing evidence that some of the most important personnel of the seventeenth-century tobacco monopoly were, in fact, committed to crypto-Judaism.[60] Historians, eschewing an older view of Marranism as a kind of perverted and impure Judaism (as it was seen by many contemporary Jewish communities), now seek to describe it on its own terms. To avoid losing life, limb, and livelihood, crypto-Jews practiced stealth and subterfuge, and these in turn dictated many of the emphases of *marrano* practice. Circumcision in Iberia was suicidal. Rites of confidence, where one declared to another his or her adherence to the Law of Moses, took on special significance. The risk and complexity of celebrating traditional Jewish holidays undercover led crypto-Jews to dispense with the full ritual calendar and instead celebrate three holy days—Purim (known as the "Fast of Esther"), Passover, and Yom Kippur (known as the "Day of the Great Fast").[61] The emphasis on fasting is illustrative—the celebratory aspects of Purim were largely ignored. Fasting was easier to disguise than active celebration, and the penitential aspects complemented the inevitable feelings of guilt and betrayal to faith that accompanied the spiritual compromises survival demanded. Purim, though of secondary importance in normative Judaism, took on particular poignancy for *marranos*, for it commemorated Esther, who became the bride of the wicked king of Persia, Haman, and who sacrificed individual religious piety for the spiritual welfare of the greater collective. Similarly, *marranos* found much resonance in the Egyptian exile and courage in the example of Moses—another Biblical hero who allowed his people to survive as a minority in hostile lands until he could help them escape. Gómez de Salazar's son-in-law told Inquisitors how Gómez de Salazar and his wife Leonor invoked the "miracles" of Moses.

Marranism, or crypto-Judaism, among seventeenth-century Portuguese New Christians cannot be fully understood without looking at the social apparatus that allowed a group formally outlawed to survive. Conversely, the organization of the tobacco monopoly—which became central to this apparatus—requires understanding the cultural milieu of those who created it. It has long been recognized that in societies without sophisticated banking institutions, economic transactions that inevitably depend on credit are made possible by family networks that can generate trust, loyalty, and confidence between individuals separated by time and space. The conditions that made Portuguese New Christians pariahs within Iberian society also allowed the community to more easily operate like an extended family, even where there were no direct family ties, though the outsider status and endogamous practices of the group assisted with the proliferation of such kinship bonds. This solidarity, however, should not be overstated. It did not prevent rifts and rivalries, such as the one that produced such animosity between Diego Gómez de Salazar and Antonio de Soria, where overlapping personal and business interests led to conflict rather than cooperation. In addition to their dispute over the monopoly, they also were estranged because one of Gómez de Salazar's sons-in-law ran off to France with Soria's wife.[62]

The *arrendadores* molded the monopoly into a structure that allowed them to simultaneously pursue their economic interests and social objectives, ensuring that their strategies in both areas were mutually supportive. This is no clearer than in the case of Diego Gómez de Salazar, who obtained the monopoly lease in 1656 and for whom there is abundant and diverse documentation, appearing in state treasury archives and those of the Inquisition, as well as published briefs.[63] Gómez de Salazar was born in 1606 in Ciudad Rodrigo, a city in the province of Extremadura, abutting Portugal, from which his parents emigrated at the end of the sixteenth century. He married Leonor de Espinosa, who hailed from Antequera, a trading city 60 miles west of Granada that was home to an important nucleus of Portuguese *conversos*. Her family was more prominent, with relatives in the Americas and an uncle who became well known as a poet. The couple raised five daughters and four sons, and husband and wife created a partnership that intertwined the business of family and commerce—Leonor appears on some of the contracts he negotiated with the state.[64] They started married life in Antequera—one of the municipalities that inaugurated a local tobacco monopoly, perhaps whetting Gómez de Salazar's appetite for the business—and then moved to Málaga, an important Andalusian port town, where Gómez de Salazar collected a small fortune by trading in various merchandise, perhaps expanding into American commodities. He also entered the business of tax farming, becoming treasurer of the *millones* in Cordoba. There were setbacks: in 1637 he and his brother fled to Barcelona after they defaulted on payments related to a tax-farming venture. But authorities caught up with him, and he endured a brief incarceration. Nevertheless, Gómez de Salazar rose from relative rags (family members worked in construction and agriculture, though his father was a silk merchant) to definitive riches, acquiring posh quarters at one of Madrid's most prestigious addresses, the Calle de Alcalá, and a luxurious horse carriage. In addition to the tobacco monopoly, he farmed the *millones* for Granada and secured the position of "accounts keeper" (*contador*) for His Majesty in return for a generous sum reckoned at 100,000 ducats.[65]

In defending himself in 1660 against the Inquisition's accusation of Judaizing, Gómez de Salazar pointed to his social and financial eminence as proof of innocence, declaring that "it is true that [I] had a carriage in Madrid and much respect, and that ministers and grandees of Spain visited [my] home in order to discuss and negotiate about issues of the treasury . . . and all these things refute [the accusations] of these proceedings."[66] Witness testimony from the Inquisition, particularly that of his estranged son-in-law Antonio de Fonseca, portray the monopolist as a witty, sharp-tongued controlling patriarch; he had a particular penchant for giving nicknames to family, friend, and foe, and even ministers of state and fellow prisoners of the Inquisition, to whom he bequeathed such epithets as "the clog" (to a son-in-law), "little monk" (to his brother), "suckler" (to his rival Antonio de Soria), "stick-face" (to a state minister), "fortress" (to a cell mate), and "the Catalana" to his wife—for having either "received her bosom from a woman of Catalan" or "been weaned in Catalonia." Fonseca, who provided this information while under interrogation, was called "musk" (*hamusco*) by his father-in-law for being of a "melancholic" nature and "a poor conversationalist."[67]

The Inquisition arrested and incarcerated Gómez de Salazar in 1659, along with his wife, children, and several sons-in-law.[68] Nonetheless, Gómez de Salazar and many family members eventually escaped Iberia and ended their days in the community of Bayonne, France's most populous and vibrant Jewish community and a refuge for Portuguese *conversos*. There he was buried as a Jew in 1671; in Madrid he was burned in effigy at an *auto-da-fé* in 1681. Gómez de Salazar viewed his worldly engagements as ways to further his belief system and foster the collective welfare of his coreligionists. The tobacco monopoly was central to these objectives. According to Fonseca, his father-in-law "had the intention of enjoying the rent of tobacco for two or three years and then to pass it afterwards to whoever would give him a nice jewel for it" and then take the proceeds to support their emigration to and exile in France.[69] But even in advance of his intended exile, Gómez de Salazar ran the monopoly in a manner keeping with his identification as a patron of the *marrano* community of Iberia.

The successful operation of the tobacco monopoly hinged on developing a pyramid—from the *arrendador general* at the top to the hundreds of retail *estanqueros* at the bottom—and forging an international network for procuring tobacco on the global market. In creating an organizational network and fostering an international supply system, *arrendadores* such as Gómez de Salazar found a synergy between the Portuguese New Christian economic enterprises and commitment to Marranism.

The *arrendador general* resided at the apex of an organizational pyramid.[70] *Arrendadores* commonly employed a kind of vice president, or lieutenant general, known as the *administrador*: during his *arrendamiento*, Méndez Enríquez apparently delegated most of the work directly to his *administrador*, Simon Fernández de Miranda, a member of another well-known Portuguese family with a commitment to crypto-Judaism.[71] During his tenure as *arrendador*, Gómez de Salazar appointed Gabriel Salazar, his nephew and son-in-law, as *administrador*. Gabriel Salazar sent him regular missives concerning the status of various provinces and districts, while Diego's uncle Juan Gómez de Salazar helped administer the monopoly in Seville.[72] To ensure the distribution of tobacco throughout

Castile, the *arrendador* divided the kingdom into provinces (whose boundaries shifted over time), including Seville, Madrid, Pastrana, Avila, Galicia, Toledo, Segovia, Burgos, Valladolid, Guadalajara, Extremadura, Jaen, Salamanca, and Oviedo. In charge of these provinces were *subarrendadores*—sometimes also known as *subadministradores*—who signed contracts with the *arrendador general* that required them to buy and sell minimum quantities of tobacco for the period of their leases. These provincial heads also kept the *arrendador general* apprised of problems within their jurisdiction (substandard shipments of product, difficulties in contracting district lessees or retail vendors, encounters with obstreperous customs' officials, incidents of smuggling) and supervised their own subordinates and factors, who, in turn, kept them informed. Many of these provinces were further subdivided into *partidos*, or districts. The "district managers" signed leases with the provincial concessionaires—or sometimes directly with the *arrendador general* or his *administrator*—and oversaw the distribution to the retail outlets.[73] From the ranks of these *subarrendadores* or district administrators came many of the *arrendadores generales* of the later seventeenth century: Jorge Baptista Carrafa, who held the monopoly concession from 1663 to 1673, cut his teeth as one of the sublessees of Seville during the administration of Gómez de Salazar. Likewise, Francisco López Pereira, who administered the province of Granada for Gómez de Salazar, became *arrendador general* between 1676 and 1684.[74] On the bottom of the pyramid were the numerous retailers—there were nearly two hundred within the first years of the monopoly's operation in Madrid alone.[75]

The *arrendador* ran a major industrial operation in a preindustrial age.[76] Some of the tobacco arrived ready for consumption, all the necessary treatments having occurred in workshops in the colonies rather than in Spain, but significant quantities were sent to factories for processing. The scented powdered tobacco, or *polvo de olor*, was treated to a multiple-stage process in Spanish factories that included initial milling, moistening, a finer milling, fermentation, and a "wash" with odiferous additives such as orange blossoms, or a fragrance known as "ambar," which combined rose, mint, clover, and oak bark.[77] Tobacco *sin olor* (without fragrance), also known as *sumonte*, and "roll" tobacco also required processing, but less than that of *olor*.[78] The most important manufacturing center was the Factory of San Pedro in Seville, but there appear to have been major tobacco processing centers in Madrid and Alicante, and smaller ones in Burgos, Valladolid, Betanzos, Gijón, Ronda, Málaga, and Cadiz.[79] Expanded over the century, San Pedro—so known for its location in front of the parish church by that name—had on its ground floor nine rooms that contained two horse-powered milling stones and additional human-operated grinders, quarters for "washing" the tobacco with scents, workshops for manufacturing cigars, storage rooms, accounting offices, and a safe. After being milled and treated with fragrance on the ground floor, the snuff moved upstairs, where workers used combs and other instruments to remove moisture. Mechanization increased over the century. The number of horses that fueled the millstones in San Pedro increased from thirteen in 1668 to sixty-five in 1691. In 1684 the Seville factory employed more than 130 people, from the bookkeeper or "auditor of the activities of the factory" to the foreman who ran the mills to the *mozos* (lads) in charge of the horses. Demand for this tobacco was such that workers labored day and night (candles providing illumination).[80]

The state tobacco monopoly allowed its *arrendador* to horizontally and vertically integrate his enterprises. It also permitted lessees such as Diego Gómez de Salazar to use the monopoly to foster solidarity among Portuguese New Christians, and even to sustain and nourish *marrano* practice. (Though it must be emphasized that many who found employment were not part of the Portuguese New Christian community and that many of the Portuguese Christians who *did* find employment with the monopoly were not "Judaizers.")[81] Each set of objectives assisted with the other: the danger faced by Judaizers or even suspected Judaizers would guarantee loyalty among cadres and operatives, while, as the head of an enormous business enterprise, Gómez de Salazar could patronize and reward those who embraced the Law of Moses and make available to his associates unique opportunities to travel abroad to interact with those who openly practiced the Jewish religion. Correspondence seized by the Inquisition shows how business and community were combined. Manuel Rodríguez Isidrio, who was for a time in charge of the Seville monopoly jurisdiction, received a note from another monopoly factor that relayed problems he was having with a "lad" in Extremadura who would not pay his debts and congratulated him on the birth of a baby girl; another associate also sent his congratulations, along with a fine bottle of wine.[82]

The historian Pilar Huerga Criado has characterized "clientelism" as an important strategy among crypto-Jews, finding instances in which prosperous Portuguese New Christians offered money and assistance to poorer members of the community, particularly those who proved themselves recondite, such as the economically precarious Doña Ines, the widow of a mule-for-hire operator, who was sought after and supported by eminent and prosperous *marranos* because of her understanding of Jewish rites (such as knowledge of prayers, the Old Testament, and the preparation of a corpse for burial).[83] According to witnesses to the Inquisition, Gómez de Salazar was known for his almsgiving to "poor followers of the Law of Moses."[84] Most significantly, running the tobacco monopoly allowed the monopolist numerous patronage opportunities. For the positions with the most responsibility, Gómez de Salazar relied heavily on members of his extended family, but he also used the monopoly to accommodate members of varying social strata of the Portuguese community in Spain—from placing someone in a factory, licensing an *estanquero*, or subcontracting a provincial jurisdiction. Manuel Rodríguez Moreira, who had overseen the monopoly administration in the province of Extremadura, testified in 1660 to the Inquisition that Diego Gómez de Salazar favored Portuguese New Christians with jobs, credit, and money, particularly those who were knowledgeable about Judaism. In his own case, there was a connection between securing the contract for administering the monopoly in Extremadura and the fact that he and Gómez de Salazar had "declared" to one another their obedience to the Law of Moses.[85] Lower on the social rung there was the man—nicknamed "the Black" for his dark coloring—whom Gómez de Salazar "accommodated in a tobacco factory" as a bribe, it seems, to keep the former from testifying against the latter to the Inquisition.[86] And then there was Josef Borjes, who had worked as a district chief in the monopoly jurisdiction of Extremadura; after that fell into bankruptcy, he was in charge of a retail outlet in Madrid. While incarcerated by the Inquisition, Borjes told a prison mate about going to Gómez de Salazar's house and, according to his denouncer, "the said Josef Borjes was selecting some rolls of tobacco in presence of the said Diego Gómez; the aforesaid one asked Josef Borjes whether he was an observer of the Law of Moses, to which the said Borjes responded yes, and the said Diego Gómez de Salazar told him that he too was an observer of the said law."[87]

Another way that in the operation of the tobacco monopoly Gómez de Salazar and other *arrendadores* found a synergism for Portuguese New Christian economic interests and religious commitments was through the international supply network. By the 1630s, the provenance of tobacco consumed by Castilians was wide-ranging. It was generally agreed that the best tobacco was that cultivated in the Spanish Indies, particularly that which came from Barinas in Venezuela (soon rivaled by Cuba), but that Brazilian and Virginian tobacco was significantly cheaper.[88] Royal officials complained in 1684 that the recent *arrendadores* had provisioned the monopoly with tobacco from Virginia that they bought for 1 or 1.5 copper *reales* per pound, while the tobacco coming from Havana cost 2 silver *reales*.[89] Seeking to balance the imperatives of quality, cost, and supply, the monopolist and his factors, mobilizing contacts throughout the Portuguese diaspora, also arranged shipments that originated in Virginia and Brazil, coming overland after disembarkation from Lisbon or overseas to port cities in France and the Netherlands.[90] Officially, all New World commodities were to arrive in designated Andalusian ports—mainly Seville—before being transported for inland distribution. But in practice *arrendadores* used a number of ports for tobacco shipments. Of particular importance was Bilbao, the northern port city in the Basque country, where shipments from Virginia or from Spanish colonies illegally traded to Dutch, French, or English merchants came through Amsterdam or Bordeaux or Bayonne.[91] During the tenure of Juan de Rosales, the subcontractor for Burgos was accused of contacting associates and brothers in the "kingdoms of France and other foreign lands" to "introduce" more than fifty thousand pounds of tobacco "in powder and leaf" by way of Bayonne, from where it traveled on "out-of-the-way paths and hidden roads" to Burgos where it was further elaborated.[92] In other instances, it appears that *arrendadores* obtained special dispensation to transport tobacco—appealing to the provision of the contracts that "obligated" the "provision and supply tobacco" throughout the Kingdom of Castile. When asked by an Inquisitor to account for travels in France in the company of Jews, Gómez de Salazar during his interrogations explained that "His Majesty had given him a license [for this]" and "that for having been *estanquero* of tobacco of all of this Kingdom," he had no choice but "to make the majority of purchases outside of [Castile] with those persons he deemed best."[93]

This defense points to another way in which *arrendadores* such as Gómez de Salazar ran the monopoly to serve religious and social objectives as well as economic interests. Those with a commitment to Judaism but residing in Iberia found it imperative, despite the substantial risk, to visit, renew ties with, and learn from "open" Jews living abroad.[94] The monopoly stipulation requiring *arrendadores* to "provision" Castile with tobacco gave them dispensation and cover to travel to otherwise forbidden or suspicious areas. A frequent destination was Bayonne, home to the Jewish community closest to the Iberian frontier. Gómez de Salazar's brother and a monopoly administrator in Valladolid, Manuel Rodríguez Franco, was accused of being an "observer of Moses" for spending four to six weeks in Bayonne in 1658.[95] Similarly, Gómez de Salazar's son, Pedro de Salazar, traveled throughout France for a month and a half before ending in Bayonne, where he oversaw tobacco cargo that would disembark in Bilbao and San Sebastian and then ship to Valencia.[96]

Just as there was a silver lining to the painful diaspora forced on Jews and *conversos*, in that it mobilized them for international trade, so it seems, the tobacco monopoly was attractive to crypto-Jews not only for its economic returns but as an organizational device to maintain religious and social identities in the face of Iberian anti-Semitic persecution. The tobacco monopoly played a critical role in sustaining Iberian Jews long after the expulsion of 1492 and even after the downfall of Prime Minister Olivares in 1643, who had a short-lived tenure as a quasi guardian of Portuguese *converso*, if not Iberian Jewish, interests.[97] The testimony that Gómez de Salazar, his family and associates, and his enemies (sometimes one and the same), provided to the Inquisition reveal that Iberian Jews could use the monopoly to protect one another, maintain contacts with Jews living abroad, create community, and fend off enemies.

THE EXPANDING LEVIATHAN

Neither *arrendadores* nor government officials implemented or organized the tobacco monopoly in an effort to increase the power of the state. Rather, each pursued objectives more particular to their circumstances. "Portuguese" *arrendadores* found a singular opportunity in leasing the monopoly to mobilize their commercial and financial expertise to bolster their precarious social and political position in xenophobic Spain during the Counter-Reformation. Government officials were enthusiastic about the monopoly as an increasingly lucrative rent that could be justified in ways that squelched opposition (in theory, if not effect). Nonetheless, a transformative *effect* of the monopoly was to create techniques of state power more often associated with France and the eighteenth century. The tobacco monopoly was unique in its centralization. Whereas other monopolies and taxes (*millones, alcabala*) were farmed separately by region, the tobacco monopoly concession encompassed the whole kingdom.[98] Centralization was accompanied by national standardization; under the tobacco monopoly, consumers across Castile were bound together by a uniformity in pricing and standardization in tobacco products. And the ubiquity of state tobacco vendors (*estanqueros*) made the state an increasing presence in the Iberian landscape. By the 1650s the terms *tabaquero* (tobacco seller) and *estanquero* (monopolist) were interchangeable.[99]

Given that gargantuan price hikes inflicted extreme distortions on the market, the monopoly has been viewed as archaic in its economic inefficiency, inevitably precipitating so much contraband that it appears the state would have benefited had it pursued more "rational" policies of lower taxation but with lower levels of avoidance. It has also been judged a failure for undermining mercantilist objectives. In *France and the Chesapeake: A History of the French Tobacco Monopoly, 1674–1791*, the most comprehensive study of any state tobacco monopoly during the ancien régime, Jacob Price argues that with the French tobacco monopoly the state followed a course driven by fiscal considerations—the immediate need to generate revenue to pay for expenditures, most often military—and thus subordinated the competing objectives of colonial expansion, commerce, or public health, despite the state's expressed desire to support these latter three.[100] In a similar fashion for Spain's tobacco monopoly, José Rodríguez

Gordillo argues that the tobacco monopoly did not serve mercantilist ends as it bought significant quantities of tobacco from imperial rivals—English and Portuguese colonies—as well as relying on "manufactured" tobacco products from its own colonies but rather is best seen as an "outstanding revenue-raising success for the state."[101] By today's standards of rationality, efficiency, and national interest, the monopoly can easily be seen as a "failure" because of the smuggling and fraud that undermined its ability to maximize revenue, exacerbated by the counterescalation of lawsuits and security measures and the economic support it gave to imperial rivals.

While there is much sense in these arguments, there is another historical approach to the tobacco monopoly, which is to understand how this institution served as a mechanism to make the state an increasing presence in people's lives. Approached this way, the challenges to implementation and deployment, which came frequently and from multiple quarters, do not (only) prove the irrationality and inefficiency of the monopoly but also demonstrate its novelty and transformative effect on society. Moreover, in combating these challenges—which came in the form of lawsuits from merchants, defamation campaigns from displaced tobacconists, and rampant and endemic fraud and smuggling by consumers colluding with traders, big and small—the state and the Crown further increased its power. This process of state growth brings to mind metaphors of the Leviathan that expands because it eats what lies in its path, or the organism that becomes more powerful when attacked by viruses because it produces antibodies.

From the moment state officials began to consider the idea, and throughout the seventeenth century, the tobacco monopoly triggered challenges from the many interests that would and did suffer under its regime. First, the powerful merchant block from Seville, with the support of the merchant guild (*consulado*) and city officials, sent petition after petition to the finance council to dissuade them from implementing the monopoly. They succeeded in preventing its implementation for two years, and begged for its repeal even after it took effect.[102] In an eight-page petition, the merchants pleaded that the monopoly would cause their imminent ruin because it "takes from them . . . the trade they have and have had for many years. . . . having invested their estates and capital in the said trade (augmenting the said commerce), and thereby sustaining their households and families" and they would "not know nor have another way to live." They estimated that their existing stocks of tobacco were worth 200,000 ducats (which they would be obliged to sell at prices advantageous to the monopolists), and they bemoaned the losses on their investments in "capital, the costs, the fleets, the port taxes" and the costly rents of the "very large houses and warehouses in which the tobacco is stored." The petitioners claimed a wave of bankruptcies would wreck the Sevillan economy. Moreover, it would cause the ruin of many a Spanish colony, as the "foreign" *arrendadores* would buy tobacco from enemy provisioners rather than from growers in the Spanish Indies. Playing to pervasive xenophobia and suspicion of Portuguese mercantile dominance, they charged that the Portuguese monopolists would defraud the Crown and collude with enemy English and Dutch. Throughout the monopoly's operation in the seventeenth century, the merchant block in Seville remained its active foe, and there were frequent lawsuits between them and the monopoly.[103]

As the Seville merchants anticipated, resistance also came from the tax farmers who would lose their ability to collect duties and imposts on tobacco in the new regime. Tax farmers of the customs duties complained in 1640 about the royal tobacco monopoly, as well as new taxes on cacao and chocolate.[104] A thick dossier from the Treasury Council contains the vestiges of more than a decade of litigation and extralegal conflict between Granada's municipal authorities, its spice and luxury goods guild (*gremio de especiería, buhonería, y joyería*), various tobacco monopoly lessees, and royal authorities acting as both interested parties and the mediating justice.[105] Distilled to its essence, the conflict in Granada revolved around the guild's efforts to continue as Granada's subcontractor for the *alcabala* on tobacco, and the monopolists' bid, at first, to deny the legitimacy of the *alcabala* and then to concede it but maintain that the monopoly, and not the guild, should collect it.[106] When appraising and dispensing judgment in the Granada case, royal officials made repeated references to parallel conflicts arising in Cáceres, Cordoba, and Antequera, not to mention Seville.[107]

Granada was particularly disgruntled and imaginative in its resistance to the tobacco monopoly. City officials commissioned an apothecarist to investigate the quality of tobacco in the wake of "having received noticed that the [tobacco] was mixed with many foreign things, and that these could cause great harm to the vassals and that it could also be infected with some kind of poison, confected by enemies of these Kingdoms." The investigating apothecarist submitted samples of the monopoly tobacco to a variety of experiments and concluded that because "the tobacco was far off in color, smell, and flavor, it was far off in goodness" and advised against consuming it.[108] Apparently the campaign was sufficiently effective to prompt a veritable boycott of the new monopoly, and the *arrendador*, Luis Méndez Enríquez, argued to the council that he should not be obligated to pay the full lease amount because of this unexpected harm to consumption levels and concomitant revenues.[109] (This contributed to his losing the monopoly and its being returned to Soria.) The monopoly became a mechanism by which the Crown could suppress local interests and contracts. It offered a basis on which to renege on earlier accords and override the privileges of powerful interest groups (Seville merchants), localities

(Granada) and tax-farmers (of the *alcabala* and *almojarifazgo* [customs duty]), and the clergy (to be exempt from excise taxes). They repeatedly referred to its New World provenance and its status as a luxury good as the criteria for a new monarchical privilege.

But the biggest impediment to the Crown's ability to maximize rents from this monopoly was the rife contraband and smuggling that took place, endemic among all sectors of the society, compelled by the huge gap between "market" and "monopoly" prices. According to the unhappy tobacco *arrendador* in 1682, one could purchase tobacco of reasonable quality for 5 *reales* per pound on the black market; meanwhile the monopoly price for the less expensive varieties was almost three times as much (14 *reales*).[110] Market realities were perhaps made more convincing by the sense that this was an unethical novelty imposed by the state. An influential critic of the monopoly asserted in a 1646 treatise that it was essentially unjust to consumers and the treasury alike, benefiting only the *arrendadores*:

> It is known that the *arrendador*, without scale or measure, sells [tobacco] however he wants, and in the maritime ports buys it wholesale at two *reales* per pound and sells it retail, in his *estanco*, for more than 50 [sic], with nothing more than a touch of supposed fragrance, mixing in such things that if it was known, horror would not allow one to consume it.[111]

However, the *arrendadores* were as much "victims" as perpetrators of fraud and contraband.[112] Contraband tobacco arrived from every provenance. The agents of contraband came from every part of society, in and out of Spain. Foreign suppliers participated. There was the French captain who purchased tobacco in Lisbon in 1661 in order to "introduce it to ports of Spain."[113] But domestic shippers were more than willing to supply contraband—the revenge of the unhappy *consulado* merchants—as well as sailors who were happy to smuggle it on board.[114] Once clandestinely brought to shore, carried overland over the Pyrenees from France, or across the long border with Portugal, there were small peddlers and powerful upper-class individuals and operations ready to sell the contraband. Gabriel Gómez de Salazar reported to his father-in-law Diego in 1656 the pervasiveness of smuggling in the frontier province [with Portugal] of Mérida, singling out in particular "friars, priests, and soldiers."[115] Nobles were also well represented. The Duke of Veragua was accused of allowing his servants to bring tobacco from his estate and distribute it, despite having been given a warning to put an end to the practice. And local officials were involved, such as the mayor of Las Casillas (Jaén), who was found to have a mill used for processing snuff along with 108 pounds of Virginia tobacco.[116] Another way of procuring contraband tobacco was to grow it oneself.[117] Contraband also came from the inside, from workers in the tobacco factory who smuggled the product out. The temptation for employees and contractors to commit fraud was enormous (given the ready demand, differential in price, and their access to the product), which helps to explain why the Portuguese New Christian *arrendadores* were so ready to keep the business in the "family." The consumption of tobacco led to a concomitant increase in contraband, along with a counterescalation of efforts to curb it.[118]

One of the reasons that the Castilian tobacco monopoly has not received the attention it deserves for its role in European state formation is the enduring hold of the interpretive framework established by Max Weber that holds that the modern state evolved in a linear trajectory from government offices held venally by private administrators or run corruptly by employees to a "rational" bureaucracy administered by disinterested civil servants. For instance, I. A. A. Thompson argues that the Spanish state experienced "devolution" in the seventeenth century, demonstrated by a path that led from the direct administration of finance and military (whose apotheosis was reached during the first half of Phillip II's regime) to decentralized private contracting in the seventeenth (the way the tobacco monopoly was run). He describes a "shift from central to centrifugal government and from public to private administration . . . that fragmented administrative authority and in fragmenting the administration it fragmented the state. Each contractor, each province, lord or city was in its own way a separate administrative and jurisdictional unit." For Thompson, this "failure" on the part of the Spanish Crown prevented it from developing a truly strong state necessary for international European competition in the early modern era.[119] The monopoly did not follow (or lead) a trajectory of state atrophy, but, rather, as it developed under indirect administration, it grew into such a powerful institution that it prompted the state to experiment with direct administration at the end of the seventeenth and permanently in the eighteenth centuries. In May 1683 the Crown decreed that the monopoly would no longer be leased but directly administered by the state—though the individual "districts" would still be farmed.[120] This foray into direct administration did not last, for the revenues fell significantly below those collected through the leasing arrangement, and the Crown reverted to the contracting arrangement in short order. Though the experiment in direct administration was short-lived, it became a blueprint for the organization of the monopoly during the Bourbon regime of the eighteenth century.[121] Rather than being an example of the "devolution" of the state as Thompson and other followers of Weber might have it, the leasing arrangements of the tobacco monopoly of the seventeenth century were the building blocks that made the emergence of a powerful state institution possible.

And this institution did not remain restricted to Castile, or even Spain. Over the course of the seventeenth and eighteenth centuries state tobacco monopolies were instituted in Spain's American colonies, in Portugal, Venice, Austria, France, and even the Papal States.[122]

Tobacco played an important role in the development of the modern state and in the fortunes of the *converso* community. Conversely, the monopoly regime influenced the place of tobacco in Iberian—and ultimately European—society. Just as the cultural valences of tobacco and chocolate helped determine state and imperial policy, their fiscalization reciprocally affected their cultural meanings. They reinforced and made legal tobacco's cultural status as a vice, or even the first "mass luxury," rather than as the medicine that Monardes had wanted it to be. In order to justify the constitutional legitimacy of the monopoly, royal jurists emphasized that tobacco was *not* a medicine but rather a *vicio* (vice) and *regalo* (luxury). The impact of the state on the meanings associated with tobacco—and chocolate—is clearly discerned in the language employed in a proposal to impose a trading monopoly on cacao in 1691–92. The author anticipated objections based on "the juridical prohibition against monopolies for restricting the right to trade freely, which is based in natural and positive law." Accordingly, he explained that "it is undeniable that the *potestad* (legitimate power) of the Prince to restrict the right of free trade . . . in those species that are not necessary for human sustenance, or because they are imbued with *vicio* and *cortesía* (honor), which is true of cacao, the main ingredient of chocolate." Throughout, he cited the constitutional legitimacy of the tobacco monopoly as a precedent.[123]

The monopoly led consumers and vendors alike to see the state and tobacco as inextricably linked, and their association had mutually determining effects. For tobacco, the association with the state—the guarantor of its supply in words and action—legitimized it. While, for the state, the association with tobacco presented it as an accessory to vice. This challenges the commonly accepted narrative about modern consumption—that dominant discourse disdained "luxury" and indulgence until eighteenth-century libertinism.

The tobacco monopoly was the "effect" of the convergence of the fiscal implosion of an overextended state, a culture of consumption that labeled tobacco as a vice, and strategies pursued by Portuguese merchants in Iberia—most of them labeled as *conversos* and a number of them self-identified as secret Jews. It also was a "cause," catalyzing state expansion that went far beyond Castile and the seventeenth century, influencing the cultural meaning of tobacco and offering a haven for (some) Iberian Jews.

10

Enchanting the Profane

❖ ❖

In his 1629 play, *Discurso de todos los diablos* (A discussion among demons), Francisco de Quevedo told the story of tobacco and chocolate's introduction into Spain as a tale of revenge:

> There came the devil of tobacco and the devil of chocolate, who, despite my suspicions, told me they were not the cause of all evil. . . . They told me that they had avenged the Indies against Spain, for they had done more harm by introducing among us those powders and smoke and chocolate cups and chocolate-frothers (*molinillos*) than the Catholic Kings had ever done through Columbus and Cortés and Almagro and Pizarro. For it was much better and cleaner and more honorable to be killed by a musket ball or a lance than by snuffling and sneezing and belching and dizziness and fever; the chocolate-bibbers idolize the cup that they raise on high and adore and go into a trance over; the tobacco consumers are like Lutherans [heretics]: taking it in smoke, they are serving their apprenticeship for hell.[1]

The satirist leaves no doubt about the centrality of tobacco and chocolate to Spanish culture. Avenging the destruction wrought by conquistadores in the Americas, these substances of New World provenance had subjected Iberians to their rule. Enthralled aficionados now behave like religious devotees, such that "chocolate-bibbers" treat chocolate like the wine consecrated during Mass and smokers risk damnation. This sacrilege connects the compulsive adoration of the acolytes back to their origins among Amerindian "idolaters." All in jest, of course.

The sentiments expressed by Quevedo were opposite to the formal conclusions reached by cultural authorities charged with investigating the nature of the goods and their effects on Christian orthodoxy. Theologians examined whether the sacrilegious potential of tobacco and chocolate could be fully contained through regulation, and they concurred that they could. A related debate sought to define the intrinsic character of the goods, considering whether the natural laws of the universe governed them fully, or whether their peculiarly powerful actions on body and mind meant that they abrogated these laws and manifested enchanted, magical properties. The former view prevailed. Yet neither the technical theological debates nor humoral medicine nor venerable theories about desire were sufficient to quell powerful associations of the demonic and the divine in discussions about these goods.

In pre-Columbian and colonial Amerindian cultures, the powerful somatic and psychological effects assigned to tobacco and chocolate were a consequence of their sacred character (and conversely, these effects were used as evidence for the existence of supernatural deified forces in the cosmos). In seeking to reconcile the increasingly central place of tobacco and chocolate in their lives with their broader understanding of the universe, Europeans were confronted with a legacy in which native religions had been deemed idolatrous at best and diabolical at worst. Despite the efforts of Monardes and his emulators to remove the taint of diabolical paganism from tobacco and chocolate, this earlier framework stymied efforts to reconcile their centrality with Christianity. European discourses about the goods, since the earliest days of the conquest, inscribed associations that were divine and diabolical, mystical and magical, reflecting the actual transcendent, sacred associations Amerindians attributed to tobacco and chocolate.

This created a counterpoint to the dominant discourse that denied tobacco and chocolate any magical or mystical properties or power to threaten Christianity's spiritual monopoly. This counterpoint that presented the goods as manifestations of an immanent divine and diabolical, that offered the succor of mystical union, was not accorded the status of orthodoxy. Mystical explanations were not granted admission into the formalized debate of early modern experts but, rather, relegated to the nebulous domain of the collective unconscious in jokes, asides, and metaphors. There tobacco and chocolate appeared as preternatural and supernatural mediums, likened respectively to a witches' unguent that dispensed powerful assistance and a Eucharistic elixir that delivered transcendental bliss. This powerful, haunting set of associations accentuated a cultural realm that was not supported by Church orthodoxy, which could not in turn support Church orthodoxy. The cultural condition in which a powerful set of somatic ritual experiences supports not the realm of formal religion but secular activity is quintessentially modern.

Secularization is commonly understood as the decline of magical and mystical beliefs along with the rise of scientific and rationalist beliefs.[2] The flip side of this process, less emphasized and generally attributed to the eighteenth and nineteenth centuries, is "reenchantment"—short-hand for a variety of phenomena that have traditionally been associated with backlash to secular values of Enlightenment: romanticism, renewed interest in the occult, psychoanalysis (rational efforts to understand the irrational), and mass movements of nationalism and dream-worlds of consumer culture.[3] The world we live in today is not secularized, for both fervent religiosity and personal spirituality are alive and well in even the most secular countries. Yet a secular world view is embraced by many, particularly those in powerful positions in the developed world. A secular outlook is commonly characterized by a lack of belief in mystical forces and a conviction in natural, disenchanted explanations for any and all phenomenon. There is an underappreciated flip side to this secular view, which is not the disappearance of transcendent mystical beliefs but their relegation to the realm of art and its uncouth twin sibling, advertising.[4] The origins of this bifurcation of the disenchanted and enchanted process accompanied the creation of a distinctly secular realm and related to Europeans' efforts to come to terms with the Americas.

DEMYSTIFYING DISCOURSE

As people recognized that tobacco and chocolate had become thoroughly entrenched in Iberian society, they pondered the implications their ubiquitous use had for Christian orthodoxy. Theologians, jurists, philosophers, inquisitors, physicians, and interested lay folk fretted: Did snuffing or smoking tobacco before Mass interfere with Holy Communion? Did the pervasive presence of tobacco in churches and usage by clergy profane that which should be most sanctified? Did chocolate drinking jeopardize the ecclesiastical fast? These controversies surfaced in the erudite debates of professors of theology and medicine, in print polemics waged in the vernacular, and in spoken arguments among the populace. They percolated into confessors' manuals and were thought to inhabit the consciousness of the "rude masses." They were spoofed in satirical verse.

At one level, the theological controversies surrounding tobacco and chocolate contributed to the discourse of the Counter-Reformation, the Catholic Church's campaign of response and renewal in the wake of the schism that Luther unleashed. Issues dividing Catholics and the nascent Protestant churches included the priesthood, the Eucharist, and ascetic practices, such as fasting, issues that were also spotlighted by the faithful's consumption of tobacco and chocolate. Theologians found a way to contain the sacrilegious ramifications of Christians' consumption of tobacco and chocolate, and the Catholic Reformation gained further legitimation through expanding its realm of authority. More particularly, the theological debates concerning tobacco in seventeenth century Spain coalesced around two major areas—whether its consumption interfered with Communion and whether its use by holy people or in holy spaces constituted sacrilege—concerns that matched general preoccupations of Catholic reform theologians, modifying clerical behavior, protecting sacred space, and protecting the principle of transubstantiation in the Eucharist.[5]

Tobacco's trespass into hallowed spaces was a concern that captured the attention of the head of the Church. In 1642 Pope Urban VIII issued a bull that forbade the smoking or taking of tobacco in churches or in their environs in the archbishopric of Seville under penalty of excommunication.[6] The bull called attention to the fact that tobacco abuse had reached the point that tobacco stained the floor and its odor pervaded church. In the same year, the vicar general of Seville also forbade ecclesiastics, "be they regulars or seculars, and men or women, and of whatever estate, trade, condition, or dignity," in the archbishopric from using tobacco "in public." The edict bemoaned the scandal caused by the uncontrolled use of tobacco by the clergy "at all hours, in all places, with publicity."

From a certain vantage point the campaign to eradicate tobacco from holy spaces and the public bodies of holy people coincided perfectly with existing efforts to revitalize the clergy and guarantee the sanctity of sacred places. By addressing the place and conspicuousness of tobacco use, ecclesiastical legislation diverted attention from the essential nature of the substance itself and reinforced Church hierarchy by emphasizing sanctity of sacred spaces and people alike. When the Jesuit priest Antonio de Quintanadueñas published his *Explicación a la bula en que N.S.P. Urbano VIII prohibe en Sevilla, y su Arçobispado el abuso del Tabaco en las Iglesias, en sus Patios y Ambito* (Explanation of the bull in which Our Supreme Pontiff Urban VIII prohibits the use of tobacco in Seville and its archbishopric in its churches, patios, and environs) the formal reason for banning tobacco on sacred grounds was based on precedents that prohibited "all kinds of dances, balls, and entertainments" and interdictions against noise, commotion, food, and drink in churches.[7] Therefore,

[the] illustrious *señores* of the chapter of the Santa Iglesia Metropolitana recognized the grave indecency that came from the Ecclesiastics profaning Churches, Sacristies, Choirs and other sacred places with the use of Tobacco, dirtying the floors, walls, and worst, in altars, mantels, and even the sacred vestuaries, making public the indecent action when they consume it, occasioning indecencies and filthiness so undignified for Ministers of the Church.[8]

The gloss on the papal bull prohibiting tobacco consumption in church provided as the legal precedent the rules from the synod that outlawed eating, dancing, and general rambunctiousness in churches.[9]

Likewise, it was no accident that reformers paired efforts to curb tobacco use with those to banish the use of inappropriate clothing.[10] When the vicar of Seville issued the 1642 edict against the clergy's public use of tobacco, he also mandated an edict prohibiting their "use of worldly clothing."[11] Just as clergy should not sport inappropriately opulent clothing because they then embodied "weakness, vanity, and human malice" and failed as moral exemplars, they should not use tobacco publicly.

This discourse worked in two directions. It contributed to the broader Catholic Church reform program, which sought to defend the practice of ordaining priests as intermediaries between lay people and salvation through administering the sacraments of the Eucharist, confession, and penance, in response to Luther and other Protestant attacks. By addressing the problems of dereliction of these holy bodies (abandonment of chastity, indulgence in worldliness, ignorance of Latin) and implementing reforms aimed at enforcing discipline among the clergy, it upheld the notion of priests as divine intermediaries.[12] Conversely, by being folded into such a discourse, tobacco was normalized, no better, but also no worse, than flashy clothing or luxurious foods.

Tobacco not only threatened the sanctity of priests, it had infiltrated the celebration of the Mass. Following their counterparts in the New World, religious authorities in Spain took up the issue of whether tobacco interfered with Communion. As with the debate about tobacco use by holy people and in holy places, in discussing tobacco in the context of the Eucharist, Catholic theologians reaffirmed the meaning and importance of the sacrament. Many of the new Protestant denominations had revised the meaning of this sacrament, some declaring that the "Lord's Supper" was purely a commemoration of Christ's sacrifice on the cross and so rejecting the miraculous "transubstantiation" of matter. In response, Catholics upheld the centrality of the Mass—"no other work can be performed by the faithful holy and divine as this tremendous mystery"—and reasserted that through consecration, priests really and truly changed—transubstantiated—the substance of the wine and wafer into the blood and flesh of Christ, and that the communicant who ingested either one, received Christ, whole and entire.[13] When theologians in Catholic Europe grappled with the effect of tobacco on Communion, they did it in such a way that both validated the sacrament and reduced the threat of tobacco. The explicit parameters of the debate were narrowly technical and thus obscured the more damning aspects of tobacco's infiltration into Communion: Citing the American councils, the authorities who insisted that priests should abstain from tobacco before administering Communion maintained that one who took tobacco (whether chewed, sniffed, or smoked) would break a natural fast, since the latter precluded any substance even if was not "something truly potable or edible."[14] Other authorities, however, took a more permissive stance. The Italian theologian Antonio Diana argued that a natural fast compelled one to forego food and drink; eating and drinking depended on the use of the mouth; ergo, if one ingested substances via orifices other than the mouth—such as snuffing tobacco—the natural fast would not be abrogated (even if the substances descended to the stomach), "for tobacco in leaf and powder is consumed through the nose and therefore does not break the natural fast because it is not consumed by an eating action which is done only with the mouth."[15] No clear consensus emerged, and local synods decided the matter themselves.[16] Yet by reducing the debate to technicalities, the theological discourse upheld the centrality of the Eucharist, one of the driving issues behind the schism of the Church.

As with tobacco, the formal parameters of the theological debate that surrounded chocolate served to bolster another aspect of Catholic belief and practice—fasting—that had come under challenge from Reformation leaders. Protestant reformers dismissed the Church's emphasis on the body as a vehicle for acquiring grace, viewing fasting and other ascetic practices as empty shows of faith that bore no relation to genuine, interior piety (leading Calvin to declare that during Lent penitents were led merely "to abstain from eating flesh and otherwise give oneself over to all delicacies and gluttonies of pleasure"). To this, Catholic reformers emphasized that a "spiritual fast" must accompany a "physical fast," but also maintained that "exterior virtues" such as fasting were *importantísimas* because they "heightened the passion for spiritual things."[17]

Assimilating chocolate into a discussion about the fast enhanced the program of the Catholic Reformation. The main controversy was whether chocolate drinking constituted a violation of the ecclesiastical fast. This question had vexed Christians at least since anxious Creoles in Chiapas had asked for a papal resolution on the issue in 1577. The pope's reaction—to laugh and offer a verbal decision that this strange Indian drink did not pose a threat to the ecclesiastical fast—created an ambiguous situation, since there was no written papal bull for Church authorities to retreat to. In Spain this debate continued in the pulpit and university lecture halls, in meetings of ecclesiastical officials, in theological compendiums in Latin and confessor's manuals in the vernacular, in treatises devoted to the topic, and in everyday conversations and comic spoofs.[18] In the spring of 1632, professors of theology—variously representing the Benedictine, Franciscan, Dominican, and Jesuit orders—met in Salamanca to discuss the matter; in attendance were a Dominican friar who later became archbishop of Santiago and a noted professor of medicine at the University of Seville, known as the "Hippocrates of Seville." The involvement of some of the most important Spanish prelates and physicians reflects the seriousness with which contemporaries viewed the matter. The author of an influential treatise published in 1636 wrote that whether chocolate could be consumed during fast days was a "circulating question" that "today is the most popularly debated."[19] In addition to attracting the attention of the highest-ranking intellectuals, the matter also penetrated the consciousness of the "vulgar masses." At one level, theological authorities contained the sacrilegious implications of tobacco and chocolate by inserting them into debates concerning religious practices incited by the religious schism of the Reformation. These worries about the effects of tobacco and chocolate on Christian orthodoxy matched generic preoccupations of the Catholic Church during its reformation—upholding the legitimacy and sanctity of the priesthood, devotion to the Eucharist, and reaffirmation of ascetic practices. Conversely, these debates served to demystify tobacco and chocolate, revealing them as incapable of inflicting any special sacrilege on hallowed rites.

Medical experts, too, participated in this demystifying process. In keeping with the tendencies among early seventeenth century intellectuals, they rejected supernatural or demonic explanations for the goods' powerful effects. [20] Instead, they drew heavily on the Galenic models already devised by the New World experts and called on neo-Aristotelian notions of desire to explain the compulsive behavior of consumers.

The need for definition, categorization, and classification was expressed in proliferating publications. Santiago Valverde Turices, a physician and professor of medicine in Seville who wrote the first treatise dedicated to chocolate use in Europe (*Un discurso de chocolate*, 1624), explained that his work was needed "because there are many people who are now using this beverage . . . discussing Chocolate when they are about to drink it and asking if it is healthy or harmful."[21] And in 1631 Antonio Colmenero de Ledesma, a Madrid physician, addressed his extremely influential *Curioso tratado de la naturaleza y calidad del chocolate* (Curious treatise on the nature and quality of chocolate) to the "*aficionado* reader," explaining the necessity of his work because "so great is the number of people who today drink Chocolate."[22]

Answers about tobacco were equally in demand, for it had set deep, strong, and multiplying "roots" in Spain, as the Cordoban apothecarist Juan de Castro y Medinilla, who wrote the first work dedicated to tobacco directed at Spanish consumers, attested: "The most illustrious, worthy, and rich people have [tobacco] as such a vice [and] they agree that among the vices never has there been one equal—neither drink, nor gambling, nor women."[23] The debate about tobacco still raged more than twenty years later, when physician and university professor Cristóbal de Hayo wrote that in "every country, especially in Spain, people speak divergently [of tobacco], some praising its use and virtues, and others vituperating its properties and use, and not only among secular people but also among lettered people, ecclesiastics, religious people, princes, nobles, and vulgar plebeians and rustics."[24] That eminent physicians took up these topics is evidence of the weightiness of these matters, as the reverberations in satirical works is evidence of widespread interest. Seventeenth-century experts recognized the thrall under which devoted consumers fell, but, in keeping with the arguments first put forth by Monardes, they did not think there was anything enchanted or supernatural about the substances. Medical and theological experts demystified tobacco and chocolate in two ways. They accounted for the substances' purported effects by the natural workings of the body. Or they characterized the effects as the delusional fantasies of people under the sway of a powerful vice.

The seventeenth century, particularly the first half, saw an intense debate throughout Europe over the health effects of tobacco. Yet both tobacco's most faithful advocates and those who held it in contempt essentially agreed on what tobacco did inside the body. Medical authorities, again following humoral classifications offered by Monardes, agreed that tobacco was hot, dry (while differing on the number of degrees), and purgative.[25] The disagreement concerned whether these effects were desirable. For those in favor, the purging effects of tobacco accounted for its ability to clear the brain and improve cognitive function; Hayo explained that snuffing tobacco "cleans the brain of its excrements, evacuating them through the nostrils and mouth." For those against, the drying effects led to the fate of those "clerics of Saint Jeronimo in Seville who died from using too much tobacco, having smoked and burned their senses, leaving in their place black ashes, like those found in chimneys after big fires" or making people's heads as "hollow gourds," causing the deterioration of "some of the senses, such as smell and hearing."[26] Likewise, the humoral arguments could support or undermine the opposite effects it was thought to have on sexuality. Some thought the heat "dried up sperm" and thus the "stimulus to mate" (*excitante acopula*), while others claimed that tobacco's "natural heat . . . causes an increase in seminal material and assists the venereal act and with its dryness helps to consume the humid excrements that debilitates the one and the other [seminal material and veneral act]."[27]

In other cases, they agreed on effects but disagreed about their desirability. Tobacco critics Bartolomé Marradón and Francisco de Leiva y Aguilar brooked no argument with those who claimed that tobacco purged cold humors and thus assisted with digestion and caused phlegm to flow out of the head.[28] Rather, Marradón—who wrote the first thoroughly antitobacco treatise aimed at Spanish consumers—argued that it was better to let nature operate on its own, without interference: "Why not let nature work . . . letting leave of the waste that offends by those sites God created for this end, which are the mouth, ears, and nose" instead of expelling the "humor by force so that the majority have [these body parts] aggravated and wounded?"[29] Tobacco adversary Leiva y Aguilar acknowledged that tobacco expedited digestion but deplored this as it enabled gluttony.[30]

There was even more consensus among experts about the effects of chocolate. The opinions of seventeenth-century medical authorities largely coincided with those of laymen as far as the effects of chocolate were concerned. Like their creole (and native American) predecessors, they esteemed chocolate for stimulating the brain, eliminating fatigue, creating happiness, exciting the libido, and ameliorating digestive difficulties. As with tobacco, Spanish authorities offered explanations based in the syncretic framework, as elaborated by Francisco Hernández, Juan de Cárdenas, and Juan de Barrios. The influence of these New World physicians was in evidence in the classifications, in their direct citation, and frequent excerpts. León Pinelo transcribed Cárdenas's chapters on chocolate and portions of Barrios's *Libro de chocolate* in an appendix to his own widely circulated work on chocolate.[31] They followed their antecessors in their humoral classification of cacao and spices commonly added to chocolate. Unanimously, they agreed that cacao was moderately cool. They inherited the disagreement about whether it was wet or dry. Colmenero de Ledesma stated the "consensus" (*la común de todo*) that cacao was predominantly "cold and dry," though a few years later León Pinelo followed Barrios and qualified it as "temperate declining toward cold and wet."[32] They generally agreed that most of the New World and Old World additives (*mecasuchil, orejuelas,* vanilla, cinnamon, anise, cloves, and the like) were hot, though, and following the difference of opinion among their predecessors, they disagreed about achiote.[33] And, like their New World forerunners, they agreed that the chocolate drink could easily be modified through its mode of preparation and addition or eschewal of ingredients to match the temperament of the consumer. Colmenero de Ledesma wrote that chocolate itself was almost neutral in its humoral makeup because of the effects of its processing and the "hot" properties of the additives that tempered the "cold" property of cacao. Urging that chocolate preparations match individual complexions, he wrote "we must recognize that those who are healthy and normal, as well as the sickly, can benefit from [chocolate], since each one can select the ingredients according to their needs."[34] However, most seemed to consider that the predominant preparation of chocolate was "hot" because of the addition of spices.[35]

❖ ❖ ❖

ALL were astounded by the sway chocolate and, in particular, tobacco held over their consumers. The *Panegírico al chocolate* described the compulsion to drink chocolate as greater than that of all else. And medical authorities bemoaned that chocolate was too often used to excess and warned of dire consequences for those who did not moderate their intake. Valverde Turices, the Seville medical professor, admonished that chocolate should be consumed no more than two or three times a week ("and not, as Doctor Barrios wants, three times a day"). He held that consumers must drink no more than three or four ounces at a sitting in the morning and that drinking chocolate in the evening led to insomnia. He admonished that "chocolate administered not according to some or all of these conditions is bad for the healthy." He reminded his readers of the counsel of Hippocrates and Aristotle to "be moderate in the pleasures, eating and drinking being among the greatest."[36]

But the compulsive behavior of tobacco consumers drew the most attention. The physician Leiva y Aguilar described how there was "a type of tobacco user, one of those people very fond of always medicating themselves, who in all times and all hours worry about their health, going over every moment and evaluating themselves from head to toe, inside and outside, and it seems to them that now they are lacking color, or now have too much color, now cold, now very hot . . . these are very afraid of death and guided by this irritating and rustic medicine, think that in evacuating phlegm they obtain the security of life."[37] Even the tobacco advocate Cordoban apothecarist Juan de Castro y Medinilla acknowledged that in "today's day" there are "among us so many barbarians who every hour and moment of the day take it without respect to order, as if they were beasts" and confessed that "friends of mine (not once but many times) have diligently renounced it, thrown out their snuff boxes with the intention of never returning to it; but it has such a hold on their hearts, that later they return, seeking its forgiveness."[38] The Dominican Tomás Ramón relayed that he had persuaded some "learned men" in Seville to promise that they would give up their habit. Nonetheless, one or two days after they quit, they went back on their word and resumed their consumption, and "when [Ramón] asked them why, they responded that they could not help it."[39] Running through the seventeenth-century treatises were many suggestions that tobacco was not simply another creation of God but rather something peculiarly perverse.

Yet, ultimately, they concurred that, when used in moderation, both substances had beneficial attributes. Someone as outraged by excessive tobacco use as Ramón recognized it as a legitimate substance when used properly.

He asked rhetorically of tobacco: "Then is this not a useless plant without virtue?" He answered his question, "Such a thing cannot be said, because God created [all plants], and as it was said at the beginning, it has [uses] and [many virtues], if it is applied like other medicines, at the appropriate time and season . . . according to the medical arts." Moreover, they sought to show that their negative effects were the product of excessive consumption. Tobacco, like wine, was safe in moderate consumption and dangerous when used profligately: the moralist Jiménez Patón acknowledged that "if wine was consumed with the frequency and disorder that tobacco is nowadays, it, too, would be pestilence." He described the dire physiological effects caused by general excess, whether wine, food, medicine, or tobacco. Hayo defended tobacco from the charge that its "superstitious" uses resulted from properties inherent to the substance, arguing, rather, that "all excess is the enemy of nature, as can be seen with bloodletting and purging, as well as immoderation in eating and drinking, whether it is partridge, chicken, rabbit, or good wine."[40] With the emphasis on the consumer giving way to his or her animal appetites, the substance itself was free of culpability.

Yet the power was such in the case of tobacco that authorities felt compelled to deny diabolical intervention. The clerical author and apologist Tomás Hurtado included a chapter in his treatise on tobacco and chocolate devoted to resolving the quandary of whether "the habit of consuming tobacco" does or does not "entail a pact with the devil." Hurtado presented the argument: "This habit obligates with such great force and solicits he who has it to rouse against his will and reason that a kind of spell and interior force drags and brings him violently to that which he does not want."[41] Continued Hurtado:

> They seem to be under a spell with this herb, which consumed seems to change nature and make slaves of the free . . . the interior force that one feels compelling one to take Tobacco does not seem to be the natural property of this herb but the work of the Devil, as in the other spells, in which because of the property of the pact excites the imagination and fantasy, so that with the acute longing that is experienced one wants to consume and appease until the desire is fulfilled.[42]

Yet he rejected this view and, instead, citing Aristotle and Aquinas explained tobacco users' compulsive behavior through the dynamic of vice, that "miserable habit . . . engendered by the repeated acts that produce a desire or pleasure that one has in the olfactory (*olfato*) and then in the cognitive (*estimativo*) part of the mind that this herb seizes."[43]

To explain the compulsive behavior of tobacco and chocolate devotees, physicians, theologians, and others resorted to a generic model of desire that had its origins in Aristotelian schema, Christianized by the medieval scholastic Thomas of Aquinas and reaffirmed and updated by the theology of the Catholic Reformation. In this schema, the body was the reservoir of senses allowing the subject to apprehend the world, while the mind "warehoused" both the animal appetites and higher human capacities. The basest part was the "sensory appetite" (*apetito sensitivo*)—the font of natural urges. From this compartment of the mind emanated all of the passions and instinctual urges such as "love, happiness, sadness, desire, fear, hope, ire and other similar passions." The "sensory appetite" was "that which makes us most like beasts, whom in every way and for everything are driven by appetites and passions." Moreover, it was "the storehouse of, the force behind, and the ammunition of sin." In the best-selling *Guía de pecadores* (Guide for sinners), the eminent sixteenth-century theologian Luis de Granada advised that "although we always need to war with our appetites, we need especially to contend with the desires of honor, pleasures, and temporal goods, because they are the principal founts and roots of evils."[44]

An often-applied descriptor for both goods was vice (*vicio*), further authorized by the state's categorization as a prerequisite for its taxation and monopoly policies. *Vicio* exemplified an overwhelming object of a desire, such that the craving for it becomes "a passion or habit . . . that obstructs the orderly living of men." The dictionary author and emblem maker explained that "the hieroglyphic of vice is a chain of gold," illustrating the enslaving attachment subjects have to the objects of their desire.[45] Even tobacco's staunchest opponents denied that its unseemly subjugation of so many consumers was based on demonic powers. In keeping with the precedent set by Monardes and the natural philosophy of their epoch, they disavowed miraculous explanations.

That cultural authorities concurred in demystifying tobacco and chocolate will come as no surprise to students of seventeenth-century European intellectual trends. Overall, the supernatural and magical were in retreat in the seventeenth century. Miracles were viewed with increasing skepticism, and though learned people believed in the agency of the devil, they denied him supernatural powers, instead crediting him with exemplary cleverness in his ability to manipulate the natural world. His powers were of the "preternatural" variety, allowing the immensely cunning devil to manipulate the world so effectively as to appear capable of producing supernatural effects, though he could not abrogate the natural order, a right reserved for God alone.[46]

DIVINE AND DIABOLICAL MAGIC

The formal conclusions of the naturalists, physicians, theologians, and jurists are only one part of the story. Lurking nervousness about the suspect origins and unseemly sway of tobacco and chocolate could not be banished by familiar frameworks organized around Catholic reform programs, humoral medicine, or Aristotelian and Thomist models of desire. In the collective imaginary, tobacco and chocolate were not disenchanted. As seen, tobacco and chocolate promised—and delivered—potent effects. They allowed people to consecrate bonds, reaffirm status hierarchies or transgress them. In solitary settings, individuals found them mighty substances that provided singular pleasures, improved faculties of mind and body, and succored the anguished soul. Recognition of these powerful properties, combined with their notorious legacy among New World pagans and Christian theories about miraculous and magical matter, made tobacco and chocolate numinous substances in the collective imagination. The discourse of theologians and physicians—and their distorted reflections in satirical literature—memorialized the goods' importance to mystical ritual among Amerindian peoples. Catholicism and diabolism offered powerful models for viewing material substances—the consecrated Eucharist and witches' unguents, respectively—as a way for humans to grasp the transcendent supernatural. These traditions taken together resulted in the proliferation of tobacco and chocolate as vehicles for the immanent divine and demonic.

Print memory ensured that Europeans could not forget the observations of their predecessors that tobacco enjoyed a sacral role among American Indians. Though historians have sometimes misread or overemphasized the role of printed works in attracting European consumers to tobacco and chocolate, the technology of print and the culture of reading ensured the persistence of memories some would have rather forgotten. While Monardes wrote about the use of tobacco by the "barbarians" to acquit the substance from the charge of idolatry and diabolism, he also inscribed an origins' story that would powerfully maintain those associations. The formal problematization provided in the papal bull for banning the use of tobacco on sacred grounds made reference to previous bans against disrespectful behavior exemplified by unruly consumption, yet there was a subtext (that sometimes surfaced explicitly) of diabolical infiltration. The Jesuit Quintanadueñas articulated what was on the forefront of his and his contemporaries' consciousness. "If we are to give credence to those qualified Historians," he declared, "sacrilegious spirits invented and introduced [tobacco] in the Temples and among the Idolatrous Priests of the Indians." He followed this with a summary of the account of Monardes as to how Indians used tobacco to communicate with the devil.[47] This substance was singular because its barbarian, pagan, even diabolical origins could not be forgotten.

Leiva y Aguilar, in the introduction to *Desengaño contra el mal uso del tabaco* (The abuse of tobacco revealed), wrote that tobacco was first taught to the Priests of those idolatrous Indians, as Monardes says, [and] they all took it in smoke to answer questions asked about the victories in wars and other things of importance, becoming with it stupefied, drunk, and demented, and when they woke they responded with what they had dreamed or what the devil by way of those qualities of tobacco showed them and put it in their imagination so they could give the oracle's answer. Who would say that this was not the invention of the Devil? Would a good Angel or Saint help with a superstition so *ridiculous* in offense of our true God and in honor of those false idols?[48]

Similarly, even though his objective was to remove the specter of diabolism from tobacco use, Hurtado cited Monardes's work to show that it was the "Devil who first taught the Idolatrous Priests to consume Tobacco in smoke" in order to induce trances and manipulate their imaginations.[49] These and similar passages demonstrate the paradoxical legacy of Monardes. Though the sixteenth-century tobacco enthusiast wrote to exorcise tobacco of its idolatrous associations, he effectively enshrined an origins' story that linked tobacco to idolatrous Indians and supernatural uses.

Chocolate, too, prompted seventeenth-century cultural authorities to contend with the legacy of Indian influence, though in a markedly different, more subtle, perhaps more insidious way. Antonio de León Pinelo was already a preeminent jurist and expert on the Spanish Indies—best known as the coauthor of a compilation of the laws of the Indies, one of the most important legal works of the seventeenth century—when he published *Questión moral: si el chocolate quebranta el ayuno eclesiástico* (A moral question: whether chocolate violates the ecclesiastical fast) in 1636.[50] León Pinelo took the conservative line that one could not drink chocolate and uphold the ecclesiastical fast. Hurtado, a theologian belonging to a religious order notorious for endorsing permissive theological views that justified the worldly lifestyles of aristocrats, issued a rebuttal to León Pinelo, first in his lectures on theology at the University of Seville and later in his 1645 *Chocolate y tabaco: ayuno eclesiástico y natural* (Chocolate and tobacco: the ecclesiastical and natural fast).[51]

As with the parameters defining the theological controversy around tobacco, the formal terms of the debate over chocolate and the ecclesiastical fast exemplified the concern during the Catholic Reformation with shoring up orthodox practice. But the participants in the debate took certain avenues that brought the pagan past of chocolate to the fore. Chocolate's origin among "Gentiles and barbarians" was actively invoked when the debate evolved to emphasize that in its essence chocolate was an "artificial drink"—or, to put it in present-day terms, a "social construct." This twist came about when the adversaries reached an impasse when trying to determine the essential nature of chocolate (drink versus food) by using traditional criteria based on physical characteristics. Invoking standard scholastic Aristotelian distinctions between "accidental" and "intrinsic" qualities, León Pinelo held that the liquid form of chocolate was an accident but its intrinsic quality was to nourish, making it a food.[52] Hurtado, however, declared that chocolate's intrinsic quality was its potability, and its nourishing effects were the "accident."[53] The turn to classical authorities could not provide answers, and technical criteria alone would not suffice to settle the matter.

So the adversaries agreed that if the resolution lay in determining a precedent, it followed that it was necessary to understand how the "originators," that is, Indians, employed chocolate in their own societies. In the prologue to *Questión moral*, León Pinelo established that the principal task was to determine the social role of the beverage. He declared that he was going to resolve a "question [that] is about an artificial drink," one that was "invented" by "art or delight in the Indies." It was a powerful statement to begin a book about ambiguities concerning a central precept of the Christian Church with a story of Indian-European transculturation. Though disputing León Pinelo's categorization, Hurtado concurred with his reasoning process and accepted that to establish the true nature of chocolate required looking at how it was used customarily in the Americas. He first offered the analogy that during the days of the "primitive Church the faithful when they fasted did not drink wine, but today *custom* has derogated this law." By corollary, he explained "if today chocolate is made and drank in Spain as a proper beverage . . . because of its nature and its *first institution*, it is a beverage, and even if it sustains in some manner, as wine sustains, it is absolutely certain, that it does not violate the Ecclesiastical fast."[54] Hence, Hurtado established that cultural criteria mattered more than chemical or physiological criteria in defining a beverage. Moreover, he, like León Pinelo, gestured toward the place of the drink's "first institution"—that is, America—in order to establish its usage. The fact that chocolate was invented in "the Indies" was not incidental to either León Pinelo or Hurtado's cultural account of chocolate.

Yet the consensus that to understand the nature of chocolate required investigating its customary use in the Americas did not bring the opposing factions to a common agreement. Those who believed that drinking chocolate would not violate the ecclesiastical fast argued that chocolate was the quintessential Mesoamerican *beverage*, as opposed to food. Hurtado wrote, "It does not matter that these drinks were introduced by Gentiles and Idolaters, because the judgment of natural reason distinguishes between food and drink and we Catholics use this distinction and from its beginning the Sacred Theology has held that beverages do not break the fast."[55] The same rationale surfaced in the confessional manual *Examen de confesores y practica de penitentes en todas las materias de teologia moral* (Disquisition for confessors and guide for penitents in all the subjects of moral theology). One question raised by the fictitious confessant was "You said that one can drink chocolate, because it is a beverage, without violating the fast: How can one be sure that it is a beverage?" The virtual confessor answered that "a *jícara* is made of one ounce of pure chocolate, one and one half ounces of sugar (without egg or milk). In this way *the Indians drank it*, and taken moderately in this way it was approved by the Pope."[56] Just as Christian Europe could acknowledge its inheritance and cultural continuity from pagan antiquity, so too it could absorb the cultural distinctions made by the pagan and idolatrous inhabitants of the New World.

León Pinelo refuted the argument by disputing the notion that chocolate's "inventors" used it akin to the way different European peoples used wine, beer, or cider. While beer and wine served as the quotidian drinks for all kinds of people, chocolate was not a common drink. León Pinelo followed the chroniclers of the Indies in asserting that only those at the summit of society because of birthright or military valor were allowed the perquisite of drinking chocolate:

> As a drink of *regalo* and considerable and singular quality, it was not permitted to all of the commoners, but only the lords, princes, captains, and courageous men as affirmed by Antonio de Herrera, and it was such that the privilege of drinking it was so esteemed that it was like an act of nobility, a reward for heroic feats.[57]

The material content of the drink altered in the process of migration—new ingredients, new recipes—but its social form remained fixed. Just as it served as a *regalo* in pre-Columbian America, so it was likewise used in Spain.

León Pinelo offered another precedent in Mesoamerican customary practice to support his brief. Referencing the ethnographic reports of Indians' religious practices found in the writings of missionaries, León Pinelo asserted that since the Mexica refrained from drinking chocolate when honoring their idols during the "fast of the festival they called Quetzalcohaut," then Christians should do likewise during their fast days: "Therefore, if the Indians, inventors of this beverage in their barbarian fasts that lack form, law, or merit, do not use it or allow it, holding that it provides much sustenance, then all the less should we use it ourselves."[58] It was also characteristic of León Pinelo's method to invoke "Historians of the Indies," such as Herrera, Toribio de Motolinia, José de Acosta (and also Peter Martyr, Francisco López de Gómara, Girolamo Benzoni, Bernal

Díaz de Castillo, among others).[59] By eschewing classical and Christian authorities and elevating New World chroniclers, León Pinelo underscored chocolate's Amerindian origins and the irrelevance of Christian antecedents. Remarkably, Hurtado did not quibble with León Pinelo's use of Mexican religion, but rather argued that "it does not matter that the Gentile Priests abstained from chocolate during their fasts, because in order to fast more rigorously, they also abstained from wine, which is not mandated of our precepts."[60] In other words, Hurtado argued that since Indians abstained from wine during their fasts and Christians did not, it would not make sense to follow the example of Indians vis à vis chocolate. The implied logic, of course, was that Indian and Christian religious practices were not comparable because those of the former were *more* "rigorous" than those practiced by contemporary Christians.

Chocolate, rather than being contained within the discourse of the Counter-Reformation, undermined it from within. Asking whether chocolate drinking and fasting could coincide was not unlike finding a loose thread, pulling on it, and discovering that one's shirt had unraveled. What seemed to begin as a simple query about the material nature of chocolate—solid or liquid—dissolved into inquiries about the social meanings of chocolate consumption. And what seemed to be a straightforward investigation well within the confines of Christendom led its detectives well beyond its limits.[61]

The powerful place of tobacco and chocolate in pre-Columbian societies contributed to their potency in seventeenth-century Europe. This potency, heightened by circulating and recirculating knowledge of their social and religious significance for Amerindians, helps explain the mystical framework that enveloped them in the Old World. For tobacco, the dominant paradigm was diabolical. Synthesizing Amerindian understandings of tobacco as a sacred element with European views of sorcery, the earliest chroniclers of the Indies, such as Oviedo, saw tobacco as a supernatural, often demonic, substance. Even Monardes, who rejected the idea that the devil "invented" tobacco, accepted that large quantities of tobacco consumed by Indians worked as a medium that allowed prophesy or access to knowledge not obtainable through natural means.

Tobacco entered Europe when concern about witches—understood as women who willingly entered a diabolical pact with the devil in return for occult powers—was high, leading to over ten thousand executions.[62] One witch hunt—that resulted in as many as eighty executions at the stake—was conducted in 1609 by Pierre de Lancre, a learned French magistrate and most influential demonologist commissioned to investigate charges of witchcraft among the peoples of Labourt in southwestern France. The Labourdins were Basque, belonging to a culture that stretched from France to

northern Spain. Lancre, a cosmopolitan Frenchman, found the Basques utterly alien, and he saw many parallels between their behaviors and those of
the idolaters of the New World, whose strange rituals he learned about
from his reading. Lancre even adduced that the triumphs of Christian missionaries in the New World had led a frustrated Satan and his devils to renew their efforts in Europe, citing travelers in Bordeaux who had seen
"demons appearing as horrific human beings," en route, flying through the
sky.[63] The presence of tobacco demonstrated a direct link between the Satanic worship of Basque witches and American Indians. Clearly familiar
with the writings of Peter Martyr—or one of his translators or
plagiarizers—the magistrate associated the smoking habits of New World
idolaters to Basque Satan worshippers:

> And like the Indians of the Spanish Isles, who, after inhaling the smoke of a
> certain herb called Cohoba, grow restless . . . [and] stay this way for a cer-
> tain period in a state of ecstasy, they finally rise all lost and confused, telling
> marvels of their false gods whom they call Cemis, just like our witches when
> they return from the Sabbath.[64]

While Lancre acknowledged that tobacco smoking might have appealed to
the impoverished Labourdins to mitigate the hunger pangs, he also viewed
its presence as evidence of diabolical rites. The French Basque witch craze
crossed the frontier and catalyzed a witch hunt in the Spanish Basque area
around Logroño—though overall Spain, relative to most other European
countries, escaped the bloody witch-hunting frenzies—and there, too, tobacco appeared as possible evidence of sorcery during prosecutions that
took place in 1610.[65] Tobacco traveled easily, in the imaginations of Europeans, from Indian diabolically inspired idolaters in the New World to
witches, sorcerers, and the other minions of Satan in the Old World.

This transposition is most dramatically displayed in a Dutch engraving,
The Sorceress (1626). (See figure 10.1.) The scene depicts a witch's Sabbath,
and tobacco serves as a diabolical sacrament. Many of the most central
tenets of diabolical witchcraft, as understood throughout seventeenth-
century Europe, are pictured in the scene.[66] The dominant trope is of inversion; central to the sixteenth- and seventeenth-century understanding
of the devil was his wont to invert Christian rites. The antithesis of the male
priest, a young, sexy female witch, her long locks enticing and seductive,
convenes over a motley crew of people, animals, and monsters (it was
well-known that those who entered a diabolical pact were prone to
shape-shift) for Satanic worship. Tobacco—the pipes, the smoke—visually
integrates the scene, reflecting its sacramental and symbolic centrality. Tobacco smoke and the sorceress's magical powers mingle into one enchanted

stream. The smokiness of the tobacco, along with the night cover, evokes the infernal, reminding viewers that the witch receives her powers from the devil—as the priest receives his from God. The crew of devils and devil worshippers find communion in their shared rite of smoking. In place of a chalice of wine and consecrated host, tobacco is the diabolical Eucharist, uniting the witch, her communicants, and the devil. Witches, it was known, entered a pact with the devil, committing themselves to Satan in return for occult powers. Tobacco, here, was the medium of this pact.

The association of tobacco as a diabolical sacrament originated with New World chroniclers' efforts to make sense of native Americans' ritual consumption of tobacco; like the consecration of bread and wine that al-

Figure 10.1. Jan van de Velde, *The Sorceress* (1626). The long-enduring trope of tobacco as the medium of diabolical consecration is dramatically represented here. Engraving. Print collection, Miriam and Ira D. Wallach Division of Art, Prints and Photographs, the New York Public Library, Astor, Lenox and Tilden Foundations. Reproduced with permission.

❖ 247 ❖

lowed transubstantiation, shamanic ingestion of tobacco allowed a union with the divine. The Jesuit ethnographer Acosta was explicit that tobacco was an inverted sacrament and discussed the mimetic tendencies of the devil in this context, and Castro y Medinilla cited this very passage in providing the natural history of tobacco.[67] To counter those who were suspicious of smoke as a medium, Castro y Medinilla defended smoke by reminding that it was a legitimate weapon in the arsenal of exorcists (this just a few pages after he described the divine powers that Indians attributed to tobacco).

The fear that tobacco ingested would interfere with Holy Communion developed not only from the idea that it was a natural fast (requiring abstention from all food or drink), a precondition for the absorption of the divine to take place, but also from the images of the inverted debauched communion rituals supposedly practiced by witches, devil worshippers, and Amerindians. Tobacco use in Christian churches indicated a perverse parody of the Christian Communion. This is why the use of tobacco by those overseeing church altars and offering Communion prompted such anxiety, anxiety so acute that it could not be fully expressed. It was easier to discuss exactly what constituted a fast—a requirement for Communion—and to show then how tobacco use violated that condition than to discuss the scary homology between the host and wine as the flesh and blood of Christ and tobacco as the essence of the Antichrist. But, when reacting to the widespread practice of tobacco sniffing, smoking, and chewing in Spain, cultural authorities could only repress their awareness of this connection, not in spite of but because of its corrosive threat.

The efforts of cultural authorities in seventeenth-century Spain to demonstrate that the devil was not involved in tobacco consumption also speak to the power of that association. In 1635 Ramón wrote, citing Monardes as a source, "And with respect to those who use so much of this powder [tobacco] in Spain, I do not know what to say, except that they have some kind of implicit pact [with the Devil]." Ten years later, the medical professor Cristóbal de Hayo countered the still persisting opinion that "tobacco in smoke was used superstitiously in order to provoke a dream in order to prophesy while awake."[68] Leiva y Aguilar, in *Desengaño contra el mal uso del tabaco*, asserted that since the creation of the world—beginning with his promise "I will make you like gods" to Adam and Eve—Satan had wrought perdition by promising illicit knowledge and powers, following up that act with the "invention" of "so many magical arts" (geomancy and necromancy, among others) and the sponsorship of "his various stewards" (conjurers and dream tellers, among others). He also included the "miserable sorcery" that abounds, which spurs people to use various magical herbs (valerian, henbane, mandragora) "with which Satan promises thousands of

illusions about love, victory, gambling, favor, riches, journeys . . . matching each one to a person's weakness and ambition, and all is lies." Tobacco
arrived "among these numbers and kinds." Leiva y Aguilar appears ambivalent about whether the various black magic and witches' potions were
"lies" promulgated by the devil or whether in fact they possessed some efficacy. (At the very least they were assigned effectiveness by their deluded
followers.) Later on in his work he compared the value people accorded to
tobacco to that they assigned to love potions, amulets, and superstitious
incantations.[69] The 1673 dictionary definition for tobacco concurred with
theological authorities that tobacco consumers' compulsive behavior was
the result of a vice, but it recognized, as well, "that there are many who say
that it casts a spell, upon seeing the exertion and solicitude expended by
those seeking it, and how those members of the tobacco confraternity become melancholy when they are without it." The entry juxtaposed this diabolical theory to its suspect origins, stating that "the first to discover it was
the devil, who made his priests and ministers take it when they were asked
to prophesy, and the devil showed them how with symbols, by means of
that drugged state."[70]

Ever since the days of St. Augustine, a Manichean view in which Satan
wielded equal power to God was considered heretical. Following principles
outlined by Aquinas, theologians and natural philosophers of the sixteenth
and seventeenth centuries were clear that the devil could not perform truly
supernatural deeds, which was the domain of God alone.[71] The devil was
no more than an extra-clever manipulator of the natural world who could
create powerful delusions or effects though the manipulation of occult
powers. Nonetheless, at a broader, symbolic level, Satan appeared like an
inverted God, and his black magic the counterpart to God's miracles. The
diabolically enchanted associations of tobacco—and chocolate—haunted
the highest quarters. Charles II (r. 1665–1700), the last Habsburg monarch
of Spain and most extreme victim of that dynasty's inbreeding, suffered
from demonic possession. The devil's channel to the sovereign was thought,
variously, to be a *jícara* of chocolate or tobacco.[72]

Overall, however, seventeenth-century representations of chocolate
evoked the divine, rather than the demonic. In his line that "chocolate-
bibbers idolize the cup that they raise on high and adore and go into a
trance over," Quevedo was making the outrageous charge that chocolate
devotees revere their *jícara* as a chalice of consecrated wine during Communion. In likening chocolate to the consecrated wine—the blood of
Christ—Europeans synthesized (again) traditions from both hemispheres.
The Eucharist offered a prototype for how ingesting a quotidian substance
could be a vehicle for divinity, a substance that on absorption gave the
body and soul new life and the spirit uplift. Just as the predilection for

chocolate reddened by achiote had crossed the Atlantic, so did the understanding of chocolate as a bloodlike substance and a divinely infused elixir of life.

Like tobacco, chocolate trespassed into the Christian Mass. Bartolomé Marradón, who wrote the first treatise about tobacco and chocolate consumption aimed at Spanish audiences, described with shock this infiltration, when he recounted how he witnessed a Spanish priest—who was supposed to be proselytizing to Indians—so dependent on chocolate that he was compelled to interrupt his Mass to guzzle chocolate. This disconcerting infiltration crossed the Atlantic. We have already seen the grouchy Madrid nobleman finding recourse in chocolate and avoiding Mass, and even the cheery commendation that "preachers find much good in taking chocolate before and after preaching."[73]

Chocolate did not only compete for the devotion of consecrants and communicants, but it was described in terms that evoked the Eucharist, as well as Mesoamerican descriptions of it as a life-infusing elixir. The decrees of the Council of Trent proclaimed that the Eucharist, in which "our Lord Jesus Christ, who gave His own beloved soul as the price of our salvation, and gave us His own flesh to eat," allowed the communicant "that supersubstantial bread" that offered "truly the life of the soul, and the perpetual health of their mind; that being invigorated by the strength thereof, they may, after the journeying of this miserable pilgrimage, be able to arrive at their heavenly country; there to eat, without any veil, that same bread of angels which they now eat under sacred veils."[74] In the late seventeenth and early eighteenth century, Jesuit writers took up the theme of the Eucharist as the ultimate comfort food, referring to the ecstasy of Communion as the "manna," "balsam," "elixir," "precious viand," and "sacred powder" that heals all infirmities, restores "all lost corporal strength," and brings "marvelous rest and peace," "immortal and incomprehensible light."[75] Central to the portrayal of the Eucharist was that beneath the "accidents" of bread and wine there was very real flesh and blood.

So it is important that the idea that chocolate worked like blood to offer a singular source of vitality flourished in the seventeenth century, a connection that Europeans in good part learned from Mesoamericans. Valverde Turices wrote that it "revives, invigorates, and uplifts the principal parts [of the body], and improves the flow of blood and vapors to the exterior parts."[76] Such an explanation was *despite*, not because of, its humoral associations, which assigned it only a moderate heating effect. The association between chocolate and blood came to the fore prominently in a manuscript of "a certain Spanish Physician of Sevil," which came into the hands of Henry Stubbe, an English physician and chocolate advocate, himself the author of *The Indian Nectar, or a Discourse Concerning Chocolata*. Stubbe reported that this Spanish authority

> made it his peculiar inquiry to search into the nature of Chocolata, as he
> doth an every occasion shew himself extraordinarily learned, and to have
> consulted all the Publick Discourses and private Manuscripts about it, so he
> manifests a great regard to the Testimony of Experience, which he avows to
> be so favourable for Chocolata, that there is not one, who doth drink it, and
> doth not feel himself to be manifestly refreshed and strengthened, as well as
> delighted by it.[77]

For this "Spanish physician" the explanation for chocolate's life-giving force lay in its effects on blood:

> Chocolata by a new quality arising to the Composition through fermenta-
> tion (as happens in Treacle) strengthens the natural heat in each part, and
> encreaesth that, which continually inflows, and begetting by a speedy and
> easie transmutation much and good Blood . . . *and it doth more speedily and
> readily refresh and invigorate the bodily strength than any other sustenance
> whatever, no other potable liquers [which yet do most quickly nourish] pro-
> ducing so speedy and sensible an effect: whereby it seems to be peculiarly
> differenced from all other Viands.*[78]

That such a view of chocolate as a near-universal panacea and containing a life-giving force was widely held is suggested by the gentle parodies of such.[79]

Chocolate's association with blood and its trespass into the Mass suggested the miracle of the consecrated wine that becomes the blood of Christ during the Mass. The Eucharistic echoes in the comic literature about chocolate were purposeful. Not only Quevedo but the *Panegírico al chocolate* asserted of chocolate, "Oh, *jícara*, exquisite miracle! To you my life is dedicated and consecrated." Another verse announced that chocolate "surpasses the pious heavens" for heating in December and cooling in July.[80] Other poems compared chocolate to "ambrosia" and "manna," terms also applied to the Eucharist. This tradition finds its culmination in *Chocolata, sive in laudem potionis indiae, quam apellant Chocolate* (Chocolata, or in honor of the Indian beverage called chocolate) (1733), an "elegy" written by the Enlightenment scholar Gregorio Mayans y Siscar (1699–1781). It is worth noting that he dedicated his paean to a Jesuit, Cardinal Álvaro Cienfuegos, during the same era in which Jesuits were writing their tributes to the Eucharist. The verses celebrate many of the salient endowments attributed to chocolate for over a century. Most of all, Mayans vividly evoked how the beverage pleased the senses, augmented the faculties, and brought comfort to the soul:

The empty breast is filled with the heavenly gift and a vital heat penetrates to the marrow of the bones. In an instant, the mind strengthens upon contact with the soft vapor, and the tired members are reinvigorated with a vitalizing strength. . . . When you [the chocolate] glide over the throat, a myriad of preoccupations distance themselves from the heart, the corrosive restlessness flees. You furnish suffering men with desired rest, and dissolve the pangs of sadness. You are the nourishing beverage of the good heart and fine mind, not only do you provide one with happiness but to the other a sprightly vigor, . . . [Chocolate] introduces life-giving sap into the drought-struck medulla; it restores the strength and gives new breath to the spirit.[81]

Mayans encapsulated the amazing effects of chocolate, of infusing the body to the marrow of the bones with an essential vigor—reminiscent of the Mesoamericans life-giving sap—that provides comfort, stills nervousness, furnishes physical strength and mental agility. The transcendent language is evocative of how spiritual writers had elegized the experiencing of ingesting the consecrated host since the Middle Ages.[82]

Serious treatises and spoofs alike suggest that people—at some level—believed that their consumption of tobacco and chocolate offered individual and social transformations not fully accounted for through "rational" explications grounded in either religion or science. These beliefs were relegated to the powerful ether of unauthorized imagination. Tobacco and chocolate helped to usher in a phase of modern consumption in which sublime attention was displaced from religious activities to secular rites.

DESACRALIZATION

Tobacco and chocolate infiltrated the institutional Church and undercut its sanctity and authority through sanctioned sacrilege and the import of a cultural relativism that belied the Church's claim to an exclusive monopoly on cosmological truth and as the only vehicle for salvation. The *Sátira contra el tabaco* did not resort to euphemism when it stated that the person who abuses tobacco "is no longer a good Christian." Other spoofs fleshed out Quevedo's charge of idolatry; they portray tobacco consumers as appropriating pagan customs, sacrificing Christian devotion for pursuit of their appetites, and worshipping false gods (manifested both in their devotion to vice and the pagan gods with which the goods and correlated behaviors were associated).[83] There was the obstreperous attachment of the clergy—those sanctified bodies responsible for consecration of the Eucharist and administration of other sacraments—to their tobacco. That tobacco-consuming clergy resisted the decrees limiting their tobacco consumption was further evidence of tobacco's insidious sacrilege. Seville clergy appealed the 1642 papal bull, protesting frankly that "upholding [the rule] would result in great problems, among those the obvious danger that the priests would incur the punishments of the said bull . . . given the custom they have of consuming tobacco without which they cannot survive, some out of necessity and others because of the said habit."[84] For those who were already alarmed, the resistance of priests must have only flamed their worries. In fact, the antitobacco moralist Tomás Ramón presciently anticipated such resistance when he related hearing "a cleric say that even if so ordered by the pontiff, he would not give up [tobacco]," and concluded that its users would kill for it,[85] a sufficiently notorious anecdote that it reappeared in the light-hearted *Sátira contra el tabaco* (Satire against tobacco). The companion work, *Romance en alabanza del tabaco* (In praise of tobacco) also hinted at the complicity and compromisedness of the clergy, for its narrator asserted that he composed the elegy of tobacco at the insistence of a friar who "with his rule required me to write it . . . under penalty of penitential discipline and harsh imprisonment, correction, and bread and water and other penalties."[86]

SATIRICAL literature also portrayed chocolate as necessarily sacrilegious.

The *Panegírico al chocolate* was irreverent, hovering around blasphemous, when it subordinated Mary and Joseph to chocolate.

> If Joseph and Mary drank
> The sweet, always majestic chocolate
> She would have the face of snow and roses
> He would be made into a robust lad
> She the envy of Diana
> And him another Apollo of famous pleasure.[87]

Thus it suggested that the sainted Mary and Joseph, family of Jesus, could have been more perfect with chocolate, and put them in the company of pagan gods of antiquity. In "Coplas al Chocolate" (Couplets of chocolate), Antonio Hurtado de Mendoza wrote of its origins among pagans and even its substitution as an object of veneration as well as source of solace: "Without a doubt chocolate is not Christian . . . it becomes my hope."[88]

The desacralizing impact of chocolate is most visible in a necessarily anonymous 1684 poem whose title translates as "A True Report of the Great Sermon that Mahomet Calipapau, of Russian nationality, the Great Prior of Escanzaona, and the Archbishop of Lepanto, Doctor Degreed in the Texts and Paragraphs of the Koran preached in the Parroquial Mosque of Babylon."[89] The main conceit of this subversive satire was a formal dispute between a Christian archbishop and the Muslim Caliph over the merits of chocolate versus coffee. The targets of this spoof were the serious theological debates over chocolate and the medical claims made for the beverage. It also ensnared for mockery the Inquisition and, generally, the Church.

The verse recounts how the Archbishop won converts for chocolate. The prelate begins by claiming that he had taken his "profound" subject from the Koran and discovered that since ancient times chocolate had been the favored drink of vestal virgins, the queen of Cathay, Amazons, fauns, giants, nymphs, and "even governing Muses and the Gods." On the other hand, "Moors invented coffee / and with it have remained / as punishment for their sin."[90] This opening joke rests on the discrepancy between the purported and known lineage of chocolate. While the fictitious Archbishop of Lepanto praised chocolate for its pedigreed classical origins, any late seventeenth-century audience would be well aware that the "angelic beverage" was being accorded a false lineage—that it in fact originated with pagan Americans. The effect is to make chocolate-drinkers appear as guilty as apostasy as Muslim infidels.

As the poem progresses, sovereigns the world over come under chocolate's thrall. The archbishop succeeds in converting the Grand Sufi, "who no longer could love / his Coffee, now only Chocolate."[91] The friar Juan de Costa, Inquisitor and Abbot of Montserrat, exorcised the "Grand Cam of Tartar" with chocolate, and the King of Japan was cured of his "crippled limbs" after imbibing the beverage. Other chapters described how chocolate revived the dead.[92]

In the poem, chocolate travels throughout the world in the care of various men of the Church. Not only did Juan de Costa visit the Tartars, but the "Jesuit Father Juan de Mota" brought chocolate to the "gran Mogor" (Great Mogul of India?). During their meetings, the latter inquired if it was a "fabulous story" that in Spain it was a "crime" to be of the wrong "birth or lineage," since "the birth one has / is not of one's choice but comes from God." In other words, the Mogul was asking about (and pointing to the hypocrisy in) Spain's infamous *limpieza de sangre* statutes (those rules that discriminated against people with Jewish or Muslim ancestry). The poem's character "Father Mota" responds by putatively defending the Inquisition but actually further indicting it by describing its penalties of "loss, life, goods, and honor" to those "who give argument to that which the Faith prescribes without reasons." The author aims yet another barb when he underscores the tribunal's hypocrisy for persecuting those of non-Christian ancestry, since on the "tribunal there preside three priests, saintly and eminent . . . among them there are various lineages."[93]

In this stanza, the author satirized Spain's religious intolerance, much in the manner that Montesquieu attacked religious intolerance in France with the *Persian Letters*. That state and church persecution of religious dissension struck the stereotyped despotic Asian tyrant as bizarre demonstrated that Spain had surpassed the famously capricious and intolerant rule of the East. The spoof of the chocolate debate metamorphosed into a jab at the intolerance of Church and state and the hypocrisy of the Inquisition.

It was no coincidence that these subjects—chocolate and the Church—were conjoined for mockery in this anonymous, unpublishable verse. Chocolate became the occasion to show the hypocrisy of the Church. This poem brought to the surface the underside of the "serious" debate over chocolate—Spanish incorporation of chocolate pointed to the internal inconsistencies of intolerance during the Counter-Reformation.

For most of its history, Christianity has demanded that its adherents accept its monopoly on truth. Part of the process of secularization has been to call into question the notion that any one religion (with the possible exception of "science") has a particular hold on truth, a phenomenon often spurred by relativism. Christian Europe's encounters with the greater world did not precipitate relativism, in large part, no doubt, because its own history was marked by struggle with non-Christian belief systems, first with Judaism, then paganism in the early classical world, and then with an expanding Islam. Scholars have thus dismissed the relativizing effects of the New World encounter until the advent of the scientific revolution and the Enlightenment's rejection of textual and, ultimately, divine authority. But the effect of the New World—in the form of the infiltration of tobacco and chocolate into the heart of the metropole—did contribute to a relativist outlook, as certain observers took note of its corrosive effects on institutional religion. It is silly to say that the assimilation of tobacco and chocolate led to relativism, as it is silly to say that *any* one factor precipitated such a significant shift in worldview, yet for those already inclined in that direction, the paradoxes engulfing the goods became powerful instigators to go further.

THE incorporation of tobacco and chocolate into European culture contributed to its secularization. They became fuel for the secular state, prompting it to become a defender, even guarantor of the consumption of "vice" goods. They became a catalyst for the retreat of mystical explanations in religious and medical discourse. Both the rise of the modern state and decline of magical thinking have long been identified as central developments of the seventeenth century, linked, respectively, to warfare and the decline of feudalism, and the Reformation and Counter-Reformation. It is my view that European expansion and its by-products must be included among the catalysts for these modern transformations.

However, the history of tobacco and chocolate in seventeenth-century Spain also demonstrates that nascent modernity encompassed more than state-building and disenchantment. It also shows that the paradox of tobacco and chocolate became a prompt for a kind of desacralizing and relativistic approach to Christianity that is conventionally associated with the eighteenth century and northern Europe. Perhaps most modern of all was the way that the magic of tobacco and chocolate did not, in the end, become extinct. Rather, the goods flourished as magical fetishes, as the devil's little helper and a divine elixir, in the collective imagination. It does not matter whether consumers "really" believed that the goods' potency derived from supernatural forces anymore than whether anyone today "really" believes that rinsing with a certain brand of conditioner will make her hip and attractive, or whether driving a particular sports utility vehicle will bring him closer to nature. Mass advertising was not, of course, in existence during the first phase of the spread of tobacco and chocolate in Europe. Yet the physiological processes that make advertising work—the body's proclivity to associate beliefs and desires with concrete sensory experiences—is what allowed tobacco and chocolate to enchant a secular realm of experience.

Epilogue:
Globalization, Gateways, and
Transformations

❖ ❖

GLOBALIZATION

Tobacco cropped up in many places around the globe, roughly simultaneously, at the end of the sixteenth century. The speed at which tobacco smoking swept across Africa, the Middle East, and Asia after initial exposure is remarkable in comparison with the time lag between Columbus's first voyages and tobacco's systemic diffusion throughout Europe. What accounts for the alacrity of tobacco's global diffusion outside of Europe?

On the "push" side, a crucial exogenous factor was the role of European mariners in introducing the habit and the commodity. Portuguese, Dutch, Arab, and French sailors and traders have been credited with bringing tobacco to the Ottoman Empire, Persia, Africa, India, Japan, China, and Java. [1] For instance, members of an expedition to the Gold Coast (West Africa) during 1597–98 commented that "the inhabitants of those regions, a short time ago, learned from the Batavians [Dutch] to use and consume the smoke of Tobacco or Nicotiana, of which they had before been completely ignorant, having been content to chew only betel leaves."[2] Likewise, in 1599 an Englishman traveling on a vessel in the Dardanelles remarked that when a captain from the Turkish navy came aboard he "desired to have some tobacko [sic] and tobacco-pipes," demonstrating that Turks had prior experience with enjoying tobacco procured from English sailors.[3] From the Ottoman Empire, tobacco traveled to neighboring Safavid Persia. However, it is also possible that it arrived in Persia, and India, before that, by way of the Portuguese mariners who traded in the Persian Gulf in the sixteenth century.[4]

The most thoroughly studied non-European region for the introduction and diffusion of tobacco is Asia. The Spanish Philippines and Portuguese Macao are thought to have been critical gateways.[5] An entrepot in tobacco's Asian trajectory was Macao, established by the Portuguese in 1557. Though Macao is very close to the south coast of China's Guangdong Province, it appears that Japanese traders first systematically adopted tobacco through their interactions with the colonists there. Japanese traders carried the custom to Korea, then Manchuria and China, resulting in the perception among some northern Chinese that the "southern herb" originated in Korea. Tobacco also entered China by way of Manila. The largest of the Philippine islands colonized by the Spanish in the 1570s, Manila attracted Chinese traders based in coastal Fujian who were interested in European goods. In this way they became acquainted with smoking, and their extensive trading networks led them to spread the custom into mainland China and beyond (Japan, Korea, and throughout Southeast Asia). By the early seventeenth century tobacco was cultivated in the Beijing area, and a visitor to the capital in 1642 found "tobacconists on every street corner," despite prohibitions against smoking.[6]

In addition to the push factor of a tobacco-loving mariner subculture, a "pull" factor that likely contributed to the rapid adoption of tobacco in many societies was the existence of *mainstream* traditions of using psychotropic substances, namely betel, cannabis, and opium. In Europe, by contrast, the strong hallucinogenic plants of the nightshade family (henbane, datura) were associated with the despised and marginal—witches and sorcerers—and wine was considered more food (or drink) than drug, despite its inebriating effects. Betel chewing is an ancient practice that has ranged from East Africa to southern and southeastern Asia to the western Pacific. It involves wrapping betel leaf around an areca palm seed treated with slaked lime. Chewing betel offers pleasant stimulating effects, compared in sensation to that of tobacco.[7] The idea that one could substitute one for the other was made explicit by the traveler in West Africa, quoted above, who wrote that before tobacco the local people had "been content to chew only betel leaves." Regular opium and cannabis consumers in the Middle East and South Asia were also likely to find tobacco amenable.[8] And, again, as anticipated by Monardes, contemporary observers were themselves quick to make such a connection. "The Turkes are also incredible takers of Opium," wrote an Englishman, "which they say explelleth all feare, and makes them courageous: but I rather thinke giddy headed and turbulent dreamers. . . . And perhaps for the selfe same cause they also delight in Tobacco."[9]

Another factor that may have contributed to Europe's relative lag and other societies' relative rapidity in embracing tobacco was in divergent attitudes toward smoke. For Europeans, tobacco connoted the diabolically infernal, bringing to mind the cauldrons of hell and witches' brews. In contrast, a friendliness toward smoke characterized many Asian cultures. For instance, in Indian legend, the fire god taught sages ways to make smoke to protect babies from evil spirits. In China, smoke was a symbol and ritual object for "the boundless natural forces that brought the invisible world into being."[10]

The spread of tobacco entailed not only the ingestion of *Nicotiana* but also the technique of smoking. In the case of opium, it is definite that tobacco smoking led to smoking opium. In the Indonesian archipelago and throughout the Malay world, smokers began to add opium to their tobacco pipes in the early seventeenth century.[11] From there, opium arrived in China at about the same time as tobacco, through exchanges with foreigners, perhaps once again by way of Portuguese in Macao. Scholars emphasize that the arrival of opium in China depended on tobacco, since the opium substance that the Chinese first began to smoke was made of tobacco leaves soaked in the sap of unripened opium poppy seeds.[12] It is less clear in the case of cannabis, but to my mind the most persuasive evidence points to its having been only chewed by inhabitants of the Near East and Africa.[13] A thirteenth-century Arabic botanical treatise discussed the narcotic effects of marijuana but failed to discuss its being smoked. A sixteenth-century Portuguese account only mentioned that East Africans *ate* hemp. But after the introduction of tobacco smoking, people began to smoke their *bangue* (marijuana) as well.[14]

GATEWAYS

While the beginnings of tobacco's diffusion across Europe lay with explorers of diverse nationalities in Spanish and Portuguese America, chocolate flowed through pathways from metropolitan Spain into the rest of Europe. Chocolate's early introduction into Europe outside of Spain remains to be thoroughly studied, but various sources suggest that it penetrated certain circles by the 1630s. Antonio Colmenero de Ledesma wrote in 1631 that "the number of people who nowadays drink Chocolate is so great that it is not only in the Indies where this drink originated and began, but also in Spain, Italy, and Flanders it is already very common."[15] This should come as no surprise when one considers the cosmopolitan, transnational communities of clergy, aristocrats, *conversos* and Jews, and even army officers that were among the chocolate vanguard. There is the corroborating archival tidbit showing that in 1634 Mexican Jesuits were shipping chocolate to their brethren in Rome by way of Seville. Portuguese New Christians and Sephardim were relays for the spread of chocolate from Iberia to northern

Europe, particularly to Flanders. In seventeenth-century Amsterdam Jews were identified as chocolate specialists, and *conversos* fleeing persecution from the Spanish Inquisition specialized in chocolate in Bayonne. Even in the late nineteenth century, in southern France, the chocolatiers who traveled from house to house in order to freshly grind chocolate with *metates* were most often Sephardic Jews.[16] One index that chocolate was established among elite habits of non-Iberian Europeans by the mid-seventeenth century was the proliferation of translations of Antonio Colmenero de Ledesma's 1631 *Curioso tratado de la naturaleza y calidad del chocolate*; at least nine editions appeared in the seventeenth century in English, French, Latin, Italian.[17]

Henry Stubbe, author of *The Indian Nectar, or a Discourse Concerning Chocolata* (1662), was very clear that he and his English compatriots looked to Spain as the chocolate epicenter. He vouched for the London chocolatier Richard Mortimer "in Sun Alley in Eastsmith-Field," better than "all others" at replicating Spanish chocolate recipes, in part because he "lived in Spain many years, and is as skillful as honest."[18] Throughout his treatise, Stubbe recommended a "Chocolate-Royal" concoction that "agrees almost altogether with that which is followed in the Court of Spain" and invoked and lengthily excerpted Spanish authorities from Hernández to Colmenero de Ledesma.[19] Willem Piso, a Dutch author, also referred to Spanish recipes as the gold standard, rather apologetically explaining that because "few of the Ingredients of Chocolata, except the Cacao nut are brought into Europe, instead of these there are, and may be substituted those common Spices of the East Indies, or other Seeds, and Flowers."[20] French treatises similarly deferred to Spanish expertise.[21] While in northern Spain in 1799, John Adams, future second president of the United States, commended Spanish chocolate "as the finest I ever saw."[22]

The historical significance of chocolate's diffusion transcends chocolate itself. That dark, stimulating beverage served as a "gateway" drink for those other ones—coffee and tea—that would overtake their predecessor in popularity across all European countries, excepting Spain, by the end of the seventeenth century.[23] It is important to note that Europeans' first *exposure* to coffee and tea was insufficient to lead them to adopt it for themselves. As early as the thirteenth century, Marco Polo encountered tea, as did the Christian missionaries who inhabited the Chinese court in the late sixteenth century.[24] Europeans also came across coffee in the sixteenth century during travels throughout the Ottoman Empire.[25] They noted it with curiosity but not as something they or their compatriots at home might want to imbibe. The Augsburg physician Leonhart Rauwolf, who wrote about his travels in the Near East in 1582, wrote that Turks and Arabs consumed a beverage called "'chaube' ... nearly black as ink."[26] In

1610 an English voyager declared of coffee that it was "black as soote, and tasting not much unlike it."[27] But coffee did not have a foothold in Europe until the mid 1600s, and tea did not take off until the end of that century.[28] What happened in the interim between Europeans' first encounters with tea and coffee and their systematic adoption? Chocolate.

Striking evidence that one who already had a taste for chocolate would more readily embrace coffee comes from a brief pamphlet published in the seventeenth century entitled *Carta qve escrivió vn Médico cristiano, que estava curando en Antiberi, a vn Cardenal de Roma, sobre la bebida del Cahuè or café* (A letter that a Christian physician, who was practicing in Antiberi, wrote to a cardinal in Rome, concerning the beverage of *cahuè* or *café*).[29] The author, a Spaniard traveling in the cardinal's retinue while he was visiting the Ottoman Empire, perhaps Palestine, wrote at the request of the prelate about "this new drink coffee."[30] Both explicitly and implicitly, the doctor viewed coffee—"a drink so common among the Turks, Persians, and Moors"—through chocolate-tinted glasses, making him much more favorably disposed toward the beverage than the earlier traveler who likened it to soot. He designated the special coffee cups used by the Turks, Moors, and Persians with the Hispanicized pre-Columbian term used for chocolate vessels: *xícaras*.[31] He referred to the vessel used to boil the water as "a glass pot or a tin-covered *chocolatera* with a spout." He noted that "they add a spoonful of ground sugar as with Chocolate, and stir it with a silver spoon and drink it by sipping it like Chocolate, as hot as they can take it." One already enamored of chocolate would be more ready to experiment with a hot, dark, sweet, stimulating beverage than one who was not.

The explanations that have been advanced for the diffusion of coffee, like those for chocolate, generally point to the role of European social phenomena, such as interest in potential medical virtues, the "Protestant work ethic," and the social appeal of coffeehouses.[32] While the latter was clearly integral to its broader penetration into European society, among the vanguard, coffee preceded coffeehouses: there was a prior phase in which a critical number of chocolate drinkers switched over to coffee (as later on a majority of English consumers abandoned coffee for tea). Evidence suggests that the earliest coffee vendors in Europe sold it alongside chocolate (perhaps persuading their customers that this was a variant but related beverage).[33] Likewise, more evidence that Europeans identified chocolate, coffee, and tea as cognates is that seventeenth-century treatises on the stimulant beverages inevitably grouped them together, with the French author of *Traitez nouveaux et curieux du café, du thé, du chocolat* (New and curious treatise on coffee, tea, and chocolate), Phillipe Dufour, explaining the "great rapport these beverages have together."[34] Chocolate would lose its place to coffee and then tea as the dominant stimulant beverage among Europeans, but the explosive popularity of these other caffeinated liquids originated in the path-breaking role of the former.

TRANSFORMATIONS

That caffeine and nicotine reign today as the first and third most-consumed psychoactive substances in the world has roots in chocolate and tobacco's integration into seventeenth-century Europe. Nonetheless, the place of these goods in the twenty-first century is at a far remove from that earlier age. Chocolate today barely registers as a stimulating beverage, with the small but notable exceptions of places in Mesoamerica and southern Europe where chocolate drinks are still being made as they have for centuries and with high-end chocolatiers who sell "Mayan" and "Aztec" dark chocolate drinks alongside truffles and other confections.[35] Globally, the relative insignificance today of chocolate as a stimulant beverage has origins partly in the price advantage that coffee and tea wielded over it, the cheapness of the latter contributing to their mass consumption among Europeans in the seventeenth and eighteenth centuries.[36] In Spain and places in southern Italy long under Spanish control, such as Naples, upper- and middle-class Spaniards stayed loyal to their first stimulant beverage at least until the end eighteenth century.[37] Yet, even for elite and middle-class consumers outside of the southern Mediterranean and Latin America, chocolate ranked as an important member of the stimulating beverage triumvirate well into the nineteenth century, largely indistinguishable in its material form, symbolic association, and ritual context from that in the seventeenth century.[38] Even in 1872, when a Boston lady published the *Dessert Book*, she referred to chocolate only as beverage, not as the candy that was becoming increasingly popular.[39]

Probably the single most important event that caused a breach between chocolate then (a drink) and now (a confection) is of a fairly recent vintage. For most people today the immediate connotation of chocolate is of a sweet wrapped in foil (whose actual cacao content may be rather marginal) or of a flavoring well-suited for cakes and ice cream. Though antecedents to chocolate candy can be found in colonial New Spain and eighteenth-century France, the origins of prevailing chocolate sweets has its roots in the invention patented in 1828 by a Dutchman named Coenraad Johannes Van Houten.[40] The Dutch chemist perfected a hydraulic press that could effectively separate much of the cacao butter from cacao, leaving behind a "cake" that could be made into fine powder, known to us today as "cocoa," which contained only about half as much fat as the end result of the traditional cacao grinding method. In order for the cocoa to mix well with water, Van Houten processed it with alkaline salts. These inventions laid the basis for efficiently producing durable candy bars with a smooth texture. Subsequent industrialists, many whose names are now synonymous with chocolate—Cadbury, Nestle, Lindt, Toblerone, and Hershey—applied techniques of mass production and further innovations in the nineteenth and twentieth centuries and brought about the transformation of chocolate into a mass-produced sweet and the general demise of small-scale chocolate artisanship.[41]

At first glance, the gap between tobacco of the seventeenth century and that of the present day is less than that which divides chocolate. On closer scrutiny, however, the rupture in many ways is even greater. In a very real sense, over the last hundred years or so, tobacco has become more dangerous to human life. According to the World Health Organization, tobacco ranks second as the cause of death worldwide and results in about five million deaths each year.[42] Modern corporations are responsible for ever more efficient ways to convey ever greater doses of nicotine. They have deployed and honed the tool of mass advertising (Marlboro Man for the macho, Virginia Slims for women, Joe Camel for kids) among other means of creating, expanding, and retaining their markets—a phenomenon in its present proportions and parameters that predates this history. Other changes also affect the safety of tobacco. Tobacco can be used in ways to alleviate pain and illness and promote health; today, all of these advantages are vastly outweighed by the concomitant exposure to lethal carcinogens, and the existence of superior medical alternatives.[43] Yet in pre-Columbian America and sixteenth- and seventeenth-century Europe, it is not clear that this was the case. The state of medical technology—a time when mercury was a common treatment for syphilis—made the antibacterial, analgesic, headache-reducing, respiratory assisting, attention-focusing, and hedonic effects of tobacco adequate compensations for its hazardous effects, particularly when the high risk of early death from childbirth, plague, famine, war, among others, reduced one's opportunity to die from cancer relatively late in life.[44]

Aside from the exogenous transformations that made life more secure for many, the nineteenth century saw some important shifts in the culture of tobacco consumption across Europe. Most significantly, smoking irrevocably became the dominant form of tobacco ingestion, while the use of snuff and other smokeless forms steadily, albeit gradually, eroded. (With some important exceptions—in the United States chewing tobacco remained the most popular form of tobacco consumption until 1900.) It was also during the nineteenth century that tobacco became gendered masculine, creating the context in which twentieth-century cigarette advertisers could market smoking to women as a feminist act.[45]

It was the rise of the modern cigarette, however, that most dramatically transformed global tobacco use.[46] The cigarette concept is not a recent invention. Mesoamericans had smoked tobacco in wrappers for millennia, and Spaniards in the early modern period had sometimes substituted the maize wrapper for paper in a device called the *papelete*. In the second half of the nineteenth century English companies began to manufacture crude cigarettes with a tissue paper and a cane mouthpiece, but these were unwieldy and their appeal limited. The *modern* cigarette was the result of the efforts of a struggling businessman in North Carolina named James Buchanan Duke to make his company profitable in a very competitive tobacco manufacturing market. By 1889 Duke was the largest cigarette company in the world. With James Duke at the helm, his company produced the prototype of the modern cigarette, which continues to dominate the world market today. The salient features of Duke's cigarette industry were (1) mass industrialization by employing the Bonsack machine that could produce quantities more quickly and cheaply than previously seen (churning out 100,000 to 120,000 cigarettes a day, Bonsack's invention did for tobacco what Van Houten's did for chocolate); (2) ever-increasing palatability, beginning with the use of flue-cured tobacco (as opposed to air dried); (3) the strenuous and escalating application of mass advertising techniques. Duke's competitors in the United States and Britain adopted and improved on these innovations. For instance, the introduction of filtered cigarettes after World War II improved palatability. And ever more sophisticated and effective means of marketing developed over the course of the twentieth century. By the late twentieth century, the cigarette had vanquished other forms of tobacco products globally. Though tobacco consumption has tapered off in developed countries, a third of the world's population aged sixteen and older smokes.[47]

In many respects, then, the modern cigarette and a Hershey's kiss are far removed from the tobacco and chocolate profiled in this book. Yet it is as true today as it was centuries ago, in America and Europe, that the powerful experiences induced by the consumption of psychotropic substances is a consequence of both the physiological effects they produce and the cultural meanings they hold.

Some of these cultural associations have endured to the present despite the radical transformations of tobacco and chocolate's material forms. In sharing a cigarette or some chocolate (and its successors, coffee and tea), people declare their affection—or at least cordiality—toward one another. "Let's have coffee" more often proposes a low-key, friendly meeting than it suggests the sipping of a bitter brew. The marketer who invented the phrase

"M&Ms make friends" capitalized on this ancient association. The more intimate bonding connected to chocolate survives in the Valentine's Day practice of bestowing red heart-shaped boxes of bon-bons to loved ones. Though everyone forty and younger who grew up in the United States cannot have escaped learning that cigarettes cause cancer, for some the promise of friendship and belonging (otherwise known as "peer pressure") overrides a long-off death sentence. And though today smokers are often solitary figures seeking protection from the wind as they stand outside work places and bars that have banned their habit, the collective output of twentieth-century Hollywood attests to tobacco's longevity as conduit of connection. These contemporary cultural investments have roots in the history of the Americas.

While one can find continuity in the history of tobacco and chocolate with respect to sociability, the sacred is another matter. For Mesoamericans, the fact of cacao and the experience of chocolate was a way to approach godhead. Its "invigorating," "uplifting" effects, the sensation of vitalizing blood, was not only a gift from a divine source but also proof of divinity itself. For native Americans across both continents, tobacco was one of the most powerful substances that allowed a sacred communion, whether sniffed, smoked, chewed, or offered to the fire. Despite European conquerors' and colonizers' overt rejection of native American religious traditions, they, too, came to feel the numinous associations of tobacco and chocolate (if ambivalently) because of the cultural immersion created by the colonial regime and because of the parallels with Christian beliefs and practices. Those raised to celebrate and revere the Eucharist, a rite that merged the mortal human body with divine flesh and blood, found familiar the notion that a body could instantiate the divine through the consumption of sacred substances.

This too-close-for-comfort familiarity of cross-cultural spirituality, and the entrenched use of tobacco and chocolate in Spanish society, lent urgency to the effort to demystify them, to deny them miraculous or diabolical properties. By the time European theologians and other cultural authorities confronted the issue, they could neither prohibit the use of tobacco and chocolate nor incorporate them into Christian practice. Instead, the solution was to insist that they were ordinary rather than extraordinary. Yet the imagery of enchantment that surrounded tobacco and chocolate, both because of their American origins and because of Europe's Eucharistic culture, did not disappear. Rather, it was displaced; the images of chocolate as divine elixir and tobacco as a diabolical, but ever-useful, substance flourished in the pretend-world of art and literature. Exile to an alternate, unreal reality is not annihilation. Their "magic" did not so much "decline" as it migrated.[48] Today, alongside tobacco and chocolate, many goods inhabit the imaginary netherworld of consumer fantasies that fuel substantial sectors of both western economies and our collective imagination. If tobacco and chocolate did not inaugurate this phenomenon, then they offered a special demonstration of how people whose worldviews were secularizing could maintain their attachment to mystical hopes.

Notes

Introduction

1. Johannes Wilbert, *Tobacco and Shamanism in South America* (New Haven: Yale University Press, 1987), 149–50; Joseph Winter, ed. *Tobacco Use by Native North Americans* (Norman: University of Oklahoma Press, 2000); Alexander Von Gernet, "Nicotian Dreams: The Prehistory and Early History of Tobacco in Eastern North America" in *Consuming Habits: Drugs in History and Anthropology*, ed. Jordan Goodman, Paul E. Lovejoy, and Andrew Sherratt (London: Routledge, 1995); Jordan Goodman, *Tobacco in History: The Cultures of Dependence* (London: Routledge, 1994), 25–36.

2. Wilbert, *Tobacco and Shamanism* offers an encyclopedic compendium of South American Amerindian tobacco uses; see also Gerardo Reichel-Dolmatoff, *The Shaman and the Jaguar: A Study of Narcotic Drugs among the Indians of Colombia* (Philadelphia: Temple University Press, 1975); Joseph Winter, "Traditional Uses of Tobacco by Native Americans," in *Tobacco Use*; J. Eric S. Thompson, *Maya History and Religion* (Norman: University of Oklahoma Press, 1970), 118–19.

3. Traditionally, Post-Classic (900–1519) Mesoamerica was defined to include the area encompassing present-day Mexico and ranging as far south and east as present-day northern Costa Rica based on shared cultural characteristics, including cacao cultivation, Paul Kirchhoff, "Mesoamérica," *Acta Americana* 1, no. 1 (1943): 92–107. More recently, scholars have reconsidered the defining elements of "Mesoamerica" and have shifted the boundaries farther north and west to include parts of northern Mexico and to exclude areas in the south and east, Shirley Gorenstein, "Western and Northwestern Mexico," in *The Cambridge History of the Native Peoples of the Americas*, vol. 2, *Mesoamerica*, ed. Richard E. W. Adams and Murdo J. MacLeod (Cambridge: Cambridge University Press, 2000), bk. 1: 318–57; Payson D. Sheets, "The Southeastern Frontiers of Mesoamerica," in *Cambridge History*, vol. 2, bk. 1: 408–10, 438. However the boundary lines for chocolate's cultural compass more closely align (though extend farther east) with the boundaries offered by Kirchoff for Mesoamerica. The northernmost instances of chocolate use that I have seen are the cacao tribute levied by rulers of the Tarascan state (Michoacán, Mexico) in Gorenstein, "Western and Northwestern Mexico," vol. 2, bk. 1: 328; and the pre-Tecuexes (in Jalisco, Mexico) also appeared to consume cacao, Carolyn Baus Czitrom, "The Tecuexes: Ethnohistory and Archaeology," in *The Archaeology of West and Northwest Mesoamerica*, ed. Michael S. Foster and Phil C. Weigand (Boulder: Westview Press, 1985), 100.

4. Larry Steinbrenner, "Cacao in Greater Nicoya: Ethnohistory and a Unique Tradition," in *Chocolate in Mesoamerica: A Cultural History of Cacao*, ed. Cameron L. McNeil (Gainesville: University Press of Florida, 2006), 253–70. Though numerous groups in South America made use of *T. cacao* and its relatives before the Spanish invaded and colonized, there is no evidence that any of them fermented the seeds to make a beverage; rather, they consumed the pods' pulp and used the fruits in other ways, Allen M. Young, *The Chocolate Tree: A Natural History of Cacao* (Washington, D.C.: Smithsonian Institution Press, 1994); Nathaniel Bletter and Douglas C. Daly, "Cacao and Its Relatives in South America," in *Chocolate in Mesoamerica*, 36.

5. Francisco de Quevedo y Villegas, "Discurso de todos los Diablos o Infierno Enmendado," in *Obras completas*, ed. Felicidad Buendía (Madrid: Aguilar, 1959), 1:223. Though Quevedo wrote the play in 1627, it was first published in 1628 in Gerona and 1629 in Valencia, see Buendía, *Obras*, 1:197, n. 1.

6. David T. Courtwright, *Forces of Habit: Drugs and the Making of the Modern World* (Cambridge: Harvard University Press, 2001), 19.

7. See the excellent synthesis, John H. Elliott, *Empires of the Atlantic World: Britain and Spain in America, 1492–1830* (New Haven: Yale University Press, 2006).

8. The paradigmatic work in this tradition is Alfred Crosby, *The Columbian Exchange: The Biological and Cultural Consequences of 1492* (Westport, Conn.: Greenwood Publishers, 1972).

9. Terrence Rafferty, "Archaeology," in *Tobacco in History and Culture: An Encyclopedia*, 2 vols. (New York: Charles Scribner's Sons; Thomson/Gale, 2004), 1: 66–71; Deborah M. Pearsall, "The Origins of Plant Cultivation in South America," in *Origins of Agriculture. An International Perspective*, eds. C. W. Cowan and P. J. Watson, 173–205 (Washington, D.C.: Smithsonian Institution Press, 1992).

10. Though a human innovation, *N. rustica* thrives without direct intervention; however, it does best in "disturbed" sites, perhaps places where animals and humans have inadvertently created nitrogen-rich plots. Hegemonic today, *N. tabacum* flourishes in humid, tropical climes, requires human cultivation, and does not survive for more than a generation or two if left without tending. At the time of the European arrival, *N. tabacum* was under cultivation in eastern South America, Central America, Mexico, and the West Indies. *N. rustica* was harvested by people in Mexico and the eastern United States as well as in the Andes in South America, Michael Nee, "Origin and Diffusion," in *Tobacco in History and Culture*, 2: 397–402; T. H Goodspeed, *The Genus* Nicotiana (Waltham, Mass.: Chronica Botanica, 1954).

11. For a synthesis of research on pre-Columbian chocolate, see Sophie D. Coe and Michael D. Coe, *The True History of Chocolate* (London: Thames and Hudson, 1996), 11–104. Since the publication of the *True History*, there has been a boom in pre-Columbian chocolate studies, well represented by the contributions in *Chocolate in Mesoamerica: A Cultural History of Cacao*.

12. At the time of the Spanish arrival, the *criollo* varietal of *T. Cacao* grew in Mesoamerica, while the *forastero* variety was indigenous to South America. *Criollo* is widely considered to have a superior, less bitter flavor, but the *forastero* is more robust and produces fruit in a shorter time, so is the prevalent variety consumed today.

13. Recent contributions and an overview to this debate are found in Nathaniel Bletter and Douglas C. Daly, "Cacao and Its Relatives in South America," in *Chocolate in Mesoamerica*, 31–68, and Nisao Ogata, Arturo Gómez-Pompa, and Karl A. Taube, "The Domestication and Distribution of *Theobrama cacao* L. in the Neotropics," in *Chocolate in Mesoamerica*, 68–89.

14. John S. Henderson, Rosemary A. Joyce, Gretchen R. Hall, W. Jeffrey Hurst, and Patrick E. McGovern, "Chemical and Archaeological Evidence for the Earliest Cacao Beverages," *Proceedings of the National Academy of Sciences* 104 (2007): 18937–18940, http://www.pnas.org/cgi/crossref-forward-links/104/48/18937; John S. Henderson and Rosemary A Joyce, "Brewing Distinction: The Development of Cacao Beverages in Formative Mesoamerica," in *Chocolate in Mesoamerica*, 141–42.

15. Terrence Kaufman and John Justeson, "The History of the Word for 'Cacao' and Related Terms in Ancient Mesoamerica," in *Chocolate in Mesoamerica*, 117–39.

16. Coe and Coe, *True History*, 43–53, and various essays in *Chocolate in Mesoamerica*.

17. Despite some differences in interpretation, this book was made possible by the research of others. I have found particularly illuminating *Tobacco: Its History Illustrated by the Books, Manuscripts, and Engravings in the Collection of George Arents Jr.* (New York: The Rosenbach Company, 1937–1952), which includes a comprehensive annotated bibliography; Fernando Ortiz, *Cuban Counterpoint: Tobacco and Sugar*, trans. Harriet de Onís (Alfred A. Knopf, 1947; Durham: Duke University Press, 1995); Sarah Augusta Dickson, *Panacea or Precious Bane: Tobacco in Sixteenth Century Literature* (New York: New York Public Library, 1954); José Pérez Vidal, *España en la historia del tabaco* (Madrid: Consejo Superior de Investigaciones Científicas, 1959); Jordan Goodman, *Tobacco in History: The Cultures of Dependence* (London: Routledge, 1993); Coe and Coe, *True History*.

18. There is, of course, a huge literature on the addictive properties of nicotine. See, for instance, John A. Dani and Steve Heinemann, "Molecular and Cellular Aspects of Nicotine Abuse," 16 *Neuron* (1996): 905–8. On cacao, see Hendrik J. Smit, Elizabeth A. Gaffan, and Peter J. Rogers, "Methylxanthines Are the Psycho-pharmacologically Active Constituents of Chocolate," *Psychopharmacology* 176 (2004): 418; Hendrik J. Smit and Rachel J. Blackburn, "Reinforcing Effects of Caffeine and Theobromine as Found in Chocolate," *Psychopharmacology* 181 (2005): 101–6.

19. On addiction as a historical cause for the spread of tobacco and other psychotropic substances, see Courtwright, *Forces of Habit*; on the "big fix," Eric Wolf, *Europe and the People without History* (Berkeley: University of California Press, 1982), 322.

20. My translation. Girolamo Benzoni, *Histoire nouvelle de nouveau monde*, trans. Urbain Chauveton (Geneva: Eustace Vignon, 1579), 505; Girolamo Benzoni, *Historia del mondo nuovo* (Venice: F. Rampazetto 1565), fol. 102; Sophie Coe, *America's First Cuisines* (Austin: University of Texas Press, 1984), 109.

21. My translation. Benzoni, *Historia del mondo nuovo*, fols. 54r–55v.

22. For a landmark study historicizing taste, in this case sweetness, see Sidney W. Mintz, *Sweetness and Power: The Place of Sugar in Modern History* (New York: Viking, 1985).

23. Among others, see Dickson, *Panacea*; Goodman, *Tobacco in History*, 41–44; Coe and Coe, *True History*, Alan Davidson, "Europeans' Wary Encounter with Potatoes, Tomatoes, and other New World Foods," in *Chilies to Chocolate: Food the Americas Gave the World*, ed. Nelson Foster and Linda S. Cordell (Tucson: University of Arizona Press, 1992), 3; Another variation in the "Europeanizing" tradition is the one articulated by Wolfgang Schivelbusch, *Tastes of Paradise: A Social History of Spices, Stimulants, and Intoxicants*, trans. David Jacobson (New York: Vintage Books, 1992), 34, 38–39, 87–93.

24. Marcel Proust, *Remembrance of Things Past* (New York: Vintage Books, 1934), 1:50–51. In thinking about the relationship between individual bodies and social organization, I have also found useful the notion of *habitus* developed in Pierre Bourdieu, *The Logic of Practice*, trans. Richard Nice (Stanford: Stanford University Press, 1990).

25. Serge Gruzinksi is also one of the few scholars who has suggested that the phenomena migrated to Europe, *The Mestizo Mind: The Intellectual Dynamics of Colonization and Globalization*, trans. Deke Dusinberre (New York: Routledge, 2002), 17–23. There have been criticisms of the conceptual utility of "syncretism"; therefore, some scholars eschew it and prefer terms such as "hybridity," or "mestisaje," Gruzinski, 127–29, 165.

1. Experiencing the Sacred and the Social

1. Bernal Díaz del Castillo, *The Conquest of New Spain*, trans. J. M. Cohen (London: Penguin Books, 1963), 214–16, 228–39; Antonio Serrato-Combe, *The Aztec Templo Mayor: A Visualization* (Salt Lake City: University of Utah Press, 2001); Jacques Soustelle, *Daily Life of the Aztecs*, trans. Patrick O'Brian (Stanford: Stanford University Press, 1961), 1–28;

Inga Clendinnen, *Aztecs: An Interpretation* (New York: Cambridge University Press, 1991), 15–21.

2. Bernal Díaz del Castillo, *Historia verdadera de la conquista de la Nueva España*, ed. Joaquin Ramírez Cabañas (Mexico City: Porrua, 1964), 155–56. All translations are my own unless otherwise noted. Bernardino de Sahagún's investigation of preconquest culture (which relied heavily on native collaborators and informants) corroborates the centrality of tobacco and chocolate to the conspicuous consumption of the Aztec ruler, emphasizing chocolate (eleven varieties) more than any other item, and referring to "precious tobacco" that was "the rightful due of the rulers": Bernardino de Sahagún, *Primeros Memoriales*, trans. Thelma D. Sullivan (Norman: University of Oklahoma Press, 1997), 201–2, 210, 226. See also Bernardino de Sahagún, *The Florentine Codex: General History of the Things of New Spain* (henceforth *FC*), trans. Arthur J. O. Anderson and Charles Dibble, 12 books in 13 vols. (Santa Fé: School of American Research, University of New Mexico Press, and Salt Lake City: University of Utah Press, 1950), 8:28, 39.

3. Victor Turner, "Social Drama and Ritual Metaphors," in his *Dramas, Fields, and Metaphors: Symbolic Action in Human Society* (Ithaca: Cornell University Press, 1974), 55–57; Inga Clendinnen, *Aztecs: An Interpretation* (New York: Cambridge University Press, 1995), 253–54.

4. Nigel Davies, *The Aztec Empire* (Norman: University of Oklahoma Press, 1997).

5. *The Essential Codex Mendoza*, ed. Frances F. Berdan and Patricia Rieff Anawalt (Berkeley: University of California Press, 1997), fols. 41v--42r, 46r, 47r, 68r.

6. John. F. Bergmann, "The Distribution of Cacao Cultivation in Pre-Columbian America," *Annals of the Association of American Geographers* 59 (1969): 87; Alonso de Molina, *Vocabulario en lengua castellana y mexicana* (1571), 2 vols., facsimile (Madrid: Ediciones Cultura Hispanica, 1944); *Hernán Cortés: The Letters from Mexico*, trans. and ed. A. R. Pagden (New York: Orion Press Book/Grossman, 1971), 94.

7. *FC* 1:44.

8. *Problemas y secretos maravillosos de las Indias*, ed. Angeles Durán (Madrid: Alianza Editorial, 1988), 145.

9. Molina, *Vocabulario*, 1:19v; 2:10v; Juan de Córdoba, *Vocabulario castellano-zapoteco*, ed. Wigberto Jiménez Moreno, facsimile (Mexico City: Instituto Nacional de Antropología e Historia, 1942), 64v; Francisco Hernández, *Obras completas*, vol. 2, *Historia natural de Nueva España* (Mexico City: Universidad Nacional Autónoma de México, 1959), bk. 1:303–5.

10. The cacao beverage made only of cacao, water, and spices was known in Nahuatl as *xochiaya cacautl* (the beverage of cacao with dried and ground-up flowers), from Molina, *Vocabulario*, 2:10v. The Coes identify the "ear" spice as the thick ear-shaped petal on blossoms of *Cymbopetalum penduliflorum*, which grows in tropical lowland forests of Veracruz, Oaxaca, and Chiapas—their taste is compared to black pepper, nutmeg, allspice, and cinnamon—and identify *mecaxóchitl* as *Piper sanctum*, offering a flavor compared to rose; see Sophie D. Coe and Michael D. Coe, *The True History of Chocolate* (London: Thames and Hudson, 1996), 89–92. In Mexico today *mecaxóchitl* is known as *acuyo* and the leaves are used to wrap fish, offering a flavor compared to tarragon or anise, but Spanish sources as well as the Nahuatl suffix (*xochitl*=flower) indicate that the flower was used in chocolate: Antonio de León Pinelo, *Questión moral: si el chocolate quebranta el ayuno eclesiástico* (Madrid: Viuda de Juan González, 1636), fol. 6v. This flower-spice constellation had an ancient lineage, appearing in the creation story of the Quiché Maya in the *Popl Vuh*: Susan D. Gillespie and Ana Lucrecia E. de MacVean, "Las flores en el *Popol Vuh*," *Revista Universidad del Valle de Guatemala* 12 (2002): 10–17. Hernández wrote that achiote was added to cacao in part in order "to realize its color and flavor," *Historia natural* 1:27–28. Based on colonial-era descriptions and current efforts to replicate Mesoamerican recipes, I would characterize this beverage as complex, rich, thick, fragrant, musky, and spicy—perhaps a distant cousin of cardamom-flavored Turkish coffee.

11. *FC* 10:93. The importance of chocolate foam is also suggested by the fact that Sahagún's informants listed aerating stirring sticks among the ruler's chocolate parapherna-

lia, *FC* 8:40; Bernardino de Sahagún, *Historia general de las cosas de Nueva España*, 3 vols., ed. and transcribed by Alfredo López Austin and Josefina García Quintana (Mexico City: Consejo Nacional para la Cultura y las Artes, 2000), 2:756. The Spanish version is more explicit about the purpose of these implements.

12. *Essential Codex Mendoza*, fols. 47r, 68r; Molina, *Vocabulario*, fols. 93r, 158v; *FC* 9: 35, 28. The *Florentine Codex* also refers to vendors who specialized in different kinds of gourd containers, including those for chocolate, *FC* 10:78.

13. *FC* 11:119. See also Hernández, *Historia natural*, 1:305.

14. Allen M. Young, *The Chocolate Tree: A Natural History of Cacao* (New York: Smithsonian Institution Press, 1994), 5, 14; Bergmann, "Distribution of Cacao Cultivation," 85–96; René F. Millon, "When Money Grew on Trees: A Study of Cacao in Ancient Mesoamerica" (PhD diss., Columbia University, New York, 1955), 107–27; Murdo J. MacLeod, *Spanish Central America* (Berkeley: University of California Press, 1973), 69–70, 236.

15. *FC* 10:88; the Nahuatl terms for "smoking tubes, pipes, and cigars" were *acacuáhuitl*, *aca;aayetl*, and *yetlalli*. The common root for tobacco in Nahuatl is *yetl*. *FC* 8:69; ibid. 11:146–47, and Sahagún, *Historia general*, 2:777. Hernández, *Historia natural*, bk. 2, chap. 109: 81–82.

16. *FC* 10:88; Diego Durán, *Historia de las Indias de Nueva España e Islas de la Tierra Firme*, ed. Angel María Garibay K. (Mexico City: Editorial Porrua, 1967), 2:310.

17. *FC* 11:147; ibid. 10:88. Juan Bautista de Pomar, "Relación Juan Bautista de Pomar, Tezcoco 1582," in *Poesía náhuatl*, vol. 1, *Romances de los señores de la Nueva España, manuscrito de Juan Bautista de Pomar, Tezcoco, 1582*, trans. and ed. Angel María Garibay K., 2nd ed., 152–219 (Mexico City: Universidad Nacional Autónoma de México, 1993), 215. See also [Francisco Hernández], *Quatro libros de la naturaleza y virtudes de las plantas y animales*, trans. Francisco Ximénes (Mexico City: Viuda de Diego Lopez Davalos, 1615), fols. 18r–v, 177v.

18. *FC* 10:88; Sahagún, *Historia general*, 1:191; *FC* 2:68.

19. Durán, *Historia de las Indias*, 2:310.

20. *FC* 11:141; Hernández, *Historia natural*, 2:82; Francis Robicsek, *Smoking Gods: Tobacco in Maya Art, History, and Religion* (Norman: University of Oklahoma Press, 1978), 38.

21. Fernando Ortiz, *Cuban Counterpoint: Tobacco and Sugar*, trans. Harriet de Onís (New York: Alfred A. Knopf, 1947; Durham: Duke University Press, 1995), 141; Johannes Wilbert, *Tobacco and Shamanism in South America* (New Haven: Yale University Press, 1987), 25–29; J. Eric S. Thompson, *Maya History and Religion* (Norman: University of Oklahoma Press, 1970), 110–12.

22. The Jay I. Kislak collection at the Library of Congress includes an extensive collection of Mayan tobacco flasks.

23. *FC* 10:94; ibid. 11:147. See also Pomar, "Relación," 215; Diego Durán, *The Book of the Gods and Rites and the Ancient Calendar by Fray Diego Durán*, trans. and ed. Fernando Horcasitas and Doris Heyden (Norman: University of Oklahoma, 1971), 115.

24. See above and *FC* 11:147.

25. Quoted in Henry B. Nicholson, introduction to *Primeros Memoriales*, 3.

26. Quoted in Alfredo López Austin, "The Research Method of Sahagún," in *Sixteenth-Century Mexico: The Work of Sahagún*, ed. Munro S. Edmonson, 111–50 (Albuquerque: University of New Mexico Press, 1974), 116–17. See also Munro S. Edmonson, introduction in the same book, 1–16; Clendinnen, *Aztecs*, 8–9, 279–80. The results of the investigation, which historians now refer to as the *Primeros Memoriales*, were completed circa 1560. This preliminary study became the basis for further extensive interviewing of informants in Tlateloco during 1560–65 and Tenochtitlan during 1565–90. From Sahagún's perspective the definitive Nahuatl version of the *Historia general* was that completed circa 1577, the copy in the Laurentian Library in Florence, now know as the *Florentine Codex*. In this version he authored a parallel Spanish text that López Austin qualifies as "a version (not a literal translation) of the *General History*," 118.

27. *FC* book 9; Clendinnen, *Aztecs*, 329, n. 39.

28. *FC* 9:7, 33. For the banquet description, see also Sophie Coe, *America's First Cuisines* (Austin: University of Texas Press, 1984), 79–81.

29. *FC*, 1:41, and n. 123; ibid. 9:17, 31.

30. *FC* 9:33.

31. *FC* 9:34. On the merchants and their role in Aztec society, see also Soustelle, *Daily Life*, 59–65; Frances Berdan, "The Economics of Aztec Luxury Trade and Tribute," in *The Aztec Templo Mayor*, ed. Elizabeth Hill Boone, 161–83 (Washington, D.C.: Dumbarton Oaks, 1983).

32. Quoted in Clendinnen, *Aztecs*, 135.

33. *FC* 8:53; Durán, *Historia de las Indias*, 2:236; Chita de la Calle, introduction to Muriel N. Porter's "Pipas precortesianas," *Acta Anthropologica* 3, no. 2 (1948): 146.

34. *FC* 9:34–35.

35. *FC* 9:37.

36. *FC* 9:37–39.

37. *FC* 9:39.

38. *FC* 9:39–40.

39. "Tres poemas sacros," Angel María Garibay K., trans. and ed. *Poesía náhuatl*, vols. 2 and 3, *Cantares mexicanos: Manuscrito de la Biblioteca Nacional de México*, 2nd ed., trans. and ed. Angel María Garibay K., (Mexico City: Universidad Nacional Autónoma de México, 1993), 2:78. *Cantares mexicanos: Songs of the Aztecs*, trans. and ed. John Bierhorst (Stanford: Stanford University Press, 1985), 245. My translation combines Garibay's Spanish and Bierhorst's English translation of the Nahuatl, following Garibay where they diverge.

40. Garibay, *Poesía náhuatl*, 2:85.

41. *FC* 9:40–41.

42. *FC* 9:41–42. For other examples of Mexica ritual that gendered maize female, see Clendinnen, *Aztecs*, 159, 203.

43. Simon Martin, "Cacao in Ancient Mayan Religion," in *Chocolate in Mesoamerica: A Cultural History of Cacao*, ed. Cameron L. McNeil (Gainesville: University Press of Florida, 2006), 154–83; Kathleen Berrin, Mary Miller, and Simon Martin, *Courtly Art of the Ancient Maya* (New York: Thames and Hudson, 2004), 61–63, 78. Scholars of the ancient Maya have posited that maize was gendered male and chocolate female (McNeil, introduction to *Chocolate in Mesoamerica*, 14–15) but they also recognize, paradoxically, Mexica allusions to chocolate's being forbidden, or at least more regulated, among women (ibid., 17).

44. *FC* 9:42.

45. Dorie Reents-Budet, "The Social Contexts of Kakaw Drinking among the Ancient Maya," in *Chocolate in Mesoamerica*, 202–23; Miller and Martin, *Courtly Art*, 277; Millon, "When Money Grew on Trees," 174.

46. Miller and Martin, *Courtly Art*, 61–62, 83; Robicsek, *Smoking Gods*, 59; Patricia A. McAnany and Satoru Murata, "Belizean Cacao Farmers through the Ages," in *Chocolate in Mesoamerica*, 442–43; Coe and Coe, *True History*, 44–49. Dorie Reents-Budet, *Painting the Maya Universe: Royal Ceramics of the Classic Period* (Durham: Duke University Press, 1994), 75–77.

47. Durán, *Book of the Gods*, 200; See also *FC* 6:256; Antonio de Herrera y Tordesillas, *Historia general de los hechos de los castellanos en las islas y tierra firme del mar océano* (Madrid: Oficina Real de Nicolás Rodríguez Franco, 1730), 5:155; MacLeod, *Spanish Central America*, 69; Coe and Coe, *True History*, 93.

48. *FC* 4:117. Durán, *Historia de las Indias*, 2:297.

49. *FC* 4:124; ibid. 10:88.

50. *FC* 10:93, 65.

51. Durán, *Historia de las Indias*, 2:336. My translation. See also chap. 39, 2:297.

52. *FC* 1:41–42, and n. 123; ibid. 9:17.

53. *FC* 9:12. That Sahagún's informants could remember speeches so well after the conquest is made credible by the practice of committing "rhetorical orations" to memory among

Nahuas: Thelma D. Sullivan, "The Rhetorical Orations, or Huehuetlatolli," in *Sixteenth-Century Mexico: The Work of Sahagún*, 82.

54. *FC* 9:9–16, esp. 13.

55. Porter, "Pipas precortesianas," 148.

56. Lynn M. Meskell and Rosemary A. Joyce, *Embodied Lives: Figuring Ancient Egypt and the Classic Maya* (London: Routledge, 2003), 140.

57. *Codex Zouche-Nuttall*, 26; Coe and Coe, *True History*, 95.

58. Ramón Cruces Carvajal, *Lo que Mexico aportó al mundo* (Mexico City: Panorama Editorial, 1986), 51; J. Eric S. Thompson, "Notes on the Use of Cacao in Middle America," *Notes on Middle American Archaeology and Ethnology* 128 (1956): 104–5, writes that "cacao is rather widely associated with the crisis of birth, marriage, and death."

59. Henry B. Nicholson, "Religion in Pre-Hispanic Central Mexico," in *Handbook of Middle American Indians*, vol. 10, *Archaeology of Northern Mesoamerica* (Austin: University of Texas Press, 1971), 403–8.

60. *FC* 4:77–78; *Primeros Memoriales*, 87–88, 179; Thompson, *Maya History*, 108–9, 112–13, 121; Porter, "Pipas precortesianas," 147, 170; Ortiz, *Cuban Counterpoint*, 142.

61. For Mesoamerican traditions of cacao as a sacred tree and "paradisical gardens" inhabited by gods and containing cacao, see McNeil, introduction to *Chocolate in Mesoamerica*, 13, 22–23.

62. Nicholson, "Religion in Pre-Hispanic Central Mexico," in *Archaeology of Northern Mesoamerica*, 434–35; *FC* 2:68.

63. On the use of these as pre-Hispanic sources, see Miguel León Portilla, trans. and ed., *Fifteen Poets of the Aztec World* (translation of *Trece poetas del mundo azteca*), (Norman: University of Oklahoma Press, 1992), 43–44, 290; cf. Bierhorst, *Cantares mexicanos*.

64. "Song of Tlaltecatzin, Cuahchinanco," in *Fifteen Poets*, 67. Also cited in M. Á. Méndez, "Una relación conflictiva: La Inquisición novohispana y el chocolate," *Caravelle* 71 (1998): 9–10.

65. Clendinnen, *Aztecs*, 221–22.

66. On *teotl*, see Arild Hvidtfeldt, *Teotl and Ixiptlatli: Some Central Conceptions in Ancient Mexican Religion* (Copenhagen: Munksgaard, 1958); Elizabeth H. Boone, *Incarnations of the Aztec Supernatural: The Image of Huitzilopochtli in Mexico and Europe* (Philadelphia: American Philosophical Society, 1989), 4.

67. On Aztec human sacrifice, see Clendinnen, *Aztecs*, 73–74; on the care and feeding of Mayan deities, including blood sacrifices, see Nancy M. Farriss, *Maya Society under Colonial Rule: The Collective Enterprise of Survival* (Princeton: Princeton University Press, 1984), 286–87, 290–91; Soustelle, *Daily Life*, 99–102.

68. Gonzalo Fernández de Oviedo, *Historia general y natural de las Indias*, 2nd ed., ed. and intro. Juan Pérez de Tudela Bueso (Madrid: Ediciones Atlas, 1992), 1:269 and chap. 2; *FC* 6:256.

69. *FC* 10:154–56, 158; Coe, *America's First Cuisines*, 143. Coe and Coe, *True History*, 45; Jill Leslie Furst, *Codex Vindobonensis Mexicanus I: A Commentary* (Albany: State University of New York, Institute for Mesoamerican Studies, 1978), 231; Elizabeth Hill Boone, *Stories in Red and Black: Pictorial Histories of the Aztecs and Mixtecs* (Austin: University of Texas Press, 2000), 95–96; McNeil, introduction to *Chocolate in Mesoamerica*, 15.

70. Diego Durán, *Libro de los dioses y ritos y el calendario antiguo*, 1:81–93. Translation is from *Book of the Gods and Rites and The Ancient Calendar*, trans. and ed. Fernando Horcasitas and Doris Heyden (Norman: University of Oklahoma Press, 1971), 156. The connection between cacao and fertilizing water may also explain why chocolate and cacao beans were typical offerings for the attendants of the sacred steam baths: Durán, *Book of the Gods*, 271; Furst, *Codex Vindobonensis*, 274.

71. For instance, Cameron L. McNeil, "Traditional Cacao Use in Modern Mesoamerica," in *Chocolate in Mesoamerica*, 355; and Johanna Kufer and Michael Heinrich, "Food for the Rain Gods: Cacao in Ch'orti' Ritual," in *Chocolate in Mesoamerica*, 385–94.

72. Meskell and Joyce, *Embodied Lives*, 140; Thompson, "Notes on the Use of Cacao," 101.

73. Joyce Marcus and Kent Flannery, "Ancient Zapotec Ritual and Religion: An Application of the Direct Historical Approach," in *The Ancient Mind*, ed. Colin Renfrew and E. Zubrow, 55–74 (New York: Cambridge University Press, 1994), 58.

74. Gregorio García, *Origen de los indios del Nuevo Mundo* (1607), ed. Franklin Pease G. Y., facsimile 1729 ed. (Mexico City: Fondo de Cultura Económica, 1981), 327.

75. Franklin Pease, estudio preliminar to García, *Origen de los indios*, xii, xxxiv.

76. García, *Origen de los indios*, 327–28. García calls the offering *beleño* (henbane), but tobacco was often mistaken as a variety of henbane in the sixteenth century: see Sahagún, *Historia general*, 1:202 and chapter 2.

77. The friar Gerónimo de Mendieta declared that "some believe that [*picietl*] was the body of a goddess named Ciuacouatl," *Historia eclesiástica indiana*, ed. Francisco Solano y Pérez-Lila (Madrid: Atlas, 1973), 66–67.

78. García, *Origen de los indios*, 328.

79. Boone, *Stories in Red and Black*, 91.

80. Nicholson, "Religion in Pre-Hispanic Central Mexico," in *Archaeology of Northern Mesoamerica*, 398. Berdan and Anawalt, *Essential Codex Mendoza*, 1:182; Porter, "Pipas precortesianas," 169. Deities with the *yetecomatl* include the Mixtec Ilamatecuhtli, and the Nahuatl Xochipilli and Xihuteuhtli: Eduard Seler, ed., *Códice Borgia y Eduard Seler: Comentarios al Códice Borgia*, trans. Mariana Frank, 3 vols. (Buenos Aires: Fondo de Cultura Económica, 1963), 1:60; 2:92, 144; *Codex Fejérváry-Mayer: An Old Mexican Picture Manuscript in the Liverpool Free Public Museums (12014/M)*, ed. Eduard Seler and trans. A. H. Keene (London: T. and A. Constable, 1901–2), 123, 176, 188; *Codex Fejérváry-Mayer*, 176; Eloise Quiñones Keber, *Codex Telleriano-Remensis: Ritual, Divination, and History in a Pictorial Aztec Manuscript* (Austin: University of Texas Press, 1995), fol. 6v, p. 150. This tradition dated back centuries, if not millennia, for frescos at Teotihuacán included depictions of priests bearing the *yetecomatl*: Porter, "Pipas precortesianas," 144.

81. *FC* 2:81. *Codex Borgia*, 2:167; Furst, *Codex Vindobonensis*, 23; Thompson, *Maya History*, 110, 112.

82. Juan de Tovar, "Tratado de los ritos y ceremonias y dioses que en su gentilidad usavan los indios de esta Nueva España," JCB, 73r–v.

83. Diego Muñoz Camargo, *Historia de Tlaxcala* (Ms. 210 de la Biblioteca Nacional de Paris), transcribed and ed. Luis Reyes García with Javier Lira Toledo (Tlaxcala, Mexico: Universidad Autónoma de Tlaxcala, 1998), 170. On the sources and influences of Muñoz Camargo, see Reyes García, introduction to *Historia de Tlaxcala*, 54.

84. Muñoz Camargo, *Historia de Tlaxcala*, 170. Durán, *Libro de los dioses*, 1:169–70. Translation is from *Book of the Gods and Rites*, 262; *Essential Codex Mendoza*, fol. 63r.

85. *Codex Vienna*, 35b, 35a, 34a, 47a, 30a, 22b, 15b, 50d, in Furst, *Codex Vindobonensis*, 18, 83, 85. See also Boone, *Stories in Red and Black*, 91. For the *Codex Zouche-Nuttall* and *Codex Selden*, see Furst, *Codex Vindobonensis*, 18. The codices also depict the tobacco gourds as accoutrements for laymen making sacrifices or ascending to power: *Essential Codex Mendoza*, fol. 63r; *Codex Magliabechiano*, facsimile (Graz, Austria: Akademische Druck u. Verlagsanstalt, 1970), fols. 63r, 71r, 84r, 88r; *Códice Tudela*, 2 vols. (Madrid: Ediciones Cultura Hispánica, 1980), fols. 50r, 54r, 55r, 69r, 76r; *Primeros Memoriales*, est. i, ii, iii, v; Berdan and Anawalt, *Essential Codex Mendoza*, 1:182; Boone, *Stories in Red and Black*, 46.

86. Hernando Ruiz de Alarcón, *Treatise on the Heathen Superstitions and Customs that Today Live among the Indians Native to this New Spain*, 1629, trans. and ed. J. Richard Andrews and Ross Hassig (Norman: University of Oklahoma Press, 1984), 83–84, 86, 94, 117–19, 121.

87. Alarcón, *Treatise on the Heathen Superstitions*, 109.

88. Ibid., 111. On the efficacy of tobacco as an insecticide, see Wilbert, *Tobacco and Shamanism*, 152–54.

89. *FC* 8:62; Porter cites the chronicler Tezozomac as well, "Pipas precortesianas," 148;

Codex Magliabechiano, fols. 70v–71r; *Códice Tudela,* fol. 54r. Elizabeth Hill Boone has shown that the *Magliabechiano, Tudela,* and at least three other contemporary manuscripts were derived from a now lost prototype created between 1529 and 1553: *The Codex Magliabechiano and the Lost Prototype of the Magliabechiano Group* (Berkeley: University of California Press, 1983), 3–5.

90. Muñoz Camargo, *Historia de Tlaxcala,* 170; Tovar, "Tratado de los ritos," fols. 73r–v. On tobacco's pain-relieving properties, see Wilbert, *Tobacco and Shamanism,* 184–86, 191–92.

91. *FC* 2:199; Durán, *Libro de los dioses,* 1:145; Clendinnen, *Aztecs,* 171, 201.

92. Clendinnen, *Aztecs,* 176.

93. Alarcón, *Treatise on the Heathen Superstitions,* 165, 171–74, 178–79, 193–95, 251. On medical uses, *FC* 10:140, 144, 149, 152; Porter, "Pipas precortesianas," 151–52, 165; Bernardo Ortiz de Montellano, *Aztec Medicine, Health, and Nutrition* (New Brunswick, N.J.: Rutgers University Press, 1990), 149–50, 155–56, 174, 187–88, 203.

94. Alfredo López Austin, *Cuerpo humano e ideología: Las concepciones de los antiguos Nahuas,* 2 vols. (Mexico City: Universidad Nacional Autónoma de México, 1980), 1:223–26, 292–93, 310–11; Montellano, *Aztec Medicine,* 44, 155. The ubiquity of *picietl* in offerings to the fire deity Xiuhtecutli may also be connected to the latter's solar association.

2. Encountering Novelties

1. Christopher Columbus, *The Diario of Christopher Columbus's First Voyage to America, 1492–1493,* transcribed and trans. Oliver Dunn and James E. Kelly Jr. (Norman: University of Oklahoma Press, 1989), 65, 81; Samuel Eliot Morison, *Admiral of the Ocean Sea: A Life of Christopher Columbus,* 2 vols., new ed. (New York: Time, 1962) 1:211–28.

I extrapolate Amerindian reactions to European appearance based on later sources that illuminate Island Carib views of European dress: Charles de Rochefort, *The History of the Caribby-Islands,* trans. John Davies (London: Printed by J. M. for T. Dring and J. Starkey, 1666), 253–54; original French in Charles de Rochefort, *Histoire Naturelle et Morale des Iles Antilles de l'Amerique* (Rotterdam: A. Leers, 1658); and Raymond Breton, *Dictionaire caraibe-françois* (Auxerre, France: Gilles Bouquet, 1665), 223. For a history of Amerindian-European relations reconstructed from Amerindian perspectives, see Daniel K. Richter, *Facing East from Indian Country: A Native History of Early America* (Cambridge: Harvard University Press, 2001).

On the unresolved debate about the location of this island, Samuel M. Wilson, *Hispaniola: Caribbean Chiefdoms in the Age of Columbus* (Tuscaloosa: University of Alabama Press, 1990), 45; Morison, *Admiral of the Ocean Sea,* 1:221–23.

2. Columbus, *Diario,* 83–85.; Morison, *Admiral of the Ocean Sea,* 1:243; Wilson, *Hispaniola,* 51.

3. Columbus, *Diario,* 118–19.

4. Ibid., 137–39. Morison, *Admiral of the Ocean Sea* 1:253–54.

5. Columbus, *Diario,* 236–37.

6. Ibid., 252–53.

7. Ibid., 171.

8. Morison, *Admiral of the Ocean Sea,* 1:362–68.

9. J. H. Elliott, *The Old World and the New, 1492–1650* (New York: Cambridge University Press, 1970); Tzvetan Todorov, *The Conquest of America: The Question of the Other,* trans. Richard Howard (New York: Harper and Row, 1984); Stephen Greenblatt, *Marvelous Possessions: The Wonder of the New World* (Chicago: University of Chicago Press, 1991). Scholarship that challenges this model include: Richard White, *The Middle Ground: Indians, Empires, and Republics in the Great Lakes Region, 1650–1815* (New York: Cambridge University Press, 1991); Natalie Zemon Davis, *Women on the Margins: Three Seventeenth-Century Lives* (Cambridge: Harvard University Press, 1995), specifically the study of the Dutch naturalist Maria Sibylla Merian's collaboration with Surinam assistants.

10. The conceptualization of the frontier draws from Richard White's *The Middle Ground*, 52. However, I will use the term "frontier," because while frontiers often created a "middle ground" in the manner described by White, it was perhaps even more unstable than the territory investigated by White and could just as easily give way to total violence as negotiated alliance.

11. For this episode, I cite the modern edition of Gonzalo Fernández de Oviedo, *Historia general y natural de las Indias*, ed. and intro. Juan Pérez de Tudela Bueso, 2nd ed. (Madrid: Ediciones Atlas, 1992), 2:132–48, but because the edition is known to have errors, I cross-checked it with the first edition, Gonzalo Fernández de Oviedo y Valdés, *La historia general de las Indias* (Seville: Juan Cromberger, 1535), fols. 140r–143r. The episode is also discussed in Fernando Ortiz, *Cuban Counterpoint: Tobacco and Sugar*, trans. Harriet de Onís (Durham: Duke University Press, 1995), 162–63. In the chapters devoted to this expedition, Oviedo followed closely the account of a participant—so closely, in fact, that he forgot to revise his informant's more favorable assessment of tobacco in favor of his own scorching views.

12. Inga Clendinnen, *Ambivalent Conquests: Maya and Spaniard in Yucatan, 1517–1570* (Cambridge: Cambridge University Press, 1987), 14–15; Oviedo, *Historia general y natural*, 2:113.

13. Oviedo, *Historia general y natural*, 2:122–29.

14. Ibid., 138.

15. Ortiz, *Cuban Counterpoint*, 163.

16. Oviedo, *Historia general y natural*, 2:138.

17. Inga Clendinnen, "Fierce and Unnatural Cruelty: Cortés and the Conquest of Mexico," *Representations* 33 (1991): 65–100.

18. Charles Gibson, *Tlaxcala in the Sixteenth Century* (New Haven: Yale University Press, 1952), 29.

19. The final chapters of Diego Durán, *Historia de las Indias de Nueva España e Islas de la Tierra Firme*, 2 vols., ed. Angel Maria Garibay K. (Mexico City: Editorial Porrua, 1967), concern the arrival of the Spanish. For his account of the conquest, completed sixty years afterward, Durán relied on conquistadores' accounts and Indian accounts (from both the "painted books" and oral recollections), Garibay, introduction to *Historia de las Indias*, 582, n. 2; Clendinnen, "Fierce," 70.

20. Durán, *Historia de las Indias*, 2:506–7, 510–11.

21. Diego Durán, *Historia de las Indias*, 2:509–10; my translation modifies that in Diego Durán, *The History of the Indies of New Spain (The Aztecs)*, ed. and trans. Fernando Horcasitas and Doris Heyden (New York: Orion Press, 1964), 266.

22. For encounters with chocolate during Cortés's march, see also Bernal Díaz del Castillo, *Historia verdadera de la conquista de la Nueva España*, ed. Joaquin Ramírez Cabañas (Mexico City: Porrua, 1964), 73.

23. Members of Cortés's expedition in residence at Tenochtitlan during Moctezuma's captivity recognized cacao's value enough to decide it was worthy of theft. Francisco Cervantes de Salazar, *Crónica de la Nueva España* (Madrid: Hispanic Society of America, 1914), 374; Sophie D. Coe and Michael D. Coe, *The True History of Chocolate* (London: Thames and Hudson, 1996), 85–86.

24. See also Girolamo Benzoni, *Historia del mondo nuovo* (Venice: F. Rampazetto, 1565), fol. 102.

25. Peter Martyr d'Anghera, *De orbe novo decades* (Alcalá de Henares, Spain: A. G. Brocar, 1516). Subsequent editions quickly appeared, including Basel (1521), Nuremberg, (1524), Alcalá de Henares (1530), and Paris (1532), among others; see Angel Delgado-Gómez, *Spanish Historical Writing about the New World, 1493–1700* (Providence, R.I.: John Carter Brown Library, 1992), 119.

26. Delgado-Gómez, *Spanish Historical Writing*, 10; and D. A. Brading, *The First America: The Spanish Monarchy, Creole Patriots, and the Liberal State 1492–1867* (Cambridge: Cambridge University Press, 1992), 16–18.

27. On the place of noble savages and the uses of antiquity in Martyr, see Michael Ryan, "Assimilating the New World in the Sixteenth and Seventeenth Centuries," *Comparative Studies in Society and History* 23, no. 4 (1981): 526; Todorov, *Conquest of America*, 36; Brading, *First America*, 16–18, 23, 25.

28. Pané's original manuscript is lost, but the son of Columbus included it in a biography he wrote, but never published, of his father. José Juan Arrom, introduction to Ramón Pané, *An Account of the Antiquities of the Indians*, ed. José Juan Arrom and trans. Susan Griswold (Durham: Duke University Press, 1999), xiii–xiv; Carl Ortwin Sauer, *The Early Spanish Main* (Berkeley: University of California Press, 1966), 47, 71.

29. Peter Martyr d'Anghera, *De Novo Orbe or The Historie of the West Indies*, trans. Richard Eden and Lok Gent (London: Thomas Adams, 1612), fols. 50r–51v. I follow Eden's edition for this and subsequent translations of Martyr.

30. Pané, *Account*, 21, 25, 26. The composition of *cohoba* is a mystery and source of controversy. There is a long tradition identifying it with tobacco, beginning with Gonzalo Fernández de Oviedo. Some have come to reject the idea—in part because the hallucinogenic experiences ascribed to *cohoba* do not correspond to contemporary notions of tobacco's effects—and propose that it derived instead from the pods of the tree *Anadenanthera peregrina*. A third, and the most persuasive position in my opinion, is that the snuffed powder was a composite of tobacco and *Anadenanthera*. This is consistent with sixteenth-century accounts from the Caribbean mainland, as well as twentieth-century anthropological studies, that describe the combined use of tobacco and *yopa* (*Anadenanthera*). However, whatever the actual content of *cohoba*, Pané's description of it (via Martyr) had a far-reaching effect on the history of tobacco, since influential early commentators viewed them as synonymous. For the controversy, see Arrom in *Account*, 15–16, n. 70; Sauer, *Early Spanish Main*, 56; William E. Safford, "Identity of the *Cohoba*, the Narcotic Snuff of Ancient Haiti," *Journal of Washington Academy of Science* 6 (1916): 547–62; Johannes Wilbert, *Tobacco and Shamanism in South America* (New Haven: Yale University Press, 1987), 16–17.

31. Martyr, *De Novo Orbe*, fols. 52r–53r.

32. Ibid., fol. 52r.

33. Ibid., fol. 50r; compare to Shirley McGinnis, "Zemi Three-Pointer Stones," in *Taíno: Pre-Columbian Art and Culture from the Caribbean*, ed. Fatima Bercht, Estrellita Brodsky, John Alan Farmer, and Dicey Taylor (New York: Monacelli Press, 1997), 92–101.

34. Martyr's work was not the first European publication to include a mention of cacao. Hernán Cortés made note of it in his second letter—published in 1522—when describing the court of Moctezuma: "Cacao is a fruit like the almond, which they grind and hold to be of such value that they use it as money throughout the land and with it buy all they need in the markets and other places": *Letters from Mexico*, trans. and ed. A. R. Pagden, and intro. J. H. Elliott (New York: Orion Press of Grossman Publishers, 1971), 94.

35. Martyr, *De Novo Orbe*, fol. 182v.

36. My emphasis. Ibid., fol. 195v.

37. Ibid., fols. 291r–v.

38. Ibid., fols. 106r–v.

39. Oviedo y Valdés, *La historia general*, fol. 47r; Oviedo, *Historia general y natural*, 1:116–17; Sarah Augusta Dickson, *Panacea or Precious Bane: Tobacco in Sixteenth-Century Literature* (New York: New York Public Library, 1954), 26.

40. Brading, *First America*, 31–34; also Antonio Barrera-Osorio, *Experiencing Nature: The Spanish American Empire and the Early Scientific Revolution* (Austin: University of Texas Press, 2006), 106; Antonello Gerbi, *Nature in the New World* (Pittsburg: University of Pittsburgh Press, 198.)

41. Anthony Pagden, *The Fall of Natural Man: The American Indian and the Origins of Comparative Ethnology* (Cambridge: Cambridge University Press, 1983), 30–31, 58, 47, 82, 87–89; Brading, *First America*, 58–62, 85–86, 91.

42. Oviedo y Valdés, *La historia general*, fol. 44v.

43. Ibid., fol. 47r.

44. Ibid.
45. For instances of henbane as ingredients of witches' concoctions, see Andrés de Laguna, *Pedacio Dioscórides Anazarbero, acerca de la materia medicinal, y de los venenos mortiferos* (Salamanca, 1555), facsimile (Madrid: Instituto de España, 1968–69), 417–22; Gustav Henningsen, *The Witches' Advocate: Basque Witchcraft and the Spanish Inquisition, 1609–1614* (Reno: University of Nevada Press, 1980), 297–300.
46. Oviedo, *Historia general y natural,* 3:28, 32, 362; 4:416–17.
47. Oviedo y Valdés, *La historia general,* fol. 47r.
48. This chapter—unpublished until the nineteenth century—appears in Oviedo, *Historia general y natural,* 1:267–73.
49. Oviedo, *Historia general y natural,* 1:268–69.
50. Ibid., 1:268, 270–73.
51. Ibid., 1:269.
52. Ibid., 1:271.
53. Ibid., 1:272.
54. Francisco López de Gómara, *Primera y segunda parte de la historia general de las Indias* (Zaragoza: Agustín Millan, 1553). At least eight Spanish editions appeared in the 1550s alone, and translations were issued in Italian, French, and English in the sixteenth century, Delgado-Gómez, *Spanish Historical Writing,* 18, 19, 124.
55. López de Gómara, *Primera y segunda,* fol. 41 [dii].
56. Compare Benzoni, *Historia del Mondo Nuovo,* fols. 54r–55v; on Benzoni's derivativeness, Dickson, *Panacea,* 121–22.

3. Adapting under Colonialism

1. Aztec views of the conquest (*Florentine Codex*) are excerpted in *Victors and the Vanquished: Spanish and Nahua Views of the Conquest of Mexico,* ed. Stuart Schwartz (Boston: Bedford, Saint Martin, 2000), 194.
2. Peter Gerhard, *A Guide to the Historical Geography of New Spain* (Norman: University of Oklahoma Press, 1993), 7–8.
3. Charles Gibson, *The Aztecs under Spanish Rule* (Stanford: Stanford University Press, 1964), 8, 14, 102; James Lockhart, *The Nahuas after the Conquest: A Social and Cultural History of the Indians of Central Mexico, Sixteenth through Eighteenth Centuries* (Stanford: Stanford University Press, 1993), 15–16, 29.
4. Lockhart, *Nahuas,* 187, and next chapter.
5. Alonso de Molina, the sixteenth-century linguist, gives four different compositions under "bebida de cacao," *Vocabulario en lengua Castellana y Mexicana* (1571), facsimile (Madrid: Ediciones Cultura Hispánica, 1944). pt. 1, fol. 19v; see also Francisco Hernández, *Obras completas,* vol. 2, *Historia natural de Nueva España* (Mexico City: Universidad Nacional Autónoma de México, 1959), bk. 1, 303–5. Diego López de Cogolludo, *Historia de Yucatán* (Mexico City: Editorial Academia Literaria, 1957), 181; *Relaciones histórico-geográficos de la gobernación de Yucatán (Mérida, Valladolid, y Tabasco)* (Mexico City: Universidad Nacional Autónoma de México, 1983), 1:82; 2:40, 44, 419; Toribio de Benavente, *Historia de los Indios de la Nueva España,* ed. Claudio Esteva Fabregat (Mexico City: Dastin, Crónicas de América, 2001), 240–41.
6. See next chapter.
7. Richard E. Greenleaf, *Zumárraga and the Mexican Inquisition, 1536–1543* (Washington, D.C.: Academy of American Franciscan History, 1961).
8. Gerhard, *Guide,* 295–97.
9. This account follows the testimony to the Inquisition transcribed in "Proceso del Santo Oficio contra Tacatetl y Tanixtetl, indios, por idólatras," *Procesos de indios idólatras y hechiceros* (Mexico City: Tip. Guerrero H[erma]nos, 1912), 1–16. The case is described in Greenleaf, *Zumárraga,* 50–52. Another idolatry case involving tobacco is documented in "Proceso del Santo Oficio contra Martin Ucelo, indio, por idolatra y hechicero," *Procesos de indios,* 17–51, especially 18 and 19.

10. "Proceso . . . contra Tacatetl y Tanixtetl," 2.

11. It is also likely that the cacao was a beverage because Suárez mentioned it between his listings of other beverages.

12. "Proceso . . . contra Tacatetl y Tanixtetl," 6. *Sahumerio* could designate a tobacco pipe or incense brazier; I tend toward the former interpretation since Suárez separately listed *incensarios* to refer to incense burners. It would be in keeping with custom to refer to tobacco and *yautle* (marigold seeds) together as herbs, which together would be sprinkled with copal into the smoking brazier to produce an odoriferous sizzle and thick smoke: J. Richard Andrews and Ross Hassig, appendix D in *Treatise on the Heathen Superstitions and Customs that Today Live among the Indians Native to this New Spain, 1629* (Norman: University of Oklahoma Press, 1984), 250.

13. "Proceso . . . contra Tacatetl y Tanixtetl," 7–8.

14. "Proceso . . . contra Tacatetl y Tanixtetl," 15.

15. "Proceso e información que se tomó contra Xpobal y su mujer, por ocultar idolos y otros idolos y contra Martin, hermano del primero," *Procesos de indios*, 141–75; Greenleaf, *Zumárraga*, 60–62. On Ocuituco, see Gerhard, *Guide*, 92–93.

16. "Proceso e información que se tomó contra Xpobal y su mujer," 151–52, 157.

17. Ibid., 161–62.

18. Introduction to *Procesos por idolatría al cacique, gobernadores y sacerdotes de Yanhuitlán 1544–46*, ed. María Teresa Sepúlveda y Herrera (Mexico City: Colección Científica, Instituto Nacional de Antropología e Historia, 1999), 43–112; Gerhard, *Guide*, 286–87; the trial testimony is transcribed in *Procesos por idolatría . . . Yanhuitlán*, 113–229.

19. The 1527 *encomienda* grant was rescinded as a result of the divisive factional politics that largely pivoted around the power struggle between Cortés and the royal officials. By 1536 Las Casas regained the *encomienda*; see Sepúlveda y Herrera, *Procesos por idolatría . . . Yanhuitlán*, 91, 123.

20. *Procesos por idolatría . . . Yanhuitlán*, 115–201 passim.

21. Ibid., 120, 170, 201, 137.

22. Ibid., 170–71.

23. Ibid., 120.

24. Greenleaf, *Zumárraga*, 48–50.

25. Lockhart, *Nahuas*, 204.

26. *Procesos por idolatría . . . Yanhuitlán*, 209, 151.

27. Grant D. Jones, *Maya Resistance to Spanish Rule: Time and History on a Colonial Frontier* (Albuquerque: University of New Mexico Press, 1989). Peter Gerhard, *The Southeast Frontier of New Spain* (Princeton: Princeton University Press, 1979), 67–71.

28. Nancy M. Farriss, *Maya Society under Colonial Rule: The Collective Enterprise of Survival* (Princeton: Princeton University Press, 1984), 38–39, 90–93, 96.

29. Inga Clendinnen, *Ambivalent Conquests: Maya and Spaniard in Yucatan, 1517–1570* (Cambridge: Cambridge University Press, 1987), chaps. 6 and 7; Farriss, *Maya Society*, 290–91.

30. The transcript of the case testimony is in a dossier Herrera sent for promotion in AGI Mex., leg. 292, "Probanza de Baltazar de Herrera, Cura de Petú 1597–98." It has been examined extensively by John F. Chuchiak in "The Indian Inquisition and the Extirpation of Idolatry: The Process of Punishment in the Provisorato de Indios of the Diocese of Yucatan, 1563–1812," (PhD diss., Tulane University, New Orleans, 2000), 1–18. I am grateful to John Chuchiak for alerting me to the existence of this fascinating trial. On Petú, see Gerhard, *Southeast Frontier*, 75–79.

31. López de Cogolludo, *Historia de Yucatán*, 206; Gerhard, *Southeast Frontier*, 79.

32. "Probanza de Baltazar de Herrera," fols. 4r–4v.

33. Ibid., fols. 16v, 11r, 13v, 18r, passim. On the Mayan *ah kin*, see Farriss, *Maya Society*, 233, 290; Matthew Restall, *The Maya World: Yucatec Culture and Society* (Stanford: Stanford University Press, 1997), 150.

34. "Probanza de Baltazar de Herrera," fols. 4v–5r.

35. Ibid., fol. 11v.

36. Ibid., fols. 12v, 13r. The deities included those of the hunt and rain.
37. Ibid., fols. 5r–5v.
38. Ibid., fols. 7v–8r, 16v.
39. Ibid., fols. 12v, 17v, 18v.
40. Ibid., fol. 16v.
41. Ibid., fols. 16v, 12v.
42. Ibid., fol. 21v.
43. Ibid., fol. 19r.
44. Ibid., fols. 26–27r.
45. Ibid., fol. 9r.
46. Chuchiak, "Self-Promotion," 16.
47. López de Cogolludo, *Yucatán*, 93.
48. "Probanza de Baltazar de Herrera," fol. 15v.
49. Toribio de Benavente, *Historia*, 213, 121–22.
50. Ibid., 125.
51. *Codex Magliabechiano*, facsimile (Graz, Austria: Akademische Druck- u. Verlagsanstalt, 1970), fols. 66v–67r, 67v–68r, 71v–72r; Elizabeth H. Boone, *The Codex Magliabechiano and the Lost Prototype of the Magliabechiano Group* (Berkeley: University of California Press, 1983), 210, 212; Henry B. Nicholson, "Religion in Pre-Hispanic Central Mexico," in *Handbook of Middle American Indians*, vol. 10, *Archaeology of Northern Mesoamerica* (Austin: University of Texas Press, 1971), table 4; Cameron L. McNeil, W. Jeffrey Hurst, and Robert J. Sharer, "The Use and Representation of Cacao during the Classic Period at Copan, Honduras," in *Chocolate in Mesoamerica: A Cultural History of Cacao*, ed. Cameron L. McNeil (Gainesville: University Press of Florida, 2006), 232–36.
52. Toribio de Benavente, *Historia*, 213–14, 241; López de Cogolludo also described Indians in the Yucatán bringing "a little cacao and vanillas and some tablets of chocolate . . . when someone comes to visit whom they recognize they must show respect," *Yucatán*, 645–46.
53. Lockhart, *Nahuas*, 237.
54. J. Richard Andrews and Ross Hassig, introduction to *Treatise on the Heathen Superstitions*, 7, 66; Hernando Ruíz de Alarcón, *Tratado de las idolatrías, supersticiones, dioses, ritos hechicerías y otras costumbres gentílicas de las razas aborígenes de Mexico*, ed., notes, and intro. Francisco del Paso y Troncoso (Mexico City: Ediciones Fuente Cultural, 1953).
55. Hernando Ruiz de Alarcón, *Treatise on the Heathen Superstitions and Customs*, ed. and trans. Andrews and Hassig, 146, 144, 149.
56. Diego Valadés, *Rhetorica christiana* (Perugia, Italy: Petrumiacobum Petrutium, 1579); Diego Valadés, *Retórica cristiana*, intro. Esteban J. Palomera, trans. Tarsicio Herrera Zapién (Mexico City: Universidad Nacional Autónoma de México, 1989).
57. Pauline Moffit Watts, "Hieroglyphs of Conversion: Alien Discourses in Diego Valadés *Rhetorica Christiana*," *Memorie Domenicane* n.s., no. 22 (1991): 405–33, esp. 408–11; Esteban J. Palomera, *Fray Diego Valadés, O.F.M: Evangelizador humanista de la Nueva España, su obra* (Mexico City: Editorial Jus, 1963); Louise M. Burkhart, *The Slippery Earth: Nahua-Christian Moral Dialogue in Sixteenth-Century Mexico* (Tucson: University of Arizona Press, 1989), 11, 20–22, 40.
58. Valadés, *Retórica cristiana*, 31, 37, 39, 41. My translations from the Spanish edition.
59. Ibid., 40, 493.
60. On the use of images, see Valadés, *Retórica cristiana*, 477, 485, 495, 501.
61. On a plate between pages 220 and 221 in *Rhetorica christiana* (1579) and page 498 in *Retórica cristiana* (1989).
62. Nicholson, "Religion in Pre-Hispanic Central Mexico," 406–7.
63. For other explications, Valadés, *Retórica cristiana* (1989), 489, 493; for the possible allusion, 501.
64. The same pairing is labeled "cacao" in another of Valadés's engravings (figure 1.6 in this book); Martyr, *De Novo Orbe*, fol. 291, also Hernández, *Historia natural*, 1:303–5; José de Acosta, *Historia natural y moral de las Indias* (Seville: Juan de León, 1590), 163.

65. As suggested by figure 0.1, monkeys played an essential ecological role in cacao reproduction, for after they eat the pulp of the pods, they distribute the seeds by discarding them or defecating. In Mesoamerican cosmogony, monkeys are attributed great creative powers and thought to have given rise to the arts: Manuel Aguilar-Moreno, "The Good and Evil of Chocolate in Colonial Mexico," in *Chocolate in Mesoamerica*, 277–81.

66. Alarcón, *Treatise*, 52.

4. Going Native

1. Though it is known that tobacco was used by Andean peoples before and after the Spanish conquests, it does not appear to have as much importance as another substance, namely *coca*. However, Spanish colonists living in the areas became sufficiently habituated that ecclesiastical officials felt compelled to prohibit its use by priests prior to Communion. The place of tobacco in colonial Andean society is a subject that requires more investigation. On pre-Columbian usage, see Johannes Wilbert, *Tobacco and Shamanism in South America* (New Haven: Yale University Press, 1987), 57–58, 122; for frequent occurrences of coca in cases of Andean "idolatry," see Kenneth Mills, *Idolatry and Its Enemies: Colonial Andean Religion and Extirpation, 1640–1750* (Princeton: Princeton University Press, 1997), 64, 79, 97, 257, and on frequent interaction between Indians and Spaniards, mestizos, and Africans in Andean Peru, see ibid., 270; on the tobacco prohibition, see chapter 6.

2. There were places in Mesoamerica that fit this category as well, such as Chiapas, where the Chol-Lancadón Maya resisted Spanish pacification for centuries and also collaborated with Spain's imperial rivals; see Grant D. Jones, *Maya Resistance to Spanish Rule: Time and History on a Colonial Frontier* (Albuquerque: University of New Mexico Press, 1989); Peter Gerhard, *The Southeast Frontier of New Spain* (Princeton: Princeton University Press, 1979), 150. Cacao remained very central to the Itza Maya, a group that resisted Spanish subjugation through the seventeenth century: Laura Caso Barrera and Mario Aliphat F., "The Itza Maya Control over Cacao," in *Chocolate in Mesoamerica: A Cultural History of Cacao*, ed. Cameron L. McNeil (Gainesville: University Press of Florida, 2006), 289–306.

3. Kathleen Deagan and José María Cruxent, *Columbus's Outpost among the Tainos: Spain and America at La Isabela, 1493–1498* (New Haven: Yale University Press, 2002); Carl Ortwin Sauer, *The Early Spanish Main* (Berkeley: University of California, 1966; with new foreword 1992).

4. Sauer, *Early Spanish Main*, 149, 178–95.

5. Ibid., 150, 155; Neil Whitehead, "The Crises and Transformations of Invaded Societies: The Caribbean (1492–1580)," in *The Cambridge History of the Native Peoples of the Americas*, vol. 3 of *South America*, pt. 1, ed. Frank Salomon and Stuart B. Schwartz (New York: Cambridge University Press, 1999), 864–903 at 868–69.

6. Precontact population estimates ranged between six hundred thousand and three million: Sauer, *Early Spanish Main*, 66–68; Whitehead, "Crises," 872.

7. Deagan and Cruxent, *Columbus's Outpost*, 211.

8. Philip D. Morgan. "Virginia's Other Prototype: The Caribbean," in *The Atlantic World and Virginia, 1550–1624*, ed. Peter C. Mancall (Chapel Hill: University of North Carolina Press for the Omohundro Institute, 2007), 372–73.

9. Gonzalo Fernández de Oviedo y Valdés, *La historia general de las Indias* (Seville: Juan Cromberger, 1535), fol. 47r.

10. Bartolomé de las Casas, *Historia de las Indias*, ed. André Saint-Lu (Caracas: Biblioteca Ayacucho, 1986), 236; Fernando Ortiz, *Cuban Counterpoint: Tobacco and Sugar*, trans. Harriet de Onís (New York: Alfred A. Knopf, 1947; Durham: Duke University Press, 1995), 110. Citation is to Duke edition.

11. Oviedo, *La historia general*, fol. 97v.

12. Solange Alberro, *Del gachupín al criollo: o cómo los españoles de México dejaron de serlo* (Mexico City: Jornadas 122; El Colegio de México, 1992); Enrique Rodríguez-Alegría, "Eating Like an Indian: Negotiating Social Relations in the Spanish Colonies," *Current Anthropology* 46 (2005): 551–73.

13. Perhaps 1.5 million people lived in the Valley of Mexico at the time of conquest; by 1570 the Indian population had declined to 325,000, and it continued to decrease until the middle of the seventeenth century: Charles Gibson, *The Aztecs under Spanish Rule* (Stanford: Stanford University Press, 1964), 141. Around eight thousand Spaniards arrived in New Spain before 1560, and almost as many again by 1580: Peter Boyd-Bowman, "Patterns of Spanish Emigration to the Indies until 1600," *Hispanic American Historical Review* 56, no. 4 (1976): 601.

14. Alberro, *Del gachupín*, 55; Ida Altman, *Emigrants and Society: Extremadura and America in the Sixteenth Century* (Berkeley: University of California Press, 1989), 325; R. Douglas Cope, *The Limits of Racial Domination: Plebeian Society in Colonial Mexico* (Madison: University of Wisconsin Press, 1994), 13–22; Colin Palmer, *Slaves of the White God* (Cambridge: Harvard University Press, 1979).

15. Women were less than 7% of the migrants before 1540 and more than 25% in the period after 1560 (583–84, 599). These latter figures apply to Spanish emigration to the Indies as a whole, but it seems obvious they would particularly characterize emigration to New Spain—an area identified as a major settlement region for Europeans and therefore in need of administrators and wives: Peter Boyd-Bowman, "Patterns of Spanish Emigration," 580–604. See Pedro Carrasco, "Indian-Spanish Marriages in the First Century of the Colony," in *Indian Women of Early Mexico*, ed. Susan Schroeder and Robert Haskell (Norman: University of Oklahoma, 1997), 88, on the role of Indian wives in the acculturation Spanish men, 123; Sophie D. Coe and Michael D. Coe, *The True History of Chocolate* (New York: Thames and Hudson, 2000), 110–11; Alberro, *Del gachupín*, 71–73.

16. Sophie Coe, *America's First Cuisines* (Austin: University of Texas Press, 1984), 75, 78, 103.

17. Alberro, *Del gachupín*, 72.

18. Nancy Farriss, *Maya Society under Colonial Rule: The Collective Enterprise of Survival* (Princeton: Princeton University Press, 1984), 112.

19. Gibson, *Aztecs*.

20. Toribio de Benavente, *Historia de los indios de la Nueva España*, ed. and intro. Claudio Esteva Fabregat (Mexico City: Dastin, Crónicas de América, 2001), 131.

21. Thomas Gage, *The English-American his Travail by Sea and Land, or, A New Survey of the West-India's* (London: B. Cotes, 1648), 25.

22. Francisco Hernández, *Antigüedades de la Nueva España*, trans. from Latin to Spanish and notes Joaquín García Pimentel (Mexico City: Editorial Pedro Robredo, 1945), 80, 82. Lists of goods sold at markets in Mexico City, Tlaxcala, and Coyocán compiled in the mid-sixteenth century include cacao, chocolate, and the gourd containers used for drinking chocolate: James Lockhart, *The Nahuas after the Conquest: A Social and Cultural History of the Indians of Central Mexico, Sixteenth through Eighteenth Centuries* (Stanford: Stanford University Press, 1993), 187; Gibson, *Aztecs*, 353, 356.

23. Bartolomé Marradón, "Dialogue du Chocolate," in *Traitez nouveaux & curieux du café, du thé, et chocolat*, trans. Phillipe Sylvestre Dufour (Lyon: Jean Girin and B. Riviere, 1685), 431–33.

24. "Local Market Tax Records, Coyoacan, Mid-Sixteenth Century," in *Beyond the Codices: The Nahua View of Colonial Mexico*, trans. and ed. Arthur J. O. Anderson, Frances Berdan, and James Lockhart (Berkeley: University of California Press, 1976), 138–47. The translators provide "tobacco sellers" as the translation for *picienamacac*, but I believe this referred more specifically to the lime-enhanced ground tobacco used for chewing and topical applications, since the pipe and cigar makers were indicated separately. Tobacco figured among goods sold at markets in Mexico City, Tlaxcala, Xochimilco, and Acolman in the mid-sixteenth century: Lockhart, *Nahuas*, 187; Gibson, *Aztecs*, 353, 356; María Teresa Sepúlveda y Herrera, ed., *Procesos por idolatría al cacique, gobernadores y sacerdotes de Yanhuitlán, 1544–46* (Mexico City: Colección Científica, Instituto Nacional de Antropología e Historia, 1999), 151, 209.

25. Francisco Hernández, *Obras completas*, vol. 2, *Historia natural de Nueva España* (Mexico City: Universidad Nacional Autónoma de México, 1959), bk. 1, 82.

26. Sepúlveda y Herrera, *Procesos por idolatría . . . Yanhuitlán*, 221, 223. This testimony was used to prove that the presence of *picietl* could not be taken as evidence of idolatry.

27. Cultural authorities changed views about whether this practice was benign, or even profitable, or a hazardous venture that led to cultural contamination, depending on whether they saw it as a way to procure purely "medical" knowledge or as succumbing to foolish superstition, or worse.

28. Nicolás Monardes, *Dos libros El uno trata de todas las cosas q[ue] trae[n] de n[uest] ras Indias Occidentales* (Seville: Sebastián Trujillo, 1565), fol. G(v); Marcy Norton, "New World of Goods: A History of Tobacco and Chocolate in the Spanish Empire, 1492–1700," (PhD diss., University of California, Berkeley, 2000), 108–9.

29. Serge Gruzinski, *The Conquest of Mexico: The Incorporation of Indian Societies into the Western World, 16th–18th Centuries*, trans. Eileen Corrigan (Cambridge: Polity Press, 1993), 145. See also Noemí Quezada, "The Inquisition's Repression of *Curanderos*," in *Cultural Encounters: The Impact of the Inquisition in Spain and the New World*, ed. Mary Elizabeth Perry and Anne J. Cruz (Berkeley: University of California Press, 1991), 37–57; Fernando Cervantes, *The Devil in the New World: The Impact of Diabolism in New Spain* (New Haven: Yale University Press, 1994), 38.

30. *Relaciones geográficas del siglo XVI: Tlaxcala*, ed. René Acuña (Mexico City: Universidad Nacional Autónoma de México, Instituto de Investigaciones Antropológicas, 1984), 4:29.

31. *Relaciones histórico-geográficos de la gobernación de Yucatán (Mérida, Valladolid, y Tabasco)* (Mexico City: Universidad Nacional Autónoma de México, 1983), 2:429.

32. *Papeles de Nueva España, segunda serie, geografía y estadística: Relaciones geográficas de la diócesis de México*, ed. Francisco del Paso y Troncoso (Madrid: Sucesores de Rivadeneyra, 1905; Mexico City: Editorial Cosmos, 1979), 111, 320, 141. Citations are to Editorial Cosmos edition. See also, *Relaciones histórico-geográficos de la gobernación de Yucatán*, 1:80, 239–20; 2:429.

33. Cope, *Limits*, 4, 14–22; Gibson, *Aztecs*, 380, and see Cope, 83.

34. Antonio Colmenero de Ledesma, *Curioso tratado de la naturaleza y calidad del chocolate* (Madrid: Francisco de Martínez, 1631), fol. 6.

35. Gage, *English-American his Travail by Sea*, 23.

36. Sauer, *Early Spanish Main*, 161–77, 218–65; Whitehead, "Crises," 864–903. On early settlements in Venezuela, see Pablo Ojer, *La Formación del Oriente Venezolano* (Caracas: Universidad Católica "Andrés Bello," Facultad de Humanidades y Educación, Instituto de Investigaciones Histórica, 1966).

37. Neil L. Whitehead, "Ethnic Plurality and Cultural Continuity in the Native Caribbean," in *Wolves from the Sea: Readings in the Anthropology of the Native Caribbean*, ed. Neil L. Whitehead (Leiden, Netherlands: KITLV Press, 1995), 105–6; Jalil Sued Badillo, *Los Caribes: Realidad o fabula* (Río Piedras, Puerto Rico: Editorial Antillana, 1978), 90; Peter Hulme, *Colonial Encounters: Europe and the Native Caribbean, 1492–1797* (London: Methuen, 1986), 4.

38. Neil Whitehead, *Lords of the Tiger Spirit: A History of the Caribs in Colonial Venezuela and Guyana, 1498–1820* (Dordrecht, Netherlands: Foris Publications, 1988), 71–72; Ojer, *Formación del Oriente Venezolano*, 353–54, 358; Whitehead, "Crises."

39. Richard White, *The Middle Ground: Indians, Empires, and Republics in the Great Lakes Region, 1650–1815* (Cambridge: Cambridge University Press, 1991), 52.

40. Quoted in Ojer, *Formación del Oriente Venezolano*, 308.

41. C. S. Alexander, "Margarita Island, Exporter of People," *Journal of Inter-American Studies* 3 (Oct. 1961): 548–57; Ojer, *Formación del Oriente Venezolano*, 83, 165, 210; Whitehead, *Lords*, 18, 75–76. On Carib alliances, see Charles de Rochefort, *The History of the Caribby-Islands*, trans. John Davies (London: Printed by J. M. for T. Dring and J. Starkey, 1666), 160.

42. José Rafael Lovera, Estudio preliminar, in Galeotto Cey, *Viaje y descripción de las Indias, 1539–1553* (Caracas: Fundación Banco Venezolano de Crédito, 1995), xxvi–xxvii.

43. Cey, *Viaje*, 129.

44. Modified translation in Wilbert, *Tobacco and Shamanism*, 11, 80; Gonzalo Fernández de Oviedo, *Historia general y natural de las Indias*, ed. and intro. Juan Pérez de Tudela Bueso (Madrid: Ediciones Atlas, 1992) 3:32–33; for an example from a later period in the Cumana region of Venezuela, see *Relaciones de las Misiones de los PP. Capuchinos en las antiguas provincias españolas hoy República de Venezuela, 1650–1817*, ed. Froilán de Rionegro (Seville: Tipografía Zarzuela, 1918), 72. Such uses were reminiscent of Nahua laymen's use of tobacco to ensure good fortune on hunting, trading, and fishing expeditions; see chapter 3.
45. Juan de Castellanos, *Elegías de varones ilustres de Indias*, ed. and intro. Miguel Antonio Caro (Bogotá: Editorial ABC, 1955), 1:7–44 (introduction by Caro), 383; Gerardo Reichel-Dolmatoff, *The Shaman and the Jaguar: A Study of Narcotic Drugs among the Indians of Colombia* (Philadelphia: Temple University Press, 1975), 12.
46. Pedro de Aguado, *Recopilación historial* (Bogota: Empresa Nacional de Publicaciones, 1956–57), 1:599; translated in Gerardo Reichel-Dolmatoff, *The Shaman*, 12–13.
47. Oviedo, *Historia general y natural*, 4:416–17; Eugenia Ibarra Rojas, *Fronteras étnicas en la conquista de Nicaragua y Nicoya: entre la solidaridad y el conflicto, 800 D.C.–1544* (San José: Editorial de la Universidad de Costa Rica, 2001) 99–109.
48. Oviedo, *Historia general y natural*, 4:416.
49. Two famous instances of this phenomenon are recounted in Bernal Díaz del Castillo, *The Conquest of New Spain*, trans. J. M. Cohen (London: Penguin Books, 1963), 57–61, and examined in Inga Clendinnen, *Ambivalent Conquests: Maya and Spaniard in Yucatan, 1517–1570* (Cambridge: Cambridge University Press, 1987), 17–18; Alvar Núñez de Vaca, *The Account: Alvar Núñez de Vaca's Relación*, ed. and trans. Martin A. Favata and José B. Fernández (Houston: University of Houston, Arte Público Press, 1993). For similar episodes, see Ojer, *Formación del Oriente Venezolano*, 167, 197, 211–12; Castellanos, *Elegías de varones*, 1:342–43, 345; Miguel Acosta Saignes, *Estudios de etnología antigua de Venezuela* (Caracas: Universidad Central de Venezuela, 1961), 249–50.
50. Juan Friede, *Los Welser en la conquista de Venezuela* (Caracas: Ediciones EDIME, 1961), 193; Juan Friede, "Geographical Ideas and the Conquest of Venezuela," *The Americas* 16, no. 2. (1959): 148–49; Oviedo, *Historia general y natural*, 3:7–8.
51. Oviedo, *Historia general y natural*, 3:8–11; Friede, *Los Welser*, 192–98; Friede, "Geographical Ideas," 151–52.
52. Friede, *Los Welser*, 197–202. I have relied on the account in Oviedo, *Historia general y natural*, 3:24–27, and Acosta Saignes, *Estudios de etnología*, 249; all used Martín's testimony, now in the AGI Justicia, leg. 1003.
53. Oviedo, *Historia general y natural*, 3:27.
54. Whitehead, *Lords*, 182; Acosta Saignes, *Estudios de etnología*, 84–85.
55. Oviedo, *Historia general y natural*, 3:28.
56. Quoted in Friede, *Los Welser*, 201–2.
57. Oviedo, *Historia general y natural*, 3:28; "taco" appears to be a faulty transcription for "tabaco."
58. Oviedo, *Historia general y natural*, 3:21.
59. Ibid., 3:22.
60. Ibid., 3:28.
61. Ibid.
62. See, for example, the ritual described by Oviedo for the Caquetio above; Wilbert, *Tobacco and Shamanism*, 86–89.
63. Friede, *Los Welser*, 202.
64. Kenneth R. Andrews, *The Spanish Caribbean: Trade and Plunder* (New Haven: Yale University Press, 1978), 65, 71, 75–77, 181; Ojer, *Formación del Oriente Venezolano*, 75; K. R. Andrews, "The English in the Caribbean 1560–1620," in *The Westward Enterprise: English Activities in Ireland, the Atlantic, and America, 1480–1650*, ed. K. Andrews, N. P. Canny, and P. E. H. Hair (Liverpool: Liverpool University Press, 1978), 103–23.
65. Whitehead, "Crises," 873–79.
66. Jalil Sued Badillo, "The Island Caribs: New Approaches to the Question of Ethnicity in the Early Colonial Caribbean," in *Wolves from the Sea*, ed. Neil L. Whitehead, 80–82;

Sued Badillo, *Los Caribes*. Many of the islands of the Lesser Antilles came under French and English rule by the mid-seventeenth century, resulting predictably in adverse consequences for the native population. However, St. Vincent and Dominica benefited from the intercolonial rivalry and retained native autonomy until the eighteenth century.

67. Joseph Borome, "Spain and Dominica," *Caribbean Quarterly* 12, no. 4 (1966): 30; Samuel Eliot Morison, *Admiral of the Ocean Sea: A Life of Christopher Columbus* (New York: Time, 1962), 2:390.

68. Borome, "Spain and Dominica," 32–33, 36–37.

69. Ibid., 33–34; 43 n. 29.

70. Ibid., 35–36.

71. Ojer, *Formacion del Oriente Venezolano*, 62, 63, 394.

72. Borome, "Spain and Dominica," 39.

73. Rochefort, *History of the Caribby-Islands*, 309, checked against the French in Charles de Rochefort, *Histoire Naturelle et Morale des Iles Antilles de l'Amerique* (Rotterdam: A. Leers, 1658).

74. Rochefort, *History of the Caribby-Islands*, 309.

75. Ibid., 309.

76. Ibid., 311–12.

77. Edmund Morgan, *American Slavery, American Freedom: The Ordeal of Colonial Virginia* (New York: Norton, 1975), 6–7, 11–12.

78. Quoted in Sarah Augusta Dickson, *Panacea or Precious Bane: Tobacco in Sixteenth Century Literature* (New York: New York Public Library, 1954), 119; Jerome Brooks, *Tobacco, Its History: Illustrated by the Books, Manuscripts, and Engravings in the Collection of George Arents Jr.* (New York: Rosenbach Company, 1937–52), 1:217–18.

79. Translation by Thomas Hacket (spelling modernized), quoted in Brooks, *Tobacco, Its History*, 2:116.

80. John Sparke, "The Voyage Made by M. John Hawkins Esquire, 1565," in *Early English and French Voyages, Chiefly from Hakluyt, 1534–1608*, ed. Henry S. Burrage (New York: C. Scribner's Sons, 1906), 125; Brooks, *Tobacco, Its History*, 1:240–41.

81. Quoted in Brooks, *Tobacco, Its History*, 1:227; Dickson, *Panacea*, 38; Pietro Andrea Mattioli, *Commentarii in sex libros Pedacii Dioscoridis Anazarbei de medica materia* (Venice: Vincenzo Valgrisi, 1554), 472–73.

82. Nicolás Monardes, *Segunda parte del libro, de las cosas que se traen de nuestras Indias Occidentales, que sirven al uso de medicina: Do[nde] se trata del Tabaco* (Seville: Alonso Escrivano, 1571), fol. 22; Dickson, *Panacea*, 44.

83. Nicolás Monardes, *Primera y segunda y tercera partes de la historia medicinal: de las cosas que se traen de nuestras Indias Occidentales, que se sirven en medicina* (Seville: Alonso Escrivano, 1574), fol. 117v.

84. Translation in Jordan Goodman, *Tobacco in History: The Cultures of Dependence* (London: Routledge, 1993), 47; also Matthias de L'Obel and Pierre Peña, *Stirpium adversaria nova* (London: Thomas Purfoot, 1570–71), 251.

85. *Noticias relativas al pueblo de Tepetlaoxtoc* (Mexico City: Vargas Rea, 1944), 13–18; for background on Tepetlaoztoc and the lawsuit, see Peter Gerhard, *A Guide to the Historical Geography of New Spain* (Norman: University of Oklahoma Press, 1993), 311–14; Gibson, *Aztecs*, 80, 429.

86. *Noticias relativas al pueblo de Tepetlaoxtoc*, 18.

87. Coe and Coe, *True History*, 130–33.

88. Some have considered that her work was actually composed by her father, who then decided to publish it under her name, but recent research by Gianna Pomata of the University of Bologna, who is working on a study of her medical theories, suggests otherwise. Though Hernández completed his influential work on cacao before Sabuco de Nantes published hers, there is no evidence that she read his work in manuscript, and no part of it was published until the seventeenth century, see chapter 5.

89. Oliva Sabuco de Nantes, *Nueva filosofía de la naturaleza del hombre* (Madrid, 1588), facsimile, ed. Florentino M. Torner (Madrid: M. Aguilar, 1935), 132, 176, 183.

90. Juan de Cárdenas criticized her ideas about physiology but did not seem aware of her mention of cacao, *Problemas y secretos maravillosos de las Indias* (1591), ed. Angeles Durán (Madrid: Alianza Editorial, 1988), 167–69; Antonio de León Pinelo wrote that Doña Oliva de Nantes was deceived in thinking cacao was of "white marrow," for it is "almost black, going toward tawny": Antonio de León Pinelo, *Questión moral: si el chocolate quebranta el ayuno eclesiástico* (Madrid: Viuda de Juan Gonzalez, 1636), fol. 3v. The views of Sabuco de Nantes and León Pinelo can be reconciled if one considers that the pulp inside the cacao pod is a white, fleshy mass, while the seeds (nibs) are dark colored.

91. Juan López de Velasco, *Geografía y descripción universal de las Indias* (Madrid: Establ. tip. de Fortanet, 1894), 9–12, 72–79.

92. López de Velasco, *Geografía y descripción*, 72–74.

93. "Descripción de Santiago de León gobernación de Venezuela ... Nuestra Señora de Caraballeda," in *Relaciones geográficas de Venezuela*, ed. and intro. Antonio Arellano Moreno (Caracas: Academia Nacional de la Historia, 1964), 130; the same was true for "Descripción de la ciudad del Tocuyo" (1578) in the same work, 141–60.

94. Gibson, *Aztecs*, 335, 348–49; Murdo J. MacLeod, *Spanish Central America* (Berkeley: University of California Press, 1973).

5. Learning from Indians

1. Nicolás Monardes, *Segunda parte del libro, de las cosas que se traen de nuestras Indias Occidentales, que sirven al uso de medicina: Do[nde] se trata del Tabaco, y de la Sassafras ...* (Seville: Alonso Escrivano, 1571), frontispiece, fols. 3r, 4r–4v. For an exhaustive bibliography of Monardes's works and translations, see Francisco Guerra, *Nicolás Bautista Monardes: Su vida y obra* (Mexico City: Compañia Fundidora de Fierro y Acero de Monterrey, 1961), 115–75. For an abridged English translation of Monardes's chapter on tobacco, see Sarah Augusta Dickson, *Panacea or Precious Bane: Tobacco in Sixteenth Century Literature* (New York: New York Public Library, 1954), 80–84. Much of the subject matter of this chapter is explored in more depth in Marcy Norton, "New World of Goods: A History of Tobacco and Chocolate in the Spanish Empire, 1492–1700," (PhD diss., University of California, Berkeley, 2000), chap. 2.

2. Nicolás Monardes, *Primera y segunda y tercera partes de la historia medicinal: de las cosas que se traen de nuestras Indias Occidentales, que se sirven en medicina* (Seville: Alonso Escrivano, 1574), fol. A(4)v.

3. José María López Piñero, José Luis Fresquet Febrer, María Luz López Terrada, and José Pardo Tomás, *Medicinas, drogas y alimentos vegetales del nuevo mundo* (Madrid: Ministerio de Sanidad y Consumo, 1992); Francisco Guerra, "La política imperial sobre las drogas de las indias," *Revista de Indias* (Madrid) nos. 103–4 (1966): 47, 50–51; Charles H. Talbot, "America and the European Drug Trade," in *First Images of America: The Impact of the New World on the Old*, ed. Fredi Chiappelli (Berkeley: University of California Press, 1976), 2:834; Jonathan D. Sauer, "Changing Perception and Exploitation of New World Plants in Europe, 1492–1800," in *First Images of America: The Impact of the New World on the Old*, ed. Fredi Chiappelli (Berkeley: University of California Press, 1976), 2:818–19; Antonio Barrera-Osorio, "Local Herbs, Global Medicines: Commerce, Knowledge, and Commodities in Spanish America," in *Merchants and Marvels: Commerce, Science, and Art in Early Modern Europe*, ed. Paula H. Smith and Paula Findlen (New York: Routledge, 2002); José Martinez Gijon, "Métodos comerciales utilizados en la Española durante el siglo xvi para la exportación de cañafistula," in *Actas y estudios del iii congreso del instituto internacional de historia del derecho indano* (Madrid: Instituto Nacional de Estudios Jurídicos 1973), 903–24; Eufemio Lorenzo Sanz, *Comercio de España con América en la época de Felipe II*, vol. 1, *Los mercaderes y el tráfico indiano* (Valladolid: Servicio de Publicaciones de la Diputación Provincial de Valladolid, 1979), 604–13, 624; Huguette Chaunu and Pierre Chaunu, *Séville et l'Atlantique, 1504–1650* (Paris: S.E.V.P.E.N., 1956), vol. 6, bk. 2: 1022–30; David C. Goodman, *Power and Penury: Government, Technology, and Science in Phillip II's Spain* (Cambridge: Cambridge University Press, 1988), 233, 248–49, 259 nn. 141–42.

4. Lorenzo Sanz, *Comercio*, 613, 624.

5. On diversity of healing traditions in Spain, see Jon Arrizabalaga, "The Ideal Christian Physician," in *Medicine and Medical Ethics in Medieval and Early Modern Spain*, ed. Samuel S. Kottek and Luis García-Ballester (Jerusalem: Magnes Press, 1996), 66, 80; Goodman, *Power and Penury*, 217–21; on *morisco* and *converso* practitioners, see Luis García-Ballester, "Academicism versus Empiricism in Practical Medicine in Sixteenth-Century Spain with Regard to Morisco Practioners," in *The Medical Renaissance of the Sixteenth Century*, ed. Andrew Wear, R. K. French, and I. M. Lonie (Cambridge: Cambridge University Press, 1985), 246, 250–53, 261–63; Luis García-Ballester, *Medicina, ciencia y minorías marginadas: Los moriscos* (Granada: University of Granada, 1977).

6. Goodman, *Power and Penury*, 222, 227–31; José María López Piñero, "The Medical Profession in Sixteenth-Century Spain," in *The Town and the State Physician in Europe from the Middle Ages to the Enlightenment*, ed. A. W. Russel (Wolfenbuttel, Germany: Herzog August Bibliothek, 1982), 85–98; Luis S. Granjel, *La medicina española renacentista* (Salamanca: Ediciones Universidad de Salamanca, 1980), 74.

7. Owsei Temkin, *Galenism: Rise and Decline of a Medical Philosophy* (Ithaca: Cornell University Press, 1973), 17–18, 112; Nancy G. Siraisi, *Medieval and Early Renaissance Medicine: An Introduction to Knowledge and Practice* (Chicago: University of Chicago, 1990), 48–77, 100–108; Granjel, *La medicina*, 47–48, 253–54; Nancy G. Siraisi, "The Changing Fortunes of a Traditional Text: Goals and Strategies in Sixteenth-Century Latin Editions of the Canon of Avicenna," in *The Medical Renaissance of the Sixteenth Century*, ed. Wear, French, and Lonie; Anthony Grafton, "Drugs and Diseases: New World Biology and Old World Learning," in his *New Worlds, Ancient Texts: The Power of Tradition and the Shock of Discovery* (Cambridge: Belknap Press of Harvard University Press, 1992); Jerry Stannard, "Pietro Andrea Mattioli: Sixteenth-Century Commentator on Dioscorides," *Bibliographical Contributions* 1 (1969): 59–81; J. M. Riddle, "Dioscorides," in F. O. Cranz and P. O. Kristeller, *Catalogus translationum et commentariorum*, vol. 4, *Medieval and Renaissance Latin Translations and Commentaries* (Washington, D.C.: Catholic University of America Press, 1980), 1–145; Pietro Andrea Mattioli, *Commentarii in libros sex Pedacii Dioscoridis Anazarbei de medica materia* (Venice: Vincenzo Valgrisi, 1554); Agnes Arber, *Herbals, Their Origin and Evolution: A Chapter in the History of Botany, 1470–1670* (Cambridge: Cambridge University Press, 1912), 8–9. See also Miguel Ángel González Manjarrés, *Andrés Laguna y el humanismo médico* (Valladolid: Junta de Castilla y Léon, 2000).

8. Guerra, *Nicolás Bautista Monardes*, 87. See also Alix Cooper, *Inventing the Indigenous: Local Knowledge and Natural History in Early Modern Europe* (Cambridge: Cambridge University Press, 2007); Christine R. Johnson, *The German Discovery of the World: Renaissance Encounters with the Strange and Marvelous* (Charlottesville: University of Virginia Press, 2008).

9. Ruy Díaz de Isla, *Tractado contra el mal serpentino: que vulgarmente en España es llamado bubas que fue ordenado en el hospital de todos los santos de Lisbona* (Seville: Dominico de Robertis, 1539); Robert S. Munger, "Guaiacum, the Holy Wood from the New World," *Journal of the History of Medicine and Allied Sciences* 4 (April 1949): 202, 215.

10. J. H. Elliott, *The Old World and the New, 1492–1650* (Cambridge: Cambridge University Press, 1970), 15.

11. Nicolás Monardes, *Dos libros. El uno trata de todas las cosas q[ue] trae[n] de n[uest]ras Indias Occidentales que sirven al uso de medicina* (Seville: Sebastián Trujillo, 1565).

12. Monardes, *Primera y segunda y tercera*, fol. A(3)r.

13. The two biographies of Monardes are Francisco Rodríguez Marin, *La verdadera biografía del doctor Nicolás de Monardes* (Madrid: Ministerio de Instrucción Pública y Bellas Artes, 1925), and Guerra, *Nicolás Bautista Monardes*. Daniela Bleichmar arrived at similar conclusions concerning Monardes and his attitudes toward New World goods in "Books, Bodies, and Fields: Sixteenth-Century Transatlantic Encounters with New World *Materia Medica*," in *Colonial Botany: Science, Commerce, and Politics in the Early Modern World*, ed. Londa Schiebinger and Claudia Swan, (Philadelphia: University of Pennsylvania Press,

2005), 84–85, 91–92, 98. Compare Marcy Norton, "New World of Goods: A History of Tobacco and Chocolate in the Spanish Empire, 1492–1700" (Ph.D. diss., University of California, Berkeley, 2000), chap. 2, esp. 105–9.

14. César E. Dübler, *La "Materia Médica" de Dioscórides: Transmision medieval y renacentista*, 6 vols. (Barcelona: Tipografía Emporium, 1953–59), 4: 8, 77–80. Like Mattioli, Laguna did include some discussion of New World plant material, but it too came as an afterthought: ibid., 4: 291, 193. Also mentioned are guaiacum, sarsaparilla, cochineal, maize, and balsam, 1:109, 135; 2:135; 4:49.

15. Guerra, *Nicolás Bautista Monardes*, 32–38.

16. On this question, see José María López Piñero, "Los primeros estudios científicos sobre la materia médica americana: *La historia medicinal* de Nicolás Monardes y la expedición de Francisco Hernández a Nueva España," in *Viejo y nuevo continente: La medicina en el encuentro de dos mundos* (Madrid: Saned, 1992), 220–79. The shift by Monardes between 1536 and 1565 is attributed to the "regenerative" arrival of pharmaceutical products from America and the East Indies: F. J. Pérez Fuenzalida, "Nicolás Monardes y Andrés Laguna: Actidudes tradicionales y renovadoras en la medicina del Renacimiento," in *Actas del IV Congreso de la Español historia de la medicina* (Granada: 1975), 81–88.

17. Lorenzo Sanz, *Comercio*, 329, 346, 351, 362–64; see also Ruth Pike, *Aristocrats and Traders: Sevillan Society in the Sixteenth Century* (Ithaca: Cornell University Press, 1972).

18. Guerra, *Nicolás Bautista Monardes*, 24.

19. Rodríguez Marin, appendix in *La verdadera biografía*, 62, 67, 70, 69; Guerra, *Nicolás Bautista Monardes*, 17.

20. Lorenzo Sanz, *Comercio*, 314, 320–21, 339, 346, 364; Guerra, *Nicolás Bautista Monardes*, 16–29, and Rodríguez Marin, *La verdadera biografía*, 25–27, 99.

21. Robert T. Gunther, *The Greek Herbal of Dioscorides* (New York: Hafner, 1959).

22. Monardes, *Primera y segunda y tercera*, fol. 77v.

23. Monardes, *Dos libros*.

24. Ken Albala, *Eating Right in the Renaissance* (Berkeley: University of California Press, 2002).

25. Monardes, *Primera y segunda y tercera*, fols. 106v–107; see also Monardes, *Dos libros*, fols. C, D(1).

26. Monardes, *Primera y segunda y tercera*, fols. 30v–31r.

27. This work was first published in Latin in Rouen, France, in 1554; Jean Liebault updated the 1567 book, Dickson, *Panacea*, 71, 81–82.

28. Charles Estienne and Jean Liebault, *L'agriculture et maison rustique* (Lyon: Jacques Carteron, 1653). This edition contains material in the section on tobacco that was not in the 1567 edition, so I also relied on the excerpt of the complete entry on tobacco from the 1567 edition in Dickson, *Panacea*, 72–75. *L'agriculture et maison rustique* was a best seller, printed over one hundred times, including translations in Dutch, German, Italian, English, and Catalan: Marc and Muriel Vigie, *L'herbe à Nicot: Amateurs de tabac, fermiers généraux et contrebandiers sous l'ancien régime* (Paris: Fayard, 1989), 16.

29. Liebault, *L'agriculture*, 208. Translation from Dickson, *Panacea*, 72.

30. Dickson, *Panacea*, 82.

31. Evidence internal to Monardes's 1565 book suggests acquaintance with tobacco even though he did not mention it by that name: he described a resin called *tacamaca* (*Elaphrium tecomaca*) that could be consumed by "taking smoke in the nose," Monardes, *Dos libros*, fols. B(1)v–B(2)r; a similar reference to liquidambar is on fol. C(1)r. An independent source confirms that *tacamaca* was added to tobacco pipes in New Spain. Juan de Barrios wrote that "to comfort the brain . . . *tecohama* is taken in smoke of *picietl* through the nostrils." "Tratado Quarto," in *De la Verdadera medicina, cirugía y astrología* (Mexico City: Fernando Balli, 1607), no fol. number. This suggests that Monardes was already familiar with the practice of smoking.

32. Jerome Brooks, *Tobacco, Its History: Illustrated by the Books, Manuscripts, and Engravings in the Collection of George Arents Jr.* (New York: Rosenbach Company, 1937–52), 1:245.

33. Monardes, *Segunda parte del libro*, fols. 3r, 4v–26r

34. Ibid., fols. 7r–17r.

35. Ibid., fol. 5r.

36. Ibid., fol. 14r.

37. Dickson, *Panacea*, 88–89.

38. See chapter 1. Juan de Barrios, a creole physician in New Spain, compiled a treatise—based on a portion of Francisco Hernández's work—organized by ailment, and *picietl* appeared as an ingredient in prescriptions to "comfort the head" and alleviate toothaches, asthma, and digestive and gynecological problems, as well as the discomfort associated with hunger and thirst": "Tratado Quarto," no fol. number. On indigenous influence in Barrios and his methodology, see Juan Comas, "Influencia de la farmacopea y terapéutica indígenas de Nueva España en la obra de Juan de Barrios," *Anales de Antropología* 8 (1971): 142; José María López Piñero, *Nuevos materiales y noticias sobre* La historia de las plantas de Nueva España *de Francisco Hernández* (Valencia: Instituto de Estudios Documentales, 1994), 115–16.

39. Monardes, *Primera y segunda y tercera*, fols. 106v–107r.

40. *Ballestero*, the juice of black hellebore, was commonly used as a poison during hunts in the sixteenth century and as recently as the 1950s in Spain: Dübler, *Don Andres de Laguna y su épcoa*, 251. Monardes, *Segunda parte del libro*, fols. 13r–13v.

41. Monardes, *Segunda parte del libro*, fol. 7r. For contemporary medical meanings for these terms, see Dübler, *La "Materia Médica"* 5: 335, 482, 813–14.

42. Hernández wrote of the "error" of those who thought tobacco cold and a species of henbane: Francisco Hernández, *Obras completas*, vol. 2, *Historia natural, de Nueva España* (Mexico City: Universidad Nacional de México, 1959), bk. 2, chap. 109. Juan de Cárdenas also characterized henbane (*beleño*) as cold: *Problemas y secretos maravillosos de las Indias* (1591), ed. Angeles Durán (Madrid: Alianza Editorial, 1988), 193.

43. Bernardo Ortíz de Montellano, *Aztec Medicine, Health, and Nutrition* (New Brunswick, N.J.: Rutgers University Press, 1990), 155. There is a long-standing debate about which aspects of postconquest medicine have Indian versus European roots; see 214–21.

44. Monardes, *Segunda parte del libro*, fols. 18v–19v. I have relied on, but altered, Dickson's translation, *Panacea*, 87.

45. Monardes, *Segunda parte del libro*, fol. 19v.

46. This paragraph follows Sabine MacCormack, *Religion in the Andes: Vision and Imagination in Early Colonial Peru* (Princeton: Princeton University Press, 1991), 39–42. See also Fernando Cervantes, *The Devil in the New World: The Impact of Diabolism in New Spain* (New Haven: Yale University Press, 1994) and Stuart Clark, *Thinking with Demons: The Idea of Witchcraft in Early Modern Europe* (Oxford: Oxford University Press, 1997), chap. 11.

47. My translation of chapter titles and sections.

48. Monardes, *Segunda parte del libro*, fol. 22v.

49. On European use of opium, see Cristóbal de Acosta, *Tractado de las drogas y medicinas de las Indias Orientales* (Burgos: Martin de Victoria, 1578), 408; Juan de Fragoso, *Discursos de las cosas aromáticas* (Madrid, 1572), fol. 40v; Antonio Castell, *Theorica y pratica de boticarios, en que se trata de la arte y forma como se han de componer las confecciones ansi interiores como exteriores* (Barcelona: Sebastián de Cormellas, 1592), fols. 125–145; and Santiago Valverde Turices, *Un discurso de chocolate* (Seville: Juan de Cabrera, 1624), fols. 2A(3)v. Opium as well as laudanum and poppy [seeds?] appear in seventeenth-century apothecary inventories: AHPM, lib. 3873 (1623), fol. 14v; lib. 5929 (1627), fol. 55v; see also Antonio Escohotado, *Historia general de las drogas* (Madrid: Alianza Editorial, 1989), 1:205, 296–97, 340–42. On Turks as barbarians, see Anthony Pagden, *The Fall of Natural Man: The American Indian and the Origins of Comparative Ethnology* (Cambridge: Cambridge University Press, 1982), 193.

50. Monardes, *Segunda parte del libro*, fols. 23r–23v.

51. Ibid., fol. 22v.

52. Ibid., fol. 23r.

53. Ibid., fols. 20v–22r. His source for *bague* is the work of Diego García da Orta and the "book he wrote of those *aromatos* of East Indies," and the Portuguese viceroy in India, Martín Alfonso de Sosa.

54. On Spanish initiatives to collect scientific information, see Paula de Vos, "The Science of Spices: Empiricism and Economic Botany in the Early Spanish Empire," *Journal of World History* 17 (2006): 399–427; and Antonio Barrera-Osorio, *Experiencing Nature: The Spanish American Empire and the Early Scientific Revolution* (Austin: University of Texas, 2006); Jorge Cañizares-Esguerra, *Nature, Empire, and Nation: Explorations of the History of Science in the Iberian World* (Stanford: Stanford University Press, 2006); Ernesto Schäfer, *El consejo real y supremo de las India*, vol. 2, *La labor del consejo de Indias en la administración colonial* (Seville: Escuela de Estudios Hispano-Americanos, 1947), 406.

55. Quoted in Goodman, *Power and Penury*, 235. The most extensive work on Hernández is in Germán Somolinos d'Ardois, *Obras completas de Francisco Hernández*, vol. 1, *Vida y obra de Francisco Hernández* (Mexico City: Universidad Nacional Autónoma de México, 1960). Biographical information is also from Germán Somolinos d'Ardois, *El doctor Francisco Hernández y la primera expedición científica en América* (Mexico City: Secretaría de Educación Pública, 1971); Raquel Álvarez Peláez, "El Doctor Hernández: Un viajero ilustrado del siglo xvi," *Revista de Indias* 47, no. 180 (1987): 614–29; Enrique Álvarez López, "El Dr. Francisco Hernández y sus comentarios a Plinio," *Revista de Indias* 3, no. 8 (1942): 251–91; López Piñero et al., *Medicinas*, 197–213. Two other excellent studies of Hernández and his impact are José María López Piñero and José Pardo Tomás, *La influencia de Francisco Hernández (1515–1587) en la constitución de la bótanica y la materia médica modernas* (Valencia: Instituto de Estudios Documentales e Históricos sobre la Ciencia, 1996) and Simon Varey, Rafael Chabrán, and Dora B. Weiner, eds., *Searching for the Secrets of Nature: The Life and Works of Dr. Francisco Hernández* (Stanford: Stanford University Press, 2000). For English translations of Hernández's work, see *The Mexican Treasury: The Writings of Dr. Francisco Hernández*, ed. Simon Varey and trans. Rafael Chabrán, Cynthia L. Chamberlain, and Simon Varey (Stanford: Stanford University Press, 2001).

56. Quoted in López Piñero et al., *Medicinas*, 200.

57. Somolinos d'Ardois, *Obras completas*, 1:194–96; Somolinos d'Ardois, *El doctor*, 30.

58. The result was Francisco Hernández, *Antigüedades de la Nueva España*, ed., trans. from Latin to Spanish, and notes Joaquín García Pimentel (Mexico City: Editorial Pedro Robredo, 1945), which, to judge by his dedication to the king, he intended to publish, but like his natural history never did.

59. Monardes, *Primera y segunda y tercera*, fols. 30v–31r.

60. For differences in the style and objective of the two doctors' works, see López Piñero et al., *Medicinas*, 209–10.

61. Barrios, "Tratado Quarto."

62. On tobacco, see Hernández, *Historia natural*, bk. 2, 80–82; on cacao, ibid., bk. 1, 303–5.

63. The first time Hernández's chapters on chocolate and tobacco from the *Historia natural* appeared in print was [Francisco Hernández], *Quatro libros de la naturaleza y virtudes de las plantas y animales*, trans. Francisco Ximénez (Mexico City: Viuda de Diego Lopez Davalos, 1615), fols. 32r–35, 93r–98r. However, Ximénez, a friar and physician in Mexico City, also added material from Juan de Barrios's book on chocolate as well as original material of his own. Hernández's chapters on tobacco and chocolate, as well as other New World goods, also circulated in two other printed works in the seventeenth century: Juan Eusebio Nieremberg, *Historia natvrae, maxime peregrinae* (Antwerp: ex officina Plantiniana B. Moreti, 1635); and Francisco Hernández, *Rerum medicarum Novae Hispaniae thesaurus, seu, Plantarum animalium mineralium mexicanorum historia* (Rome: Vitalis Mascardi 1651). None of the compilers/translators worked directly from his original manuscript, which was lost, but rather from an abridged summary prepared by a court physician named Nardo Antonio Recchi at the request of Philip II. For the trajectory and dissemination of Hernández's work, through these printed works and manuscript circulation of the digest, see López Piñero and Pardo Tomás, *La influencia de Francisco Hernández*; Simon Varey and

Rafael Chabrán, "Mexican Medicine Comes to England," *Viator* 26 (1995): 333–53, and the relevant chapters in *Searching for the Secrets of Nature*.

64. Hernández, *Historia natural*, 1:303–4.

65. Hernández, *Historia natural*, 1:304.

66. Comas, "Influencia," 125; López Piñero et al., *Medicinas*.

67. Valverde Turices, *Un discurso*, fol. 1A(4)v.

68. Hernández, *Antigüedades*, 11.

69. Hernández, *Historia natural*, 1:303–4.

70. Anthony Pagden, *Spanish Imperialism and the Political Imagination: Studies in European and Spanish-American Social and Political Theory, 1513–1830* (New Haven: Yale University Press, 1990), 92.

71. López Piñero et al., *Medicinas*, 212.

72. Quoted in Somolinos d'Ardois, *Obras completas*, 1:195.

73. Hernández, *Historia natural*, 1:305. On *caquexia*, see Dübler, *La "Materia Médica"*, 5:288; he offers Ruyces de Font's 1606 definition: "mal hábito de cuerpo abuhado y hinchado, descolorido."

6. Enduring Idolatry

1. Fernando Cervantes identifies 1585 as a key turning point: "Lapsed Indians could no longer be seen as gullible simpletons who had been deluded by the devil nor even as malicious sorcerers who used demonic power to harm their fellow beings. Much more serious than this, idolatrous Indians were active devil-worshippers, members of a counter-church set up by a devil anxious to be honoured like God," *The Devil in the New World: The Impact of Diabolism in the New World* (New Haven: Yale University Press, 1994), 25, 34–35. For reasons indicated, I think the shift began earlier.

2. Quoted in Cervantes, *Devil*, 34–35. See also Serge Gruzinski, *The Conquest of Mexico*, trans. Eileen Corrigan (Cambridge: Polity Press, 1993), 147, 187, and 193.

3. Lewis Hanke, *Las Casas: Bookman, Scholar, and Propagandist* (Philadelphia: University of Pennsylvania Press, 1952), 29.

4. Georges Baudot, *Utopie et histoire au Mexique* (Toulouse: Privat, 1977), 489–92; for a different view, see Germán Somolinos d'Ardois, *Obras completas de Francisco Hernández*, vol. 1, *Vida y obra de Francisco Hernández* (Mexico City: Universidad Nacional Autónoma de México, 1960), 264.

5. My emphasis. Quoted in Baudot, *Utopie*, 492. There was basis for such fears, for some Indians successfully appropriated the medium of print to preserve pre-Columbian practices; see Gruzinski, *Conquest*.

6. Solange Alberro, *Les Espagnols dans le Mexique colonial: Histoire d'une acculturation* (Paris: Armand Colin, 1992), 56–57.

7. Gonzalo Aguirre Beltrán, *Medicina y magia: El proceso de aculturación en la estructura colonial* (Mexico City: Instituto Nacional Indigenista, 1963), 263–64. He notes that between 1580 and 1640, with the influx of African slaves, it was noticed that the black population adopted many indigenous customs, such as consuming peyote. The Inquisition was particularly busy with these cases between 1614 and 1630.

8. Lope de Montoya, "Summa de muchos capítulos generales y de todas las Actas, Ordinaciones, Visitas y avisos de Capítulos Provinciales desde que se fundó esta Provincia de Sn. Vicente Chiapa," at the Library of the Hispanic Society of America in New York City, is an eighteenth-century manuscript copy that includes the two opinions that the "Doctissimo Doctor Navarro" wrote as to "si era licito beber el día de Ayuno Chocolate, o Chilate." Navarro's original letters were dated April 21 and 22, 1577, and posted from the Convent of Santo Domingo in Ciudad Real, Chiapas; Alonso de Noreña, who copied the letters written by Navarro *and* the notes that were returned with it from Rome, records that when presented with the letter from Navarro, the pope and the cardinals did not take it seriously and laughed instead ("se reían"), fol. 23v. Noreña's copy with his notes was recopied by Montoya, which were recopied by Salazar. Lope de Montoya, "Copia manuscrita moderna hecha

por del Dr. Ramon A Salazar, director de la Biblioteca Nacional de Guatemala, 1897," in the Library of the Hispanic Society of America. See also Agustín Dávila y Padilla, *Historia de la fundacíon y discurso de la provincia de Santiago de México* (Mexico City: Editorial Academia Literaria, 1955), 626; Antonio de León Pinelo, *Questión moral: si el chocolate quebranta el ayuno eclesiástico* (Madrid: Viuda de Juan Gonzalez, 1636), fol. 86r; and Tomás Hurtado, *Chocolate y tabaco: ayuno eclesiástico y natural* (Madrid: Francisco García, [1645]), fols. 14v, 20r, 34r, 18v, 27r–27v.

9. AGN Inq., vol. 141, no. 18, fol. 2 (March 21, 1584).

10. *Concilios limenses, 1551–1772*, ed. Rubén Vargas Ugarte (Lima: Tipografía Peruana, 1951), 1:354; for the Latin, 293.

11. *Coleccion de canones y de todos los concilios de la Iglesia de España y de America*, ed. Juan Tejada y Ramiro (Madrid: Montero, 1859), 5:608. Concilio III Provincial de Mexico, tit. xv.

12. D. A. Brading, *The First America: The Spanish Monarchy, Creole Patriots, and the Liberal State, 1492–1867* (Cambridge: Cambridge University Press, 1992), 200, 297 (on creole patriotism, see 199–200, 293–313); Jorge Cañizares-Esguerra, "New World, New Stars: Patriotic Astrology and the Invention of Indian and Creole Bodies in Colonial Spanish America, 1600–1650," in *American Historical Review* 104 (Feb. 1999): 33–68.

13. Acosta left Spain for Peru in 1571 and was there until 1586, at which time he went to Mexico en route to Spain, which he reached in 1587. Anthony Pagden, *The Fall of Natural Man: The American Indian and the Origins of Comparative Ethnology* (Cambridge: Cambridge University Press, 1982), 147–48.

14. José de Acosta, *Historia natural y moral de las Indias* (Seville: Juan de León, 1590), fols. 163r–164v.

15. Juan de Barrios, "Tratado Quarto," in *Verdadera medicina, cirugía y astrología* (Mexico: Fernado Balli, 1607). On this work, see Juan Comas, "Influencia de la farmacopea y terapéutica indígena de la Nueva España en la obra de Juan de Barrios," in *Anales de Antropología* 8 (1971): 142, and José María López Piñero, *Nuevos materiales y noticias sobre La historia de las plantas de Nueva España de Francisco Hernández* (Valencia: Instituto de Estudios Documentales, 1994), 103–7.

16. No exemplars survive of Juan de Barrios's work, but portions were excerpted as "Lo que del chocolate escrive el Doctor Juan de Barrios" in León Pinelo, *Questión moral*, fols. 116r–120v. Other authors who excerpted this work include Santiago Valverde Turices, *Un discurso de chocolate* (Seville: Juan de Cabrera, 1624), fol. A(2); Francisco Ximénez, *Quatro libros de la naturaleza y virtudes de las plantas y animales* (Mexico City: Viuda de Diego Lopez Davalos, 1615), fols. 34v–35r.

17. I follow Germán Somolinos d'Ardois, *Capítulos de historia médica mexicana*, vol. 3, *Relación alfabética de los profesionistas médicos* (Mexico City: Sociedad Mexicana de Historia y Filosofía de la Medicina, 1980? [n.d.]), 204–9 in this paragraph. On Cárdenas, see also Angeles Durán, introduction to *Problemas y secretos maravillosos de las Indias*, ed. Angeles Durán (Madrid: Alianza Editorial, 1988), 7–17, and Xavier Lozoya, estudio preliminar in *Primera parte de los problemas y secretos maravillosos de las Indias* (Mexico City: Academia Nacional de Medicina, 1980).

18. Oliva Sabuco de Nantes's passing mention of cacao in 1588 is the only exception.

19. Juan de Cárdenas, *Problemas y secretos maravillosos de las Indias* (1591), ed. Angeles Durán (Madrid: Alianza Editorial, 1988), 21, 192–200, 135–36.

20. Cárdenas, *Problemas*, 265–66.

21. Ibid., 270, 273.

22. Ibid., 206, 208, 242–43. See also Brading, *First America*, 200, 298; Anthony Pagden, "Dispossessing the Barbarian," in *The Languages of Political Theory in Early Modern Europe*, ed. Pagden (Cambridge: Cambridge University Press, 1987), 57; and Cañizares-Esguerra, "New World, New Stars."

23. Cárdenas, *Problemas*, 140, 143.

24. Barrios in León Pinelo, *Questión moral*, fol. 116.

25. Acosta, *Historia natural*, fol. 117v.

26. Cárdenas, *Problemas*, 146.

27. Ibid., 144.

28. Ibid., 248–49. Augustín Farfán similarly discussed the habit of women in New Spain of consuming chocolate ("eaten and drunk") "at all hours of the day and many of the night": *Tractado breve de medicina y de todas las enfermedades* (Mexico City: Pedro Ocharte, 1592), fol. 33v. See also Cárdenas, *Problemas*, 248, n. 68, and Luis Castillo Ledón, *El Chocolate* (Mexico City: Dir. Gen. de Bellas Artes, 1917), 22.

29. Cárdenas, *Problemas*, 146.

30. Cárdenas also intervened in the still unsettled controversy concerning whether drinking chocolate violated the ecclesiastical fast—he thought it did—desiring to "refute and banish from the populace the ignorance and terrible error surrounding these drinks of poçole, cacao, chocolate, pinole, chicha, and others of this type one has in the Indies," *Problemas*, 148–49.

31. My emphasis. Barrios in León Pinelo, *Question moral*, fol. 116v. Even in choosing Hernández as his main authority, Barrios was already situating chocolate closer to Nahua cultural practices than Cárdenas did.

32. Barrios in León Pinelo, *Question moral*, fols. 116v–117r. In *Chocolate y tabaco*, the cleric Tomás Hurtado adopted this view in order to provide another piece of evidence that chocolate was in fact a "drink" and hence could be consumed during a fast.

33. Barrios in León Pinelo, *Question moral*, fol. 117r; León Pinelo echoed this sentiment, fol. 9r.

34. Cárdenas, *Problemas*, 274, 34. On the hallucinogenic effects and idolatrous associations of *poyomatli* (Nah.), see Alberro, *Les Espagnols*, 70; for peyote and morning glory seeds, see Aguirre Beltrán, *Medicina*, 130–37, 140.

35. Cárdenas, *Problemas*, 195–96.

36. Ibid., 268.

37. Ibid.

38. Sánchez de Aguilar, "Idolatrías, supersticiones, hechicerías," in *Tratado de las idolatrías, supersticiones, dioses, ritos hechicerías y otras costumbres gentílicas de las razas aborígenes de Mexico*, ed., notes, and intro. Francisco del Paso y Troncoso (Mexico City: Ediciones Fuente Cultural, 1953), 2:279; see also Diego López de Cogolludo, *Historia de Yucatán* (1688), facsimile ed. (Mexico: Editorial Academia Literaria, 1957), 1:184; Gruzinksi, *Conquest*, 148.

39. Hernando Ruiz de Alarcón, *Treatise on the Heathen Superstitions and Customs that Today Live among the Indians Native to this New Spain, 1629*, eds. and trans. J. Richard Andrews and Ross Hassig (Norman: University of Oklahoma Press, 1984), 83.

40. Prior to 1571, deterring and punishing Indian paganism was the job of regular and secular clergy armed with "special dispensation to . . . carry out inquisitorial functions." Once the Holy Office came to Mexico City in 1571, "Indians were now exempted from the Inquisition's attentions. Vigilance over their faith was left to the bishops, who were, however, no longer inquisitors. But the rest of the colonial population, Spanish or mixed-blood . . . were grist to the inquisitorial mill": Peter Bakewell, *A History of Latin America: Empires and Sequels, 1450–1930* (Oxford: Blackwell, 1977), 135, 139.

41. Jacinto de la Serna, "Manual de ministros de indios para el conocimiento de sus idolatrías y extirpación de ellas," in *Tratado de las idolatrías*, 1:239.

42. On chocolate and Juana de Sossa, see "Proceso y causa criminal contra María de Rivera mulata libre natural y vezina de la Ciudad de la Puebla de los Angeles," Banc. Mss 96/95 1652, fols. 3r–3v; on chocolate and María de Riviera, fol. 121r.

43. María Agueda Méndez has found numerous cases of this sort in the archives of the Inquisition of New Spain: "Una relación conflictiva: La Inquisición novohispana y el chocolate," *Caravelle* 71 (1998): 9, as has Martha Few, "Chocolate, Sex, and Disorderly Women in Late-Seventeenth- and Early-Eighteenth-Century Guatemala," *Ethnohistory* 52, no. 4 (2005): 673–87. There is also a mention of chocolate in the case footnoted by Aguirre Beltrán, *Medicina*, 340.

44. This is suggested by the ambiguous setting of the dialogue and references to consumption in both the Americas and Spain. Bartolomé Marradón, *Diálogo del uso del tabaco, los*

daños que causa, etc. Y de chocolate y otras bebidas (Seville: Gabriel Ramos Vejarano, 1618). The only surviving exemplar of the original Spanish edition is in the Vatican Library. Unable to consult it, I relied on Bartolomé Marradón, "Dialogue du Chocolate," in *Traitez nouveaux & curieux du café, du thé, et du chocolat*, trans. Phillipe Sylvestre Dufour (Lyon: Jean Girin and B. Riviere, 1685), 423–25, and the excerpts on tobacco in Silvia Monti, ed., *Il tabaco fa male? Medicina, ideologia, letteratura nella polemica sulla diffusione di un prodotto del Nuevo Mondo* (Milan: Franco Angeli, 1987) 88, n. 15.

45. Marradón was nicknamed "the physician of Marchena" in reference to his hometown near Seville (in other documents he appeared as an apothecarist). It seems likely the opinions of his characters reflected some of his own experiences—and increasing opportunities to use it in Spain. AGI Contrat., leg. 5360, no. 8; on his daughter's request for a license to unite with her husband in the Indies, leg. 5407, no. 8.

46. Culling from Ximénez's translation of Francisco Hernández, the Indian personage compared the cacao tree to an orange tree and its pod to "a large cucumber, though red and grooved": Marradón, "Dialogue du Chocolate"; cf. Francisco Hernández, *Quatro libros de la naturaleza y virtudes de las plantas y animales*, trans. Francisco Ximénez (Mexico: Viuda de Diego Lopez Davalos, 1615), fol. 33v; following Acosta, he remarked that the cacao beans resembled almonds and were the object of a lucrative trade. He noted four varieties of the cacao tree and their need for companion trees to provide protective shade: Acosta, *Historia natural*, fols. 163r–164.

47. Marradón, "Dialogue du Chocolate," 425–26.
48. Ibid., 430–32; Cárdenas, *Problemas*, 145–46.
49. Marradón, "Dialogue du Chocolate," 436–38.
50. Ibid., 444–45.

7. Commodifying across the Atlantic

1. *Cartas privadas de emigrantes a Indias, 1540–1616*, ed. Enrique Otte ([Seville?]: Consejería de Cultura, Junta de Andalucía, 1988).
2. The *avería* (fleet) tax was collected to pay for the defense of the Spanish fleets.
3. Sophie D. Coe and Michael D. Coe provide 1585 as the date of the "first official shipment of beans" to Seville but do not indicate their source, *The True History of Chocolate* (London: Thames and Hudson, 1996), 133.
4. Sarah Augusta Dickson, *Panacea or Precious Bane: Tobacco in Sixteenth Century Literature* (New York: New York Public Library, 1954), 5, 57–58; Jordan Goodman, *Tobacco in History: The Cultures of Dependence* (London: Routledge, 1993), 41–44; Sophie D. Coe and Michael D. Coe, *The True History of Chocolate* (New York: Thames and Hudson, 1996), 126; Alan Davidson, "Europeans' Wary Encounter with Potatoes, Tomatoes, and Other New World Foods," in *Chilies to Chocolate: Food the Americas Gave the World*, ed. Nelson Foster and Linda S. Cordell (Tucson: University of Arizona Press, 1992), 3; Ken Albala, "The Use and Abuse of Chocolate in 17th Century Medical Theory," *Food and Foodways* 15, no. 1–2 (2007): 53–74.
5. The account books for the apothecary of Seville's Hospital Cinco Llagas for the years 1595, 1624, 1625, 1635, and 1636 revealed regular imports of New World medicines *Cassia fistula*, sarsaparilla, and *mechoacan*, with scattered imports of *jalapa*, *caraña*, and *palo de China*: "Gastos de despensa," Hospital Cinco Llagas, ADS, leg. 110. There are numerous purchases of sarsaparilla, *Cassia fistula*, and a few of *mechoacan* and *palo santo* in 1624 and 1625, leg. 114, fol. 61r (*jalapa*), fol. 65v (*mechoacan* and *caraña*); fol. 65r (*palo santo*); 1635, leg. 116, fol. 67r (*jalapa, mechoacan, palo de china*, sarsaparilla); and 1636, leg. 116, fol. 68r (*Cassia fistula*), fol. 70r (tobacco purchased on Nov. 30 and Dec. 14). Tobacco does appear in the apothecary account book of 1636, but by then it was already well established as a recreational drug, thus not giving any support to the interpretation it arrived *first* as medicine.

In addition, several pharmaceutical inventories in notarial archives in Madrid and Seville showed *mechoacan*, *palo santo*, *tacama* (*tacamahaca* or *Elaphrium tecomaca*), sassafras, but no tobacco or chocolate. *Mechoacan* appears in two of three of the pharmaceutical inventories I consulted in the Madrid notarial archive: "media libra de mechoacan, 4 reales," AHPM, lib. 3873 (1623), fol. 13r; lib. 1733 (1589), fol. 188r; and in the two 1570 inventories from Seville in Mercedes Fernández-Carrión and José Luis Valverde, *Farmacia y sociedad en Sevilla en el siglo XVI* (Seville: Servicio de Publicaciones del Ayuntamiento de Sevilla, 1985), 51, and another in a Valladolid apothecary in Félix Francisco Pastor Frechoso, *Boticas, boticarios, y materia médica en Valladolid, S. XVI–XVII* (Salamanca: Junta de Castilla y León, 1993), 270; *Palo sancto* is in the 1589 inventory (lib. 1733, fol. 189v) and 1623 (lib. 3873, fol. 11r). Four ounces of *tacama* also appear in 1623 (fol. 12r). "[S]axafras de la yndia" appears in the 1628 inventory (lib. 5929, fol. 55r). On these and other American drugs, see Fernández-Carrión and Valverde, *Farmacia y sociedad*, 51, 80, 81, 83.

6. Antonio Castell, *Theorica y pratica de boticarios, en que se trata de la arte y forma como se han de componer las confecciones ansi interiores como exteriores* (Barcelona: Sebastián de Cormellas, 1592), fols. 292v, 292r. He also quoted the section by Hernández on tobacco; Juan de Castro y Medinilla, *Historia de las virtudes y propiedades del tabaco* (Cordoba: Salvador de Cea Tesa, 1620).

7. Castro y Medinilla, *Historia de las virtudes*, fols. 13v, 15r; for examples of indigenous use of green tobacco topical applications, see Johannes Wilbert, *Tobacco and Shamanism in South America* (New Haven: Yale University Press, 1987), 189, 191–92.

8. AGI Contrat., leg. 2595, fol. 66r.

9. AGI Contrat., leg. 4389, shipment no. 221.

10. AGI Contrat., leg. 4389.

11. Eufemio Lorenzo Sanz, *Comercio de España con América en la epoca de Felipe II*, vol. 1., *Los mercaderes y el trafico indiano* (Valladolid: Servicio de Publicaciones de la Diputación Provincial de Valladolid, 1979), 380.

12. AGI Contrat., leg. 1786, "Ambrosio Sofia, 1602, venida de Santo Domingo," fols. 9v–10r.

13. "El fiscal contra Ambrosio Sofia maestre sobre lo que resulto de su visita" (1607), AGI Contrat., leg. 5733, no. 11. The biographical details are from this case. Another clue linking Sofia to the Portuguese network was that one of the witnesses testifying on his behalf was a Lisbonite temporarily residing in Seville.

14. Lorenzo Sanz, *Comercio de España con América*, 1:336, 395. Their chocolate purchases were registered in AGI Contrat., legs. 4389, 4412. The prominent merchant Cristóbal de Ribera shipped chocolate in 1595, leg. 4424, fols. 60r–60v. The small quantities (one box apiece, which ranged between twenty and one hundred pounds), particularly in comparison with the massive amounts of bullion and dye goods they were importing, suggest autoconsumption.

15. Quoted in Enriqueta Vila Vilar, *Los Corzo y los Mañara: Tipos y arquetipos del mercader con Indias* (Seville: Consejo Superior de Investigaciones Científicas, 1991), 115; chocolate purchase in AGI Contrat., leg. 4452, shipment no. 649.

Other prominent merchants who appear as precocious chocolate buyers were Martín de Tirapau, one box of chocolate in 1615, leg. 4440, fol. 125r; four boxes of chocolate in 1625, leg. 4452, fols. 128v, 98r; Cristóbal de Barrionuevo, one box of chocolate in 1615, leg., 4440, fol. 166r. The Honduran Carmona shipping family (Hernando, Bartolomé, and Juan) bought one box of chocolate in 1602 (leg. 4412, shipment no. 70), one box in 1612 (leg. 2129, fol. 53), and two boxes in 1615 (leg. 4440, fols. 174v, 176r). In 1625 the Neve brothers purchased seven boxes of chocolate (and a box of achiote), leg. 4452, fols. 111r, 125r, 130r, 149r; by 1634 it is clear they were significant chocolate and cacao importers, for that year they shipped eleven thousand pounds of cacao, as well as five boxes of chocolate (leg. 4462, fols. 143r, 261r, 261v, 301r). In 1615 Jorge Reynoso imported three boxes of chocolate (leg. 4440, fols. 133r, 166r); in 1625, fifteen boxes of chocolate (leg. 4452, fols. 114r, 116v, 124r, 125, 128v, 129r, 199r). Tomás Mañara bought a thirty-pound box of chocolate (leg. 4462, fol. 320v) in 1635. Antonio María Bucarelli was registered for a box of chocolate in 1625, two boxes in 1634, and one in 1635 (the latter box was duty free, indicating that it was for personal consumption), leg. 4452, fol. 90v; leg. 4462, fols. 137r, 265r.

Martín de Tirapau was a merchant-guild officeholder in 1622 and 1629; the Neve brothers also held office in the guild, and their descendants became the marquéses of Moscoso; Jorge Reynoso was an established Sevillan merchant by 1594, when he sold goods worth 311,525 *maravedís*; Antonio María Bucarelli was administrator of the fleet tax in 1631, and his descendants became the marquéses de Vallehermoso. Tomás Mañara was one of the most famous merchants of his day. Enriqueta Vila Vilar, "El poder del Consulado sevillano y los hombres del comercio en el siglo XVII: Una aproximación," in *Relaciones de poder y comercio colonial: Nuevas perspectivas*, ed. Enriqueta Vila Vilar and Allan J. Kuethe (Seville: Escuela de Estudios Hispano-Americanos; Lubbock: Texas Tech University, 1999), 30–31; Lorenzo Sanz, *Comercio de España con América*, 1:394; Vila Vilar, *Los Corzo y los Mañara*.

16. AGI Contrat., leg. 4424, fols. 41r, 105r.

17. Vila Vilar, "El poder del Consulado sevillano," 12–20. Precocious chocolate purchasers who held office in the guild included Juan and Miguel de Neve, Tomás Mañara, Rodrigo de Vadillo, Cristobal de Barrionuevo, and Martín de Tirapu. Vila Vilar, "El poder del Consulado sevillano," 30–31; Vila Vilar, *Los Corzo y los Mañara*, 118

18. Vila Vilar, *Los Corzo y los Mañara*, 102, 121–31, 138, 153, 156, 172, 192, 206–7; Vila Vilar, "El poder del Consulado sevillano," 10, 14–16, 30–31.

19. On use of agents, see Vila Vilar, *Los Corzo y los Mañara*, 106.

20. Auke P. Jacobs, *Los movimientos migratorios entre Castilla e Hispanoamérica durante el reinado de Felipe III, 1598–1621* (Atlanta: Rodopi, 1995), 160.

21. AGI Contrat., leg. 4424, shipment no. 770; leg. 2129, fol. 43; leg. 4462, fol. 282: chocolate shipments from 1608, 1612, 1634.

22. "Juan de Obiedo vezino de la villa de Poza con Alváro González de la Fragata el Rosario—sobre cobrarle el importe de una partida de tabaco" (1612), AGI Contrat. 781, no. 2; "Autos de Antón Martín, maestre, con Ruy Pérez Cabrera, vecino de Sevilla, sobre que recibiese una pipa de tabaco" (1612), ibid., leg. 782, no. 3; the shipment was consigned to the canon Juan de la Villanueva and Baltasar de Sepúlveda, fol. 3r.

23. AGI Contrat., leg. 825, no. 8; see also Marradón, *Diálogo*.

24. AGI Contrat., leg. 4464, fols. 261, 264, 281.

25. *Thomas Gage's Travels in the New World*, ed. J. Eric S. Thompson (Norman: University of Oklahoma Press, 1958), 7–8.

26. AGI Contrat., leg. 4389, shipment no. 180.

27. AGI Contrat., leg. 4440, fol. 130v; in 1625 the Marqués of Montesclaros shipped a considerable quantity of chocolate, leg. 4452, fol. 116r.

28. Alonso Ulloa de Toro to Esteban Ulloa de Toro, "escribano mayor," AGI Contrat., leg. 2411, fol. 816r; Gerónimo Pedro de Alvares, a regidor of Santo Domingo was the shipper, fol. 851r; Quesada de Figueroa, fol. 859v.

29. Vila Vilar, *Los Corzo y los Mañara*, 102, 121–31, 138, 153, 156, 172, 192, 206–7; Vila Vilar, "El poder del Consulado sevillano," 10, 14–16, 30–31.

30. "Autos de Diego Jiménez de Encisco, tesorero de la contratación, con Francisco Goicoechea, sobre que le entregue tres arrobas de chocolate," (1633) AGI Contrat., leg. 824ᵃ no. 8.

31. AGI Contrat., leg. 4389, shipment no. 225.

32. Ibid. The two clear prices were for thirty and twenty *reales*, which indicates that the boxes could contain no more than thirty pounds of chocolate. At a *very* conservative estimate of a small serving size of one ounce, twice a day, for a household of eight for a consumption of sixteen ounces a day, the fifty pounds would last fifty days.

33. AGI Contrat., leg. 4412, shipment no. 13; leg. 4424, fol. 196v; leg. 4440, fol. 149r.

34. AGI Contrat., leg. 2129, fols. 78v–79r, 138v.

35. Indian demographic catastrophe and Spanish pressure to overproduce led traditional pre-Hispanic cacao-producing regions to go into decline in southern Mexico (Tabasco and Soconusco) and to the development of new regions for cultivation or intensification (the Sonsonate region in Guatemala and El Salvador). By the late sixteenth century, Guatemala was the prime producer of cacao. In 1560, the captaincy-general of Guatemala supplied Mexico with over one million pounds of cacao, and by 1576 the number reached 2.5 million. In time,

the pattern of overexploitation and subsequent collapse repeated itself. At the beginning of the seventeenth century, Guatemalan export crops of cacao for central Mexico are estimated to be between six and nine million pounds, but by the end of the seventeenth century, the region exported only three hundred thousand pounds: Dauril Alden, "The Significance of Cacao Production in the Amazon Region during the Late Colonial Period: An Essay in Comparative Economic History," *Proceedings of the American Philosophical Society* 120, no. 2 (April 1976): 104–6; for shortsighted Spanish exploitation of cacao producers in Soconusco and then the Sonsonate, see Murdo J. MacLeod, *Spanish Central America* (Berkeley: University of California Press, 1973), 68–94, 235–52; Juan López de Velasco, *Geografía y descripción universal de las Indias,* ed. Marcos Jiménez de la Espada (Madrid: Atlas, 1971), 150, 153.

36. This section follows Marcy Norton and Daviken Studnicki-Gizbert, "Imperial Rivalries and Commercial Collaboration: Portuguese and English Merchants and the Formation of an Atlantic Tobacco Trade, 1492–1650," in *The Atlantic World and Virginia, 1550–1624,* ed. Peter C. Mancall (Chapel Hill: University of North Carolina Press for the Omohundro Institute, 2007), 251–73.

37. Huguette Chaunu and Pierre Chaunu, *Séville et l'Atlantique, 1504–1650,* 8 vols. (Paris: S.E.V.P.E.N., 1956–59), vol. 8, bk. 1; Kenneth R. Andrews, *The Spanish Caribbean: Trade and Plunder* (New Haven: Yale University Press, 1978), 11, 14, 54–70; Engel Sluiter, "Dutch–Spanish Rivalry in the Caribbean Area, 1594–1609," *Hispanic American Historical Review* 28 (May 1948): 165–96; Pedro Pérez Herrero, "La estructura comercial del Caribe en la segunda mitad del siglo xvi," *Revista de Indias* 47, no. 181 (1987): 788–810.

38. Andrews, *Spanish Caribbean,* 54–55, 59, 70; Sluiter, "Dutch–Spanish Rivalry," 171.

39. See chap. 4 of this book and Arie Boomert, "The Arawak Indians of Trinidad and Coastal Guiana, ca. 1500–1650," in *Journal of Caribbean History* 19, no. 2 (Nov. 1982): 132; Neil Whitehead, *Lords of the Tiger Spirit: A History of the Caribs in Colonial Venezuela and Guyana, 1498–1820* (Dordrecht: Foris Publications, 1988), 18; Cornelius Ch. Goslinga, *The Dutch in the Caribbean and on the Wild Coast, 1580–1680* (Gainesville: University of Florida Press, 1971), 76.

40. Francis Drake, *Sir Francis Drake's West Indian Voyage 1585–86,* ed. Mary Frear Keeler (London: Haklyut Society, 1981), 111, 193, 236.

41. Joyce Lorimer, "The English Contraband Tobacco Trade in Trinidad and Guiana, 1590–1617," in *The Westward Enterprise: English Activities in Ireland, the Atlantic, and America, 1480–1650,* ed. K. Andrews, N. P. Canny, and P. E. H. Hair, 124–50 (Liverpool: Liverpool University Press, 1978), 125; Andrews, *Spanish Caribbean,* 225.

42. C. T., *An Advice how to plant tobacco in England* (London: Nicholas Okes, 1615), fol. B.

43. Andrews, *Spanish Caribbean,* 75–107, 175–81.

44. Norton and Studnicki-Gizbert, "Imperial Rivalries and Commercial Collaboration," 261; Domingo de Vera Ybargoien to Philip II, 1595, BL Add. Mss. 36315, fol. 264v.

45. Mercedes Ruiz Tirado, *Tabaco y sociedad en Barinas, siglo XVII* (Mérida, Venezuela: Universidad de los Andes, 2000), 77; "Memorial de López de Castro para el remedio de los rescates en la Isla Española" (1598), in Emilio Rodríguez Demorizi, *Relaciones históricas de Santo Domingo* (Ciudad Trujillo, Dominican Republic: Editoria Montalvo, 1945), 2:166; E. Arcila Farias, *Economía colonial de Venezuela* (Caracas: Italgrafica, 1973), 1:113, 131.

46. It's not clear whether this began at the end of the sixteenth century or at an earlier date: Goodman, *Tobacco in History,* 140.

47. Daviken Studnicki-Gizbert, *A Nation upon the Ocean Sea: Portugal's Atlantic Diaspora and the Crisis of the Spanish Empire, 1492–1640* (New York: Oxford University Press, 2007), 28–29; Clarence H. Haring, *Trade and Navigation between Spain and the Indies* (Cambridge: Harvard University Press, 1918).

48. Andrews, *Spanish Caribbean,* 178–79, 226–27.

49. Sancho de Alquiza, "Por una real cédula de 26 agosto del año pasado," June 15, 1607; see also C. T., *An Advice,* fol. A3.

50. Royal decree to the Audiencia de Santo Domingo, Aug. 26, 1606, AGI SDom., leg. 869, l. 5, fols. 59v–63r; Andrews, *Spanish Caribbean*, 214.

51. "Real cedula a los gobernadores de las provincias de Indias levantando la prohibición del cultivo de tabaco en las islas de Barlovento y Venzuela," Oct. 20, 1614; AGI SDom., leg., 869, l. 6, fols. 206v–207r; leg. 193, r. 16, n. 70.

52. Fleet tax records indicate shipments of tobacco from Margarita and Caracas in 1608, AGI Contrat., leg. 4424.

53. Referring to "Indians of War of Cumanagote" cultivating tobacco: "Copia de un capitulo de carta que Pedro Suarez Coronel, Governador de la Provincia de Cumana escrivio a su Majestad en 25 de Junio de 1610," AGI SDom., leg. 187, r. 4, n. 26; Whitehead, *Lords of the Tiger Spirit*, 84–85.

54. "Suministro de tabaco a ingleses por García Girón," May 29, 1612, AGI SDom., leg. 869, l. 6, fol. 142r.

55. Lorimer, "English Contraband Tobacco," 124–50.

56. Quoted in ibid., 131–32.

57. Quoted in ibid., 132–33, 136.

58. "Real cedula a los gobernadores de las provincias de Indias levantando la prohibición del cultivo de tabaco en las islas de Barlovento y Venzuela," Oct. 20, 1614; AGI SDom., leg., 869, l. 6, fols. 206v–207r.

59. In addition to the specific sources cited, the following draws from Norton and Studnicki-Gizbert, "Imperial Rivalries and Commercial Collaboration," 266–73. For the "Portuguese Mercantile Nation" more generally, see chap. 9 and Studnicki-Gizbert, *A Nation upon the Ocean Sea*.

60. Studnicki-Gizbert, *A Nation upon the Ocean Sea*, 17–18, 25–26.

61. Ibid., 50; Pablo E. Pérez Mallaína, *Spain's Men of the Sea: Daily Life on the Indies Fleets in the Sixteenth Century*, trans. Carla Rahn Phillips (Baltimore: Johns Hopkins University Press, 1998).

62. Andrews, *Spanish Caribbean*, 38; Pérez Herrero, "La estructura comercial del caribe," 788.

63. "Relación de los estrangeros flamencos yngleses franceses ytalianos Portugueses que residen en la ciudad de Santiago de León y otras desta provinica de Venezuela son los siguientes en esta manera," AGI SDom., leg. 193, r. 15, n. 50.

64. Andrews, *Spanish Caribbean*, 38; Pérez Herrero, "La estructura comercial del Caribe," 788; Sluiter, "Dutch–Spanish Rivalry," 169, 175; Lorimer, "English Contraband Tobacco," 138–39, 144, 149.

65. Norton and Studnicki-Gizbert, "Imperial Rivalries and Commercial Collaboration," 271.

66. Among those purchasing tobacco in 1598 and 1599 were Diego Pérez de Porras, Gaspar de Acosta, Pedro Miranda Belas, and [missing or illegible first name] Pereira, AGI Contrat., leg. 2411, fols. 859v–861r–v, 965v–966r, 1002r–v, 1029r–v.

67. "Real Cedula de Instrucción ... Don Diego Pinelo nombrandole Factor y Administrador del Tabaco que se cria y coge en los lugares Maritimos y Mediterraneos de las Indias Occidentales ...," May 25, 1620, BPR, Mss. II/2889, fols. 21r—33v. This is an eighteenth-century copy. See also documents from the Casa de Contratación concerning Pinelo's tenure in Chaunu and Chaunu, *Séville*, 4:575–78.

68. "Real Cedula de Instrucción dada ... a Don Diego Pinelo ... ," fols. 22v–23r.

69. See also "Con los despachos para firmar sobre el estanco del tabaco en Indias, y el nombramiento Diego Pinelo para administrador," May 9, 1620, AGI Indif., leg. 753; Garzon Pareja, "El tabaco," 240.

70. Chaunu and Chaunu, *Séville*, 4:578.

71. Prominent Portuguese merchants purchasing tobacco from Maracaibo in 1635 were Enrique de Andrade, Simon Fonseca Piña, and Manuel Duarte, AGI Contrat., leg. 4462. Studnicki-Gizbert identified these as Portuguese, referring to Andrade as "probably the patron of the Portuguese merchant community in Seville": *A Nation upon the Ocean Sea*, 102.

72. George Louis Beer, *The Origins of the British Colonial System, 1576–1660* (New York: MacMillan Company, 1908), 79. For English concerns about the importation of Spanish tobacco, see Theodore Rabb, *Jacobean Gentleman: Sir Edwyn Sandy, 1561–1629* (Princeton: Princeton University Press, 1998), 229–40.

73. Goodman, *Tobacco in History*, 138–55.

74. Norton and Studnicki-Gizbert, "Imperial Rivalries and Commercial Collaboration," 251–73; Philip R. Morgan, "Virginia's Other Prototype: The Caribbean," in *The Atlantic World and Virginia, 1550–1624*, ed. Peter C. Mancall (Chapel Hill: University of North Carolina Press for the Omohundro Institute, 2007), 361–64.

75. C. T., *An Advice*, fol. A3.

76. Morgan, "Virginia's Other Prototype," 359.

77. Norton and Studnicki-Gizbert, "Imperial Rivalries and Commercial Collaboration," 253–54.

78. Morgan, "Virginia's Other Prototype," 362.

79. Castro y Medinilla, *Historia de las virtudes*, fol. 20v; Goodman, *Tobacco in History*, 43.

80. Pérez Mallaína, *Spain's Men of the Sea*, 23, 115.

81. Ibid., 6–7, 15–17.

82. *Romance en alabanza del tabaco* (Barcelona: Gabriel Nogués, 1644).

83. Pérez Mallaína, *Spain's Men of the Sea*, 38–39.

84. Ibid., 150.

85. Haring, *Trade and Navigation*, 67.

86. "Los Interessados mercaderes y personas vezinos . . . ," fol. 41v, 41r, AGS DGT, inv. 4, leg. 29. Though this observation dates from the 1630s, by which time tobacco was an Atlantic staple, it seems all the more likely this phenomena was in place in earlier years.

87. Pérez Mallaína, *Spain's Men of the Sea*, 50.

88. Castro y Medinilla, *Historia de las virtudes*, fols. 20v, 39. Francisco del Leiva y Aguilar, *Desengaño contra el mal vso de tabaco* (Cordoba: Salvador de Cea Tesa, 1634), fol. 5v.

89. In works by Miguel de Cervantes inns appear as places frequented by those of different social status and even places where those of the upper classes sometimes succumbed to the attractions of the picaresque life. For instance, see Miguel de Cervantes, "The Illustrious Kitchen Maid," in *Exemplary Stories*, trans. Lesley Lipson (Oxford: Oxford University Press, 1998), 185–235.

90. Quiñones de Benavente, *Dos Gaiferos: Entremés famoso*, quoted in José Romera Castillo, "Los entreméses y el descubrimiento," in *Las Indias (América) en la literatura del siglo de oro*, ed. Ignacio Arellano ([Pamplona]: Gobierno de Navarra, Departamento de Educación y Cultura; Kassel: Edition Reichenberger, 1992), 124.

91. Of 295 retailers selling chocolate in 1721, one of them was identified as a tavern: AVM Sec. 3, leg. 277, no. 8.

92. Brian Cowan, *The Social Life of Coffee: The Emergence of the British Coffeehouse* (New Haven: Yale University Press, 2005).

93. Castro y Medinilla, *Historia de las virtudes*, fols. 21r, 20v.

94. Leiva y Aguilar, *Desengaño*, fols. 8v, 263v; Cristóbal de Hayo, *Las excelencias y maravillosas propiedades del tabaco, conforme a gravissimos Autores, y grandes experiencias* (Salamanca: Diego de Cossío, 1645), proemio.

95. AFTS, series 2.1, leg. 132, "Cartas del superintendente general de la renta," Feb. 21, 1722; see also letter from Feb. 17, 1722 in ibid. A number of Dutch painters showed women smoking, as does figure 8.5. Note, too, that a number of the registered tobacco vendors in 1641 were women.

96. El Capitán Castro de Torres, *Panegírico al chocolate*, ed. Manuel Pérez de Guzmán (Segovia, 1640; Seville: E. Rasco, 1887), 12. Citation is to E. Rasco edition. BL Eg. Mss. 2055, fol. 192.

97. Lutgardo García Fuentes, *El comercio español con América, 1650–1700* (Seville: Escuela de Estudios Hispano-Americanos, 1980), 353, 359, 369.

98. Luis Márquez Cardoso and Manuel Cáceres, *Memorial dado a su Mgd por D[o]n Luis Marquez Cardoso sobre estancar la oja de tavaco q[ue] viene de Indias* (Madrid, 1682), fol. 1v, NYPL Arents no. 375.

99. Wim Klooster, *Illicit Riches: The Dutch Trade in the Caribbean, 1648–1795* (Leiden: KITLV Press, 1998), 182–86, 188–91, 228–231; the statistic is on 240.

100. Márquez Cardoso and Cáceres, *Memorial*, fol. 1v.

101. José Manuel Rodríguez Gordillo, "Las estadísticas de la Renta del Tabaco en el siglo XVIII: nuevas aportaciones," in *El mercado del tabacdo en España durante el siglo XVIII*, ed. Santiago de Luxán Meléndez, Sergio Solbes Ferri, and Juan José Laforet (Las Palmas de Gran Canaria: Fundación Altadis [2000]), 66. I derived a population estimate of about 6 million for Castile for the late seventeenth century and eight million for 1739 based on the figures in Jordi Nadal, *La población española, siglos XIV a XX* rev. ed. (Barcelona: Ariel, 1984), 74–75. Both figures are probably maximums, so per capita levels were probably higher for this reason as well.

102. On annual per capita pipe estimates, see Carole Shammas, "Changes in English and Anglo-American consumption from 1550 to 1800," in *Consumption and the World of Goods*, ed. John Brewer and Roy Porter (London: Routledge, 1994), 180; on lesser amounts needed for snuff tobacco, Goodman, *Tobacco in History*, 73.

103. On English estimates, Shammas, "Changes," 180; for Europe, Goodman, *Tobacco in History*, 73.

104. David R. Ringrose, *Madrid and the Spanish Economy, 1560–1850* (Berkeley: University of California Press, 1983); José Luis de los Reyes Leoz, "Evolución de la población, 1561–1857," in *Madrid: Atlas histórico de la ciudad*, ed. Virgilio Pinto Crespo and Santos Madrazo Madrazo (Madrid: Fundación Caja de Madrid, 1995), 140–49.

105. AVM Sec. 3, leg. 277, exp. 8. I am grateful to José Ubaldo Bernardos Sanz for telling me about this document.

106. For proportions, see recipes of chocolate guild, AVM Sec. 2, leg. 245, exp. 1, "Expedientes con motivo del establecimiento del gremio de chocolateros," Aug. 29, 1774. The best grade of chocolate had 25 lbs. cacao, 16.5 lbs. sugar, and 10 oz. cinnamon; medium grade had 25 lbs. cacao, 18 lbs. sugar, and 8 oz. cinnamon; low grade had 19 lbs. cacao, 21 lbs. sugar, and 4 oz. cinnamon. The lower grades of chocolate combined Guayaquil and Caracas cacao, which dictated larger quantities of sugar to reduce bitterness; the best chocolate grade used solely Caracas cacao. Thus, my figures underestimate the amount of chocolate that would be produced from the cacao, since they assume the 2:1 ratio of the better grade.

107. The "typical" number of servings ranged from several weekly to several daily; typical serving amount seemed to range from one to six ounces. One "expert" recommended several times a week: Santiago Valverde Turices, *Un discurso de chocolate* (Seville: Juan de Cabrera, 1624). Antonio de León Pinelo wrote that three servings per day was standard [*de tabla*], *Questión moral: si el chocolate quebranta el ayuno eclesiástico* (Madrid: Viuda de Juan González, 1636), fol. 8v. Municipal and chocolate guild sources frequently describe chocolate being sold by the ounce: a price list from February 1775 lists chocolate sold "by the ounce, retail" for 18 *maravedís*, "Expedientes con motivo del establecimiento del gremio de chocolateros." A late eighteenth-century manuscript asserted that the norm was for "ecclesiastics and *gentes de estudio* to consume a large one of two ounces, and others to consume a medium size of 1.5 ounces, and children a small one of one ounce, which often serves adults on fasting days in the morning as *parva materia*, many [on those days] customarily have a large *jícara* in the evening *colación*": "Apuntamientos sobre el chocolate" (San Sebastian, April 23, 1790), RAH, papeles varios, 9/5876.

108. This assumes chocolate costing eight *reales* per pound, the price set by the guild for the medium grade—the superior was nine and the inferior seven *reales* per pound, "Expedientes," Aug. 29, 1774. Note, however, that the estimate, based on tax records amounts, for Madrid's cacao imports in 1789 is 1,198,837 pounds (which would result in about 1,798,300 pounds of chocolate), Ringrose, *Madrid and the Spanish Economy*, 364. Fraud and smuggling could account for some but probably not all of the discrepancy.

109. I am grateful to Jesús Cruz for shedding light on the retail structure of Madrid in this period.

110. The contracts are in AHPM, libs. 5655 and 5668 (1641), notary Domingo Alvárez.

111. For this and subsequent estimates for the population of Madrid, see Reyes Leoz, "Evolución de la población," 141.

112. AHPM lib. 5655, fol. 433.

113. AHPM, lib 5668 (1641), fol. 2. other contracts with female vendors are in lib. 5668, fols. 59, 90, 137, 253, 359, 360, and lib. 5655, fols. 385, 433.

114. AHPM, lib 5668, fol. 113. Also in this elite group was Miguel Nuñez (whose name hints at Portuguese ancestry), obligated to sell the largest amount of tobacco among the vendors, whose establishment was known as "the Seville store," indicating that he, too, specialized in luxuries from the Indies.

115. AHN Cons., lib. 1173, fol. 98v.

116. Matilde Santamaría Arnaïz, "La alimentación de los españoles bajo el reinado de los Austrias," Ph. diss., Universidad Complutense, Facultad de Farmacía, Madrid, 1986, 723, 725–26.

117. "Expedientes," 1777.

118. Ringrose, *Madrid and the Spanish Economy*, 345–346.

119. "Molenderos de Chocolate" (1788), AVM Sec. 2, leg. 245, exp. 1.

120. AHN Cons., lib. 1173, fol. 98v.

121. Xavier Lencina Pérez, "Los inventarios post-mortem en el estudio de la cultura material el consumo. Propuesta metodológica. Barcelona, siglo XVII," in *Consumo, condiciones de vida y comercialización: Cataluña y Castilla, siglos XVII–XIX*, ed. J. Torras and B. Yun Casalilla (Valladolid: Junta de Castilla y León, Consejería de Educación y Cultura, 1999), 52.

122. Juan de Cárdenas, *Problemas y secretos maravillosos de las Indias*, ed. Angeles Durán (Madrid: Alianza Editorial, 1988), 145–46.

123. Cárdenas, *Problemas*, 146.

124. Ibid., 140–42.

125. Alonso de Molina, *Vocabulario en lengua Castellana y Mexicana* (1571), facsimile (Madrid: Ediciones Cultura Hispanica, 1944), pt. 2, fol. 10v. There is a lot of debate over the linguistic origins of the word "chocolate." I think that it may have derived from the Nahuatl term for "the drink of cacao with dried and ground-up flowers," which Molina referred to as *xochiaya cacautl*, pt. 1, fol. 19v.

126. Cárdenas, *Problemas*, 140, 142–43, 145–46.

127. Ibid., 142–43.

128. For instance, in 1602 fleet tax records indicate six boxes of chocolate and two boxes of cacao, AGI Contrat., leg. 4412.

129. Santamaría Arnaïz, "La alimentación," 712–13.

130. "Sobre el 'servicio' de los dos millones y medio" (1634), AGI Consul., leg. 93, no. 9; BL Eg. Mss. 2055, fol. 146.

131. AGI Contrat., leg. 825, no. 8.

132. Valverde Turices, *Un discurso*, fol. A1–v.

133. On the preference for chilies, see Antonio Colmenero de Ledesma, *Curioso tratado de la naturaleza y calidad del chocolate* (Madrid: Francisco de Martínez, 1631), fols. 4v, 6r, 8r.

134. Molina, *Vocabulario*, 93r, 158v.

135. AGI Contrat., leg. 4389, shipment no. 392; leg. 4412, shipment nos. 13, 601; leg. 4413, shipment no. 708; leg. 4424, fols. 19, 210, 245, 296v; leg. 4440, fols. 132, 133, 139; 4462, fol. 315r. That these were meant to be used with chocolate is indicated by their pairing with chocolate in the manifest, e.g., "un caxon de chocolate y xicaras," AGI Contrat., leg. 4424, fol. 245.

136. "Expedientes . . . gremio de chocolateros." Various classes of chocolate are described, priced between seven and nine *reales* per pound depending on whether the cacao

came from Caracas (the best), Guayaquil, or Brazil. The only listed additives are sugar and cinnamon.

137. Juan Bautista de Pomar, *Relación de Tezcoco: siglo XVI*, facsimile, ed. and intro. Joaquín García Icazbalceta (Mexico City: Biblioteca Enciclopédica del Estado de México, 1975), xviii, 64.

138. Cárdenas, *Problemas*, 198.

139. Pomar, *Relación de Tezcoco*, xviii, 64.

140. "Descripción de Santiago de Leon gobernación de Venezuela . . . Nuestra Señora de Caraballeda," in *Relaciones geográficas de Venezuela*, ed. and intro. Antonio Arellano Moreno (Caracas: Academia Nacional de la Historia, 1964), 130; "Descripción de la ciudad del Tocuyo" (1578), in *Relaciones geográficas de Venezuela*, ed. Arellano Moreno, 141–60.

141. Pedro Simón, *Noticias historiales de las conquistas de Tierra Firme en las Indias occidentales* (Bogota: M. Rivas, 1882–1892), 4:361–62.

142. Molina, *Vocabulario*. It is suggested that the Spanish employed *picietl* as the generic term for tobacco because of its similarity to the Spanish word *pebete*, which refers to the smoking brands used in festivals in Spain: Chita de la Calle, introduction to Muriel N. Porter's "Pipas precortesianas," in *Acta Anthropolgica* 3, no. 2 (1948): 142–43.

143. Castro y Medinilla, *Historia de las virtudes*, fols. 21v–22r; see also Fernando de Almirón Zayas, *Discurso de la anathomia [sic] de algunos miembros del cuerpo humano necessaria en orden a los daños q de continuo uso del tabaco suceden . . .* (Seville: Gabriel Ramos Vejerano, 1623), prologue, fol. 3v; Leiva y Aguilar, *Desengaño*, fols. 44r–v, 263v.

144. Fernando Ortiz, *Cuban Counterpoint: Tobacco and Sugar*, trans. Harriet de Onís (New York: Alfred A. Knopf, 1947; Durham: Duke University Press, 1995), 76–77. Citations are to Duke edition.

145. Castro y Medinilla, *Historia de las virtudes*, fols. 21v–22r, 48v.

146. Goodman, *Tobacco in History*, 67; for the dizzying array of tobacco varieties, see José Manual Rodríguez Gordillo, *Diccionario histórico del tabaco* ([Spain]: Cetarsa, 1993), 206–49.

147. Klooster, *Illicit Riches*, 182, 189–90; *Consulta que propusieron los Arrendadores del efecto del tabaco* (Madrid, 1698), 23; NYPL Arents no. 435, fol. 19v; Goodman, *Tobacco in History*, 67, 79.

8. Consuming Rituals

1. Melchor Valenciano de Mendiolaza, "Quintillas. Chocolate, dulce nombre," *En Real Academia celebrada en el Real de Valencia . . . a los años de Carlos Segundo . . .* (Valencia: Jerónimo Vilagrasa, 1669), 96–91 [error in pagination in original]; Eliseo Armengol, "Mi Musa por ser muger," *En Real Academia celebrada en el Real de Valencia* (Valencia, 1669), 91–92. The presence of these goods is suggested by the poetry topic itself. The inference about the manner of chocolate's presentation comes from the proceedings describing the party accompanying a poetry competition in 1669: Pasqual Mas i Usó, "Justas, Academias, y Convocatorias literarias en la Valencia Barroca (1591–1705): Teoría y práctica de una convención," (PhD diss., Universitat de València, Spain, 1991), 433, http://www.cervantesvirtual.com/FichaObra.html?Ref=12321&ext=pdf&portal=0; and the depiction of chocolate in the aristocratic party in the tile painting *La Xocolatada*. Tobacco's place at such parties is suggested by the descriptions of its use in poems, as well as the gifts of *tabaqueras* at the poetry competitions, since all of the other gifts are items that one would expect to see at aristocratic gatherings (fans, silk stockings, chocolate, silver dining ware, an so forth). On these gifts, see Mas i Usó, "Justas, Academias, y Convocatorias," 302–3, 1067, 1119, 1151, 1157–58.

2. Sebastían de Covarrubias Orozco and Benito Remigio Noydens, *Primera parte del tesoro de la lengua castellaña o española* (Madrid: Melchor Sánchez, 1674), 157. The first edition appeared in 1611. See also Natalie Zemon Davis, *The Gift in Sixteenth-Century France* (Madison: University of Wisconsin Press, 2000).

3. *Sentencia jocosa sobre que dio un juez este presente año en un litigio, que tuvieron*

dos camaradas sobre el . . . el vino, y chocolate, BL Raros (n.p.: Officina de Pedro Ferreira, n.d. [seventeenth century]), 2.

4. Antonio de León Pinelo, *Questión moral: si el chocolate quebranta el ayuno eclesiástico* (Madrid: Viuda de Juan González, 1636), fols. 1v, 15v.

5. *Poética festiva celebridad a los años y nombre de Carlos II* (Valencia: Francisco Mestre, 1691), 43–44, quoted in Mas i Usó, "Justas, Academias, y Convocatorias," 583.

6. *Sentencia jocosa*, 1; also Capitán Castro de Torres, *Panegírico al chocolate*, ed. Manuel Peréz de Guzmán, (Seville: E. Rasco, 1887 [1st ed., Segovia, 1640]), 22.

7. León Pinelo, *Questión moral*, fol. 8v.

8. Sebastián Villaviciosa y Francisco de Avellaneda, *Comedia famosa. Cuantas veo, tantas quiero*, in *Parte veinte y cinco de Comedias nuevas y escogidas de los mejores ingenios de España* (Madrid: Domingo García Morras, 1666), fol. 78v; also fol. 80v.

9. M. Mercè Gras i Casanovas, "Cuerpo y alma en el carmelo descalzo femenino: Una aproximación a la alimentación conventual en la Cataluña moderna," *Studia Historica: Historia Moderna*, 14 (1996): 213–15.

10. "Memoria de las pinturas y alaxas elexidas en las tres casas del Almirante para en parte de pago del credito que contar sus bienes tienen los testamentarios y herederos de Don Jacome [Jacinto?] María Pedesina, que este en el cielo," no date, AHN Cons. leg. 7022, fols. 133r–136v. This was an inventory of paintings in the different rooms of these three houses, referred to as the "Casa del Jardín del Prado" of "Don Pedro de Aragon" and as the "Casa de los Monterrey." I infer the spatial position of the "pieza de chocolate" in the layout because inventory takers normally proceeded sequentially in the properties they were investigating. It is not clear whether these rooms were for the consumption or preparation of chocolate. It seems that the "aposento" designation in the first house suggests that was where servants stored and prepared chocolate. The "pieza" designation in the second house indicates that it was a room used by its lofty owners. It is also suggested by the presence of paintings that were fine enough to be resold. I am grateful to Julianne Gillard for this reference.

11. Antonio Colmenero de Ledesma, *Curioso tratado de la naturaleza y calidad del chocolate* (Madrid: Francisco de Martínez, 1631), fol. 10r.

12. León Pinelo, *Questión moral*, fol. 73; Matilde Santamaría Arnaíz, "La alimentación de los españoles bajo el reinado de los Austrias" (PhD diss., Universidad Complutense, Facultad de Farmacia, Madrid, 1986), 714–17.

13. "Proceso contra Simón Fernández," AHN Inq. Toledo, leg. 148, exp. 1, fols. 68r–68v.

14. Cited in C. Pérez de Bustamente, "El chocolate y el ayuno," *Correo erudito* 1, no. 2 (1941): 36.

15. Antonio Hurtado de Mendoza, "Coplas al Chocolate. Decima 115 a una Señora Rubia," PRB Mss. II/2802, fols. 252r–252v. The wordplay in the title "Couplets of Chocolate," sounding like "cups of chocolate," exists in the Spanish original, since *coplas* (couplets or verse) resembles *copas* (cups). On Hurtado de Mendoza's attendance at literary academies, see Willard F. King, *PMLA* 75, no. 4 (1960): 368, 372 n. 32.

16. Hurtado de Mendoza, "Coplas al Chocolate," fols. 252r–252v. Sor Juana Inés de la Cruz also made the relationship between sex and chocolate a conceit in one of her poems, see María Agueda Méndez, "Una relación conflictiva: La Inquisición novohispana y el chocolate," *Caravelle* 71 (1998): 18–19.

17. Juana Inés de la Cruz, "Romance a la misma . . . Señora, embiandole un zapato bordado segun estillo de Mexico, y un recado de Chocolate," in *Segundo volumen de las obras de soror Juana Ines de la Cruz* (Seville: Thomas López de Haro, 1692), 332–33.

18. Castro de Torres, *Panegírico al chocolate*, 12.

19. For literary competitions, see Mindy N. Taggard, "'Ut Pictura Poesis': Artists' Status in Early Modern Cordoba," *Artibus et Historiae* 17, no. 34. (1996): 78, and Mas i Usó, "Justas, Academias, y Convocatorias," 303; for the others, Albert Garcia Espuche, "El món de Joan Kies i Arnold de Jager: economia i política," in his *Barcelona entre dues guerres: Economia i vida quotidiana, 1652–1714* (Vic: EUMO, 2005), 261–365. Another convincing

example comes from the account books of a Sevillan hospital where the food inventory reflected a fairly Spartan diet, yet justified in 1645 "twelve boxes of chocolate that were bought in order to gift (*regalar*) Señor Don Juan Pérez de Lara, judge of Granada." That this was the sole reference to chocolate in the account books for 1595, 1625, 1635, and 1636 demonstrates that chocolate was seen as a luxury inappropriate for the wards of charity but necessary for diplomacy: ADS, Hospital Cinco Llagas, leg. 118, fol. 55v. For the other years, see legs. 110, 114, 116. On the Hospital de Cinco Llagas (or Hospital de Sangre): Luis de Peraza, *Historia de Sevilla*, ed. Francisco Morales Padrón (Seville: Asociación Amigos del Libro Antiguo, 1996), 56.

20. Antonio Paz y Meliá, introduction to *Avisos de don Jerónimo de Barrionuevo, 1654–1658*, ed. Antonio Paz y Meliá, Biblioteca de Autores Españoles (Madrid: Ediciones Atlas, 1968), 3–5.

21. *Avisos de don Jerónimo de Barrionuevo*, letter 27.

22. See Norbert Elias, *The Court Society*, trans. Edmund Jephcott (New York: Pantheon Books, 1983).

23. Juan de Castro y Medinilla, *Historia de las virtudes y propiedades del tabaco* (Cordoba: Salvador de Cea Tesa, 1620), fols. 19v–20r.

24. Mary Miller and Karl Taube, *An Illustrated Dictionary of the Gods and Symbols of Ancient Mexico and the Maya* (London: Thames and Hudson, 1993), 69.

25. Fernando de Almirón Zayas, *Discurso de la anathomia [sic] de algunos miembros del cuerpo humano necessaria en orden a los daños q[ue] de continuo uso del tabaco suceden en los que le usan sin orden y methodo medicinal* (Seville: Gabriel Ramos Vejerano, 1623), fol. 3v.

26. Cristóbal de Hayo, *Las excelencias y maravillosas propriedades del tabaco, conforme a gravissimos Autores, y grandes experiencias* (Salamanca: Diego de Cossio, 1645), fol. 2v; Tomás Hurtado, *Chocolate y tabaco: ayuno eclesiástico y natural* (Madrid: Francisco García, [1645?]), fol. 56v; *Al ill.mo y R.mo señor don Diego Castreion, dignisimo Obispo de Lugo y Gouernador del Arzobispado de Toledo* [1634–35], BN, fol. 1r.

27. *Romance en alabanza del tabaco* (Barcelona: Gabriel Nogués, 1644), BL. This and a companion poem, *Sátira contra el tabaco* (n.p., n.d. [1644–45?]), BN VE were published anonymously in broadsheets; for publication history and transcriptions, see Silvia Monti, ed., *Il tabaco fa male? Medicina, ideologia, letteratura nella polemica sulla diffusione di un prodotto del Nuevo Mondo* (Milan: Franco Angeli, 1987), 115–30, quotation on 128.

28. *Sátira contra el tabaco*, in Monti, *Il tabaco*, 118.

29. Luis Antonio, "A una Dama, que pidiéndola tabaco, sacó una caxa con un coraçon pintado en la tapa, y una flecha que le penetrava. Letra," in *Nuevo plato de varios manjares. Para divertir el ocio* (Zaragoza: Juan de Ybarra, a costa de Tomás Cabeças, 1658), fols. 31v–32r.

30. Simon Schama, *The Embarrassment of Riches: An Interpretation of Dutch Culture in the Golden Age* (Berkeley: University of California Press, 1988), 203–7.

31. A search through the Getty Provenance Index Database revealed eight paintings that explicitly mention tobacco or smoking in the title belonging to Spanish patrons in the seventeenth century, of which two were attributed to David Teniers the Younger, another to Adriaen Brouwer, and the rest anonymous. The following lists the artist's name (if known), title, the owners at the time of the inventories, and the date at which the inventory was taken: Anon., *Paiz con un flamenco tomando tabaco*, Nicolás de Cardona, Maestro de la Cámara de S. M., 1643; Anon., *Marina con esclavos que estan Tomando Tabaco*, Juan Alfonso Enríquez de Cabrera, Duque de Medina de Ríoseco y IX Almirante de Castilla, 1647; Adriaen Brouwer, *Tres figurillas q[ue] la una esta en pie con una taza en la mano, la otra durmiendo y la tercera tomando tavaco*, Antonio Mesía de Tovar, Conde de Molina, 1675; Anon., *Un hombre sentado ttomando Una pipa de tabaco*; and Anon., *Medio cuerpo de Un hombre que tiene en Una mano Una tabaquera de Umo y en la otra Un copa*, Gregorio Genaro de Bracamonte y Guzmán, Conde de Peñaranda, 1689; Anon., David Teniers the Younger, *Soldados que estan tomando Tabaco*, and *Hombres q Estan tomando Tavaco*, Gaspar de Haro y Guzmán Carpio, Conde-Duque de Olivares, 1689; *Rretratto de hombre senttado en una silla arrevozado con sombrero negro y una pluma blanca en el arrimado a un caxon y sobre*

el ay una chirimia un clarin un papel de musica y una pipa de Tavaco, Juan Gaspar Enríquez de Cabrera, Duque de Medina de Ríoseco y X Almirante de Castilla, 1691. In addition, several Flemings based in Spain owned tobacco-themed paintings. Obviously, other paintings in the database may depict tobacco but not mention it in the title. Getty Provenance Index Database, http://piweb.getty.edu/cgi-bin/starfinder/28800/collab.txt. On Teniers as a procurer of art for Spanish patrons, see W. Alexander Vergara, "The Count of Fuensaldaña and David Teniers: Their Purchases in London after the Civil War," *Burlington Magazine* 131, no. 1031 (1989): 127–32.

32. Faith Paulette Dreher, "The Artist as Seigneur: Chateaux and Their Proprietors in the Work of David Teniers II," *Art Bulletin* 60, no. 4 (1978): 682–83, 686 n. 29.

33. Jordan Goodman, *Tobacco in History: The Culture of Dependence* (London: Routledge, 1993), 70.

34. Hayo, *Las excelencias,* 15. That elites continued to smoke tobacco is suggested by the award of a tobacco box, as well as Quevedo's description of his smoking habits.

35. Francisco Ramírez Pacheco, *Parecer de el doctor Francisco Ramírez Pacheco sobre si el tabaco de polvo beneficiado con los polvillos que vulgarmente se dizen de ámbar, puede ser dañoso a la salud por causa de dichos polvillos* (Seville: Juan Gomes de Blas, 1659).

36. Though *tabaquera* is often clearly associated with snuff boxes, a poetry prize competition referred to a prize of a *"tabaqauera* of silver for tobacco in smoke": Mas i Usó, "Justas, Academias, y Convocatorias," 1070.

37. *Sátira contra el tabaco* in Monti, *Il tabaco,* 118.

38. The seminal work is Mikhail Bakhtin, *Rabelais and His World,* trans. Hélène Iswolsky (Cambridge: MIT Press, 1968; Bloomington: Indiana University Press, 1984), 4–5, 12–15, 34, 217–21. Citations are to Indiana edition; Peter Burke, *Popular Culture in Early Modern Europe* (1st ed. Maurice Temple Smith, 1978; New York: Harper and Row, 1978), 178–204; Peter Stallybrass and Allon White, *The Politics and Poetics of Transgression* (Ithaca: Cornell University Press, 1986); for Lenten Carnival in Spain, see María José del Río Barredo, "Burlas y violencia en el Carnaval madrileño de los siglos xvii y xviii," *Revista de Filología Románica* 3 (2002): 111–29, http://www.ucm.es/BUCM/revistasBUC/portal/modulos.php?name=Revistas2_Titulo&id=RFRM.

39. A. M. García Gómez, "El Corpus de 1636 en Córdoba: Estructuras y sentidos," *Bulletin of Hispanic Studies* 70 (1993): 75. I am very grateful to James Amelang for this reference (and for many others).

40. Francisco de Leiva y Aguilar, *Desengaño contra el mal uso del tabaco* (Cordoba: Salvador de Cea Tesa, 1634), fols. 12r–12v. The professor of medicine Cristóbal de Hayo explained that he was motivated to write his treatise defending tobacco to refute the view that smokers and snuff takers inhabit "the paradise of pigs" and that tobacco consumption is a violation of "civil and decent customs": *Las excelencias,* 4, 5.

41. Tomás Ramón, *Nueva prematica de reformacion contra los abusos de los afeytes, calçado . . . trajes y excesso en el uso del tabaco* (Zaragoza: Diego Dormer, 1635); the section on tobacco, Tomás Ramón, "Del abuso del tabaco o necociana," is in Monti, *Il tabaco,* 72–87; this citation, 78.

42. Ramón, "Del abuso del tabaco," 82, also 73.

43. Dreher, "Artist as Seigneur," 683–86.

44. Other verses that include ribald references to tobacco are in Francisco de Quevedo y Villegas, *Obras Completas,* ed. Felicidad Buendía (Madrid: Aguilar, 1959), 2:11, 260; 3:377, 857; Pablo Jaraulde Pou, *Francisco de Quevedo (1580–1645)* (Madrid: Editorial Castalia, 1999).

45. Teniers seems to have painted himself into *Tavern Scene* (1658), now at the National Gallery of Art in Washington, D.C. He is not actually smoking but holding a drink, looking out at the viewer, and accompanying a card-playing group who are smoking.

46. Quoted in José Luis Colomer, " 'Dar a Su Majestad algo bueno': Four Letters from Velázquez to Virgilio Malvezzi," *Burlington Magazine* 135, no. 1079 (1993): 71 n. 30; James O. Crosby, "¿De qué murió Quevedo? (Diario de una enfermedad mortal)," *MLN* 115, no. 2 (2000): 170–71.

47. The crude bodily associations of tobacco are emphasized in a number of Teniers paintings by the juxtaposition of other kinds of open bodies. For urinating, see *Peasants in a Tavern* (1633) and *Tavern Scene* (1658) at the National Gallery of Art in Washington, D.C.; for groping, see Jan Steen, *Tavern Scene* at the National Gallery in London; the latter is reproduced in Schama, *Embarrassment of Riches*, 205. Benno Tempel also notes the tendency among Dutch artists to represent smoking and "physical functions of the body" in proximity, though he offers a different explanation for the juxtaposition: "Symbols and Image: Smoking in Art since the Seventeenth Century," in *Smoke: A Global History of Smoking*, ed. Sander Gilman and Zhou Xun (London: Reaktion Books, 2004), 208.

48. Ramón, "Del abuso del tabaco," 81.

49. For other examples of chocolate still lives from the seventeenth century, see Peter Cherry, *Arte y naturaleza: el bodegón español en el Siglo de Oro*, ed. Conchita Romero (Aranjuez, Spain: Doce Calles, 1999), 258, 268, n. 29.

50. Vicente Suárez, "A un galán que por descuydo auia echado tabaco en un papel amoroso que tenía que dar a su Dama, y por el mismo descuydo se lo dio en forma de billete. Quintillas," in *Academia que se celebró en casa de Don Melchor de Fonseca de Almeyda* (Madrid: Francisco Nieto, 1663), fols. 20v, 22r.

51. Luis Antonio, "A un galán, que yendole a besar su Dama, la mordió de las narizes. Sátira," in *Nuevo plato*, fols. 12v–13r.

52. Jacinto Alonso de Maluenda, "Sátira contra el tabaco," in *Tropezón de Risa* (Valencia: Silvestre Esparaza, [n.d., after 1631]), in Monti, *Il tabaco*, 109; this is a different poem than the anonymous *Sátira contra el tabaco* published circa 1644, discussed above; Miguel Cejudo, "In Eos Qui Summut Naribus Tabacum," epigraph in Bartolomé Jiménez Patón, *Reforma de trages: doctrina de Fray Hernando de Talavera . . . Enséñase el buen uso del tabaco* (Baeza: Juan de la Cuesta, 1638), fols. 61v, 63r, 64v–65r.

53. "Eating, drinking, defecation and other elimination (sweating, blowing of the nose, sneezing) . . . all these acts are performed on the confines of the body and the outer world, or on the confines of the old and new body, in all these events the beginning and end of life are closely linked and interwoven": Bakhtin, *Rabelais*, quote at 223; 19, 317, 281, 223; see also Stallybrass and White, *Politics and Poetics*, 9, 21–22.

54. Bakhtin, *Rabelais*, 246; Burke, *Popular Culture*, 188–90; Stallybrass and White, *Politics and Poetics*, 4–5, 8, 16–17, 56–58, 183–190.

55. Hannah E. Bergman, "A Court Entertainment of 1638," *Hispanic Review* 42, no. 1 (1974): 76–77.

56. *Sátira contra el tabaco*, in Monti, *Il tabaco*, 120.

57. Armengol, "Mi Musa por ser muger," 91.

58. Francisco de Quevedo, *Obra poética*, ed. José Manuel Blecua (Madrid: Editorial Castalia, 1969–81), 3:377.

59. *Sátira contra el tabaco*, in Monti, *Il tabaco*, 118.

60. Burke, *Popular Culture*, 270–81; Río Barredo, "Burlas y violencia."

61. Norbert Elias, *The Civilizing Process: Sociogenetic and Psychogenetic Investigations*, trans. Edmund Jephcott, ed. Eric Dunning, Johan Goudsblom, and Stephen Mennell (Oxford: Blackwell, 2000).

62. Juan Francisco Marañon, "Tratado nuevo y curioso del chocolate, del café y del thé, traducido y recopilado de muy graves autores," (1690), fol. 40v, HSA.

63. Marañon, "Tratado nuevo," fols. 28r–28v; León Pinelo, *Questión moral*, fols. 8v, 73.

64. Bartolomé Marradón, "Diálogo del uso del tabaco . . . y de chocolate y otras bebidas," in Phillipe Sylvestre Dufour, *Traitez nouveaux et curieux du Café, du Thé, & du Chocolat* (Lyon: Jean Girin and B. Riviere, 1685), translated excerpt from *Diálogo del uso del tabaco, los daños que causa, etc. Y de chocolate y otras bebidas* (Seville: Gabriel Ramos Vejarano, 1618); Castro de Torres, *Panegírico al chocolate*, 13; Vicente Lardizabal, *Memoria sobre las utilidades del chocolate* (Pamplona: Antonio Castilla, 1788), 18, 44; *Thomas Gage's Travels in the New World*, ed. J. Eric S. Thompson (Norman: University of Oklahoma Press, 1958), 157.

65. Francisco Santos, *Día y noche de Madrid. Discursos de lo mas notable que en el passa* (Madrid: Joseph Fernández de Buendía, [1663], 1674), 39–40. I am grateful to María José del Río Barredo for this reference.

66. Quoted in Sherry M. Velasco, *Demons, Nausea, and Resistance in the Autobiography of Isabel de Jesús, 1611–1682* (Albuquerque: University of New Mexico Press, 1996), 17–18. I thank Luis Corteguera for this reference.

67. *Confortar* has the English meaning of *to comfort*, but in the more active sense of "dar vigor, espiritu, y fuerzas, corroborar en cierta manera vificar," DAE 2:505.

68. Castro de Torres, *Panegírico al chocolate*, 21.

69. Ibid., 13.

70. Ibid., 12.

71. Gregorio Mayans, *Chocolata, sive in laudem potionis indiae, quam apellant Chocolate* (1733), trans. and ed. José Maria Estrelles i González, in "Una pincelada frívola en la obra de Mayans: Elegía al Chocolate," *Estudios dedicados a Juan Peset Aleixandre* (Valencia: Universidad de Valencia, 1982), 1:591.

72. "Experience" demonstrates that after drinking chocolate "one does not sleep": Santiago Valverde Turices, *Un discurso de chocolate* (Seville: Juan de Cabrera, 1624), fol. C3–v. Castro de Torres, *Panegírico al chocolate*, 13.

73. Though Francisco Leiva y Aguilar doubted that tobacco could assist in scholarly pursuits, he took for granted chocolate's usefulness in this capacity, *Desengaño*, fols. 125r–125v.

74. Eliseo Armengol, "Vituperio al Tabaco, y devida alabança al chocolate. Quintillas," in *En Real Acadaemia celebrada en el Real de Valencia* (Valencia, 1669), 92; also Castro de Torres, *Panegírico al chocolate*, 7; *Sentencia jocosa*, 1.

75. Mayans, *Chocolata*, 1:591.

76. Juan Francisco Marañon, "Tratado nuevo," fol. 38v.

77. Jiménez Patón, *Enseñase el buen uso del tabaco*, fol. 61r; for excessive use in New Spain, Francisco Ximenes, trans., Francisco Hernández, *Quatro libros de la naturaleza y virtudes de las plantas y animales* (Mexico: Viuda de Diego Lopez Davalos, 1615), fols. 96r–98r.

78. Pedro Simón, *Noticias historiales de las conquistas de Tierra Firme en las Indias Occidentales* (Bogota: M. Rivas, 1882–1892), 4:361; see also Castro y Medinilla, *Historia de las virtudes*, fols. 42r–42v.

79. Castro y Medinilla, *Historia de las virtudes*, fols. 38v–39r, 46v, 47r; see also Hayo, *Las excelencias*, 12, 23.

80. *El médico del tabaco* (1653), in Monti, *Il tabaco*, 102–6.

81. Hayo, *Las excelencias*, 12.

82. John A. Baron, "Beneficial Effects of Nicotine and Cigarette Smoking: The Real, the Possible, and the Spurious," *British Medical Bulletin* 52, no. 1 (1996): 66–67.

83. Castro y Medinilla, *Historia de las virtudes*, fols. 41r, 47r; Hayo, *Las excelencias*, 12; Hurtado, *Chocolate y tabaco*, fol. 41r; Leiva y Aguilar, *Desengaño*, fols. 266v—267r. *Sátira contra el tabaco*, 118; *Romance en alabanza del tabaco*, 126.

84. Castro y Medinilla, *Historia de las virtudes*, 44r–44v; Hayo, *Las excelencias*, 26; also Suárez, "A un galán," fols. 20v, 22r; and Leiva y Aguilar, *Desengaño*, 239r–239v.

85. When nicotine binds to receptors in the brain, it facilitates the release of various neurotransmitters, including norepinephrine, serotonin, and dopamine, among others. In addition, other compounds in tobacco smoke appear to inhibit monamine oxidase, an enzyme responsible for breaking down the above-mentioned neurotransmitters; see Elizabeth Quattrocki, Abigail Baird, and Deborah Yurgelun-Todd, "Biological Aspects of the Link between Smoking and Depression," *Harvard Review of Psychiatry* 8, no. 3 (2000): 99–110.

9. Monopolizing Vice

1. "Relación de lo que ha pasado en la administración y arrendamiento del tabaco y es la joia mejor mas considerable de la R[ea]l Haz[ien]da desde el año de 1684," PRB Ms. II/2841, 174–77.

2. My characterization of the revisionism and older historiography of the Spanish state was greatly informed by James S. Amelang, "The Peculiarities of the Spaniards: Historical Approaches to the Early Modern State," in *Public Power in Europe: Studies in Historical Transformation*, ed. James S. Amelang and Siegfried Beer (Pisa: CLIOHRES-Edisud, 2006), 39–56; Pablo Fernández Albaladejo, *Fragmentos de monarquía* (Madrid: Alianza Universal, 1992); Bartolomé Clavero, *Tantas personas como estados: Por una antropología política de la historia europea* (Madrid: Editorial Tecnos, 1986); António M. Hespanha, *Vísperas del Leviatán: Instituciones y poder político: Portugal, siglo XVII*, trans. Fernando J. Bouza (Madrid: Taurus Humanidades, 1989).

3. Amelang, "Peculiarities," 42–43; such revisionism accords with Perry Anderson's understanding of the absolutist "feudal state" in *Lineages of the Absolutist State* (London: Verso, 1979) and similar analyses of the social bases of absolutism in early modern France, such as William Beik, *Absolutism and Society in Seventeenth-Century France: State Power and Provincial Aristocracy in Languedoc* (Cambridge: Cambridge University Press, 1988); see also Timothy Mitchell, "The Limits of the State: Beyond Statist Approaches and Their Critics," *American Political Science Review* 85, no. 1 (1991): 77–96.

4. Amelang, "Peculiarities," 43.

5. Mitchell, "The Limits of the State," 92; Michel Foucault, *Discipline and Punish: The Birth of the Prison* (New York: Vintage Books, 1995).

6. Mitchell, "The Limits of the State," 92; Foucault, *Discipline and Punish*.

7. J. H. Elliott, *Imperial Spain, 1469–1716* (Edward Arnold, 1963; London: Pelican Books/Penguin Books, 1970), 321–41. Citation is to Penguin edition. Antonio Domínguez Ortiz, *Política y hacienda de Felipe IV*, 2nd ed. (Madrid: Ediciones Pegaso, 1983), 7–13.

8. J. H. Parry, *The Spanish Seaborne Empire* (New York: Knopf, 1966; Berkeley: University of California Press, 1990), 246–47.

9. Elliott, *Imperial Spain*, 285–86; J. H. Elliott, *Revolt of the Catalans: A Study in the Decline of Spain, 1598–1640* (New Haven: Yale University Press, 1986).

10. Modesto Ulloa, *La hacienda real de Castilla en el reinado de Felipe II*, 2nd ed. (Madrid: Fundación Universitaria Española, Seminario Cisneros, 1977), 317–32. Citation is to Madrid edition. Juan E. Gelabert, *La bolsa del rey: Rey, reino y fisco en Castilla, 1598–1648* (Barcelona: Crítica, 1997); for fraud in *millones*, see Beatriz Cárceles de Gea, *Fraude y administración fiscal en Castilla: La comisión de millones, 1632–1658* (Madrid: Banco de España—Servicio de Estudios, 1994).

11. Ulloa, *La hacienda real*, 318, 322.

12. Quoted in Ulloa, *La hacienda real*, 322–23.

13. AHN Cons., leg. 7132, fols. 1r–1v, 24r–24v.

14. J. H. Elliott, *The Count-Duke of Olivares: The Statesman in an Age of Decline* (New Haven: Yale University Press, 1986), 425–42; Fernández Albaladejo, *Fragmentos*, 340–45; Domínguez Ortiz, *Política*, 235; Gelabert, *La bolsa del rey*, 239–40.

15. For the importance of salt to the European diet, see Fernand Braudel, *The Structures of Everyday Life: The Limits of the Possible*, trans. Sian Reynolds (New York: Harper and Row, 1979), 209–10, and Ulloa, *La hacienda real*, 236, 246; Mark Kurlansky, *Salt: A World History* (New York: Walker, 2002); on clerical resistance, see Elliott, *Count-Duke of Olivares*, 342; on the northern riots, see Domínguez Oritz, *Política*, 235.

16. Domínguez Ortiz, *Política*, 31.

17. AHN Est., lib. 856, fols. 77r, 79r, 80r.

18. Ibid., fols. 80, 147, 154v–155r.

19. Ibid., fols. 155r–155v.

20. Ibid., fols. 3, 9.

21. *Sobre el 'servicio' de los dos millones y medio* (1634), AGI Consul., leg. 93, no. 9; *Acuerdo que el Reyno hizo de lo que se impone en el açucar, conserva, papel, pescados frescos y salados, tabaco y chocolate, para la paga del servicio de dos millones y medio* (1638), BN VE; Juan García de Torres, *El Tabaco: Consideraciones sobre el pasado, presente, y provenir de esta renta* (Madrid: Imprenta de J. Norguera, 1876), 13–14; Francisco

Gallardo Fernández, *Origen, progreso y estado de las rentas de la Corona de España* (Madrid: Imprenta Real, 1805), 1:59.

22. *Sobre el 'servicio' de los dos millones y medio*; García de Torres, *Tabaco*, 13–14.

23. Quoted in Gelabert, *La bolsa del rey*, 256.

24. For theories of just taxation in the sixteenth century, see John Laures, *The Political Economy of Juan de Mariana* (New York: Fordham University Press, 1928), 99, 125.

25. AHN Est., lib. 856, fols. 83v–84.

26. García de Torres, *Tabaco*, 12.

27. AGS DGT, inv. 4, leg. 29, fols. 2v–3r.

28. Alonso Acerco, "La renta del tabaco en Orán y Mazalquivir: Fortuna y fracaso de un estanco pionero," *Cuadernos de Historia Moderna* 17 (1996): 11–40, 26.

29. *Acuerdo que el Reyno hizo*; on the pepper monopoly, see Domínguez Ortiz, *Política*, 220.

30. Ulloa, *La hacienda real*, 241; Cristóbal Espejo, "La renta de salinas hasta la muerte de Felipe II (continuación)," *Revista de archivos, bibliotecas y museos* 48 (1918): 44–45.

31. My emphasis. *Recud[imiento] a Di[ego] Gómez de Salaz[a]r de la Renta de Tabaco* (Madrid, 1656), AVM Sec. 3, leg. 462, exp. 9; *Arrendamiento que se hace a Diego Gómez de Salazar de la renta del estanco del tabaco de los Reinos de Castilla y León* (Madrid, 1656), BN VE.

32. AGS DGT, inv. 4, leg. 29, fol. 40v.

33. "Aragon" was the name of both the kingdom in northeastern Spain and the moniker for all those united under the Crown of Aragon (Aragon, Valencia, Catalonia, Mallorca).

34. Valencia also implemented a tobacco monopoly in the seventeenth century, but little is known about it, including the starting date; for this and monopolies in the Crown of Aragon, see Andreu Bibiloni Amengual, *Contrabandistes i agents de rendes: Supervivents i acumuladors entorn al negoci del tabac a Mallorca durant els segles XVII i XVIII* (Palma de Mallorca: El Tall, 2000), 26–28; in Catalonia, see Jaume Carrera Pujal, *Historia política y económica de Cataluña, siglos XVI al XVIII* (Barcelona: Bosch, 1946–47), 2:314–15; Albert Garcia Espuche, "El món de Joan Kies i Arnold de Jager: Economia i política," in his *Barcelona entre dues guerres: Economia i vida quotidiana, 1652–1714* (Vic: EUMO, 2005), 261–365; in Navarre, see Sergio Solbes Ferri, "El arriendo de la renta del tabaco a través de la Real Hacienda: Una eficaz formula de intervencionsimo regio en Navarra (1717–1749)," 319–20 and Conchita Hernández Escayola, "Los últimos arrendatarios del estanco del tabaco en Navarra (1700–1717)," 354, both in *Tabaco y economía en el siglo XVIII*, ed. Agustín González Enciso y Rafael Torres Sánchez (Pamplona: EUNSA, 1999).

35. *Avisos de don Jerónimo de Barrionuevo, 1654–1658*, ed. Antonio Paz y Meliá, Biblioteca de Autores Españoles (Madrid: Ediciones Atlas, 1968), 190, 191, 210.

36. Daviken Studnicki-Gizbert, *A Nation upon the Ocean Sea: Portugal's Atlantic Diaspora and the Crisis of the Spanish Empire, 1492–1640* (New York: Oxford University Press, 2007), 153, 166–67.

37. AGS DGT, inv. 4, leg. 29; for that of Diego Gómez de Salazar that began in 1656, *Recud[imiento] a Di[ego] Gómez de Salaz[ar] de la Renta de Tabaco*; García de Torres, *Tabaco*, 15.

38. AGS DGT, inv. 4, leg. 29, fol. 4r.

39. Records of the bidding are in AGS DGT, inv. 4, leg. 29, fols. 1–36; it is described in detail in Marcy Norton, "New World of Goods: A History of Tobacco and Chocolate in the Spanish Empire, 1492–1700" (PhD diss., University of California, Berkeley, 2000), chap. 4; and José Manuel Rodríguez Gordillo, *La creación del estanco del tabaco en España* (Madrid: Fundación Altadis, 2002), 124–35.

40. AGS DGT, inv. 4, leg. 29, fols. 4–9, 17v.

41. Ibid., fols. 122r–122v.

42. Ibid., fols. 33r–34; Julio Caro Baroja, *Los Judios en la España moderna y contemporánea* ([Madrid]: Ediciones Arión, 1962), 2:85.

43. AGS DGT, inv. 4, leg. 29, fol. 75.

44. Ibid., fols. 122r–122v.

45. Paolo de Vitoria, *Por Antonio de Soria Tesorero de la renta del tabaco con Diego Gómez Salazar* [1637?], BN Raros. I thank Paola Volpini for informing me of the "Por-Con" collection. Her research suggests that they were printed with the intention of reaching a wider readership than the immediate judges involved.

46. "Testimonio de el tabaco," fols. 9v–12v; AGS CJH, leg. 713, 1–7.

47. *Recud[imiento] a Di[ego] Gómez de Salaz[ar]; Arrendamiento que se hace a Diego Gómez de Salazar.* The monopoly contracts stipulated these prices and specified that the *arrendador* could not increase prices without the consent of the *millones* committee; likewise, neither the Crown nor any other entity could levy new taxes on tobacco. The *alcabala* sales tax would still be levied, but only once, for retail, not wholesale, transactions.

48. AHN Inq. Toledo, lib. 223, fol. 35r. The first fifty-two folios of this book were account records confiscated by the Inquisition.

49. Markus Schreiber, *Marranen in Madrid, 1600–1670* (Stuttgart: F. Steiner, 1994), 124–26; Julio Caro Baroja, "La sociedad criptojudia en la corte de Felipe IV," in his *Inquisición, brujas, y criptojudaismo*, 2nd. ed. (Barcelona: Ediciones Ariel, 1972), 108.

50. The *arrendador* who definitely did not belong to the Portuguese community was Gregorio Centani; see Sabino Lizana Fernández, "Administración y administradores de la renta del tabaco en la segunda mitad del siglo XVII en Castilla," in *Tabaco y economía en el siglo XVIII*, ed. Agustín González Enciso and Rafael Torres Sánchez (Pamplona: Ediciones Universidad de Navarra, 1999), 299–300. Lizana Fernández includes Parada among the Portuguese *conversos*, but I have not seen other evidence for this. Like most other historians, he also designates Juan Baptista Carrafa as not being Portuguese, and Carrafa is frequently identified as an "Armenian," but his name appears on a 1641 list of naturalized Portuguese residents: Lutgardo García Fuentes, *El comercio español con América, 1650–1700* (Seville: Escuela de Estudios Hispano-Americanos de Sevilla, Consejo Superior de Investigaciones Científicas, 1980), 40.

51. Antonio Domínguez Ortiz, *Los Judeoconversos en la España moderna* (Madrid: Editorial MAPFRE, 1992), 197–98.

52. Studnicki-Gizbert, *A Nation upon the Ocean Sea*, 22–24.

53. James C. Boyajian, *Portuguese Bankers at the Madrid Court, 1626–1650* (New Brunswick, N.J.: Rutgers University Press, 1983), 3–4, 17–24; Mauricio Ebben, "Un triángulo imposible: La corona española, el Santo Oficio, y los banqueros portugueses, 1627–1655," *Hispania: Revista española de historia* 53, no. 184 (May 1993): 504, 541–56; Caro Baroja, *Los Judios*, 2:58–60; Domínguez Ortiz, *Política*, 126–27; Jonathan I. Israel, *Empires and Entrepots: The Dutch, the Spanish Monarchy and the Jews, 1585–1713* (London: Hambledon Press, 1990), 361.

54. Studnicki-Gizbert, *A Nation upon the Ocean Sea*, 112–19; Boyajian, *Portuguese Bankers*, 46.

55. Israel, *Empires and Entrepots*, 374. A 1622 government official reported that a minimum of twenty-two Dutch ships had brought cargo to Bayonne and St. Jeanne to be smuggled into Madrid via Navarre with the cooperation of the Portuguese *arrendador* of the customs of the *puertos secos* (literally "dry ports" or overland checkpoints). Bayonne was a key point for channeling contraband.

56. Cárceles de Gea, *Fraude y administración.*

57. Important works on Portuguese New Christians and *marranos* include Yosef Yerushalmi, *From Spanish Court to Italian Ghetto: Issac Cardoso; A Study in Seventeenth-Century Marranism and Jewish Apologetics* (New York: Columbia University Press, 1971); David M. Gitlitz, *Secrecy and Deceit: The Religion of the Crypto-Jews* (Philadelphia: Jewish Publication Society, 1996); Yosef Kaplan, *From Christianity to Judaism: The Story of Isaac Orobio de Castro*, trans. Raphael Loewe (Oxford: Littman Library by Oxford University Press, 1989); Pilar Huerga Criado, *En la Raya de Portugal: Solidaridad y tensiones en la comunidad Judeoconversa* (Salamanca: Ediciones Universidad de Salamanca, 1994); Schreiber, *Marranen in Madrid*; Antonio Domínguez Ortiz, *Los Judeoconversos*; Julio Caro Baroja, *Los Judios en la España moderna y contemporánea*, vol. 2,

and "La sociedad criptojudia en la corte de Felipe IV"; Miriam Bodian, *Hebrews of the Portuguese Nation: Conversos and Community in Early Modern Amsterdam* (Bloomington: Indiana University Press, 1997); David L. Graizbord, *Souls in Dispute: Converso Identities in Iberia and the Jewish Diaspora, 1580–1700* (Philadelphia: University of Pennsylvania Press, 2004); Renée Levine Melammed, *Heretics or Daughters of Israel?: The Crypto-Jewish Women of Castile* (New York: Oxford University Press, 1999). For their trade networks, see Israel, *Empires and Entrepots*, and Studnicki-Gizbert, *A Nation upon the Ocean Sea*.

58. Studnicki-Gizbert, *A Nation upon the Ocean Sea*, 72.

59. Yerushalmi, *From Spanish Court*, 39–40, 12; Graizbord, *Souls in Dispute*, 63–65.

60. Huerga Criado has a good description of "Marranism" with several examples based on the practices of the family of Gómez de Salazar and his associates, *En la Raya de Portugal*, 176–88.

61. Gitlitz, *Secrecy*, 391–402. For specific instances: AHN Inq. Toledo, leg. 137, exp. 1, fol. 2v; leg. 137, no. 17, fols. 83r–83v, 178r–180r.

62. Lizana Fernández, "Administración y administradores," 305 n. 37.

63. Enormous amounts of biographical information about Gómez de Salazar are available in the dossiers on him and his associates assembled by the Inquisition: AHN Inq. Toledo, leg. 151, exp. 8, particularly, fols. 116, 224r–224v, leg. 137, exp. 17 (Josef de Borjes), particularly fol. 211v, and leg. 148, no. 272 (Antonio de Fonseca). The following paragraph is based on these and biographical synopses based on these and other sources in Caro Baroja, *Los Judios*, 2:84–91; Yerushalmi, *From Spanish Court*, 178–81; Huerga Criado, *En la Raya de Portugal*, 25–27, 119–20, 193–96; Lizana Fernández, "Administración y administradores," 293–95, 304–5. There are serious methodological issues related to using testimony from the Inquisition as it was elicited under duress, often including torture, and inquisitors were quick to assume that all those of New Christian heritage were secretly "Judaizing," even when they were not. However, Gómez de Salazar's commitment to Judaism seems indubitable, since he eventually fled Iberia and lived openly as a Jew. For a discussion of these methodological issues and strategies for effectively employing testimony from the Inquisition, see Graizbord, *Souls in Dispute*.

64. *Recud[imiento] a Di[ego] Gómez de Salaz[a]r].*

65. AHN Inq. Toledo, leg. 151, exp. 8, fol. 262r.

66. Ibid., fol. 282r.

67. AHN Inq. Toledo, leg. 148, no. 272, fols. 340–341.

68. Caro Baroja, "La sociedad," 108–10; Caro Baroja, *Los Judios*, 2:88.

69. AHN Inq. Toledo, leg. 151, exp. 8, fol. 125v; Caro Baroja, *Los Judios*, 2:86–87 n. 72.

70. This organization is described for Gómez de Salazar's *arrendamiento* in Huerga Criado, *En la Raya de Portugal*, 119–20; Lizana Fernández, "Administración y administradores," 306–15.

71. Huerga Criado, *En la Raya de Portugal*, 193–94.

72. Lizana Fernández, "Administración y administradores," 311–12.

73. For instance, the *administrador* Fernández de Miranda signed a contract with Francisco Fernández Cardoso that empowered the latter to "represent my behalf allowing him to come and go to all of the towns and villages included in the land and district of this town of Madrid and to make whatever provisions for tobacco *estancos* in the said towns and villages for the sale and consumption in this present year of 1641": AHPM, lib. 5668 (1641), fol. 53. AHN Inq., lib. 223 contains correspondence between the provincial and district levels, as well as between the *arrendador general* and subordinates for 1658 and 1659, fols. 1–52.

74. Lizana Fernández, "Administración y administradores," 300 n. 24; 307 n. 46; 316. Luis Márquez Cardoso, who held the monopoly 1680–82, also worked as a factor during Gómez de Salazar's administration: AHN Inq., lib. 223.

75. See chapter 7.

76. For comparison with other industries: Antonio Domínguez Ortiz, *Orto y ocaso de Sevilla*, 2nd ed. (Seville: Universidad de Sevilla, 1974), 53.

77. Francisco Ramírez Pacheco, *Parecer de el doctor Francisco Ramírez Pacheco sobre si el tabaco de polvo beneficiado con los polvillos q[ue] vulgarmente se dizen de ambar,*

puede ser dañoso a la salud por causa de dichos polvillos (Seville: Juan Gómez de Blas, 1659), fol. 4r.

78. José Manuel Rodríguez Gordillo, *Diccionario histórico del tabaco* ([Spain]: Cetarsa, 1993), 237; and José Manuel Rodríguez Gordillo, "Sobre la industria sevillana del tabaco a fines del siglo XVII," *Cuadernos de Historia*, no. 7 (1977): 533–52.

79. García Fuentes, *Comercio*, 364–68; "Relación de lo que ha pasado en la administración y arrendamiento del tabaco," fol. 175v; Rodríguez Gordillo, "Sobre la industria sevillana del tabaco," 536. Not much is known about these factories, but the Madrid one appears to have been quite large: *Consulta que propusieron los Arrendadores del efect del tabaco* (Madrid, 1698), 23, NYPL Arents no. 435.

80. Rodríguez Gordillo, "Sobre la industria sevillana del tabaco," 543–46, 549–50.

81. Lizana Fernández, "Administración y administradores," 299.

82. AHN Inq., lib. 223, fols. 45r–47v.

83. Huerga Criado, *En la Raya de Portugal*, 191–96.

84. AHN Inq. Toledo, leg. 137, exp. 17, fol. 214r; AHN Inq. Toledo, leg. 151, exp. 8, fols. 78r–80r, 249r–v.

85. AHN Inq. Toledo, leg. 151, exp. 8, fols. 107r–114r.

86. AHN Inq. Toledo, leg. 151, exp. 8, fol. 120r; for a similar case for the *arrendador* of Granada, see Martín González, fols. 209v–213v.

87. AHN Inq. Toledo, leg. 137, exp. 17, fols. 63r–v.

88. García Fuentes, *Comercio*, 362–63, 372–76; a royal proclamation in England acknowledged "the difference, or, at least, the opinion of difference betweene Spanish or forreine Tobacco, and Tobacco of the plantations of Virginia . . . is such, that Our Subjects can hardly be induced totally to forsake the Spanish tobacco": Charles I, *By the King a proclamation touching tobacco* (London: Bonham Norton and Iohn Bill, 1627), 1,
http://gateway.proquest.com/openurl?ctx_ver=Z39.88   2003&res_id=xri:eebo&rft_id=xri:eebo:citation:33152843.

89. "Relación de lo que ha pasado en la administración y arrendamiento del tabaco," fols. 176r–176v.

90. García Fuentes, *Comercio*, 376–78.

91. Lizana Fernández, "Administración y administradores," 313, 315; García Fuentes, *Comercio*, 86–87.

92. "Don Miguel Pérez de Mendoza, veedor de comercio y contrabando de la ciudad de Logroño," (8/1656), AGS DGT, inv. 4, leg. 29.

93. AHN Inq. Toledo, leg. 151, exp. 8, fols. 243v, 258v–260v.

94. Huerga Criado, *En la Raya de Portugal*, 189.

95. AHN Inq. Toledo, leg. 151, exp. 8, fols. 140v–141r.

96. AHN Inq. Toledo, leg. 151, exp. 8, fols. 197r–197v.

97. Studnicki-Gizbert, *A Nation upon the Ocean Sea*, 160–61, 173–74.

98. In its first years, two communities, Antequera and Ecija, resisted incorporation by arguing that their prior establishment of regional tobacco monopolies made them exempt, but later leases made no mention of any such exemption: AHN CJH, leg. 421, exp. 6, no. 1.

99. AHN Inq. Toledo, leg. 137, exp. 17, fols. 270r–v, 159v.

100. Jacob Price, *France and the Chesapeake: A History of the French Tobacco Monopoly, 1674–1791* (Ann Arbor: University of Michigan, 1973).

101. José Manuel Rodríguez Gordillo, "Spanish Empire," in *Tobacco in History and Culture: An Encyclopedia* (New York: Charles Scribner's Sons—Thomson/Gale, 2004), 2:592, 585–93. See also Rodríguez Gordillo, *La creación del estanco*, and José Manuel Rodríguez Gordillo, *La difusión del tabaco en España* (Seville: Universidad de Sevilla/Fundación Altadis, 2002).

102. AHN CJH, leg. 713 (1–7); AGS DGT, inv. 4, leg. 29, fols. 40r–43r; on the support of the *consulado*, see fols. 55r–v.

103. García Fuentes, *Comercio*, 366–67.

104. Domínguez Ortiz, *Política*, 204, 128; on the jurisdictional dispute with tax farmer for older tobacco tax: AGS CJH, leg. 421, no. 17.

105. "El gremio de especieros . . . y buhoneria de la Ciudad de Granada con el señor fiscal y Antonio de Soria, arrendador de la renta del tabaco sobre pago de la alcabála del tabaco," (1638–50), AHN Cons., leg. 33966, no. 6.

106. The monopolists who became involved in this suit were successively Luis Méndez Enríquez, Antonio de Soria, and Diego Gómez de Salazar.

107. AHN Cons., leg. 33966, no. 6.

108. Francisco de Dueñas, *Declaración de la vista del tabaco del estanquero, por comisión del Consejo a el señor don Alvaro Queypo de Llano y Valdes, . . . Por. . . . Boticario de la dicha Ciudad* (s.a. Granada), NYPL Arents no. 365. The Arents catalog dates the document 1680, but the document in AHN Cons., leg. 7256, no. 52 (below) suggests that this document could not have been written before May 1641.

109. AHN Cons., leg. 7256, no. 52 (1641).

110. Luis Márquez Cardoso and Manuel Cáceres, *Memorial dado a su Mgd por Dn Luis Marquez Cardoso sobre estancar la oja de tavaco q[ue] viene de Indias* (Madrid, 1682), fol. IV, NYPL Arents no. 375.

111. Jacinto Alcázar Arriaza, *Medios políticos para el remidio único y universal de España* (Madrid: Diego Díaz de la Carrera, 1646), 13, quoted in José Manuel Rodríguez Gordillo, "El fraude en el estanco del tabaco (siglos XVII–XVIII," *Hacienda pública española* no. 1 extraordinario (1994): 67.

112. Tobacco contraband and smuggling in the eighteenth century has been more extensively researched. See relevant essays in *Tabaco y economía en el siglo XVIII* and *El mercado del tabaco en España durante el siglo XVIII*, ed. Santiago de Luxán Meléndez, Sergio Solbes Ferri, and Juan José Laforet (Las Palmas de Gran Canaria: Fundación Altadis [2001?]).

113. AGS Rentas Cont. Gen., leg. 3836, pl. 1, "Diego Gómez de Salazar arrendador del estanco del tavaco detos Reynos."

114. García Fuentes, *Comercio*, 365, 371; Márquez Cardoso and Cáceres, *Memorial*.

115. José Manuel Rodríguez Gordillo, "El fraude en el estanco," 69; Lizana Fernández, "Administración y administradores," 313 n. 37; Márquez Cardoso and Cáceres, *Memorial*, fol. IV.

116. Juan A. Sánchez Belén, *La política fiscal en Castilla durante el reinado de Carlos II* (Madrid: Siglo XXI, 1996), 184–85, 187.

117. Rodríguez Gordillo, "El fraude en el estanco," 71; this explains why domestic cultivation was prohibited in countries that established tobacco monopolies (in France as well as Spain). In Holland, however, domestic cultivation accounted for an important proportion of total tobacco consumed, estimated at between nine and fourteen million pounds a year in the mid-seventeenth century, much more than amounts imported from Virginia: Wim Klooster, *Illicit Riches: The Dutch Trade in the Caribbean, 1648–1795* (Leiden: KITLV Press, 1998), 33, 189.

118. Sánchez Belén, *La política fiscal*, 178; Rodríguez Gordillo, "El fraude en el estanco," 70–77.

119. I. A. A. Thompson, *War and Government in Habsburg Spain, 1560–1620* (London: University of London, Athlone Press, 1975), 275, 283; Max Weber, "Bureaucracy," in *From Max Weber: Essays in Sociology*, trans. and ed. H. H. Gerth and C. Wright Mills (New York: Oxford University Press, 1946; new edition, 1958), 196–244. Citations are to new edition.

120. "Relación de lo que ha pasado en la administración y arrendamiento del tabaco," 174–77; Rodríguez Gordillo, "Sobre la industria sevillana del tabaco"; Sánchez Belén, *La política fiscal*, 181–82.

121. There still needs to be a systematic comparison of the seventeenth and eighteenth-century monopolies, but see José Manuel Rodríguez Gordillo, *Un archivo para la historia del tabaco* ([Spain]: Tabacalera, 1984); Rafael Escobedo Romero, *El tabaco del rey: La organización de un monopolio fiscal durante el Antiguo Régimen* (Pamplona: Ediciones Universidad de Navarra, 2007).

122. Jacob M. Price, "Tobacco Use and Taxation: A Battle of Interests in Early Modern Europe," in *Consuming Habits: Drugs in History and Anthropology*, ed. Jordan Goodman,

Paul E. Lovejoy, and Andrew Sherratt (London: Routledge, 1995), 167; Price, *France and the Chesapeake*; Ciniza Capalbo, *L'economia del vizio: Il tabaco nello Stato pontificio in età moderna fra produzione e consume* (Naples: Edizioni scientifiche italiane, 1999); Susan Dean-Smith, *Bureaucrats, Planters, and Workers: The Making of the Tobacco Monopoly in Bourbon Mexico* (Austin: University of Texas, 1992).

123. BL Eg. Mss 2055, fols. 145r–218v.

10. Enchanting the Profane

1. Fernando Ortiz, *Cuban Counterpoint: Tobacco and Sugar,* trans. Harriet de Onís (New York: Alfred A. Knopf, 1947; Durham: Duke University Press, 1995), 210–11 (citations are to Duke edition; my modification of original translation); Francisco de Quevedo y Villegas, *Discurso de todos los Diablos o Infierno Enmendado* (Valencia, 1629), in *Obras completas,* ed. Felicidad Buendía (Madrid: Aguilar, 1959), 1:223. Quevedo wrote the play in 1627, and it was first published in 1628 in Gerona. In 1629, when the author tried to include the play in an anthology of his satirical-moral works, an unfriendly censor required him to make revisions and change the play's title to *El entremetido, la dueña y el soplón* (1631), *Obras completas,* 197 n. 1.

2. The now-classic definition of disenchantment appears in Max Weber, *The Protestant Ethic and the Spirit of Capitalism,* trans. Talcott Parsons (1st ed., 1920; London: Harper-Collins Academic, 1991), 26–27. The classic history is Keith Thomas, *Religion and the Decline of Magic* (New York: Scribner, 1971). For "enchantment" in the modern world see the review essay and works cited in Michael Saler, "Modernity and Enchantment: A Historiographic Review," *The American Historical Review* 111 (June 2006): 692–716.

3. One of reenchantment's greatest theorists, Walter Benjamin, argued that "industrialization had brought about the reenchantment of the social world and through it a 'reactivation of mythic powers,'" Susan Buck-Morss, *The Dialectics of Seeing: Walter Benjamin and the Arcades Project* (Cambridge: MIT Press, 1989), 253.

4. Buck-Morss, *Dialectics of Seeing,* 254–55, 267–69.

5. For a discussion of tobacco in the history of Christianity over the *longue durée,* see Marcy Norton, "Christianity," in *Tobacco in History and Culture: An Encyclopedia,* ed. Jordan Goodman (New York: Charles Scribner's Sons/Thomson Gale, 2005), 1:135–44.

6. Urbano VIII, *Nos Don Juan Jacobo Pancirolo . . . Patriarca de Constantinopola, y de nuestro Santissimo Padre . . . A todas y qualquier personas . . . (sigue el texto latino del Breve prohibiendo el uso del tabaco en las iglesias del Arzobispo de Sevilla).* Authorized January 30, 1632; publicized July 27, 1642. In BCol, sig. 63-7-9 (32), and Biblioteca General y Archivo Histórico, Universidad de Sevilla, sig. 110/130 (21). Similarly, in 1650, Pope Innocent X threatened excommunication for those who committed sacrilege by using tobacco in St. Peter's. Sarah Augusta Dickson, *Panacea or Precious Bane: Tobacco in Sixteenth Century Literature* (New York: New York Public Library, 1954), 154.

7. Antonio de Quintanadueñas, *Explicación a la bula en que N.S.P. Urbano VIII prohibe en Sevilla, y su Arçobispado el abuso del Tabaco en las iglesias, en sus Patios y Ambito* (Seville: Simón Fajardo Arias Montano, 1642), 1.

8. Quintanadueñas, *Explicación,* 2.

9. Ibid., 1–2.

10. Bartolomé Jiménez Patón, *Reforma de trages: Enseñase el buen vso del tabaco* (Baeza, Spain: Juan de la Cuesta, 1638).

11. *Edicto del vicario de Sevilla prohibiendo a los Eclesiasticos del Arzobispado el uso de trages profanes, y del tabaco en publico* (Seville, 1642), RAH, Jesuitas 90 n. 91, 9/3663.

12. "Session 23," in *The Canons and Decrees of the Sacred and Oecumenical Council of Trent,* ed. and trans. J. Waterworth (London: Dolman, 1848), 170–92, http://history.hanover.edu/texts/trent/ct23.html; Sara Tilghman Nalle, *God in La Mancha: Religious Reform and the People of Cuenca, 1500–1650* (Baltimore: Johns Hopkins University Press, 1992), 31, 44–46, 70.

13. *The Canons and Decrees of the Sacred and Oecumenical Council of Trent,* 75–91,

140–44, 152–61; Robert Sauzet, "Discours clericaux sur la nourriture," in *Pratiques et discours alimentaires à la Renaissance. Actes du colloque de Tours de mars 1979, Centre d'études supérieures de la Renaissance*, ed. Jean-Claude Margolin and Robert Sauzet (Paris: G.-P. Maisonneuve et Larose, 1982), 251; Luis de Granada, *Guía de pecadores*, ed. José Mallorquí Figuerola (Barcelona: Editorial Molino, 1942), 39.

14. Antonio de León Pinelo, *Questión moral: si el chocolate quebranta el ayuno eclesiástico* (Madrid: Viuda de Juan Gonzalez, 1636, fol. 37v.

15. Antonino Diana, *Resolutiones morales* (Venice: F. Baba, 1650–63), pt. 5, tract. 13, res. 1. This decision must have also appeared in an edition before 1644, since it was cited in Zacharias Pasqualigo, *Praxis jejunii ecclesiastici et naturalis* (Rome: Francisci Corbelletti, 1644); Tomás Hurtado, *Chocolate y tabaco: ayuno eclesiástico y natural* (Madrid: Francisco García, [1645?]), fols. 59v–60r; Antonio Escobar y Mendoza, *Examen de confesores y practica de penitentes en todas las materias de teologia moral*, 39th ed. (Madrid: Maria de Quiñones, 1650), 433.

16. For instance, in 1685 the Council of Tarragona threatened excommunication to those who smoked or chewed tobacco before (or an hour after) saying Mass or receiving Communion: *Colección de cánones y de todos los concilios de la Iglesia de España y de América*, ed. Juan Tejada y Ramiro (Madrid: Montero, 1859), 6:136, 138–39.

17. Sauzet, "Discours clericaux," 247, 251, 253; Granada, *Guía*, 90, 115, 141–43, 147.

18. For instance, *Sentencia jocose, que dio un juiz este presente año en un litigio, que tuvieron dos camaradas sobre el vino, y chocolate* (Lisbon: Pedro Ferreira, n.d.).

19. León Pinelo, *Questión moral*, dedication; the more permissive stance garnered unwelcome attention from authorities of the Inquisition, AHN Inq., leg. 4474, exp. 26, who worried about its effect on the *pueblo rudo*.

20. On the convergence of medical and religious rejections of the supernatural, Andrew Keitt, "The Miraculous Body of Evidence: Visionary Experience, Medical Discourse, and the Inquisition in Seventeenth-Century Spain," *The Sixteenth Century Journal* 36, no. 1 (2005): 77–96.

21. Santiago Valverde Turices, *Un discurso de chocolate* (Seville: Juan de Cabrera, 1624), fol. A–2r.

22. Antonio Colmenero de Ledesma, *Curioso tratado de la naturaleza y calidad del chocolate* (Madrid: Francisco Martinez, 1631), fol. 1r.

23. Juan de Castro y Medinilla, *Historia de las virtudes y propiedades del tabaco* (Cordoba: Salvador de Cea Tesa, 1620), fols. 19r, 21r.

24. Cristóbal de Hayo, *Las excelencias, y marivillosas [sic] propriedades del Tabaco, conforme a gravissimos Autores, y grandes experiencias* (Salamanca: Diego de Cossio, 1645), proemio.

25. Nicolás Monardes, *Primera y segunda y tercera partes de la historia medicinal: de las cosas que se traen de nuestras Indias Occidentales, que se sirven en medicina* (Seville: Alonso Escrivano, 1574), fol. 25r.

26. Hayo, *Las excelencias*, 12v; Fernando de Almirón Zayas, *Discurso de la anathomia de algunos miembros del cuerpo humano necessaria en orden a los daños q[ue] de continuo uso del tabaco suceden en los que le usan sin orden y methodo medicinal con lo qual les sera menos dañoso su uso* (Seville: Gabriel Ramos Vejarano, 1623), fol. 8v; Tomás Ramón, *Nueva prematica de reformacion contra los abusos de los afeytes, calçado . . . trajes y excesso en el uso del tabaco* (Zaragoza: Diego Dormer, 1635); the section on tobacco: Tomás Ramón, "Del abuso del tabaco o necociana," is in Silvia Monti, ed., *Il tabaco fa male? Medicina, ideologia, letteratura nella polemica sulla diffusione di un prodotto del Nuevo Mondo* (Milan: Franco Angeli, 1987), 72–87.

27. Castro y Medinilla, *Historia de las virtudes*, fol. 44r; Hayo, *Las excelencias*, 4r, 26r–v.

28. Francisco de Leiva y Aguilar, *Desengaño contra el mal uso del tabaco* (Cordoba: Salvador de Cea Tesa, 1634), fols. 7v, 8r; Ramón, "Del abuso del tabaco," 76.

29. Bartolomé Marradón, "Dialogue du Chocolate," in *Traitez nouveaux et curieux du café, du thé, du chocolat*, trans. Phillipe Sylvestre Dufour (Lyon: Jean Girin and B. Riviere, 1685), 436–38. Excerpts from the tobacco section are in Monti, *Il tabaco*, 88 n. 15.

30. Leiva y Aguilar, *Desengaño*, fols. 264r, 268v, 269v.

31. León Pinelo excerpted Cárdenas and Barrios in *Questión moral*, fols. 105v–120. Eminent physician Gaspar Caldera de Heredia similarly relied on Cárdenas and Barrios in *Tribunal medicum, magicum et politicum* (Leiden: J. Elsevir, 1658), 467, 469, 473, 476, 478.

32. Colmenero de Ledesma, *Curioso tratado*, frontispiece, fol. 1v; Valverde Turices, *Un discurso*, fol. A–4v; Isaac Cardoso, *Utilidades del agua i de la nieve, del bever frío i caliente* (Madrid: Viuda de Alonso Martin, 1637), fol. 107r; León Pinelo, *Questión moral*, fol. 3v; Caldera de Heredia, *Tribunal Medicum*, 469–70.

33. Caldera de Heredia, *Tribunal Medicum*, 471.

34. Colmenero de Ledesma, *Curioso tratado*, fols. 1v, 6v, 7v; Valverde Turices, *Un discurso*, fols. D–3v, C–4v; León Pinelo, *Questión moral*, 9r; Caldera de Heredia, *Tribunal medicum*, 470–71.

35. Valverde Turices, *Un discurso*, fols. D–1r.

36. Ibid., fols. C–2v–C–3v.

37. Leiva y Aguilar, *Desengaño*, fols. 266r–v.

38. Castro y Medinilla, *Historia de las virtudes*, fols. 19r–v, 45v, 46r–v, 51r–v.

39. Ramón, "Del abuso del tabaco," 75.

40. Jiménez Patón, *Enseñase*, fols. 61v, 65v; Ramón, "Del abuso del tabaco," 80–81, 86; Hayo, *Las excelencias*, 25; see also Leiva y Aguilar, *Desengaño*, fols. 5v, 6, 268r–v.

41. Hurtado, *Chocolate y tabaco*, fols. 34r–35r.

42. Ibid., fols. 36r–v, 37r; Leiva y Aguilar mentions "diabolical pact," *Desengaño*, fol. 241r.

43. Hurtado, *Chocolate y tabaco*, fols. 37v, 40r; see also, Sebastían de Covarrubias Orozco, *Tesoro de la lengua castellana o española*, ed. Felipe C. R. Maldonado (Madrid: Editorial Castalia, 1994), 907.

44. Granada, *Guía*; on this work as a best-seller, see Sara T. Nalle, "Literacy and Culture in Early Modern Europe," *Past and Present* 125 (1989): 80.

45. Covarrubias, *Tesoro*, 963.

46. Lorraine Daston and Katharine Park, *Wonders and the Order of Nature, 1150–1750* (New York: Zone Books, 1998), 121–22. My thinking on these matters has also greatly benefited from the work of Stuart Clark, *Thinking with Demons: The Idea of Witchcraft in Early Modern Europe* (Oxford: Clarendon, 1997); Fernando Cervantes, *The Devil in the New World: The Impact of Diabolism in the New World* (New Haven, CT: Yale University Press, 1994); and Andrew Keitt, "The Miraculous Body of Evidence," 77–96.

47. Quintanadueñas, *Explicación*, no fol., dedication.

48. Leiva y Aguilar, *Desengaño*, fols. 4r–5r.

49. Hurtado, *Chocolate y tabaco*, fols. 36r–v, 37r; Hayo, *Las excelencias*, fols. 4r, 14v–15r, 25r–v.

50. D. A. Brading, *The First America: The Spanish Monarchy, Creole Patriots, and the Liberal State, 1492–1867* (Cambridge: Cambridge University Press, 1992), 213–14. León Pinelo eventually secured a prestigious appointment on the Council of the Indies in 1658, Ernesto Schäfer, *El consejo real y supremo de las India*, vol. 2, *La labor del consejo de Indias en la administración colonial* (Seville: Escuela de Estudios Hispano-Americanos, 1947), 416–18. León Pinelo himself regarded his contribution to the chocolate debate as one of his most substantial publications: Antonio de León Pinelo, *Memorial de los libros, tratados y obras que ha impresso y tiene escritos el Licenciado Antonio de León Pinelo, Relator del Consejo Real de las Indias* [Madrid?: n.p., 1642?], Banc.

51. Hurtado, *Chocolate y tabaco*, preface.

52. León Pinelo, *Questión moral*, fol. 15r.

53. Ibid., fol. 12r; Hurtado, *Chocolate y tabaco*, fols. 3r, 114v.

54. Hurtado, *Chocolate y tabaco*, fols. 2r–v.

55. Ibid., fol. 23v.

56. My emphasis. Escobar y Mendoza, *Examen*, 453–54; this opinion also appeared in the 53rd edition (Paris: Antonio Bertier, 1650), 294.

57. León Pinelo, *Questión moral*, fols. 1r–v.

58. Ibid., fols. 17r–18v, 19r–v.

59. Ibid., fols. 4v–5r.

60. Hurtado, *Chocolate y tabaco*, fol. 23v.

61. I explore the idea that León Pinelo's treatise on chocolate and the ecclesiastical fast could also be read as a brief for cultural relativism and that such a viewpoint may be related to his identity as a Portuguese New Christian in Marcy Norton, "New World of Goods: A History of Tobacco and Chocolate in the Spanish Empire, 1492–1700" (PhD diss., University of California, Berkeley, 2000), chap. 5.

62. Joseph Klaits, *Servants of Satan: The Age of Witch Hunts* (Bloomington: Indiana University Press, 1985), 1. More than ten thousand deaths have been documented, but estimates of actual numbers killed are much larger.

63. Gerhild Scholz Williams, *Defining Dominion: The Discourses of Magic and Witchcraft in Early Modern France and Germany* (Ann Arbor: University of Michigan Press, 1995), 90–93 n. 11, 102–3; Lancre published *Tableau de l'inconstance des mauvais anges et demons, ou il est emplement traicté des sorciers et de la sorcelerie* (1612).

64. Lancre, *Tableau de l'inconstance*, 38, quoted in Williams, *Defining Dominion*, 34, 90–92 n. 11.

65. Gustav Henningsen, *The Witches' Advocate: Basque Witchcraft and the Spanish Inquisition, 1609–1614* (Reno: University of Nevada Press, 1980); Williams, *Defining Dominion*, 91; on the presence of tobacco, see *Curiosidades de mística parda* (Madrid: Imprint de los Sucesores de Cuesta, 1897).

66. These elements of witchcraft and satanic practice are described in Williams, *Defining Dominion*, 95, 97, 103–4, 111–12; Stuart Clark, *Thinking with Demons: The Idea of Witchcraft in Early Modern Europe* (New York: Oxford University Press, 2005), 13, 15, 24, 56, 84–85, 352, 427, particularly on inversion; Gustav Henningsen, *Witches' Advocate*, 70–86.

67. José de Acosta, *Historia natural y moral de las Indias* (Seville: Juan de Léon, 1590), fol. 239v.

68. Hayo, *Las excelencias*, fols. 4r, 14v–15r.

69. Leiva y Aguilar, *Desengaño*, fol. 262v.

70. Covarrubias Orozco, *Tesoro de la lengua castellana*, 907.

71. Keitt, "The Miraculous Body of Evidence," 84–85; Daston and Park, *Wonders and the Order of Nature*; Clark, *Thinking with Demons*.

72. *Curiosidades*, 228, 238.

73. Juan Francisco Marañon, "Tratado nuevo y curioso del chocolate, del café y del thé, traducido y recopilado de muy graves autores" (1690), unpublished manuscript at the HSA, 38–39.

74. *The Canons and Decrees of the Sacred and Oecumenical Council of Trent*, 82.

75. Piero Camporesi, "The Consecrated Host: A Wondrous Excess," in *Fragments for a History of the Human Body*, trans. Anna Cancogne, ed. Michael Feher, Ramona Naddaff and Nadia Tazi (New York: Zone, 1989), 1:221–23, 227.

76. Valverde Turices, *Un discurso*, fol. C–2v.

77. Henry Stubbe, *The Indian Nectar, or a Discourse Concerning Chocolata* (London: Printed by J. C. for Andrew Crook, 1662), 97–98. There is good reason to believe that such a manuscript, though now lost, once did exist, for Stubbe is a faithful reporter of the many texts that he cites and quotes that do exist.

78. Quoted in Stubbe, *Indian Nectar*, 99–100. My emphasis.

79. "Relación verdadera del gran sermón que predicó en la mesquita parroquial" (1684), HSA, frontispiece, 7v, 9v, 54r–v; Capitán Castro de Torres, *Panegírico al chocolate*, ed. Manuel Peréz de Guzmán (Seville: E. Rasco, 1887 [1st ed., Segovia, 1640]), 21.

80. Castro de Torres, *Panegírico al chocolate*, 5, 7, 16, 15. For another poem that associates chocolate and the Mass, see *Sentencia jocosa*, 16.

81. My English translation from the Spanish translation of the original Latin, Gregorio Mayans, *Chocolata, sive in laudem potionis indiae, quam apellant Chocolate* (1733), trans. and ed. José Maria Estrelles i Gonzalez, in "Una pincelada frívola en la obra de

Mayans: Elegía al Chocolate," *Estudios dedicados a Juan Peset Aleixandre* (Valencia: Universidad de Valencia, 1982), 1:589–93.

82. Caroline Walker Bynum, *Holy Feast and Holy Fast: The Religious Significance of Food to Medieval Women* (Berkeley: University of California Press, 1987).

83. *Sátira contra el tabaco* (n.p., n.d. [1644–1645?]), in Monti, *Il tabaco*, 120.

84. Jerónimo de Prado, June 30, 1642, Sección I, Libros de Autos Capitulares, no. 57, 292–93, BCol.

85. Ramón, "Del abuso del tabaco," 74–75; "Sátira contra el tabaco," 121. The moralist Jiménez Patón suggested that tobacco "has a *nosequé* [the same as *je ne sais quoi* or "a quality or attribute that is difficult to describe"] of the spell, because some of those who consume confessed to me that, even knowing that it does them no good, rather harm, want to give it up but without success," *Enseñase*, fol. 62v.

86. *Romance en alabanza del tabaco* (Barcelona: Gabriel Nogués, 1644), no fol., BL. *Romance en alabanza del tabaco*, in Monti, *Il tabaco*, 124; *Sátira contra el tabaco*.

87. Castro de Torres, *Panegírico al chocolate*, 5, 7, 15, 16. For another poem that associates chocolate and the Mass, see *Sentencia jocosa*, 16.

88. Antonio Hurtado de Mendoza, "Coplas al Chocolate. Décima 115 a una Señora Rubia," PRB Mss. II/2802, fols. 252r–v.

89. "Relación verdadera del gran sermón."

90. Ibid., fols. 1v–2r.

91. Ibid., fol. 7r.

92. Ibid., fol. 13r.

93. Ibid., fol. 25r.

Epilogue: Globalization, Gateways, and Transformations

1. Jerome Brooks, *Tobacco, Its History: Illustrated by the Books, Manuscripts and Engravings in the Collection of George Arents Jr.* (New York: Rosenbach Company, 1937–1952), 1:41, 149–50; Berthold Laufer, "The Introduction of Tobacco into Africa," in *Tobacco and Its Use in Africa*, Anthropology Leaflet no. 29 (Chicago: Field Museum of Natural History, 1930), 3, 6, 10, 11; Allen F. Roberts, "Smoking in Sub-Saharan Africa," in *Smoke: A Global History of Smoking*, 47–48. On mariner culture in a later period, see Marcus Rediker, *Between the Devil and the Deep Blue Sea: Merchant Seamen, Pirates, and the Anglo-American Maritime World, 1700–1750* (Cambridge: Cambridge University Press, 1987).

2. Brooks, *Tobacco, Its History*, 1:487, 2:118; Laufer, "The Introduction of Tobacco into Africa," 7.

3. Brooks, *Tobacco, Its History*, 1:540.

4. Rudi Matthee, *The Pursuit of Pleasure: Drugs and Stimulants in Iranian History, 1500–1900* (Princeton: Princeton University Press, 2005), 119–23.

5. See relevant chapters in *Smoke: A Global History of Smoking*; Frank Dikötter, Lars Laamann, and Zhou Xun, *Narcotic Cultures: A History of Drugs in China* (Chicago: University of Chicago Press, 2004), 25–26; Carol Benedict, *Golden Silk Smoke: The Social and Cultural History of Tobacco Smoking in China, 1550–1950* (Berkeley: University of California Press, forthcoming), chap. 1. I am grateful to the author for allowing me to read this in manuscript.

6. Quoted in Timothy Brook, "Smoking in Imperial China," in *Smoke: A Global History of Smoking*, ed. Sander Gilman and Zhou Xun (London: Reaktion Books, 2004), 85.

7. Anthony Reid, "From Betel-Chewing to Tobacco-Smoking in Indonesia," *Journal of Asian Studies* 44, no. 3 (1985): 529–47; David T. Courtwright, *Forces of Habit: Drugs and the Making of the Modern World* (Cambridge: Harvard University Press, 2001), 54. It is thought that about 10 percent of today's inhabitants of the globe are betel chewers.

8. Matthee, *Pursuit*, 124, 131; George Bryan Souza, "Developing Habits: Opium and Tobacco in the Indonesian Archipelago, c. 1619–c. 1794," in *Drugs and Empires: Essays in Modern Imperialism and Intoxication, c. 1500 to c. 1930*, ed. James H. Mills and Patricia Barton (Basingstoke: Palgrave, 2008).

9. Brooks, *Tobacco, Its History*, 1:540.

10. The quote is from Timothy Brook in a personal communication; P. Ram Manohar, "Smoking and Ayurvedic Medicine in India," in *Smoke*, 68.

11. Souza, "Developing Habits." I am grateful to the author for showing me his work in manuscript.

12. Jonathan Spence, "Opium Smoking in Ch'ing China," in *Conflict and Control in Late Imperial China*, ed. Frederic Wakeman and Carolyn Grant (Berkeley: University of California Press, 1975), 148–49.

13. Matthee, *Pursuit*, 131.

14. Laufer, "The Introduction of Tobacco into Africa," 13, 15.

15. Antonio Colmenero de Ledesma, *Curioso tratado de la naturaleza y calidad del chocolate* (Madrid: Francisco de Martínez, 1631), 1r.

16. Henry Stubbe, *The Indian Nectar, or a Discourse Concerning Chocolata* (London: Printed by J. C. for Andrew Crook, 1662), 15; Susan J. Terrio, *Crafting the Culture and History of French Chocolate* (Berkeley: University of California Press, 2000), 73–79; Sophie D. Coe and Michael D. Coe, *The True History of Chocolate* (New York: Thames and Hudson, 1996), 236.

17. Wolf Mueller, *Bibliographie des Kaffee, des Kakao, der Schokolade, des Tee und deren Surrogate bis zum Jahre* (Bad Bocklet, Germany: Krieg, 1960).

18. Stubbe, preface to *Indian Nectar*; see also John Chamberlayne, *The Natural History of Coffee, Thee, Chocolate, Tobacco* (London: Printed for Christopher Wilkinson, 1682), 16–17.

19. Stubbe, *Indian Nectar*, 3–4, 8, 35–36, 73, 78, 83, 85, 97, 108.

20. Quoted in ibid., 89.

21. Phillipe Sylvestre Dufour, *Traitez nouveaux et curieux du café, du thé, du chocolat* (Lyon: Jean Girin & B. Riviere, 1685), 305, 317; Dutch author Willem Piso relied on Colmenero de Ledesma as well: Stubbe, *Indian Nectar*, 87–88.

22. Quoted in Coe and Coe, *True History*, 212.

23. Most of the scholarship on stimulant beverages has mistakenly assumed that chocolate followed rather than preceded coffee and tea. On chocolate being outpaced by coffee and tea in the later seventeenth century, see Jordan Goodman, "Excitantia: Or How Enlightenment Europe Took to Soft Drugs," in *Consuming Habits: Drugs in History and Anthropology*, ed. Jordan Goodman, Paul E. Lovejoy, and Andrew Sherratt (London: Routledge, 1995), 126.

24. Paul Butel, *Histoire du Thé* (Paris: Editions Desjonqueres, 1997), 28, 45–47.

25. On the development and spread of coffee in the Near East, see Ralph S. Hattox, *Coffee and Coffeehouses: The Origins of a Social Beverage in the Medieval Near East* (Seattle: University of Washington Press, 1985).

26. Quoted in Wolfgang Schivelbusch, *Tastes of Paradise: A Social History of Spices, Stimulants, and Intoxicants*, trans. David Jacobson (New York: Vintage Books, 1992), 17.

27. Mark Pendergrast, *Uncommon Grounds: The History of Coffee and How It Transformed Our World* (New York: Basic Books, 1999), 8; see also Schivelbusch, *Tastes of Paradise*, 15, 17.

28. Schivelbusch, *Tastes of Paradise*, 17; Brian Cowan, *The Social Life of Coffee: The Emergence of the British Coffeehouse* (New Haven: Yale University Press), 58–60; Jean Leclant, "Coffee and Cafés in Paris, 1644–1693," in *Food and Drink in History*, ed. Robert Forster and Orest Ranum (Baltimore: Johns Hopkins University Press, 1979), 87; S. D. Smith, "Accounting for Taste: British Coffee Consumption in Historical Perspective," *Journal of Interdisciplinary History* 272, no. 2 (1996).

29. "Carta qve escrivió vn Médico cristiano, que estava curando en Antiberi, a vn Cardenal de Roma, sobre la bebida del Cahuè or café" [n.p., 16—], Banc. and BN.

30. The location of Antiberi is not clear; one possibility is that it was the Palestinian city of Tiberias, under Ottoman suzerainty.

31. "Carta qve escrivió vn Médico cristiano," 1.

32. Schivelbusch, *Tastes*; Woodruff D. Smith, *Consumption and the Making of Respectability, 1600–1800* (New York: Routledge, 2002); Cowan, *Social Life*.

33. Ulla Heise, *Coffee and Coffee-houses* (West Chester, Penn.: Schiffer, 1987), 17; Pendergrast, *Uncommon Grounds*, 8; Jean Leclant, "Coffee and Cafés," 87.

34. Dufour, preface to *Traitez nouveaux et curieux;* Nicolas de Blegny, *Le bon usage du thé, du caffé et du chocolat pour la preservation & pour la guerison des maladies* (Lyon: Chez T. Amaulry, 1687), 247; John Chamberlayne, *The Natural History of Coffee, Thee, Chocolate, Tobacco* (London: Printed for Christopher Wilkinson, 1682); *Tractatvs novi de potv caphé; de Chinensivm thé; et de chocolata* (Paris: P. Maguet, 1685).

35. Coe and Coe, *True History*, 236; see Cameron L. McNeil, "Traditional Cacao Use in Modern Mesoamerica," 341–66, and other relevant essays in *Chocolate in Mesoamerica: A Cultural History of Cacao*, ed. Cameron L. McNeil (Gainesville: University Press of Florida, 2006); Brian Cazeneuve, "All Chocolate, No Oompa-Loompas," *New York Times*, Dec. 22, 2004. Kakawa Chocolate House, http://www.kakawachocolates.com. The revival of interest among chocolatiers in traditional Mesoamerican and European drinking chocolate may well have been spurred by the 1995 publication of Coe and Coe's *True History*.

36. Smith, "Accounting for Taste."

37. At the end of the eighteenth century, when the Spanish elite looked to France for cultural cues, coffee began its triumphant ascendance: Charles E. Kany, *Life and Manners in Madrid, 1750–1800* (Berkeley: University of California, 1932), 151.

38. Compare the descriptions in Coe and Coe, *True History*, 210–15, 224–29, with those in earlier chapters of this book.

39. Ibid., 247.

40. Ibid., 136, 234, 241–42.

41. Ibid., 242–45, 248–59.

42. World Health Organization, "Tobacco Free Initiative," http://www.who.int/tobacco/health_priority/en/index.html; Courtwright, *Forces*.

43. Warren E. Leary, "Researchers Investigate (Horrors!) Nicotine's Potential Benefits," *New York Times*, Jan. 14, 1997, B11; John A. Baron, "Beneficial Effects of Nicotine and Cigarette Smoking: The Real, the Possible, and the Spurious," *British Medical Bulletin* 52, no. 1 (1996): 58–73; "Editorial: What Aspects of Human Performance Are Truly Enhanced by Nicotine?" *Addiction* 93, no. 3 (1998): 317–20.

44. On the "mortality crises" that characterized Europe before the nineteenth century, see Michael W. Flinn, *The European Demographic System, 1500–1820* (Baltimore: Johns Hopkins University Press, 1988); Massimo Livi Bacci, *A Concise History of World Population*, 4th ed. (Malden, Mass.: Blackwell, 2007), pt. 4.

45. Jordan Goodman, *Tobacco in History: The Cultures of Dependence* (London: Routledge, 1993), 90–94, 102, 106.

46. This synopsis is based on Goodman, *Tobacco in History*, 93–114, 230–36; Courtwright, *Forces*, 114–25.

47. Courtwright, *Forces*, 19.

48. Keith Thomas, *Religion and the Decline of Magic* (New York: Scribner, 1971). Michael Saler, "Modernity and Enchantment: A Historiographic Review," *The American Historical Review* 111 (June 2006): 692–716.

Glossary

achiote (**Nah./Sp./Eng.**). *Bixa orellana*, also known in English as annatto, a red, somewhat musky spice used to color chocolate red.

ah kin (**Maya**). Traditional priest.

alcabala (**Sp.**). Sales tax levied since the Middle Ages.

almojarifazgo (**Sp.**). Customs duty.

aloja (or *aloxa*) (**Sp.**). A spiced, honey-sweetened beverage of Spanish-Muslim origin.

Arawak. Native inhabitants of the Greater Antilles and other parts of the circum-Caribbean region at the time of Spanish arrival.

arrendador (**Sp.**). Tax farmer, such as for the tobacco monopoly.

arrendamiento (**Sp.**). Lease, such as that held by a tobacco tax farmer.

atole (**Sp.** from *atextli*, **Nah.**). A maize-based beverage that could be sweetened with honey.

baile (**Sp.**). Dance; in the seventeenth century referred to brief theatrical performance with dance and song.

beleño (**Sp.**). See henbane.

boitios (**Araw.**). Shaman or priest among Arawak who could communicate with supernatural spirits and prophesy.

cabildo (**Sp.**). Town or city council.

cacáhoatl or *cacauatl* (**Nah.**). See *kakaw*.

cacahoaquáhuitl (**Nah.**). Cacao tree (*Theobroma cacao*).

cacique (**Araw./Sp./Eng.**). A chieftain in the native Caribbean; used by the Spanish for indigenous rulers throughout the American dominions.

Casa de Contratación (**Sp.**). House of Trade, Spanish body overseeing transatlantic trade.

casta (**Sp.**). Someone of mixed racial ancestry.

cemi (**Araw.**). Object made of wood, stone, or fabric in which supernatural spirits were thought to reside.

chocolatera (**Sp.**). Copper vessel for making hot chocolate.

cohoba (**Araw.**). Either tobacco or *Anadenanthera peregrina* or a composite of the two, or some other psychoactive substance(s) snuffed by Taino. See also *yopa*.

consulado (**Sp.**). Merchant guild representing interests of Seville's merchants.

converso (Sp.). A convert from Judaism to Christianity or a descendant of such a convert.

Cortes (Sp.). Parliament in Castile.

Creole (Sp.). See *criollo*.

criollo (Sp.). Someone of Spanish descent born or raised in the Americas.

curandero (Sp.). A healer, often referring to someone of indigenous or mixed ethnic background.

ducado (Sp). See *maravedí*.

encomendero (Sp.). Spanish colonist in possession of an *encomienda*.

encomienda (Sp.). Land grant given to conquistadores that gave them rights to tribute in goods and labor from indigenous subjects.

entremés (Sp.). A brief theatrical performance, often humorous.

estanco (Sp.). A monopoly.

estanquero (Sp.). Someone with a monopoly concession; synonymous with a tobacco vendor by the mid-seventeenth century.

estrado (Sp.). Room in a house where upper-class Spanish women socialized.

guaiacum (Lat., Sp. *guayaco* from Taino *guayacan*). Wood from a tree used to treat syphilis in the sixteenth century.

gueynacaztle (Nah.). See *hueinacaztli*.

henbane (Eng.). See *Hyoscyamus*.

Hyoscyamus (Lat.). A plant of the solanaceous family that can produce hallucinations; strongly associated with witchcraft in early modern Europe. Europeans first took tobacco to be a variety of tobacco henbane.

hololisque (Sp.). See *ololiuhqui*.

hueinacaztli (Nah.). "Great ear" flower, probably *Cymbopetalum penduliflorum*. One of the three floral flavorings, along with vanilla and *mecaxóchitl*, favored for chocolate drinks among pre-Columbian Mesoamericans.

indiano (Sp.). Someone returned from the Americas, likely having obtained a fortune.

jícara (Sp.). Hispanicized version of Nahuatl *xicalli* (gourd cup) that came to denote a ceramic or porcelain cup for drinking chocolate.

joyería (Sp.). Retail shop specializing in luxury goods.

kakaw (Maya). Cacao. Word borrowed by Nahuatl (and many other languages), *kakaw-atl* is drink made with cacao.

liquidambar (Sp./Eng.): A resinous gum from the bark of the tree *Liquidambar styraciflua* used, among other purposes, to scent tobacco among Mesoamericans, and later, Europeans.

maravedí (Sp.). During the period under study, in early modern Castile, 34 *maravedís* were equivalent to one *real*, and 375 *maravedís* equaled one *ducado*.

marrano (Sp.). A clandestine Jew.

materia medica (Lat./Eng.). Substances with medical value.

mecasuchil (Sp.). See *mecaxóchitl*.

mecaxóchitl (Nah.). Probably *Piper sanctum*. One of the three floral flavorings, along with vanilla and *hueinacaztli*, favored for chocolate among pre-Columbian Mesoamericans.

mechoacán. Also known as *jalapa*. Root of *Convolvulus mechoacan*, used by Mesoamericans and later Spaniards as a purgative.

millones (Sp.). Excise tax levied on specially designated goods that came to include tobacco and chocolate in the seventeenth century.

molinillo (Sp.). Wooden utensil for frothing chocolate.

morisco (Sp.). A Muslim converted to Christianity or someone with Muslim ancestry.

ololiuhqui (Nah.). The seeds of morning glory (*Rivea corymbosa*), ingested by Mesoa-mericans in order to produce hallucinations.

orejuelas (Sp.). See *hueinacaztli*.

piciete, pisiete (Nah./Sp.). See *picietl*.

picietl (Nah.). Among pre-Columbian Mesoamericans, "small" or "fine" tobacco, per-haps referring to species *N. rustica*; in the colonial period, often referred to as chew-ing, as opposed to smoking, tobacco.

pochteca (Nah.). A long-distance merchant.

polvo de olor (Sp.). Snuff with fragrance.

polvo de sumonte (Sp.). Snuff without fragrance.

pozol (Nah.). Soaked maize, sometimes combined with cacao in a beverage.

procurador (Sp.). A representative; can refer to ones attending parliament (Cortes) or religious councils.

pulque (Nah.). Alcoholic beverage made from fermented maize.

puyulcha (Maya). Beverage of cacao and maize.

real (Sp). See *maravedí*.

regalía (Sp.). Goods belonging to the royal patrimony, and thus subject to taxation and monopolies without parliamentary consent.

regalo (Sp.). Gift or luxury.

rescate (Sp.). Literally "hostage"; used to describe illegal trade between Spanish set-tlers and non-Spanish traders.

rollo (Sp.). "Roll"; used to describe tobacco processed into rolls intended for smoking.

sahumerios (Sp.). Something that makes smoke, often applied to incense braziers, but sometimes used by Spaniards to describe tobacco pipes during early Colonial pe-riod.

sumonte (Sp.). See *polvo de sumonte*.

Taíno. Language spoken by Indians of Antilles and parts of northern South America, sometimes used interchangeably with Arawak.

tabaquera: (Sp.). A small container used for carrying tobacco, most often snuff but also smoking tobacco.

tecomatl (Nah.), *tecomate* (Sp.). Ceramic vessel, such as that used for drinking choco-late.

tenderos (Sp.). Shopkeepers.

teotl (Nah.). Sacred energy force.

tianguis (Nah.). Marketplace.

tienda: (Sp.). Store.

tlatoani (Nah.). Ruler.

tlilxochitl (Nah.). Vanilla (*Vanilla planifolia*); one of the three floral flavorings, along with *mecaxóchitl* and *hueinacaztli*, favored for chocolate among pre-Columbian Mesoamericans.

vicio (Sp.). Vice or luxury.

xicalli (Nah.). A gourd, such as that used for drinking chocolate.

xícara (Sp.). See *jícara*.

xochinacaztli (Nah.). "Flowery ear," probably another term for *cymbopetalum pen-duliflorum*.

yetecomatl (Nah.). Gourd container for holding tobacco.

yetl (Nah.). Tobacco.

yopa. Pods from the tree *Anadenanthera peregrina* that were snuffed by Indians in northern South America for narcotic and hallucinogenic effects.

Index

Italic page numbers refer to figures, maps and tables.

Asia, 258, 259

Atlantic trade: and *avería* (fleet) tax, 142, 143, 147, 151, 294n2; and chocolate-drinking vessels, 144, 147, 148, 162, 169, *170*; chocolate in records of, 142, *143*, 147–48, 162; and chocolate prices, 296n32; chocolate's absence from, 141; elite Spanish network of, 145–48; individuals involved in, 144–45; infrastructure for, 144, 148; plebeian trade, 156–61; Portuguese role in, 154–55, 298n66; spreading the market, 161–67; tobacco in records of, 142, *143*, 162; and tobacco monopoly, 151, 201; tobacco production for, 11, 151, 153–54; tobacco's absence from, 141

Augustine of Hippo, 249

Avicenna, 109–10

Bakhtin, Mikhail, 189, 193, 306n53

ballestero, 117, 289n40

balsam, 109, 113

Barrionuevo, Cristóbal de, 295n15, 296n17

Barrionuevo, Jerónimo de, 180–81, 209

Barrios, Juan de, 132–34, 136–37, 237, 238, 289n38, 290n63, 292n16

Benavente, Toribio de (Motolinia), 77–78, 130, 244

Benjamin, Walter, 314n3

Benzoni, Girolamo, 8, 60, 61, 118, 139, 244

betel, 257, 258

betrothal, 30, 40, 43, 179

biological determinism, 7–8

blood sacrifice, 33–35, 65, 66, 67, 71, 72. *See also* chocolate

Brazil, 101–2, 151, 221

Brouwer, Adriaen, *The Smokers*, *186*, 190

Bucarelli, Antonio María, 295–96n15

cacao: as currency, 1, 16, 59, 64, 65, 74, 126; in detail of *Codex Mendoza*, *17*; hearts associated with, 35; and humoral balance, 237; and monkeys, 2, 83, 281n65; monopoly on, 228; provenance of, 166, 301–2n136; taxes on, 205, 206, 225; and theobromine, 3, 7; as tribute levied by Mexica, 16, *17*

cacao production: colonial encouragement of, 64; depictions of, 26; in Guatemala, 296–97n35; in Mesoamerica, 7, 18, 267n3; pre-conquest systems of, 11, 296n35; regions of, 16; and Spanish colonists, 105–6

cacao tree. *See Theobrama cacao*

caffeine, 3, 262

cannabis, 56, 120, 121, 258, 259

cannibalism, 95–96, 98

Cárdenas, Juan de, 132–37, 139, 167, 168, 237, 286n90, 293n30

Caribbean, *viii*, 149–50, 151, 153–56

Carib people, 90–92, 98–101, 116, 149, 150

Carmona shipping family, 148, 158, 295n15

Carrafa, Juan Baptista, 219, 310n50

Casa de Contratación, 99, 112, 147

Cassia fistula, 109, 113, 142, 150, 294n5

caste stratification: and Amerindian medical expertise, 134; and chocolate consumption, 15, 20, 27–28, 43, 52, 54, 55, 59, 65, 74; and merchants' feasts, 22–23, 23, 27–28; and resistance to colonialism, 66, 72, 73–74; and tobacco consumption, 15, 20, 22–23, 23, 27–28, 43, 50, 58, 65. *See also* social relations; social status

Castile: and Portuguese New Christians, 214; and Spanish state, 202, 203–4; and tobacco monopoly, 201, 203, 207, 208, 210, 221–23, 227, 228

Castro y Medinilla, Juan de, 171–72, 181–84, 188, 197, 199, 235, 238, 248

Catholic Church: on chocolate, 65, 131, 230, 231–32, 234–35, 242–45, 252, 255, 291–92n8, 293n30; and diffusion of chocolate, 146; on tobacco, 65, 131, 230, 231–34, 235, 241, 248, 252. *See also* clergy

ceramic vessel, Maya, Late Classic Period, 6

Charles II (king of Spain), 173–74, 175, 177, 249, 302n1

Charles V (emperor), 53, 95

childbirth, 31, 40, 43, 83, 138, 273n58

chili peppers, 18, 113, 123, 168, 169

chocolate: and adaptations to Christianity, 77, 80, *81*, 82; aphrodisiacal qualities of, 15, 30, 126, 138, 140, 179, 237; Barrios on, 132, 133, 134, 136, 137; blood associated with, 33, 35, 43, 59, 67, 77, 250–51, 265; as candy, 262–63, 264; dance linked with, 24, 25, 32, 43, 78, 178; demysticification of, 235–36, 240, 255, 265; and elite Atlantic trade, 145–46; ennoblement of, 15, 16; European commodification of, 11, 148; fiscal policies related to, 203; on frontier, 51–52; as gift, 27, 87, 90, 103, 146–47, 174–75, *176–77*, 180–81, 190, 244, 304n19; intrinsic hedonic qualities of, 8; as link to past traditions, 53, 64, 72, 77; as magical potion, 138; maize juxtaposed with, 27, 30, 272n43; in markets, 88, 282n22; medicinal uses of, 8, 12, 35, 43, 59–60, 65, 89, 106, 135, 139, 237, 250–51; and

merchants' feasts, 21–24, 25, 27, 28; as numinous substance, 240–41, 265; physiological effects of, 35; and pre-Hispanic associations, 76; preparation methods of Amerindian women, 6, 16, 19, 26, 59, 74, 75, 87, 103; price of, 164, 165, 296n32, 300nn107, 108; processing of, 7; provenance of, 229; psychotropic effects of, 18, 196–97, 200, 251–52, 264, 307n72; recipes for, 164, 167, 168–70, 300n106; retailers of, 164, 165–66, *166*; sacred force within, 33–35, *34*, 230, 250, 256, 265–66; satire on, 3, 229, 231, 251, 252, 253–55; and still-life genre, 169, *170*, 191; taste for, 9, 167–70, 172; taxes on, 205, 206, 208, 225, 240; tobacco's relationship with, in Mesoamerica, 1, 2; as vice, 240, 255
chocolate consumption: and caste stratification, 15, 20, 27–28, 43, 52, 54, 55, 59, 65, 74; diffusion of, 3, 64, 87, 146–48, 162, 163–64, 166, 168, 255, 259–62; and diplomatic meetings, 28, 43, 48, 49, 51–52, 146; and European medical practice, 238, 239–40; and luxury tax, 208; in Mesoamerica, 1, 267n3; pre-Columbia compared with European, 199–200; in private, 195–97, 199; in South America, 268n4
chocolate-drinking vessels (*jícaras* and *tecomates*): and Atlantic trade, 144, 147, 148, 162, 169, *170*; and chocolate retailers, 165; and colonialism, 64; in detail of *Codex Mendoza*, *17*; in markets, 282n22; and ritual, 74, 75, 177; and status distinctions, 23, 68, 173; theobromine found in, 7; as tribute levied by Mexica, 16, *17*, 18
chocolate drinks: and All Souls' Day, 78; availability of, 64; and Catholic doctrine, 131, 231, 234–35, 242–45, 291–92n8, 293n30; Díaz on, 15; and diplomatic meetings, 28, 51–52; European market for, 145–46; European reaction to, 8; foamy head of, 6, 15, 18, 19, 28, 35, 43, 59, 65, 69, 74, 78, 132, 169, 177, 270–71n11; Hernández on, 123, 128; ingredients of, 7, 18, 64, 123, 167–70, 206, 237, 260, 270n10; and Inquisition, 315n19; Marradón on, 139–40; marriage associated with, 30, 31, 179, 273n58; Martyr on, 54–55; preparation of, *176*–77, *177*; protocol for serving, 22–23; and sacred uses, 35, 67, 74–75, 77, 245; servings of, 164, 300n107; stirring sticks for, 18, 21, 64, 68, 270–71n11; terms for, 167–68, 301n125

Christian conversion: and Amerindian's adaptations to Christianity, 77, 80, 82; and Amerindians' remaking of Christianity, 64, 93; and colonialism, 63; and Columbus, 46; and European ideology, 48; Martyr on, 53–54, 56; success of, 73; superficiality of, 129–30, 134; and tobacco use, 100, 101–2; in Yanhuitlán, 69–70
Christianity: Amerindian adaptations to, 10, 63–64, 68, 77–83, *81*; desecration of holy places, 72; and liturgical calendar, 188–89. *See also* Catholic Church; clergy; Protestant Church
cigarettes, 171, 264, 265
cinnamon, 18, 45, 168, 169, 237, 270n10
clergy: and chocolate, 250, 259; chocolate use of, 139–40, 197, 250; and taxes, 204–5, 226; tobacco use of, 131, 182–83, 187, 231–34, 248–49, 252–53, 315n16; transatlantic trips of, 146. *See also* missionaries
cochineal, 144
Codex Borbonicus, *39*
Codex Fejérváry-Mayer, *34*, *83*
Codex Madrid, *36*
Codex Mendoza, *17*
Codex Tudela, *19*, *42*
Codex Vindobonensis Mexicanus I, *31*,*37*
Coe, Michael D., 270n10, 294n3, 320n35
Coe, Sophie D., 270n10, 294n3, 320n35
coffee, 161, 254, 260–62, 264, 319n23, 320n37
cohoba, 54, 55, 277n30
Colmenero de Ledesma, Antonio, 169, 235, 237, 259, 260
colonialism: in borderlands, 84–85, 90–92; and chocolate as link to past traditions, 53, 64, 72, 77; and European rivalries, 98–100, 149, 150, 285n66; regime of, 63; resistance to, 65–70, 72, 73, 74–76, 138, 291n1; and tobacco as link to past traditions, 64, 72, 77; and tribute system, 63, 64, 73, 106. *See also* Spanish colonists
Columbus, Christopher, 3, 44–47, 53, 85, 99, 201
Communion, 131, 231, 232, 233–34, 248, 249, 250
consulado, 146, 296n15
contraband. *See* smuggling
conversos. *See* Portuguese New Christians
copal: and Mesoamerican beliefs and rituals, 40, 41, 65, 67, 69, 70, 71, 74, 76; Monardes on, 113; trade in, 109

Cortés, Hernán, 13, 51, 78, 87
cosmological traditions, 2, 10, 12, 30, 32, 34, 36–42, 37, 48, 81, 82, 83, 274n76, 281n65
Counter-Reformation (Catholic Reformation), 223, 231–33, 234, 240, 242, 245, 255
Creoles: and Amerindian medical expertise, 133–34; and Atlantic trade, 146; on chocolate, 132–36, 137, 237; chocolate consumption of, 167, 170, 234; and chocolate socialization, 89–90, 132; identity of, 131–34, 136, 137; and Maya women as domestics, 87; on tobacco, 136–38; tobacco use of, 132, 158; women, 183
Cristobal (cacique of Ocuituco), 68–69
crypto-Jews. *See* Marranism
Cuba, 45, 51, 85, 151, 154, 221
cultural constructivism, 8
cultural hybridity, 21, 64. *See also* syncretism
cultural relativism, 255
culture: artifacts of, 4; European ideology of supremacy, 3, 11, 48, 53; homogeneity of, 16, 18, 20; intercultural encounters, 47; and meaning, 203, 228, 264; of mestizos, 137; transmission of, 76

deities: bloodletting onto cacao, 35, 36; chocolate and tobacco as tributes to, 30–31, 32, 65; chocolate associated with, 64, 65–66, 74–75; memory of, 83; and resistance to colonialism, 66–69, 72, 73; tobacco and chocolate consumption of, 32–33; tobacco associated with, 15–16, 33, 64, 65–66, 79
desire, 235, 239–40, 241
diabolism: chocolate associated with, 65, 140, 230, 239, 249; European conceptions of, 58, 60, 92, 93, 119, 230, 241; and Francisco Martín, 97, 98; tobacco associated with, 65, 118–21, 230, 239, 240, 241–42, 245–49, 247, 259
Díaz del Castillo, Bernal, 13, 15, 30, 52, 244–45
Dickson, Sarah Augusta, 116
Dioscorides, Pedanius, 109, 110, 111, 112–13, 115, 116, 122, 127–28
"divine ear" spice, 18, 21, 167, 169, 270n10
Dominicans, 70–71, 90, 130, 131, 234–325
Drake, Francis, 99–100, 150
drinking vessel, Maya, Late Classic Period, 2
Durán, Diego, 27–28, 29, 35, 40, 51–52, 276n19

England: and chocolate, 260; and cigarettes, 264; and Portuguese traders, 154; as rival of Spanish colonists, 98, 99–100, 149, 150; and Spanish Armada, 204; and Spanish tobacco monopoly, 224, 225; and tea, 261; tobacco consumption in, 163; and tobacco trade, 151, 153, 154, 155, 156, 222, 312n88; and tobacco use, 102, 257
enslaved Africans: and colonialism, 85, 90; as cultural go-betweens, 60; and Inquisition, 138, 291n7; as mariners, 157; and native acculturation, 88, 291n7; runaways, 91, 149; syncretic culture forged with Awarak, 86; tobacco production of, 105; tobacco use of, 86, 102
Erasmus of Rotterdam, 194–95
Eucharist, 131, 188, 230–34, 235, 241, 247, 249–52, 265
European/Amerindian interactions: and borderlands, 90–98; and chocolate drinks, 51–52; and chocolate socialization, 89–90, 199–200; and cultural improvisation, 62; and disease, 47–48, 63, 85, 87; and tobacco, 49–50, 93–94, 199–200; and trade, 47–50, 52, 62, 98
European medical practice: and academic medicine, 109; and Amerindian medical expertise, 11, 88–89, 108–9, 141; and chocolate use, 135, 235, 237, 238; and demystification process, 235–36; eclectic approach of, 109, 110; and New World materia medica, 109–11, 142, 294–95n5; and tobacco use, 235–39
Europeans: early experiences of tobacco and chocolate, 48, 276n11; ideology of religious and cultural supremacy, 3, 11, 48, 53; rivals of Spanish colonists, 98–100, 149, 150
European society: assimilation of tobacco and chocolate, 7, 8–12, 138–39, 140, 158, 199–200, 231, 255, 257, 259, 293n44; early reaction to tobacco and chocolate, 8, 102–3, 105, 107–8, 127, 132–34; effects of tobacco and chocolate on, 4; and tobacco monopoly, 228

fasting: and chocolate, 131, 179, 231, 234–35, 242–45, 291–92n8, 293n30; and shamanism, 97; and tobacco, 231, 234, 248
Ferdinand (king of Spain), 44, 46–47, 202
Fernández de Miranda, Simon, 218, 311n73
fertility celebrations, 35, 273n70
Figueroa, Juan Quesada de, 147, 148
Flanders, 184, 259, 260

Index

Flemish art works, 184, 304–5n31

Florentine Codex, 21, 23, 33, 178

flowers, and chocolate drinks, 18, 64, 167, 168, 169, 270n10

Fonseca, Antonio de, 217–18

Foucault, Michel, 202–3

France: and Brazil, 101–2; and *converso* communities, 218, 260; as rival of Spain, 98, 99–101, 149, 150; state power in, 202, 223; and tobacco monopoly, 223, 228, 313n117; and tobacco trade, 151, 222

Franciscans, 66, 89, 93, 130, 234

frontier, 47–52, 62, 90, 93, 95, 98, 101, 276n10

Gage, Thomas, 90, 146, 180

Galen: and Cárdenas, 135, 136; and Hernández, 128, 135; models of, 235; and Monardes, 111, 113, 115, 117, 127–28, 135; and Renaissance Europe, 109, 110; and Valverde Turices, 124

García, Gregorio, 274n76

gender differentiation: and juxtaposition of chocolate and maize, 27, 30; and tobacco and chocolate consumption, 20, 24, 25, 69, 77, 272n43

gold, 45, 46, 48–50, 55, 90, 95, 125, 126, 149

Gómez de Salazar, Diego, 210–12, 216, 217–23, 311n63, 313n106

Gómez de Salazar, Gabriel, 226

Gómez de Salazar, Juan, 218

Gómez de Salazar, Leonor, 216, 217, 218

Greater Antilles, 53–55, 84–86, 88, 90, 283n27

Grijalva, Juan de, 48–50, 51, 98

guaiacum, 109, 110, 113, 158

hallucinogens, 24, 39–40, 120, 127

Hayo, Cristóbal de, 183, 198, 199, 236, 239, 248, 305n40

henbane, 58, 102, 110, 116, 117, 258

Hernández, Francisco: and Amerindian medical expertise, 108, 122–26, 128–29; and Barrios, 289n38; on chocolate, 108, 121, 122–23, 126–28, 130–31, 135, 136, 139, 237, 260, 270n10, 290n63, 294n46; and Monardes, 108, 122, 125, 126; on tobacco, 88, 121, 123, 126, 127–28, 289n42, 290n63, 295n6

Herrera, Baltasar de, 73, 75, 76, 137–38, 244

Hippocrates, 109, 110, 111, 113, 135, 136, 238

Hispaniola, 85, 149, 151, 201

Hondius, Hendrik, *Venezula, cum parte Auftrali Novae Andalausiae, 152*

hueinacaztli, 18. *See also* "divine ear" spice

Huerga Criado, Pilar, 220, 311n60

human sacrifice, 13–14, 32–35, 48–49, 51, 64–68, 70, 73, 78

human/spirit world relationship: and chocolate use, 12, 30–35, 31, 34, 43, 174, 265; and *cohoba,* 54; and merchants' feasts, 23–24; and sensory experience, 9, 15–16; and tobacco use, 12, 15–16, 30–33, 43, 54, 92, 118, 174, 248

humor, 173, 189, 190, 191–94, 196, 198, 230, 251, 253

humors, balancing of, 113, 117, 123, 124, 135, 139, 236–37, 250

Hurtado, Tomás, 198, 239, 242, 243, 245

Hurtado de Mendoza, Antonio, 179, 253, 303n15

idolatry: contagious effects of, 131, 134, 137, 140; and extirpators, 71–73, 76, 79, 130; and Inquisition, 66–68, 130, 138, 278n9, 293n40; and missionaries on, 73, 129–30; Quevedo's satire on, 229; and tobacco use, 54, 58, 98

indianos (New World returnees), 112, 141, 148, 158, 160

indigo, 141, 144, 148, 158

Innocent X (pope), 314n6

Inquisition: and chocolate as medium for love potions, 179; and chocolate drinks, 315n19; and Gómez de Salazar, 217–18, 221–23, 311n63; and idolatry, 66–68, 130, 138, 278n9, 293n40; and Portuguese New Christians, 209, 214, 260; satire of, 254, 255; Suárez's testimony for, 66–67; targets of, 72, 138, 291n7; and tobacco use, 71, 72, 131

Isabella (queen of Spain), 44, 46–47, 202

Italy, 259, 262

Jesuits, 146, 169, 234, 241, 250, 251, 259

Jews and Judaism: and chocolate, 259, 260; Spanish expulsion of Jews, 46, 66, 109, 154, 212, 214, 222. *See also* Marranism; Portuguese New Christians

Jiménez Patón, Bartolomé, 197, 239, 318n85

Juana Inés de la Cruz, Sor, 180, 303n16

Laguna, Andrés, 111, 288n14

Lancre, Pierre de, 245–46

Las Casas, Bartolomé de, 56, 85, 86

Las Casas, Francisco de, 70, 279n19

Leiva y Aguilar, Francisco de, 189, 198–99, 236–38, 241–42, 248–49, 307n73

❖ 329 ❖

Index

Steen, Jan: *The Dancing Couple, 187*; and
social status, 194; *Tavern Scene,* 306n47
Stubbe, Henry, 250–51, 260, 317n77
Studnicki-Gizbert, Daviken, 215
Suárez, Lorenzo, 66–67, 84
syncretism: and adaptations to Christianity,
80, *81,* 82; and Cárdenas, 137; and
European medical practice, 237; and
Hernández, 123, 125, 128; and Monardes,
115, 125, 128; and Portuguese New
Christians, 12; and reception of American
goods, 9–10; use of term, 9, 269n25. *See
also* cultural hybridity
syphilis, 58, 109, 110, 263

tabaqueras, 188, 305n36
La Taberna, 159, 160
Tacatetl (Amerindian shaman), 66–68, 72,
278n9
Tanixtetl (Amerindian shaman), 66–68, 72,
278n9
taverns: and chocolate, 160, 161, 299n91;
and tobacco use, 159–60, *160,* 184, 190,
299n89, 305n45, 306n47
taxes: *avería* (fleet) tax, 142, 147, 151,
294n2; on luxury goods, 203, 205, 206,
208, 225, 226, 228; and *millones,* 204–5,
206, 207, 208, 210, 223; tax farms,
215, 217, 225, 313n106; vice taxes, 203,
205–9, 240
tea, 260, 261, 262, 264, 319n23
Teniers, David, the Younger: *Monkeys
Smoking,* 184, 191, *192*; *Peasants in a
Tavern,* 306n47; *Peasants Smoking in
an Inn, 184, 185*; and social status, 190,
194; *Tavern Scene,* 305n45, 306n47; and
tobacco consumers, 193
Tenochtitlan, 13, 16, 52, 63, 66
teotl (sacred energy), 33–35, 41–42
Theobrama cacao: characteristics of, 7;
and cosmological traditions, 34, 82–83;
depictions of, 26; fruits of, 1; growing
range of, 18; and human/spirit world
relationship, 24; varieties of, 123, *124,*
268n12
Thevet, André, 101–2
Thompson, I. A. A., 227
Thompson, J. Eric S., 30, 273n58
Tirapau, Martín de, 295–96n15, 296n17
Tlatelolco, 13, 16, 18, 20
tobacco: and adaptations to Christianity,
77, 78–79; as addictive, 7–8; in
Amerindian markets, 88, 105, 282n24;
Amerindians' uses for, 1, 10, 11,
40–42; and Andean peoples, 281n1;
in borderlands, 91–92; Cárdenas on,

136–37; as carnivalesque outlet, 188–95,
200; colonial discourses on, 53; and
Columbus, 44–47; commodification
of, 11, 148–51, 153–56, 214; dance
linked with, 32, 93; dangers of, 263;
demysticification of, 232–36, 240, 255,
265; ennoblement of, 15, 16; and Euro-
pean/Amerindian interactions, 49–50,
93–94, 199–200; in European markets,
142, 144, 147–48, 149, 156–57, 158,
159, 161; European reaction to, 8; and
exchange of goods, 45; on frontier,
47–50, 101; generative power of, 36–42;
as gift, 27, 100–101, 188, 190; and
grotesque body, 188–93, 200, 306n53;
and idolatry cases, 70–72; lasciviousness
associated with, 183, *187*; as link to
pre-Columbian traditions, 64, 72, 77;
Martyr on, 54, 58; medicinal uses of, 8,
11, 12, 15, 20, 40–41, 43, 58, 65, 88, 98,
106, 107, 115–16, 137, 142–44, 228, 263;
and merchants' feasts, 21–22; Monardes
on, 107–9, *108,* 114–17, 126, 127–28,
130–31, 136, 137, 141, 142–43, 228,
230, 236, 245, 248, 288n31; as numinous
substance, 240–41, 265; physiological
effects of, 40, 264; price of, 155, 161,
162, 212, 223, 226, 310n47; processing
of, 219–20, 224; provenance of, 172,
221, 226, 229; psychotropic effects
of, 118, 119, 136, 198, 200, 258, 264;
retailers of, 164–65, 301n114; Ruiz de
Alarcón on, 138; sacred force within, 33,
41–42, 58, 230, 241, 245, 256, 265–66;
satire on, 3, 183, 193, 194, 199, 229,
231, 236, 241, 252, 253; and sexuality,
183, 199, 236; taste for, 9, 170–71, *172*;
taxes on, 206, 240; terms for, 65, 171,
302n142; transgression associated with,
174, 182–83, 188, 190; as vice, 203, 228,
235, 236, 239, 240, 249, 255. *See also*
cigarettes; *picietl* (pulverized tobacco);
snuff
tobacco consumption: and caste
stratification, 15, 20, 22–23, *23,*
27–28, 43, 50, 58, 65; and Catholic
Church, 232–33; and contraband, 227;
diffusion of, 3, 64, 157, 161, 162–63,
166–67, 171, 255, 257–59, 300n101;
and diplomatic meetings, 28, 43, 48,
49–50, 100–101; and European medical
practice, 238–40; and luxury tax, 208;
pre-Columbian compared with European, 199–200; in private, 195, 197–98;
rate of, 3; and tobacco monopoly,
162–63, 228

❖ 333 ❖

CPSIA information can be obtained
at www.ICGtesting.com
Printed in the USA
LVHW010836150723
752409LV00002B/179